POPULATION IN PERSPECTIVE

Population in Perspective

EDITED BY LOUISE B. YOUNG

SCIENCE EDITOR

AMERICAN FOUNDATION FOR CONTINUING EDUCATION

OXFORD UNIVERSITY PRESS

NEW YORK   LONDON   TORONTO

1968

Copyright © 1968 by Oxford University Press, Inc.
Library of Congress Catalogue Card Number: 68-17620
Printed in the United States of America

Foreword

The population of the world is increasing at the rate of about 180,000 people every 24 hours. In effect, we add enough people each month to make a new city the size of Chicago. This rapid growth in population is a problem of crucial importance to everyone in the world. Although the situation is more critical in some areas than others, it cannot be ignored even in those areas where it is less serious because it affects international relations, economic development, and eventually the quality of life which can be lived in a rapidly unifying world.

Population has gone through surges of growth at other periods in history, as the graph below illustrates. The current upsurge started about 1600 and has been accelerating (with only minor setbacks) ever since. There is one feature, however, which is new in the past fifty years. The principal cause of the present growth is different in nature from the changes that brought about growth in the past. Historically, each important increase in population followed a major invention that made more natural resources available to mankind: the invention of agriculture, the harnessing of nonhuman power, the opening up of new lands, the organization of people into urban centers, and the industrial revolution. In all cases the population grew until it had absorbed the new supply of food, power, and usable space. Then a new balance was automatically struck between population and the means of subsistence.

The present surge in population, however, results from a different kind of discovery, the control of death by modern medicine and sanitation. Death control has upset nature's automatic balance by allowing more people to live

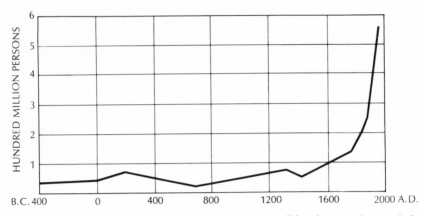

European Population. Estimates showing the recent striking increase in population, compared with the relatively steady state during the previous millennium.
(From Anthony Barnett, *The Human Species,* MacGibbon & Kee, London. Copyright © 1961 by Anthony Barnett. Reprinted with permission.)

while not providing, in itself, new sources of subsistence. Fortunately, during this same era technology has also been increasing, making available more food and energy; new ways have been found to decrease human fertility. However, these factors are not linked in the simple cause and effect relationship that automatically maintained the balance before. Equilibrium between the new death rate and the new birth rate can only be re-established by the use of human intelligence.

The first step in meeting this challenge is to understand the problem. There are many factors, physical, cultural, and psychological, which influence the fertility of a population. These factors are complex and are interrelated in ways that are only partially understood. The people of India, for instance, want more children than the people of France, and they want them for different reasons. Methods of family planning which are acceptable to Germans or Scandinavians may not be acceptable to the Puerto Ricans for aesthetic or religious reasons. An understanding of these differences, a sensitivity to the beliefs and aspirations of all the world's peoples will help to achieve a wise population policy. Oversimplification, on the other hand, is likely to do more harm than good.

The readings in this book have been brought together to help the reader achieve perspective on the population problem both in historical depth and in breadth of total cultural pattern. The essays, which begin with Thomas Malthus, demonstrate how our understanding of human population growth has evolved; how it has passed through periods of changing emphasis and concern. Selections from writers in many different disciplines—demographers, economists, anthropologists, biologists, novelists, and poets—give a broad panorama of the diverse influences that affect human fertilty. In many cases the readings have been excerpted from longer works. Titles have sometimes been changed or added to indicate the selection's function in this book. Occasionally, footnotes and illustrations have been omitted because in this context they did not contribute to the central issue; editorial notes have been added where they were deemed useful.

As with other publications sponsored by the American Foundation for Continuing Education, the editor does not represent or support any particular viewpoint with respect to the public policy questions or the philosophical, religious, or social issues contained in these readings. The AFCE is a non-profit educational organization devoted to the development of study programs in the liberal disciplines for adults concerned with their own continuing education. Conflicting opinions on controversial issues have been presented as fairly as possible and editorial comment kept to a minimum to encourage the reader to think for himself and draw his own conclusions. The only definite editorial bias is that people can and should understand this issue in all its complexity. It is only through widespread concern and an educated response that mankind will be able to take responsible action toward planning his own future.

Most of the readings in demography are not technical enough to cause any problem for the layman. However, there are a few terms which have a special meaning in this context and, therefore, require explanation. Demographers use *fecundity* to refer to reproductive capacity. *Fertility* denotes the amount of reproduction actually achieved.

There are several different ways of computing fertility and population growth. The simplest and most usual statistic is the number of births or deaths per thousand population. This is sometimes called the *gross,* or *crude, birth rate* or *death rate.* It is a statistic that must be treated with caution when comparing the birth rates of different countries or of the same country in different eras because it takes no account of the age composition of the population. For instance, in India a larger segment of the population is in the child-bearing years than in England, where the population is older (see Fig. 7, p. 59). In England the age composition has changed greatly over the past hundred years. The statistic known as the *fertility rate* takes these differences into account. It measures the births per year per thousand women in the reproductive ages (15–45.) *Specific fertility rate* refers to a more detailed breakdown of this information, for example, the fertility rate of women between the ages of 20 and 24. The specific fertility rates can be used to compute the number of girls that would be born to 1000 mothers over their reproductive period. If they bear, on the average, 1000 girl babies the *gross reproductive rate* of that population is said to be one.

Although the fertility and gross reproductive rates provide very useful estimates of the reproductive rate of a population, they do not tell us how fast the population is changing. The difference between the crude birth rate and the crude death rate gives the *rate of natural increase* and tells how many people are actually being added every year. However, it should be borne in mind that this rate does not contain any information about the age distribution of the population or how many of the children born today are likely to grow up and have children of their own. A girl born in China has much less chance of living to reproductive age than a girl born in the United States. Information of this kind is contained in the *net reproductive rate,* which measures the rate at which the population is replacing itself.

The chart below shows in a simplified manner how this calculation is made. Suppose that in a certain year 1000 women between the ages of 15 and 19 had 100 girl babies and 1000 women between 20 and 24 had 400 girl babies, and so on. These specific fertility rates are tabulated in the second column. Suppose also that of each 1000 women only 800 can be expected to reach the ages 15–19, 750 to reach the ages of 20–24, and so on. These average figures are recorded in the third column. Then, assuming that the same specific fertility and mortality continue to prevail, we can compute the number of surviving women by whom present women will replace themselves. (See column three.) In the imaginary

Illustration of the Calculation of the Net Reproductive Rate

Age Groups	Number of female children born to 1000 women passing through each age group	Number of survivors out of each 1000 female children born	Number of surviving women by whom present women replace themselves
15–19	100	800	80
20–24	400	750	300
25–29	200	700	140
30–34	150	650	97.5
35–39	100	600	60
40–44	50	550	27.5
	1000		705

From A. M. Carr-Saunders, *World Population,* Oxford at the Clarendon Press, 1936. Reprinted by permission.

example used, we find that the original 1000 girls can be expected to bear a total of 705 girl babies. In this case we say that the net reproductive rate is 0.705. If the rate is one (unity) the population is assumed to be exactly replacing itself. However, we must remember that the life expectancy rates and fertility rates could change during the time the babies of today are growing up, especially in those countries just beginning to use modern medicine and sanitation. These changes would alter the replacement rate. Nevertheless, the net reproductive rates do give the most accurate estimate of the consequences of present population growth. It is unfortunate that there are many countries where the statistics necessary for this sophisticated type of calculation are not available.

The projection of a future population from a present growth rate is a hazardous undertaking at best. These rates contain many variables and are sensitive to small changes in these variables. Furthermore, since population growth is cumulative, very slight changes in present rates can make enormous differences when projected 100, 200, or more years into the future.

In reading some of the more extreme predictions about the crowded state of our planet many centuries from now we are reminded of Mark Twain's amusing comment about using present rates of change to calculate what happened in the past or will happen in the future:

> In the space of one hundred and seventy-six years the Lower Mississippi has shortened itself two hundred and forty-two miles. That is an average of a trifle over one mile and a third per year. Therefore, any calm person, who is not blind or idiotic, can see that in the old Oolitic Silurian Period, just a million years ago next November, the Lower Mississippi River was upward of one million three hundred thousand miles long, and stuck out over the Gulf of Mexico like a fishing-rod. And by the same token any person can see that seven hundred and forty-two years from now the Lower Mississippi will be only a mile and three-quarters long, and Cairo and New Orleans will have joined their streets together, and be plodding comfortably along under a single mayor and a mutual board of aldermen. There is something fascinating about science. One gets such wholesale returns of conjecture out of such trifling investment of fact.[1]

Actually, in projecting present rates of growth into the future most demographers are not making predictions in the sense of something which they believe will happen. Rather they are putting into vivid terms the dangers of a present course of action, realizing that a knowledge of this danger will help to alter the outcome. As Philip Hauser expresses it:

1. From Mark Twain, *Life on the Mississippi*, 1883.

Projections of future populations are admittedly fictions. No one can actually predict future population and anyone who claims he can is either a fool or a charlatan. Yet the projections of the demographers are more than exercises in arithmetic: they make it possible for us to see the implications of observed rates of growth. The fact that man is able to consider these implications is one reason why the projected numbers will never be reached, for recognition of the problems posed by his birth rate will move man to modify it. Such a modification, however, will not be automatic. It requires policy decisions and implementation of policy . . . [2]

No effective policy can be created without a careful appraisal of the goals that we want that policy to achieve. Do we want to stabilize the population as rapidly as possible and attempt to hold it at that level? Many people fear that the concept of stability in population connotes stagnation and old age. A declining population is often considered to be a symptom of decadence. On the other hand, stability as it is used in Physics to describe a condition of equilibrium would allow for future population growth as new discoveries made available more natural resources. A population balanced with the means of subsistence would be in a constantly changing state of equilibrium.

Furthermore, there are other and more significant kinds of growth than the purely physical growth involved in population expansion. Cultural and spiritual growth could continue, indeed might even be favored, in a society with a relatively stable population, just as the individual human being achieves full physical growth quite early in life and thereafter goes on growing in other ways for many more years before old age and decadence set in. The prime of creativity comes long after physical growth has ceased. A wise population policy would involve planning not only for a comfortable physical balance between population and the means of subsistence but also for the fostering of those special qualities which give human existence its creative and dynamic character.

Achievement of this goal can be accelerated by a more widespread understanding of the dangers and difficulties involved and an appreciation of the many complex factors that influence the fertility of a people. It is our belief that perspective on the problem will contribute toward the formulation of an intelligent and consistent long-term policy. Therefore, the readings in this book have been planned to encourage the individual to think through the various issues himself, to question stereotypes, and to be aware of the future which is being created today by the actions and decisions of individuals everywhere on earth. "The world's greatest need,"

2. Philip Hauser, *Population Perspectives,* New Brunswick, N.J., Rutgers University Press, 1960.

says C. P. Snow, "is an appetite for the future . . . All healthy societies are ready to sacrifice the existential moment for their children's future and for children after these. The sense of the future is behind all good policies. Unless we have it, we can give nothing either wise or decent to the world." [3]

3. C. P. Snow, "What Is the World's Greatest Need?" *New York Times Magazine,* April 2, 1961.

Contents

Birth Control

PART II   ECONOMIC AND POLITICAL FACTORS

Population and Prosperity

Population and Policy

Population and Power

I BIOLOGICAL FACTORS

Introduction

Thomas Malthus is generally given the credit for initiating the study of the growth of human populations, although many writers before Malthus had recognized the importance of population size and had discussed its influence on political and economic well-being. Plato and Aristotle [1] both dealt with the problem and suggested ways in which population could be controlled. Tertullian, a Carthiginian writing in the third century A.D., anticipated Malthus by almost sixteen centuries:

> We find in the records of the Antiquities of Man that the human race has progressed with a gradual growth of population . . . What most frequently meets our view is our teeming population; our numbers are burdensome to the world, which can hardly supply us from its natural elements; our wants grow more and more keen, and our complaints more bitter in all mouths, whilst nature fails in affording us her usual sustenance. In very deed, pestilence, and famine, and wars, and earthquakes have to be regarded as a remedy for nations, as a means of pruning the luxuriance of the human race. [2]

Thomas Malthus, however, was the first writer to set forth a consistent theory of population, suggesting in mathematical terms its potential rate of increase and the factors which keep it under control. The first edition of his book was published anonymously in London in 1798, entitled *An*

1. See p. 112.
2. As quoted by Harrison Brown, *The Challenge of Man's Future*. The Viking Press, New York, 1954.

Essay on the Principle of Population as it Affects the Future Improvement of Mankind with Remarks on the Speculations of Mr. Godwin, M. Condorcet and Other Writers. His theory set forth the logical relationship between two known biological facts: (1) all living things have a reproductive potential much greater than the realized rate of increase and (2) the natural resources for growth and nourishment of these living things are limited. It is this limitation, Malthus postulated, which keeps the population within the bounds that can be supported by the given environment, and, therefore, the population must constantly press upon the means of subsistence.

This little book immediately stirred up a great deal of discussion and controversy, which is still active today. Even now the mere mention of the "Malthusian dilemma" or the "Neo-Malthusian theory" is enough to generate a heated discussion, revolving as much around religion and political ideology as around scientific principles.

It is not surprising that Malthus's theory has aroused so much interest among politicians and humanists. Although the theory itself was based solely on biological fact, the consequences of the theory had direct applications to the possibility of improving the conditions of the poor. In fact, it was this very implication that had first aroused Malthus's interest. His formal theory of population was developed as a result of his interest in the new social ideas. The eighteenth century had produced such philosophers as Rousseau and Condorcet who believed that science and human reason could create a world of plenty and a social system in which men could live more happily. Malthus saw in his law of population an inexorable barrier to the achievement of these dreams. Small wonder that his book aroused so much angry criticism! We can see here, also, one of the reasons why the Malthusian theory has never been reconciled with the Communistic doctrine.

In answer to the criticism of many of his contemporaries that man is not motivated entirely by biological instincts, that his reason and ethical principles also enter into such matters as the procreation of children, Malthus revised and amplified his original theory. He added "moral restraint" as a factor that could act as a preventive check to population growth but he himself did not appear to have any great faith in its effectiveness. His later editions were longer, more balanced, and more scholarly. He also dropped the cloak of anonymity.

The statement is often made today that Malthus has been disproven by history but most demographers would agree that this is not a fair or accurate statement. It is true that Malthus's prediction, that population if unchecked would increase geometrically while food can increase only arithmetically, has not proven to be accurate. But many new factors have appeared since Malthus's day which have affected the course of events. The rapid advance of technology and the opening up of new lands have allowed production to keep pace with population growth in a way which Malthus could not have anticipated. On the other hand, modern medicine has altered the death rate so that it no longer acts as an effective check on population. There are other new factors, also, such as modern methods of birth control, urbanization, changing social and economic aspirations. In addition to these new circumstances, studies in social sciences are increasing our understanding of cultural factors that affect the degree of "moral restraint" practised by people in different environments. And in the biological sciences, experiments with animals indicate that it may be an oversimplification to think that populations actually reproduce up to the starvation limit. All these new insights are still but dimly perceived; however, they are of interest in that they suggest how the laws of demography may be modified in the future.

It is frequently true that important scientific theories become modified as increasing knowledge in the field reveals the fuller complexities of the problem. Newton's laws of motion, for instance, are now known to be inaccurate for computing the motion of bodies moving very close to the speed of light. This is not to say that the original theory was wrong or has been disproven. It was a first approximation to the truth and formed a basis of study through which the more complex relationships were revealed. Except under extreme conditions Newton's laws still provide the most useful relationships for computing the path and acceleration of bodies in motion.

In a similar way, Malthus's law of population can be considered a first approximation of the relation between the reproductive rate of a population and the means of its subsistence. It is true, as Malthus pointed out, that there is a fundamental difference between the rate at which populations grow (like compound interest) and the rate at which food production can be increased. In the last few decades we have become very conscious of this fact as world population growth begins to outpace the food supply. It is apparent that the limit will soon be reached when further growth will result in widespread misery and starvation such as Malthus predicted.

Although in his later editions Malthus did add the element of preventive checks and was thereby able to "soften some of the harshest conclusions" at which he had arrived in his earlier edition, the main emphasis in his work was on the simple relation between life, death, and the means of subsistence. It is in terms of this relationship that he is most often quoted today. The Malthusian dilemma, for example, postulates that we cannot ameliorate the conditions of the poor or starving people without at the same time causing their population to increase and thereby reduce them to a poorer state than they had been in before. Some biologists question the validity of this conclusion, rejecting it on humanitarian as well as scientific grounds.

The readings in later parts of this book will explore the more complex economic and cultural factors which apply only to human populations and the implications for the future of man of more crowded living conditions. In this part we will concentrate on the biological relationship which Malthus proposed as the basis of his theory. We will see how these facts have changed since Malthus's time through modern medicine, which has brought about the control of death as well as the control of birth.

In suggesting that there could be preventive checks to population growth Malthus did not advocate the physiological control of conception. In fact, he called such devices "improper arts" and classified them as a form of vice. However, his name has been associated with the birth control movement from the beginning, and in a sense it represents a modern extension of his theory.

Malthus, of course, was interested primarily in the significance of his theory for human populations. However, the relationship he proposed led directly to one of the greatest biological insights, the theory of natural selection. Both Charles Darwin and Alfred Russell Wallace found in Malthus's law of population a clue to the mechanism which could bring about the evolution of the species. Darwin says in his autobiography:

> In October 1838, that is, fifteen months after I had begun my systematic enquiry, I happened to read for amusement "Malthus on Population," and being well prepared to appreciate the struggle for existence which everywhere goes on from long-continued observation of the habits of animals and plants, it at once struck me that under these circumstances

favourable variations would tend to be preserved, and unfavourable ones to be destroyed. The result of this would be the formation of new species. Here then I had at last got a theory by which to work.[3]

In *The Origin of the Species* which Darwin published twenty years later, he refers again to the Malthusian doctrine which had suggested to him the mechanism of natural selection:

A struggle for existence inevitably follows from the high rate at which all organic beings tend to increase. Every being, which during its natural lifetime produces several eggs or seeds, must suffer destruction during some period of its life, and during some season or occasional year, otherwise, on the principle of geometrical increase, its numbers would quickly become so inordinately great that no country could support the product. Hence, as more individuals are produced than can possibly survive, there must in every case be a struggle for existence, either one individual with another of the same species, or with the individuals of distinct species, or with the physical conditions of life. It is the doctrine of Malthus applied with manifold force to the whole animal and vegetable kingdoms; for in this case there can be no artificial increase of food, and no prudential restraint from marriage. Although some species may be now increasing, more or less rapidly, in numbers, all cannot do so, for the world would not hold them.

There is no exception to the rule that every organic being naturally increases at so high a rate, that, if not destroyed, the earth would soon be covered by the progeny of a single pair. Even slow-breeding man has doubled in twenty-five years, and at this rate, in less than a thousand years, there would literally not be standing-room for his progeny.[4]

3. From Charles Darwin, *Life and Letters,* Murray, London, 1887.
4. Charles Darwin, *The Origin of the Species,* The New American Library of World Literature, Inc., New York.

The Malthusian Laws

Essay on the Principle of Population
THOMAS R. MALTHUS (1816)

Statement of the Subject—Ratios of the Increase of Population and Food

In an inquiry concerning the improvement of society, the mode of conducting the subject which naturally presents itself, is,

1. To investigate the causes that have hitherto impeded the progress of mankind towards happiness; and,

2. To examine the probability of the total or partial removal of these causes in future.

To enter fully into this question, and to enumerate all the causes that have hitherto influenced human improvement, would be much beyond the power of an individual. The principal object of the present essay is to examine the effects of one great cause intimately united with the very nature of man; which, though it has been constantly and powerfully operating since the commencement of society, has been little noticed by the writers who have treated this subject. The facts which establish the existence of this cause have, indeed, been repeatedly stated and acknowledged; but its natural and necessary effects have been almost totally overlooked; though probably among these effects may be reckoned a very considerable portion of that vice and misery, and of that unequal distribution of the bounties of nature, which it has been the unceasing object of the enlightened philanthropist in all ages to correct.

The cause to which I allude is the constant tendency in all animated life to increase beyond the nourishment prepared for it.

From Thomas R. Malthus, *Essay on the Principle of Population,* Seventh Edition, 1816, J. M. Dent & Sons Ltd.

It is observed by Dr. Franklin that there is no bound to the prolific nature of plants or animals but what is made by their crowding and interfering with each other's means of subsistence. Were the face of the earth, he says, vacant of other plants, it might be gradually sowed and overspread with one kind only, as for instance with fennel: and were it empty of other inhabitants, it might in a few ages be replenished from one nation only, as for instance with Englishmen.[1]

This is incontrovertibly true. Through the animal and vegetable kingdoms Nature has scattered the seeds of life abroad with the most profuse and liberal hand; but has been comparatively sparing in the room and the nourishment necessary to rear them. The germs of existence contained in this earth, if they could freely develop themselves, would fill millions of worlds in the course of a few thousand years. Necessity, that imperious, all pervading law of nature, restrains them within the prescribed bounds. The race of plants and race of animals shrink under this great restrictive law; and man cannot by any efforts of reason escape from it.

In plants and irrational animals, the view of the subject is simple. They are all impelled by a powerful instinct to the increase of their species; and this instinct is interrupted by no doubts about providing for their offspring. Wherever therefore there is liberty, the power of increase is exerted; and the superabundant effects are repressed afterwards by want of room and nourishment.

The effects of this check on man are more complicated. Impelled to the increase of his species by an equally powerful instinct, reason interrupts his career, and asks him whether he may not bring beings into the world for whom he cannot provide the means of support. If he attend to this natural suggestion, the restriction too frequently produces vice. If he hear it not, the human race will be constantly endeavouring to increase beyond the means of subsistence. But as, by that law of our nature which makes food necessary to the life of man, population can never actually increase beyond the lowest nourishment capable of supporting it, a strong check on population, from the difficulty of acquiring food, must be constantly in operation. This difficulty must fall somewhere, and must necessarily be severely felt in some or other of the various forms of misery, or the fear of misery, by a large portion of mankind.

That population has this constant tendency to increase beyond the means of subsistence, and that it is kept to its necessary level by these

1. Franklin's Miscell. p. 9.

causes, will sufficiently appear from a review of the different states of society in which man has existed. But, before we proceed to this review, the subject will, perhaps, be seen in a clearer light if we endeavour to ascertain what would be the natural increase of population if left to exert itself with perfect freedom; and what might be expected to be the rate of increase in the productions of the earth under the most favourable circumstances of human industry.

It will be allowed that no country has hitherto been known where the manners were so pure and simple, and the means of subsistence so abundant, that no check whatever has existed to early marriages from the difficulty of providing for a family, and that no waste of human species has been occasioned by vicious customs, by towns, by unhealthy occupations, or too severe labour. Consequently in no state that we have yet known has the power of population been left to exert itself with perfect freedom.

Whether the law of marriage be instituted, or not, the dictate of nature and virtue seems to be an early attachment to one woman; and where there were no impediments of any kind in the way of an union to which such an attachment would lead, and no causes of depopulation afterwards, the increase of the human species would be evidently much greater than any increase which has been hitherto known.

In the northern states of America, where the means of subsistence have been more ample, the manners of the people more pure, and the checks to early marriages fewer than in any of the modern states of Europe, the population has been found to double itself, for above a century and a half successively, in less than twenty-five years.[2] Yet, even during these periods, in some of the towns, the deaths exceeded the births,[3] a circumstance which clearly proves that, in those parts of the country which supplied this deficiency, the increase must have been much more rapid than the general average.

In the back settlements, where the sole employment is agriculture, and vicious customs and unwholesome occupations are little known, the population has been found to double itself in fifteen years.[4] Even this extraordinary rate of increase is probably short of the utmost power of population. Very severe labour is requisite to clear a fresh country; such situ-

2. It appears, from some recent calculations and estimates, that from the first settlement of America to the year 1800, the periods of doubling have been but very little above twenty years.
3. Price's Observ. on Revers. Pay. vol. i. p. 274, 4th edit.
4. Id. p. 282.

ations are not in general considered as particularly healthy; and the inhabitants, probably, are occasionally subject to the incursions of the Indians, which may destroy some lives, or at any rate diminish the fruits of industry.

According to a table of Euler, calculated on a mortality of 1 in 36, if the births be to the deaths in the proportion of 3 to 1, the period of doubling will be only 12 years and 4-5ths. And this proportion is not only a possible supposition, but has actually occurred for short periods in more countries than one.

Sir William Petty supposes a doubling possible in so short a time as ten years.[5]

But, to be perfectly sure that we are far within the truth, we will take the slowest of these rates of increase, a rate in which all concurring testimonies agree, and which has been repeatedly ascertained to be from procreation only.

It may safely be pronounced, therefore, that population, when unchecked, goes on doubling itself every twenty-five years, or increases in a geometrical ratio.

The rate according to which the productions of the earth may be supposed to increase, it will not be so easy to determine. Of this, however, we may be perfectly certain, that the ratio of their increase in a limited territory must be of a totally different nature from the ratio of the increase of population. A thousand millions are just as easily doubled every twenty-five years by the power of population as a thousand. But the food to support the increase from the greater number will by no means be obtained with the same facility. Man is necessarily confined in room. When acre has been added to acre till all the fertile land is occupied, the yearly increase of food must depend upon the melioration of the land already in possession. This is a fund, which, from the nature of all soils, instead of increasing, must be gradually diminishing. But population, could it be supplied with food, would go on with unexhausted vigour; and the increase of one period would furnish the power of a greater increase the next, and this without any limit.

From the accounts we have of China and Japan, it may be fairly doubted whether the best-directed efforts of human industry could double the produce of these countries even once in any number of years. There are many parts of the globe, indeed, hitherto uncultivated, and almost un-

5. Polit. Arith. p. 14.

occupied; but the right of exterminating, or driving into a corner where they must starve, even the inhabitants of these thinly-peopled regions, will be questioned in a moral view. The process of improving their minds and directing their industry would necessarily be slow; and during this time, as population would regularly keep pace with the increasing produce, it would rarely happen that a great degree of knowledge and industry would have to operate at once upon rich unappropriated soil. Even where this might take place, as it does sometimes in new colonies, a geometrical ratio increases with such extraordinary rapidity, that the advantage could not last long. If the United States of America continue increasing, which they certainly will do, though not with the same rapidity as formerly, the Indians will be driven further and further back into the country, till the whole race is ultimately exterminated, and the territory is incapable of further extension.

These observations are, in a degree, applicable to all the parts of the earth where the soil is imperfectly cultivated. To exterminate the inhabitants of the greatest part of Asia and Africa is a thought that could not be admitted for a moment. To civilise and direct the industry of the various tribes of Tartars and Negroes would certainly be a work of considerable time and of variable and uncertain success.

Europe is by no means so fully peopled as it might be. In Europe there is the fairest chance that human industry may receive its best direction. The science of agriculture has been much studied in England and Scotland; and there is still a great portion of uncultivated land in these countries. Let us consider at what rate the produce of this island might be supposed to increase under circumstances the most favourable to improvement.

If it be allowed that by the best possible policy, and great encouragements to agriculture, the average produce of the island could be doubled in the first twenty-five years, it will be allowing, probably, a greater increase than could with reason be expected.

In the next twenty-five years, it is impossible to suppose that the produce could be quadrupled. It would be contrary to all our knowledge of the properties of land. The improvement of the barren parts would be a work of time and labour; and it must be evident to those who have the slightest acquaintance with agricultural subjects that, in proportion as cultivation extended, the additions that could yearly be made to the former average produce must be gradually and regularly diminishing. That we may be the better able to compare the increase of population and food, let us make a supposition, which, without pretending to accuracy, is clearly more favourable to the power of production in the earth than any experience we have had of its qualities will warrant.

Let us suppose that the yearly additions which might be made to the former average produce, instead of decreasing, which they certainly would do, were to remain the same; and that the produce of this island might be increased every twenty-five years by a quantity equal to what it at present produces. The most enthusiastic speculator cannot suppose a greater increase than this. In a few centuries it would make every acre of land in the island like a garden.

If this supposition be applied to the whole earth, and if it be allowed that the subsistence for man which the earth affords might be increased every twenty-five years by a quantity equal to what it at present produces, this will be supposing a rate of increase much greater than we can imagine that any possible exertions of mankind could make it.

It may be fairly pronounced, therefore, that, considering the present average state of the earth, the means of subsistence, under circumstances the most favourable to human industry, could not possibly be made to increase faster than in an arithmetical ratio.

The necessary effects of these two different rates of increase, when brought together, will be very striking. Let us call the population of this island eleven millions; and suppose the present produce equal to the easy support of such a number. In the first twenty-five years the population would be twenty-two millions, and the food being also doubled, the means of subsistence would be equal to this increase. In the next twenty-five years, the population would be forty-four millions, and the means of subsistence only equal to the support of thirty-three millions. In the next period the population would be eighty-eight millions, and the means of subsistence just equal to the support of half that number. And, at the conclusion of the first century, the population would be a hundred and seventy-six millions, and the means of subsistence only equal to the support of fifty-five millions, leaving a population of a hundred and twenty-one millions totally unprovided for.

Taking the whole earth, instead of this island, emigration would of course be excluded; and, supposing the present population equal to a thousand millions, the human species would increase as the numbers, 1, 2, 4, 8, 16, 32, 64, 128, 256, and subsistence as 1, 2, 3, 4, 5, 6, 7, 8, 9. In two centuries the population would be to the means of subsistence as 256 to 9; in three centuries as 4096 to 13, and in two thousand years the difference would be almost incalculable.

In this supposition no limits whatever are placed to the produce of the earth. It may increase for ever and be greater than any assignable quantity; yet still the power of population being in every period so much superior, the increase of the human species can only be kept down to the level of the means of subsistence by the constant operation of the strong law of necessity, acting as a check upon the greater power.

Of the General Checks to Population, and the Mode of Their Operation

The ultimate check to population appears then to be a want of food, arising necessarily from the different ratios according to which population and food increase. But this ultimate check is never the immediate check, except in cases of actual famine.

The immediate check may be stated to consist in all those customs, and all those diseases, which seem to be generated by a scarcity of the means of subsistence; and all those causes, independent of this scarcity, whether of a moral or physical nature, which tend prematurely to weaken and destroy the human frame.

These checks to population, which are constantly operating with more or less force in every society, and keep down the number to the level of the means of subsistence, may be classed under two general heads—the preventive and the positive checks.

The preventive check, as far as it is voluntary, is peculiar to man, and arises from that distinctive superiority in his reasoning faculties which enables him to calculate distant consequences. The checks to the indefinite increase of plants and irrational animals are all either positive, or, if preventive, involuntary. But man cannot look around him and see the distress which frequently presses upon those who have large families; he cannot contemplate his present possessions or earnings, which he now nearly consumes himself, and calculate the amount of each share, when with very little addition they must be divided, perhaps, among seven or eight, without feeling a doubt whether, if he follow the bent of his inclinations, he may be able to support the offspring which he will probably bring into the world. In a state of equality, if such can exist, this would be the simple question. In the present state of society other considerations occur. Will he not lower his rank in life, and be obliged to give up in great measure his former habits? Does any mode of employment present itself by which he may reasonably hope to maintain a family? Will he not at any rate subject himself to greater difficulties, and more severe labour, than in his single state? Will he not be unable to transmit to his children the same advantages of education and improvement that he had himself possessed? Does he even feel secure that, should he have a large family, his utmost exertions can save them from rags and squalid poverty, and their consequent degradation in the community? And may he not be reduced to the grating necessity of forfeiting his independence, and of being obliged to the sparing hand of Charity for support?

These considerations are calculated to prevent, and certainly do prevent, a great number of persons in all civilised nations from pursuing the dictate of nature in an early attachment to one woman.

If this restraint do not produce vice, it is undoubtedly the least evil that can arise from the principle of population. Considered as a restraint on a strong natural inclination, it must be allowed to produce a certain degree of temporary unhappiness; but evidently slight, compared with the evils which result from any of the other checks to population; and merely of the same nature as many other sacrifices of temporary to permanent gratification, which it is the business of a moral agent continually to make.

When this restraint produces vice, the evils which follow are but too conspicuous. A promiscuous intercourse to such a degree as to prevent the birth of children seems to lower, in the most marked manner, the dignity of human nature. It cannot be without its effect on men, and nothing can be more obvious than its tendency to degrade the female character, and to destroy all its most amiable and distinguishing characteristics. Add to which, that among those unfortunate females, with which all great towns abound, more real distress and aggravated misery are, perhaps, to be found than in any other department of human life.

When a general corruption of morals, with regard to the sex, pervades all the classes of society, its effects must necessarily be to poison the springs of domestic happiness, to weaken conjugal and parental affection, and to lessen the united exertions and ardour of parents in the care and education of their children—effects which cannot take place without a decided diminution of the general happiness and virtue of the society; particularly as the necessity of art in the accomplishment and conduct of intrigues, and in the concealment of their consequences, necessarily leads to many other vices.

The positive checks to population are extremely various, and include every cause, whether arising from vice or misery, which in any degree contributes to shorten the natural duration of human life. Under this head, therefore, may be enumerated all unwholesome occupations, severe labour and exposure to the seasons, extreme poverty, bad nursing of children, great towns, excesses of all kinds, the whole train of common diseases and epidemics, wars, plague, and famine.

On examining these obstacles to the increase of population which I have classed under the heads of preventive and positive checks, it will appear that they are all resolvable into moral restraint, vice, and misery.

Of the preventive checks, the restraint from marriage which is not followed by irregular gratifications may properly be termed moral restraint.[6]

Promiscuous intercourse, unnatural passions, violations of the marriage bed, and improper arts to conceal the consequences of irregular connections, are preventive checks that clearly come under the head of vice.

Of the positive checks, those which appear to arise unavoidably from the laws of nature, may be called exclusively misery; and those which we obviously bring upon ourselves, such as wars, excesses, and many others which it would be in our power to avoid, are of a mixed nature. They are brought upon us by vice, and their consequences are misery.[7]

6. It will be observed that I here use the term *moral* in its most confined sense. By moral restraint I would be understood to mean a restraint from marriage from prudential motives, with a conduct strictly moral during the period of this restraint; and I have never intentionally deviated from this sense. When I have wished to consider the restraint from marriage unconnected with its consequences, I have either called it prudential restraint, or a part of the preventive check, of which indeed it forms the principal branch.

In my review of the different stages of society, I have been accused of not allowing sufficient weight in the prevention of population to moral restraint; but when the confined sense of the term, which I have here explained, is adverted to, I am fearful that I shall not be found to have erred much in this respect. I should be very glad to believe myself mistaken.

7. As the general consequence of vice is misery, and as this consequence is the precise reason why an action is termed vicious, it may appear that the term misery alone would be here sufficient, and that it is superfluous to use both. But the rejection of the term vice would introduce a considerable confusion into our language and ideas. We want it particularly to distinguish those actions, the general tendency of which is to produce misery, and which are therefore prohibited by the commands of the Creator, and the precepts of the moralist, although, in their immediate or individual effects, they may produce perhaps exactly the contrary. The gratification of all our passions in its immediate effect is happiness, not misery; and, in individual instances,

The sum of all these preventive and positive checks, taken together, forms the immediate check to population; and it is evident that, in every country where the whole of the procreative power cannot be called into action, the preventive and the positive checks must vary inversely as each other; that is, in countries either naturally unhealthy, or subject to a great mortality, from whatever cause it may arise, the preventive check will prevail very little. In those countries, on the contrary, which are naturally healthy, and where the preventive check is found to prevail with considerable force, the positive check will prevail very little, or the mortality be very small.

In every country some of these checks are, with more or less force, in constant operation; yet, notwithstanding their general prevalence, there are few states in which there is not a constant effort in the population to increase beyond the means of subsistence. This constant effort as constantly tends to subject the lower classes of society to distress, and to prevent any great permanent melioration of their condition.

These effects, in the present state of society, seem to be produced in the following manner. We will suppose the means of subsistence in any country just equal to the easy support of its inhabitants. The constant effort towards population, which is found to act even in the most vicious societies, increases the number of people before the means of subsistence are increased. The food, therefore, which before supported eleven millions, must now be divided among eleven millions and a half. The poor consequently must live much worse, and many of them be reduced to severe distress. The number of labourers also being above the proportion of work in the market, the price of labour must tend to fall, while the price of provisions would at the same time tend to rise. The labourer therefore must do more work to earn the same as he did before. During this season of distress, the discouragements to marriage and the difficulty of rearing a family are so great that the progress of population is retarded. In the meantime, the cheapness of labour, the plenty of labourers, and the necessity of an increased industry among them, encourage cultivators to employ

even the remote consequences (at least in this life) may possibly come under the same denomination. There may have been some irregular connections with women, which have added to the happiness of both parties, and have injured no one. These individual actions, therefore, cannot come under the head of misery. But they are still evidently vicious, because an action is so denominated, which violates an express precept, founded upon its general tendency to produce misery, whatever may be its individual effect; and no person can doubt the general tendency of an illicit intercourse between the sexes to injure the happiness of society.

more labour upon their land, to turn up fresh soil, and to manure and improve more completely what is already in tillage, till ultimately the means of subsistence may become in the same proportion to the population as at the period from which we set out. The situation of the labourer being then again tolerably comfortable, the restraints to population are in some degree loosened; and, after a short period, the same retrograde and progressive movements, with respect to happiness, are repeated.

This sort of oscillation will not probably be obvious to common view; and it may be difficult even for the most attentive observer to calculate its periods. Yet that, in the generality of old states, some alternation of this kind does exist though in a much less marked, and in a much more irregular manner, than I have described it, no reflecting man, who considers the subject deeply, can well doubt.

One principal reason why this oscillation has been less remarked, and less decidedly confirmed by experience than might naturally be expected, is, that the histories of mankind which we possess are, in general, histories only of the higher classes. We have not many accounts that can be depended upon of the manners and customs of that part of mankind where these retrograde and progressive movements chiefly take place. A satisfactory history of this kind, of one people and of one period, would require the constant and minute attention of many observing minds in local and general remarks on the state of the lower classes of society, and the causes that influenced it; and to draw accurate inferences upon this subject, a succession of such historians for some centuries would be necessary. This branch of statistical knowledge has, of late years, been attended to in some countries, and we may promise ourselves a clearer insight into the internal structure of human society from the progress of these inquiries. But the science may be said yet to be in its infancy, and many of the objects, on which it would be desirable to have information, have been either omitted or not stated with sufficient accuracy. Among these, perhaps, may be reckoned the proportion of the number of adults to the number of marriages; the extent to which vicious customs have prevailed in consequence of the restraints upon matrimony; the comparative mortality among the children of the most distressed part of the community and of those who live rather more at their ease; the variations in the real price of labour; the observable differences in the state of the lower classes of society, with respect to ease and happiness, at different times during a certain period; and very accurate registers of births, deaths, and marriages, which are of the utmost importance in this subject.

A faithful history, including such particulars, would tend greatly to elucidate the manner in which the constant check upon population acts; and would probably prove the existence of the retrograde and progressive movements that have been mentioned; though the times of their vibration must necessarily be rendered irregular from the operation of many interrupting causes; such as, the introduction or failure of certain manufactures; a greater or less prevalent spirit of agricultural enterprise; years of plenty or years of scarcity; wars, sickly seasons, poor laws, emigrations, and other causes of a similar nature.

A circumstance which has, perhaps, more than any other, contributed to conceal this oscillation from common view is the difference between the nominal and real price of labour. It very rarely happens that the nominal price of labour universally falls; but we well know that it frequently remains the same while the nominal price of provisions has been gradually rising. This, indeed, will generally be the case if the increase of manufactures and commerce be sufficient to employ the new labourers that are thrown into the market, and to prevent the increased supply from lowering the money-price.[8] But an increased number of labourers receiving the same money-wages will necessarily, by their competition, increase the money-price of corn. This is, in fact, a real fall in the price of labour; and, during this period, the condition of the lower classes of the community must be gradually growing worse. But the farmers and capitalists are growing rich from the real cheapness of labour. Their increasing capitals enable them to employ a greater number of men; and, as the population had probably suffered some check from the greater difficulty of supporting a family, the demand for labour, after a certain period, would be great in proportion to the supply, and its price would of course rise, if left to find its natural level; and thus the wages of labour, and consequently the condition of the lower classes of society, might have progressive and retrograde movements, though the price of labour might never nominally fall.

In savage life, where there is no regular price of labour, it is little to be doubted that similar oscillations took place. When population has increased nearly to the utmost limits of the food, all the preventive and the positive checks will naturally operate with increased force. Vicious habits

8. If the new labourers thrown yearly into the market should find no employment but in agriculture, their competition might so lower the money-price of labour as to prevent the increase of population from occasioning an effective demand for more corn; or, in other words, if the landlords and farmers could get nothing but an additional quantity of agricultural labour in exchange for any additional produce which they could raise, they might not be tempted to raise it.

with respect to the sex will be more general, the exposing of children more frequent, and both the probability and fatality of wars and epidemics will be considerably greater; and these causes will probably continue their operation till the population is sunk below the level of the food; and then the return to comparative plenty will again produce an increase, and, after a certain period, its further progress will again be checked by the same causes.[9]

But without attempting to establish these progressive and retrograde movements in different countries, which would evidently require more minute histories than we possess, and which the progress of civilization naturally tends to counteract, the following propositions are intended to be proved:—

1. Population is necessarily limited by the means of subsistence.

2. Population invariably increases where the means of subsistence increase, unless prevented by some very powerful and obvious checks.[10]

3. These checks, and the checks which repress the superior power of population, and keep its effects on a level with the means of subsistence, are all resolvable into moral restraint, vice, and misery. . . .

Of Poor-Laws

To remedy the frequent distresses of the poor, laws to enforce their relief have been instituted; and in the establishment of a general system of this kind England has particularly distinguished herself. But it is to be feared that, though it may have alleviated a little the intensity of individual misfortune, it has spread the evil over a much larger surface. . . .

9. Sir James Stuart very justly compares the generative faculty to a spring loaded with a variable weight (Polit. Econ. vol. i. b. i. c. 4, p. 20), which would of course produce exactly that kind of oscillation which has been mentioned. In the first book of his Political Economy, he has explained many parts of the subject of population very ably.

10. I have expressed myself in this cautious manner, because I believe there are some instances where population does not keep up to the level of the means of subsistence. But these are extreme cases; and, generally speaking, it might be said that,

2. Population always increases where the means of subsistence increase.

3. The checks which repress the superior power of population, and keep its effect on a level with the means of subsistence, are all resolvable into moral restraint, vice, and misery.

It should be observed that, by an increase in the means of subsistence is here meant such an increase as will enable the mass of the society to command more food. An increase might certainly take place, which in the actual state of a particular society would not be distributed to the lower classes, and consequently would give no stimulus to population.

The poor-laws of England tend to depress the general condition of the poor in these two ways. Their first obvious tendency is to increase population without increasing the food for its support. A poor man may marry with little or no prospect of being able to support a family without parish assistance. They may be said, therefore, to create the poor which they maintain: and as the provisions of the country must, in consequence of the increased population, be distributed to every man in smaller proportions, it is evident that the labour of those who are not supported by parish assistance will purchase a smaller quantity of provisions than before, and consequently more of them must be driven to apply for assistance.

Secondly, the quantity of provisions consumed in workhouses, upon a part of the society that cannot in general be considered as the most valuable part, diminishes the shares that would otherwise belong to more industrious and more worthy members, and thus, in the same manner, forces more to become dependent. If the poor in the workhouses were to live better than they do now, this new distribution of the money of the society would tend more conspicuously to depress the condition of those out of the workhouses by occasioning an advance in the price of provisions.

Fortunately for England, a spirit of independence still remains among the peasantry. The poor-laws are strongly calculated to eradicate this spirit. They have succeeded in part; but had they succeeded as completely as might have been expected, their pernicious tendency would not have been so long concealed.

Hard as it may appear in individual instances, dependent poverty ought to be held disgraceful. Such a stimulus seems to be absolutely necessary to promote the happiness of the great mass of mankind; and every general attempt to weaken this stimulus, however benevolent its intention, will always defeat its own purpose. If men be induced to marry from the mere prospect of parish provision, they are not only unjustly tempted to bring unhappiness and dependence upon themselves and children, but they are tempted, without knowing it, to injure all in the same class with themselves.

The poor-laws of England appear to have contributed to raise the price of provisions, and to lower the real price of labour. They have therefore contributed to impoverish that class of people whose only possession is their labour. It is also difficult to suppose that they have not powerfully contributed to generate that carelessness and want of frugality observable among the poor, so contrary to the disposition generally to be remarked among petty tradesmen and small farmers. The labouring poor, to use a vulgar expression, seem always to live from hand to mouth. Their present wants employ their whole attention; and they seldom think of the future. Even when they have an opportunity of saving, they seldom exercise it; but all that they earn beyond their present necessities goes, generally speaking, to the ale-house. The poor-laws may therefore be said to diminish both the power and the will to save among the common people; and thus to weaken one of the strongest incentives to sobriety and industry, and consequently to happiness.

It is a general complaint among master manufacturers, that high wages ruin all their workmen; but it is difficult to conceive that these men would not save a part of their high wages for the future support of their families, instead of spending it in drunkenness and dissipation, if they did not rely on parish assistance for support in case of accidents. And that the poor employed in manufactures consider this assistance as a reason why they may spend all the wages which they earn, and enjoy themselves while they can, appears to be evident from the number of families that upon the failure of any great manufactory immediately fall upon the parish; when perhaps the wages earned in this manufactory while it flourished were sufficiently above the price of common country labour to have allowed them to save enough for their support till they could find some other channel for their industry.

A man who might not be deterred from going to the ale-house from the consideration that on his death or sickness he should leave his wife and family upon the parish, might yet hesitate in thus dissipating his earnings, if he were assured that in either of these cases his family must starve, or be left to the support of casual bounty.

The mass of happiness among the common people cannot but be diminished when one of the strongest checks to idleness and dissipation is thus removed; and positive institutions, which render dependent poverty so general, weaken that disgrace which for the best and most humane reasons ought to be attached to it.

The poor-laws of England were undoubtedly instituted for the most benevolent purpose; but it is evident they have failed in attaining it. . . . The improved condition of the labouring classes in France since the revolution has been accompanied by a greatly diminished proportion of births, which has had its natural and necessary effect in giving to these classes a greater share of the produce of the country, and has kept up the advantage arising from the sale of the church lands and other national domains, which would otherwise have been lost in a short time. The effect of the revolution in France has been to make every person depend more upon himself and less upon others. The labouring classes are therefore become more industrious, more saving, and more prudent in marriage than formerly; and it is quite certain that without these effects the revolution would have done nothing for them. An improved government has, no doubt, a natural tendency to produce these effects, and thus to improve the condition of the poor. But if an extensive system of parochial relief, and such doctrines as have lately been inculcated, counteract them, and prevent the labouring classes from depending upon their own prudence and industry, then any change for the better in other respects becomes comparatively a matter of very little importance; and under the best form of government imaginable, there may be thousands on thousands out of employment and half starved.

If it be taught that all who are born have a *right* to support on the land, whatever be their number, and that there is no occasion to exercise any prudence in the affair of marriage so as to check this number, the temptations, according to all the known principles of human nature, will inevitably be yielded to, and more and more will gradually become dependent on parish assistance. There cannot therefore be a greater inconsistency and contradiction than that those who maintain these doctrines respecting the poor should still complain of the number of paupers. Such doctrines and a crowd of paupers are unavoidably united; and it is utterly beyond the power of any revolution or change of government to separate them.
. . .

The Only Mode of Improvement

The object of those who really wish to better the condition of the lower classes of society must be to raise the relative proportion between the price of labour and the price of provisions, so as to enable the labourer to command a larger share of the necessaries and comforts of life. We have hitherto principally attempted to attain this end by encouraging the married poor, and consequently increasing the number of labourers, and overstocking the market with a commodity which we still say that we wish to be dear. It would seem to have required no great spirit of divination to foretell the certain failure of such a plan of proceeding. There is nothing however like experience. It has been tried in many different countries, and for many hundred years, and the success has always been answerable to the nature of the scheme. It is really time now to try something else.

When it was found that oxygen, or pure vital air, would not cure consumptions as was expected, but rather aggravated their symptoms, trial was made of an air of the most opposite kind. I wish we had acted with the same philosophical spirit in our attempts to cure the disease of poverty; and having found that the pouring in of fresh supplies of labour only tended to aggravate the symptoms, had tried what would be the effect of withholding a little these supplies.

In all old and fully-peopled states it is from this method, and this alone, that we can rationally expect any essential and permanent melioration in the condition of the labouring classes of the people.

In an endeavour to raise the proportion of the quantity of provisions to the number of consumers in any country, our attention would naturally be first directed to the increasing of the absolute quantity of provisions; but finding that, as fast as we did this, the number of consumers more than kept pace with it, and that with all our exertions we were still as far as ever behind, we should be convinced that our efforts directed only in this way would never succeed. It would appear to be setting the tortoise to catch the hare. Finding, therefore, that from the laws of nature we could not proportion the food to the population, our next attempt should naturally be to proportion the population to the food. If we can persuade the hare to go to sleep, the tortoise may have some chance of overtaking her.

We are not, however, to relax our efforts in increasing the quantity of provisions, but to combine another effort with it; that of keeping the population, when once it has been overtaken, at such a distance behind as to effect the relative proportion which we desire; and thus unite the two grand *desiderata*, a great actual population and a state of society in which abject poverty and dependence are comparatively but little known; two objects which are far from being incompatible.

If we be really serious in what appears to be the object of such general research, the mode of essentially and permanently bettering the condition of the poor, we must explain to them the true nature of their situation, and show them that the withholding of the supplies of labour is the only possible way of really raising its price, and that they themselves, being the possessors of this commodity, have alone the power to do this.

I cannot but consider this mode of diminishing poverty as so perfectly clear in theory, and so invariably confimed by the analogy of every other commodity which is brought to market, that nothing but its being shown to be calculated to produce greater evils than it proposes to remedy can justify us in not making the attempt to put it into execution.

Objections to This Mode Considered

One objection which perhaps will be made to this plan is that from which alone it derives its value—a market rather understocked with labour. This must undoubtedly take place in a certain degree; but by no means in such a degree as to affect the wealth and prosperity of the country. But putting this subject of a market understocked with labour in the most unfavourable point of view, if the rich will not submit to a slight inconvenience necessarily attendant on the attainment of what they profess to desire, they cannot really be in earnest in their professions. Their benevolence to the poor must be either childish play or hypocrisy; it must be either to amuse themselves or to pacify the minds of the common people with a mere show of attention to their wants. To wish to better the condition of the poor by enabling them to command a greater quantity of the necessaries and comforts of life, and then to complain of high wages, is the act of a silly boy who gives away his cake and then cries for it. A market overstocked with labour, and an ample remuneration to each labourer, are objects perfectly incompatible with each other. In the annals of the world they never existed together; and to couple them even in imagination betrays a gross ignorance of the simplest principles of political economy.

A second objection that may be made to this plan is the diminution of population that it would cause. It is to be considered, however, that this diminution is merely relative; and when once this relative diminution has been effected, by keeping the population stationary, while the supply of food has increased, it might then start afresh, and continue increasing for ages, with the increase of food, maintaining always nearly the same relative proportion to it. I can easily conceive that this country, with a proper direction of the national industry, might, in the course of some centuries, contain two or three times its present population, and yet every man in the kingdom be much better fed and clothed than he is at present. While the springs of industry continue in vigour, and a sufficient part of that industry is directed to agriculture, we need be under no apprehensions of a deficient population; and nothing perhaps would tend so strongly to excite a spirit of industry and economy among the poor as a thorough knowledge that their happiness must always depend principally upon themselves; and that, if they obey their passions in opposition to their reason, or be not industrious and frugal while they are single, to save a sum for the common contingencies of the married state, they must expect to suffer the natural evils which Providence has prepared for those who disobey its repeated admonitions. . . .

Future Improvement of Society

If the principles which I have endeavoured to establish be false, I most sincerely hope to see them completely refuted; but if they be true, the subject is so important, and interests the question of human happiness so nearly, that it is impossible they should not in time be more fully known and more generally circulated, whether any particular efforts be made for the purpose or not.

Among the higher and middle classes of society, the effect of this knowledge will, I hope, be to direct without relaxing their efforts in bettering the condition of the poor; to show them what they can and what they cannot do; and that, although much may be done by advice and instruction, by encouraging habits of prudence and cleanliness, by discriminate charity, and by any mode of bettering the present condition of the poor which is followed by an increase of the preventive check; yet that, without this last effect, all the former efforts would be futile; and that, in any old and well-peopled state, to assist the poor in such a manner as to enable them to marry as early as they please, and rear up large families, is a physical impossibility. This knowledge, by tending to prevent the rich from destroying the good effects of their own exertions, and wasting their efforts in a direction where success is unattainable, would confine their attention to the proper objects, and thus enable them to do more good.

Among the poor themselves, its effects would be still more important. That the principal and most permanent cause of poverty has little or no *direct* relation to forms of government, or the unequal division of property; and that, as the rich do not in reality possess the *power* of finding employment and maintenance for the poor, the poor cannot, in the nature of things, possess the *right* to demand them; are important truths flowing from the principle of population, which, when properly explained, would by no means be above the most ordinary comprehensions. And it is evident that every man in the lower classes of society who became acquainted with these truths, would be disposed to bear the distresses in which he might be involved with more patience; would feel less discontent and irritation at the government and the higher classes of society, on account of his poverty; would be on all occasions less disposed to insubordination and turbulence; and if he received assistance, either from any public institution or from the hand of private charity, he would receive it with more thankfulness, and more justly appreciate its value.

If these truths were by degrees more generally known (which in the course of time does not seem to be improbable from the natural effects of the mutual interchange of opinions), the lower classes of people, as a body, would become more peaceable and orderly, would be less inclined to tumultuous proceedings in seasons of scarcity, and would at all times be less influenced by inflammatory and seditious publications, from knowing how little the price of labour and the means of supporting a family depend upon a revolution. The mere knowledge of these truths, even if they did not operate sufficiently to produce any marked change in the prudential habits of the poor with regard to marriage, would still have a most beneficial effect on their conduct in a political light; and undoubtedly, one of the most valuable of these effects would be the power that would result to the higher and middle classes of society, of gradually improving their governments,[11] without the apprehension of those revolutionary excessess, the fear of which, at present, threatens to deprive Europe even of that degree of liberty which she had before experienced to be practicable, and the salutary effects of which she had long enjoyed.

From a review of the state of society in former periods compared with the present, I should certainly say that the evils resulting from the principle of population have rather diminished than increased, even under the disadvantage of an almost total ignorance of the real cause. And if we can indulge the hope that this ignorance will be gradually dissipated, it does not seem unreasonable to expect that they will be still further diminished.

11. I cannot believe that the removal of all unjust grounds of discontent against constituted authorities would render the people torpid and indifferent to advantages which are really attainable. The blessings of civil liberty are so great that they surely cannot need the aid of false colouring to make them desirable. I should be sorry to think that the lower classes of people could never be animated to assert their rights but by means of such illusory promises as will generally make the remedy of resistance much worse than the disease which it was intended to cure.

The increase of absolute population, which will of course take place, will evidently tend but little to weaken this expectation, as everything depends upon the relative proportion between population and food, and not on the absolute number of people. In the former part of this work it appeared that the countries which possessed the fewest people often suffered the most from the effects of the principle of population; and it can scarcely be doubted that, taking Europe throughout, fewer famines and fewer diseases arising from want have prevailed in the last century than in those which preceded it.

On the whole, therefore, though our future prospects respecting the mitigation of the evils arising from the principle of population may not be so bright as we could wish, yet they are far from being entirely disheartening, and by no means preclude that gradual and progressive improvement in human society which, before the late wild speculations on this subject, was the object of rational expectation. To the laws of property and marriage, and to the apparently narrow principle of self-interest which prompts each individual to exert himself in bettering his condition, we are indebted for all the noblest exertions of human genius, for everything that distinguishes the civilised from the savage state. A strict inquiry into the principle of population obliges us to conclude that we shall never be able to throw down the ladder by which we have risen to this eminence; but it by no means proves that we may not rise higher by the same means. The structure of society, in its great features, will probably always remain unchanged. We have every reason to believe that it will always consist of a class of proprietors and a class of labourers; but the condition of each, and the proportion which they bear to each other, may be so altered as greatly to impove the harmony and beauty of the whole. It would indeed be a melancholy reflection that, while the views of physical science are daily enlarging, so as scarcely to be bounded by the most distant horizon, the science of moral and political philosophy should be confined within such narrow limits, or at best be so feeble in its influence, as to be unable to counteract the obstacles to human happiness arising from a single cause. But however formidable these obstacles may have appeared in some parts of this work, it is hoped that the general result of the inquiry is such as not to make us give up the improvement of human society in despair. The partial good which seems to be attainable is worthy of all our exertions; is sufficient to direct our efforts, and animate our prospects. And although we cannot expect that the virtue and happiness of mankind will keep pace with the brilliant career of physical discovery; yet, if we are not wanting to ourselves, we may confidently indulge the hope that, to no unimportant extent, they will be influenced by its progress and will partake in its success.

Death and Death Control

Role of War, Famine, and Disease in Controlling Population

MARSTON BATES (1955)

Man Against Man

War and famine and disease—those are the words around which one must organize any discussion of human mortality. And of these, war now seems the most important, the most insoluble. . . . Warfare seems to be one of the most persistent of human traits, and one that has perhaps been important in shaping population development for a very long time.

"War" probably is a sort of wastebasket word that has caught a variety of rather different things. It is particularly dangerous to try to trace any direct line of evolution from possible territorial squabblings among Pleistocene food-gatherers to the organized ferocity of modern Western states with their complicated rituals of international "law" and violations thereof. About all that can be found in this spectrum, from the bashed skulls of Peking man to the atomic bombs of World War II, is the continuing history of intraspecific violence. . . .

It is clear that man has been killing man for a very long time, whatever the biological origins of the habit. A remarkable number of the fossil bones that have survived from the Stone Age show that the individual met a violent death of a sort that could only have been inflicted by some fellow-man. Thus, in the case of Peking man (Sinanthropus), everyone of the skulls shows evidence of heavy blows, and the limb bones were all split open—something that only man would do, in seach of marrow. The

"King Death on Horseback," Albrecht Dürer, 1505. Charcoal drawing. London, British Museum. Illustration added by editor.

fossil evidence, as far as Peking man is concerned, seems to show that the principal cause of death was murder with cannibal intent.

Murder also seems to have been a leading cause of death with later Paleolithic man in China. Franz Weidenreich, in his study of "The Duration of Life of Fossil Man in China" gives a nice, scholarly description of the evidence. Of the skulls from the Upper Cave at Choukoutien, Weidenreich writes:

> The first skull, that of an old man . . . displays a typical round depressed fracture on the left side above the temporal region. It must have been caused by a pointed implement. The second skull, probably that of a woman, shows a long and wide slit-like hole at the superior part of the left temporal region. This hole breaks through the wall of the skull from above downward giving the impression that it was caused by a spear-like

implement piercing through the wall from above. In addition, the entire skull is crushed into numerous smaller and larger fragments still in their natural connections. At least two centers are distinguishable from which these fractures radiate, indicating that the crushing was produced by heavy blows from club-like implements. The third skull is likewise fractured but not broken into such numerous fragments as in the second one. Also in this the fragments are in place in natural arrangement, the markings of the blows being located at the frontal region of the left side. The fourth skull consists of only the frontal and two parietal bones. Here the injuries are represented by a large fractured and deeply depressed area corresponding to the frontal sinus, the splinters of the outside are still in place and those of the inner side form a far protruding elevation. Both parietal bones display a large fractured depression with a typically split interior table. In this instance clubs and a more pointed weapon must have been used.[1]

Our sample of skeletons, of course, is small, and the chances of preservation may have been greater for men who were murdered and dragged into caves to be eaten at leisure than for men killed out in the open by lions or accidents or disease. But even so, it looks as though life had its grim aspects in that Old Stone Age. . . .

Cannibalism might easily follow from the nature of in-group out-group relations among social mammals. An individual not belonging to the group or territory would be regarded as foreign, hardly more "human" than any other animal. Once killed, for territorial transgression or any other reason, there would be no point in allowing the meat to go to waste. A survey of the eating habits of modern man shows quite conclusively that there is no such thing as "instinctive" aversion to any food. Whether man eats man or not seems to be just as clearly a cultural trait as whether man eats dog, or cow, or rattlesnake, or any other digestible, non-poisonous food.

Certain peoples, like the pre-Columbian Caribs of the West Indies, have taken to cannibalism as a way of life, and this may have been true of the inhabitants of the Choukoutien cave. I can hardly believe that cannibalism was a universal among early men, in the sense of hunting and killing other men as a major source of food, because surely in that case man would have succeeded in exterminating himself quite early. Cannibalism may, though, have been common enough to be an important cause of death.

The anthropologists have found examples of every imaginable kind of

1. Franz Weidenreich, *The Duration of Life of Fossil Man in China and the Pathological Lesions Found in His Skeleton*, Chinese Medical Journal, Vol. 55, pp. 34–44. (Reprinted in *Anthropological Papers of Franz Weidenreich*, New York, The Viking Fund, 1949.)

cannibalism among recent peoples. There are cultures that eat only friends, others that eat only enemies; cultures in which old people are eaten, others in which infants are eaten. Sometimes only certain members of the society, such as warriors or priests, can do the eating; sometimes the eating takes place only under special circumstances. There is no clear relation between cannibalism and availability of other food. Cannibalism may occur among starving groups of almost any culture (including our own), and cannibalism is habitual among some peoples who have an abundance of other food and thus eat man either for some ritual reason or because they like the taste.

Cannibalism is closely associated with human sacrifice—especially where the cannibalism is of a ritual kind. On the one hand, the eating of human flesh easily takes on a religious significance; and on the other, where men are sacrificed to the gods, the sacrifice may involve the eating of some part of the victim—most often, perhaps, his heart. Both cannibalism and human sacrifices are biological luxuries possible only for a population with a credit balance in reproduction.

Human sacrifice reached its most staggering proportions with the ancient Mexicans. "Scarcely any author," says Prescott, in the *History of the Conquest of Mexico,* "pretends to estimate the yearly sacrifices throughout the empire at less than twenty thousand, and some carry the figure as high as fifty thousand." The Aztec sacrificial victims were mostly prisoners of war—and wars were waged for the express purpose of capturing prisoners for sacrifice. The Aztec tactics, which aimed at capturing the enemy rather than killing him, put them at a considerable disadvantage in the fights with the Spaniards.

The sacrifice of first-born children has been a curiously widespread practice, found among a variety of cultures in many parts of the world. The sacrifice of the first-born is commonly explained as a method of promoting fecundity, though the effect would seem to be to lower fertility. The reasoning behind human sacrifice, however, is almost endlessly diverse, as has been so well documented in the writings of Sir James Frazer and Edward Westermarck.[2]

There is reason to suppose that human sacrifice is not a very ancient human pastime. It seems to go with the stages of "barbarism" and "civilization," with the development of settlements and the acquisition of leisure for the elaboration of complicated religious ideas. It also seems to be a transitory stage, since the great civilizations of the past seem indepen-

2. Edward Westermarck, *The Origin and Development of Moral Ideas,* 2nd ed., London, Macmillan & Co.

dently to have evolved through the sacrifice stage to the use of various sorts of substitute symbols or to some less bloody sort of religious ritual. . . .

There is no way, from the literature, of gaining any quantitative measure of the extent of either infanticide or abortion now or in past times. One would expect abortion to replace infanticide as societies become more sophisticated, but there seems to be no clear pattern, and in many instances both practices are reported as occurring in a given society. Infanticide has certainly persisted into quite sophisticated civilizations, and contrariwise, relatively unsophisticated peoples may be quite skillful in inducing abortions.

The general prevalence of infanticide and abortion among contemporary peoples of food-gathering or gardening culture might be taken as an indication that such forms of population control were of great antiquity. There is no direct evidence for Pleistocene man; and the fact that food-gathering peoples today have a given custom is no proof that men in the Old Stone Age had comparable customs. When traces of a given behavior pattern can be found in contemporary men and in various sorts of living primates, the argument for the antiquity of the pattern is much stronger; but I know of no evidence of infanticide (let alone abortion) in subhuman primates, nor in any other animals except under very unusual conditions. How far back in time such methods of reproductive control extend is, then, purely a matter of speculation. . . .

War and civilization have certainly generally gone together; whether there is any cause-and-effect relationship between the two is another matter. It would seem to me likely that civilization developed in spite of war, rather than because of it, and that the development of warlike habits has as often arrested the evolution of a culture as promoted it.

The addiction to social warfare by primitive gardening cultures in many parts of the world seems a case in point. This institution is admirably adapted to the maintenance of a static, "balanced" population situation—and to the arresting of possible cultural development. This relation between warfare, population and cultural development among the Indians of eastern North America has been described by Professor A. L. Kroeber:

> Of social factors, the most direct may be considered to have been warlike habits. Reference is not to systematic, decisive war leading to occasional great destructions but also to conquest, settlement, and periods of consolidation and prosperity. Of all this the Eastern tribes knew nothing. They waged war not for any ulterior or permanent fruits, but for victory;

and its conduct and shaping were motivated, when not by revenge, principally by individual desire for personal status within one's society. It
was warfare that was insane, unending, continuously attritional, from
our point of view; and yet it was so integrated into the whole fabric of
Eastern culture, so dominantly emphasized within it, that escape from it
was well-nigh impossible. Continuance in the system became self-
preservatory. The group that tried to shift its values from war to peace
was almost certainly doomed to early extinction. This warfare, with its
attendant unsettlement, confusion, destruction, and famines, was probably the most potent reason why population remained low in the East. It
kept agriculture in the role of a contributor to subsistence instead of the
basis of subsistence. On the other hand, such farming as was practiced
yielded enough of added leisure, concentration, and stability to make
pretty continuous warfare possible. A population of pure hunter-
gatherers would probably, except on the immediate coast, have been too
scattered in minute bands, too unsettled in a country of rather evenly
distributed food possibilities, too occupied with mere subsistence, to have
engaged in war very persistently. Just this seems to have happened
among Montagnais, Cree, and Ojibwa, for instance, as compared with
Muskogians, Iriquoins, and Siouans. The latter were caught in a vicious
circle, which at the same time gave them a stable adjustment. Agriculture made their wars possible; but their warfare kept the population
down to a point where more agriculture was not needed.[3]

It is probable, then, that through much of the period of cultural evolution, intraspecific strife has been an important limiting factor on the
growth of human population. When we come to modern times and historic
wars, the effect, curiously, is far less clear. There is, in fact, a widely held
theory that war has little influence on the growth of population, and this
theory is based mostly on observation of the actual statistical effects of the
last two world wars.

It is very difficult to assess the effect of historic wars on population because so many factors are involved. Through most of history, the battle
casualties have clearly been less important than the environmental disrup-
tions accompanying war, especially famine and disease. As more efficient
methods of inflicting battle casualties have developed, more efficient
methods of controlling famine and disease have also developed, so that
comparisons among wars in different periods of history become very difficult.

If the birth rate drops during a war—as it generally does—because of
the disruption of families, the deficit in births should be counted as part of

3. From A. L. Kroeber, *Cultural and Natural Areas of Native North America*, Berkeley, University of California Press, pp. 148–49.

the population loss due to the war. But the birth rates may rise to abnormal heights immediately after the war, and thus make up in some degree for the deficit.

Certainly the period from 1650 to 1950, when mankind showed such a spectacular rate of growth, could hardly be called a period of peace. If the recurring wars have slowed population growth at all, they have clearly not slowed it effectively.

• • •

Famine

> I am mourning on my high throne for the vast misfortune, because the Nile flood in my time has not come for seven years! Light is the grain; there is lack of crops and of all kinds of food. Each man has become a thief to his neighbor. They desire to hasten and cannot walk. The child cries, the youth creeps along, and the old man; their souls are bowed down, their legs are bent together and drag along the ground, and their hands rest in their bosoms. The counsel of the great ones in the court is but emptiness. Torn open are the chests of provisions, but instead of contents there is air. Everything is exhausted.—(Inscription on tomb on the Island of Sahal in the first cataract of the Nile, probably from time of Tcheser.) [4]

History, from Tcheser on, is about as full of famines as it is of wars. The famines get less attention than the wars in the history books, but their effect on human population may have been just as great, or greater. War and famine are often so entangled as to be hardly separable, but the war-caused famines, resulting from the disorganization of distribution and the disruption of ordinary farming routines, are still a rather special case. In general, famines result from crop failure, and while crop failure may have political causes, the causes more often are to be found in the vicissitudes of climate—droughts, floods or unseasonable cold.

Famine, then, is characteristically a phenomenon of an agricultural people with a population close to the maximum number that can be supported by the usual harvests. Failure of these harvests thus may be disastrous. In such a situation we would expect, according to the Malthusian propositions, a chronic misery and malnutrition as the population pressed against its food supply even in times of normal harvests. These

4. As quoted in Ancel Keys, J. Brozek, A. Henschel, O. Michelsen, and H. L. Taylor, *The Biology of Human Starvation,* Minneapolis, University of Minnesota Press, 1950.

Malthusian conditons have long applied in areas like India and China, where both chronic malnutrition and epidemic starvation are notorious.

The population effects on chronic malnutrition, among people living close to the limits of available food, are difficult to assess. Statistics of all sorts for such a population are scarce and uncertain. Even if accurate figures were available, "starvation" might not appear as a major cause of death. The effect would rather be indirect, through increased susceptibility to disease. Only with epidemic famine does starvation come to figure directly, but then the mortality may be startlingly great.

A study of the famines of China has shown that between 108 B.C. and A.D. 1911, there were 1,828 famines, or one nearly every year in some part of that vast and teeming land. There is considerable information about some of these famines. The worst in modern times was caused by a great drought in the years 1876 to 1879. "The area affected was 300,000 square miles (about the area of New England, the Middle Atlantic States, Ohio, Indiana and Illinois), and somewhere between 9,000,000 and 13,000,000 people perished from hunger and the disease and violence accompanying prolonged want." Again, in 1920 and 1921, "not less than 20,000,000 people were made destitute by crop failures, and in spite of the most efficient famine relief ever known in China, by which more than 7,000,000 people were fed, at least 500,000 died of want." (Quoting from Warren Thompson, *Population Problems.*)

Famine is far from an exclusively Oriental phenomenon. There are records of 201 famines in the British Islands between A.D. 10 and 1846, when existence in those Islands tended to accord with the Malthusian propositions. The contemporary West has escaped famine except for the special conditions of war; but the contemporary West seems also to have (temporarily?) escaped the Malthusian propositions. The closing date for the list of British famines, 1846, is the date of the great famine of Ireland. This is probably the most carefully studied and fully documented of all historic famines. It also makes a valuable case study from the point of view of general population behavior.

The Irish famine, of course, turns on the potato. How and when the potato got to Ireland is one of those historical mysteries. It is a crop of the Andean region of South America which was not cultivated in North America, Central America or the West Indies in pre-Columbian times; and it attracted relatively little attention from the early Spanish explorers. It was introduced into Spain at least as early as 1570, and by 1588 it was an established garden vegetable in various parts of Spain and Italy. One theory is that the potato got to Ireland by way of a shipwreck after the defeat of the Armada (1588). The first definite reference to the potato in Ireland is in a manuscript about the household arrangements of Lady Montgomery in the year 1606; among the inducements she offered to men working on her estates were "a garden plot to live on and some land for flax and potatoes."

However it got there, the potato soon became an important part of the Irish environment. How rapidly it became the basic food of the Irish people is not entirely clear. One authority considers that this was true as early as 1630; but other scholars consider that its adoption was considerably slower. Certainly, however, the Irish population had become completely dependent on this single crop by the end of the eighteenth century, so that crop failure in 1845 could become a gigantic disaster.

Dr. Redcliffe Salaman, who has written a fascinating book on the history of the potato, devotes several chapters to an examination of this problem of the adoption of the potato in Ireland.[5] Human beings are very conservative in their food habits, and great changes in diet have generally been slow indeed; yet here, within the space of perhaps a hundred years, a whole country became completely dependent on an entirely new crop.

Like most aspects of history, this episode of the Irish and the potato turns out to be a complex affair in which cause and effect seem to be all tangled up. My impression, after reading Salaman, is that any understanding of this period of Irish history requires about equal attention to relations with the English and to relations with the potato—and even these are not separable, since the adoption of the potato may have been partly a consequence of the activities of the English.

The potato plant, to be sure, turned out to be admirably adapted to the Irish climate and soil, but people don't adopt new foods just because they grow easily. Dr. Salaman shows that the explanation lies in politics as much as in climate—that the new crop fitted neatly into a region where the previous cattle economy had been badly disrupted by the wars, revolutions and continuous unrest caused by the English adventures in Ireland.

The spread of the potato in Ireland thus may have been caused, in part, by the circumstances of history; but it also, in turn, had historical effects. In particular, it changed the whole picture of the relations between

5. R. N. Salaman, *The History and Social Influence of the Potato,* Cambridge, University Press, 1949.

the population and the food supply. The population of Ireland grew from something like two million in 1687 to 8,175,000 in 1841, a fourfold increase in 150 years (not counting several hundred thousand who emigrated to England or America). A very careful and scholarly investigation of this extraordinary population growth, made by K. H. Connell, concludes that the primary "cause" was the potato.[6]

This Irish population growth is one of the neatest illustrations of the Malthusian theory that a population tends to expand to the limit of its food supply. The evidence, though hazy and indirect, tends to indicate that the population of Ireland remained fairly stable through the middle ages, as did that of England, limited somewhat indirectly by the food supply possible with the nature of the crops and the kind of land tenure. In the medieval world, before a man could marry and raise children, he had to find some means of support, even as a serf, by gaining rights to land for crops or pasturage. The various systems of land tenure, individual and communal, differed greatly in detail, but they tended to stabilize population-subsistence relationships—though, to be sure, at a level that we would find uncomfortable, or miserable.

The civil disturbances of Ireland, the varying laws and policies enforced by the English in their attempts to subjugate and exploit the country, and the advent of the potato, all combined to break down whatever "balance" the Irish population had maintained during the medieval period. The Irishman, like everybody else, was probably always inclined to marry early; with the breakdown of the old social structure and the easy availability of potato subsistence, there was nothing to stop him from indulging in this inclination. All he needed was an acre of land which, planted to potatoes, would support a family of five through the year, according to a contemporary estimate. A sod hut for living quarters was easily built in a few days with the help of neighbors and friends—the value of such a hut, according to another contemporary account, would be about 30 shillings! Children, instead of a liability, were a help from an early age in tending the potato patch. So everything combined to allow the Irish to embark upon a spectacular spree of reproducing themselves.

The first regular census, of 1821, showed a population of 6,802,000; the census of 1831, 7,767,000; the census of 1841, 8,175,000. There were local crop failures, there were all sorts of internal and external political troubles, and the poverty and miserable living conditions of the Irish

6. K. H. Connell, *The Population of Ireland, 1750–1845,* Oxford, Clarendon Press, 1950.

peasant became notorious in a world where poverty and misery were common everywhere. Yet the breeding spree, supported by the miraculous potato, continued.

Disaster appeared in 1845 in a form of a disease, the potato blight, new to Europe, which immediately became epidemic everywhere that potatoes were grown on the continent. Dr. Salaman writes:

> The disease attacked without warning the growing plants, destroying in a few days, fields of potatoes which till then had been proudly resplendent in all their pomp of dark green leaf and purple bloom, leaving nothing but black and withered stalks. Nor were its ravages halted by the death of the tops: before the peasants had time to harvest the crop, the tubers were found to be stained and beginning to rot. Those who had gathered their crop and placed them in the clamps, found them rotten and useless within a few weeks.[7]

There were many theories about the cause of the disease: that it was due to volcanic action within the earth, that it was a "gangrene" produced by the aphids, that it was a form of cholera that had spread to the potato, that it was an act of God to punish the lazy and sinful Irish. The British government tried a variety of relief measures, but there were many who thought this interference with the ways of Providence unwise, and that the Irish should be left to starve. The point of view was expressed by Alfred Smee, one of the leading surgeons of his day:

> This effect of depending too exclusively on the culture of the Potato is fearfully exhibited in the Irish people where the potato has begotten millions of paupers who live but are not clothed, who marry but do not work, caring for nothing but their dish of potatoes. . . . If left to itself this fearful state of things would have remedied itself: for had the people the control of their own community, and had the potato crop failed to the extent to which it has this year, these people having no relation with any other, would have been left to their own resources, which being destroyed, would have left them without food.

The blight struck again in 1846, and in these two years more than a million people died directly of starvation or of the diseases consequent on famine conditions. Large efforts were made at relief through soup kitchens and government work projects, but no man who owned as much as a half acre of ground was eligible for relief. Many starved rather than abandon their life-line to the future, but others by this very mechanism of re-

7. R. N. Salaman, *The History and Social Influence of the Potato.*

lief were rendered homeless and still greater numbers were forcibly evicted from their homes for failure to pay rent. For these, the only possible way out was emigration, and the great wave of Irish movement to the United States began.

Irish emigration had started before the famine. Connell has estimated that an average of about 4,000 a year emigrated to America between 1780 and 1815, giving a total of something like 140,000; and that about a million Irish emigrated to America between 1815 and 1845. He thinks that some 600,000 moved to England and Scotland during this same period. The census figures for the population of Ireland itself, then, are not a complete measure of the astonishing fertility of these people in the prefamine era.

The movement out of Ireland increased greatly with the onset of the famine: 61,242 persons left in 1845, according to the Irish census; 105,953 in 1846; double that in 1847. There was a good potato crop in 1848 and emigration dropped to 178,000; but in 1849 it rose again to 214,000; and the outward movement continued high all through the century.

The population of Ireland in 1952 (Northern Ireland and the Republic of Ireland) was about 4,300,000, hardly more than half the prefamine population of 1841, and the population has been about this figure for the last fifty years. The actual drop in numbers was a consequence of the emigration, but the continuing stability reflects a basic change in the habits of the people. The marriage pattern has changed, land tenure systems have changed, agriculture has become more diversified and the economy has changed in other ways. The resulting population stability, however, seems to be not so much the consequence of conscious planning and legislation, as of more or less unconscious changes in the Irish culture. It is a situation that would surely warrant detailed sociological study, though I do not know of any such study.

The population-resources adjustment of Ireland may have a high cost in some ways. The lowered population has been achieved primarily through "moral restraint" in the sense of Malthus. Ireland now has about the lowest marriage rate of any European country and one cannot help but wonder whether this is "desirable" or "healthy" from the point of view of the social and psychological well-being of the people.

The Irish story is unique in that the consequence of a famine or series of famines has been the long-term decline of population and the establishment of conditions which make the recurrence of famine unlikely. The repeated famines of the Orient have led to no such population readjustment, no such drastic change in the social habits of the people. There the population continues to live precariously at the limit possible with normal food supply, with resulting catastrophe when normal conditions fail. The Malthusian propositions seem to apply in full force.

The areas of occasional catastrophic famine are also the areas of chronic malnutrition, of dense agricultural populations with high death rates, low standards of living, undeveloped technology, and all of the other classic symptoms of overpopulation. Since the planet has become a neighborhood, the problems of these areas have become problems of concern to everyone, and we have a growing literature on the ways of implementing technological aid to these "backward" and overpopulated countries. . . .

Conditions of overcrowding, with chronic malnutrition, are also classically the conditions that breed disease—not only the deficiency diseases that clearly result directly from the food situation, but also the infectious diseases. War and famine, dramatic though they may be in human history, are dwarfed by the third major cause of ecological death in man, disease.

•   •   •

Disease

There can be little doubt but what infectious disease has been the chief cause of death in man during most of his recent history. This is no longer true in the modern West where medicine has made such dramatic progress in the control of infection, so that death generally is now the direct result of some noninfectious thing like heart disease, cancer or "accident"; and it may not have been true way back in the Old Stone Age when man was much more directly an element in the "natural" community of the forest and savannah. But through all of the period of complex culture, of civilization, while man flourished and increased so abundantly, disease was surely the chief agent of destruction, outrunning war and famine. Indeed, war and famine did not operate so much directly, as indirectly by favoring disease.

These are sweeping statements, but I doubt whether anyone will quarrel with them because the importance of disease is accepted as a truism. It would be nice, though, if we could document them, if we could say, surely, what diseases afflicted the Egyptians or the Greeks or the Mayans or the ancient Chinese, and assess the relative importance of different diseases among these different people. But the study of the history of disease is loaded with difficulties, and there are very few things we can say with certainty, despite the brilliant detective work that has gone into its study.

I have a feeling that this great importance of infectious disease is something that has come to man along with civilization, or at least along with agriculture and the possibility thus of supporting densely crowded populations. But this "feeling" can be supported only by the most indirect of evidence, and by shaky deductions from doubtful premises. We really know very little about the origins of any of our diseases; and new diseases may be forming right under our noses, but proof would be difficult to come by.

We have a fine documentation of the increasing importance of poliomyelitis in recent years. But is this a "new" disease, or an old disease that is only now becoming commonly recognized, or an old disease that is changing its appearance because of changes in human habits? The same sort of question may be asked about a whole family of diseases called the "encephalitides" or, in a slightly changed form, of the influenza that swept the world at the close of World War I. And there are similar questions about the puzzling sudden notoriety of syphilis in Europe at the beginning of the sixteenth century.

The converse of the problem of new diseases is that of old diseases that have disappeared. Sometimes we are sure what the disease was. The Black Death of medieval Europe, for instance, was the bubonic plague that smolders in many parts of the world today and breaks out occasionally in epidemic form. It appeared with dramatic suddenness in central Europe in 1348, when it is estimated that a quarter of the population were killed. Successive epidemics in 1361, 1371 and 1382 were calamitous enough, but successively less severe. Plague persisted locally, and in restricted epidemics, during the fifteenth and sixteenth centuries; and then broke out again in the great plagues of 1663 to 1668, including the London plague of 1664. Then plague gradually disappeared, not appearing in Europe in epidemic form after 1800. Why? I think no one can be sure of the answer. Isolated cases have appeared often enough, but no epidemic sweep has

started; though in the eighteenth and early nineteenth centuries, knowledge of how to control an epidemic was no better than it had been in the
seventeenth century.

The history of leprosy in Europe is another mystery. It apparently was
a common disease in Europe in the middle ages, judging from the number
of leprosaria and frequency of reference to the disease. But after the middle of the fifteenth century, it began to decline, and by the seventeenth
century it had practically disappeared from Europe. Again there is no
clear explanation. Possible improvement in sanitary conditions, treatment,
or economic changes seem hardly adequate explanations. One trouble, of
course, is that we still have no thorough knowledge of the epidemiology of
this disease.

Leprosy and plague are diseases with long and continuous histories in
the Orient; and their rise and decline in Europe can be looked at as a
problem in the geography of disease; though it remains equally inexplicable whether considered as geography or history. There are some diseases,
however, that are purely historical, that seem to have disappeared completely. One of these is the "English sweating sickness," described by
Hans Zinsser in his delightful book on *Rats, Lice and History.*

> The disease began without warning, usually at night or toward morn-
> ing, with a chill and with tremors. Soon there was fever, and profound
> weakness. Accompanying this were cardiac pains and palpitation, in
> some cases vomiting, severe headache, and stupor, but rarely delirium.
> . . . The profuse sweating, which was the most notable characteristic,
> began soon after the onset of the fever. Death came with astonishing
> speed. It is stated that many cases died within a day, and some even
> within a few hours.[8]

This sweating sickness first turns up in history in 1485, in the army of
Henry VII, after the battle of Bosworth, spreading over England rapidly
from east to west. "In London it killed, within the first week, two Lord
Mayors and six Aldermen." There was a second epidemic in 1507, much
like the first; and a third in 1518. In 1529 there occurred the most severe
epidemic of all, which swept over much of Europe. "It reached Vienna
during the siege of the city by the Sultan Soliman and, probably ravaging
the Turkish army, may have had some effect on the raising of the siege."
The fifth and last epidemic occurred in 1551. Since then no epidemic dis-

8. Hans Zinsser, *Rats, Lice and History,* Little, Brown & Co., Boston. My remarks
about the history of diseases are in general based on Zinsser's account.

ease with these symptoms has appeared, and it is impossible to identify the sweating disease with anything that we know.

So we have diseases that are apparently "new" in modern times, diseases that have changed greatly in geographical pattern, and diseases that have disappeared—without deliberate interference from man, without benefit of science or medicine. In fact, the pattern of disease, as we look back over history, seems constantly to have been changing. The relation between disease and mortality, the effect of disease on human populations, has thus never been a constant or easily calculable factor. When we try to figure out the role of disease in the history of human populations, we are thus on uncertain ground.

Infectious disease is a special form of the parasitic relationship so common among organisms. And parasitism itself, on examination, turns out to be difficult to define, to set off as a special kind of relationship. Animals and plants have all sorts of ways of living off each other and with each other. Biologists use many words, like parasitism, predation, symbiosis and saprophytism, to label such relationships, but the distinctions have a tendency to blur, and the student is apt to end up completely confused, particularly if he is enamored of nice, precise definitions for the words he uses.

For our present purposes, we can probably get along well enough with the general idea of parasitism, of some small organism living at the expense of a big organism, usually inside it, and not being of any direct help to the big organism, the host. If the parasite causes obvious harm, it is causing "disease"; and there can be every gradation in the amount of harm, in the severity of the disease.

A considerable variety of parasites are capable of causing disease in man—bacteria, viruses, protozoa, parasitic worms of several kinds, and a few parasitic fungi. Diseases with quite similar symptoms, be they fever, rash, cough, diarrhea, or what not, may be caused by quite different parasites; and the identification of the parasite, the precise diagnosis of the disease, may thus require elaborate laboratory study. The disease itself, the impairment of health, is the end result of many sorts of factors affecting the host, the parasite, and the environment in which the host-parasite relation occurs. This all adds up to make epidemiology, the study of the natural history of disease, a complex subject. . . .

With an immunity-producing contagious disease, such as smallpox, the continuing existence of the disease requires a large population in frequent contact; and with such diseases, in general, the larger the population, the more likely the persistence of the disease. In such cases, the disease is "endemic," always present, with most everyone acquiring the disease at an early age.

Where a contagion is not constantly maintained within a population, large numbers of people may grow up without immunity; and the contagion, once introduced, may sweep through the population as an epidemic. Some contagions seem almost everywhere to spread only periodically, as epidemics; while others have foci where they persist in endemic form under particularly favorable conditions, to break out periodically as epidemics in other parts of the world.

Where transmission is indirect, or involves vectors or alternate hosts, the relation between the disease and population density is more complex. Malaria, for instance, can rarely maintain itself in the centers of large cities because, while people are numerous enough, the vector mosquitoes do not breed in urban situations. It is most commonly a disease of villages and the fringes of cities, where marshes, ponds or streams provide suitable breeding places for the mosquitoes. Plague, on the other hand, dependent on rats and fleas, may be most severe in unsanitary cities.

It would be difficult to overestimate the importance of changes in the geography of disease over the globe since about 1400, for it has been associated with the modern movements of people in exploration or settlement. Both the contagions and the vector-transmitted diseases are involved.

The vector-transmitted diseases are, in general, more chained by geography than the contagions, because of their complex life-histories. But the parasite of malaria, for instance, can be transmitted by almost any species of anopheline mosquito; and there are several hundred different kinds of anopheline mosquitoes, and one or another of them occurs in almost every part of the world. The parasite thus often finds favorable conditions in quite new situations. It seems to me most probable that malaria was first brought to America by the Spaniards, and that yellow fever came over with some of the early African slaves. In the case of malaria, American mosquitoes proved excellent vectors; in the case of yellow fever, the vector was brought in with the disease—a mosquito that bred in the water tanks of the ships.

The most dramatic effects, however, were caused by the contagions which move easily with new contacts among populations; and of these contagions, smallpox has probably been the most important from the population point of view. It seems quite reasonable, in fact, to consider smallpox as the most effective agent in the Spanish conquest of America. We get only glimpses of it in the chronicles, but these make it clear enough that the smallpox arrived with the Spaniards and, in the campaigns of conquest, generally spread through the population ahead of them. As one missionary noted, "the Indians die so easily that the bare look and smell of a Spaniard causes them to give up the ghost."

All accounts agree that the island of Hispaniola was teeming with people when Columbus first landed there. Plausible estimates for the population go as high as a million, and we are fairly safe in assuming that there were at least several hundred thousand aboriginal inhabitants. But they became extinct in a remarkably short time after the intrusion of a few hundreds of Spaniards. The histories mostly explain this on the basis of the cruelty of the Spaniards on the one hand, and the lack of stamina of the Indians on the other. But the gunpowder and ferocity of the Spaniards, however potent, seem completely inadequate to explain the events without the addition of a few new viruses and bacteria.

Smallpox clearly was with Cortez in his conquest of Mexico. As the Stearns tell the story in their study of *The Effect of Smallpox on the Destiny of the Amerindian:*

> At the time of the departure of Narvaez from Cuba in order to join Cortez, smallpox was raging there severely. A pioneer vessel of the fleet brought the disease to Cozumel, whence it spread to the continent. . . . After desolating the coast regions, the disease crossed the plateau region and in the summer broke out around the lakes in passing to the land along the "western sea." For sixty days it raged with such virulence that the period of the raging of "hueyzahuatl," or great pest, fixed itself as a central point in the chronology of the natives. In most districts half the population died, towns became deserted, and those who recovered presented an appearance which horrified their neighbors. . . . In December, 1520, Cortez, on his way to Montezuma and the capital city of Mexico, stopped at Cholula, where he was asked to nominate new Indian chiefs to replace those dead from smallpox. Cuitlahuatzin, the younger brother of Montezuma, who had tried to rectify his elder brother's blunders, died of smallpox after a reign of three months. King Totoquihuatzin of Tlacopan was also an early victim of the disease.[9]

9. E. W. Stearn and A. E. Stearn, *The Effect of Smallpox on the Destiny of the Amerindian,* Boston, Humphries, Inc., 1945.

We have, of course, no nice statistics on the mortality rates of smallpox among the American Indians. One can only guess that it killed a respectable proportion of the population. When the disease appeared for the first time in Iceland, in 1707, it was said to have killed 18,000 out of a population of 50,000; and what evidence there is indicates that the mortality rates among some of the Indian epidemics were much higher than this.

There is ample evidence of the havoc caused by smallpox among the North American Indians—and here the Europeans sometimes, at least, appreciated their advantage. There seems to be no question about the occasional use of smallpox in a sort of "germ warfare." Sir Jeffrey Amherst, a British commander facing an Indian revolt, was explicit: "You will do well to try to inoculate the Indians by means of blankets as well as to try every other method that can serve to extirpate this execrable race." A Captain Ecuyer of the Royal Americans noted that "out of regard" for two Indian chiefs, "we have given them two blankets and a handkerchief out of the smallpox hospital. I hope it will have the desired effect." [9]

Smallpox may have been the most important ally of the Europeans in the depopulation of America, but it surely was not the only one. Among the islands of the Pacific where contacts were made later, and where more reliable accounts of the effects of new diseases are available, measles and mumps were prime agents of mortality, along with smallpox, tuberculosis, and various intestinal and respiratory diseases apparently new to the people. Venereal disease, which has generally been one of the "blessings" brought by Europeans to isolated peoples, has also had important population effects through reducing fertility, if not as a direct cause of mortality.

It seems to me that in tropical Africa we have had a nice reversal of this picture of the spread of disease through Western contact. Here the indigenous people were, for a long time, protected from Europeans by their diseases—yellow fever, potent local strains of malaria, and special diseases like sleeping-sickness. Of course, tropical Africa had had an indirect contact with the civilizations of the Mediterranean and the Near East for a very long time, and it may be that the special diseases of civilization spread to them at an early period, well ahead of the explorers and colonizers, so that the population had a chance to adapt to the disease situation. It also looks as though Africa, possibly the main focus of much of human evolution, may also have seen the evolution of many of the human diseases, which again would give the long-exposed indigenous population the advantage.

The present pattern of disease in the world, then, in many ways seems to be a consequence of the pattern of exploration, conquest and trade of the modern West. Contagious diseases in particular have tended to become cosmopolitan, and we now have a situation where an epidemic, like that of influenza in 1918, can sweep over the entire globe in a remarkably short time. Shared diseases seem to be one of the consequences of living on a planet that has become a neighborhood.

However unfortunate this has been in the past, there seems no reason it should continue so, because we can share knowledge of the diseases too. Surely, however one measures the accomplishments of Western civilization, one of its greatest achievements has been the understanding and control of infectious disease. So far this knowledge has been applied most effectively within the Western area itself, where the habits of the people and the economics of the situation permit great attention to public and private health. The knowledge is not as contagious as the disease, and the knowledge itself is often useless in the face of economic handicaps that seem insuperable. But infectious disease surely can be controlled, not only in the West, but everywhere, so that the prime causes of death will be physiological instead of ecological.

We have made no progress toward abolishing death; but by controlling the ecological causes, we have postponed it. . . .

Increase in Life Expectancy Due to Modern Medicine
HARRISON BROWN (1954)

Two thousand years ago the average baby born in the heavily populated city of Rome had a life expectancy of little more than 20 years. His contemporaries who were born in the provinces of Hispania and Lusitania, away from the unhealthy congestion of the capital of the empire, could expect to live for a considerably longer time—girls had a life expectancy of about 35 years, and boys, of about 40 years. In Roman Africa the chances of survival were even greater. Girls could expect to live about 45 years, and boys had nearly a 50-year life expectancy.

Life expectancy did not rise appreciably about those levels until very recent times. In 1850 the life expectancy at birth of a girl born in Massa-

From Harrison Brown, *The Challenge of Man's Future,* The Viking Press, New York. Coypright 1954 by Harrison Brown. Reprinted by permission.

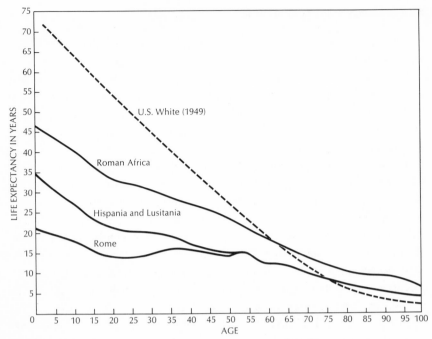

Figure 1. Female expectation of life in the ancient Roman Empire.

chusetts was little more than 40 years—only a little greater than that in ancient Hispania and Lusitania. In England, at the same time, the life expectancy at birth was very nearly the same as in the United States. Between 1850 and 1900 some decrease in mortality was achieved, and female life expectancy at birth rose to 47 years in England and to 50 years in the United States. Nevertheless, the life-expectancy figures at the turn of the century were not far removed from those which had existed in Roman Africa.

During the first half of the twentieth century enormous reductions were made in mortality rates in the United States, particularly in the younger age groups. Female infant mortality decreased from approximately 110 deaths per thousand births in 1900 to 26 per thousand in 1946. In 1900 only 80 per cent of the girls who were born could be expected to reach the age of 15. In 1953 over 96 per cent of all white girls born were expected to reach the onset of the breeding period. In 1900 only 65 per cent of newborn girls could be expected to survive until the end of the breeding period. In 1953 over 90 per cent of all white girls born in the United States could expect to reach their forty-fifth birthdays. The most impor-

tant single factor associated with the enormous decrease in mortality during the past 50 years has been the increase in knowledge, which permits
us to control many epidemic and endemic infections which are themselves
associated with the existence of civilization—diseases which were practically unknown in primitive societies. As we have seen, civilization has
resulted in the crowding of many people into small areas. This, in turn,
has created conditions for rapid incubation and spread of disease.

Since the time of Pasteur we have accumulated a vast amount of
knowledge concerning the nature of various infections and the ways in
which they are spread. Our knowledge permits us to control infections by
blocking the routes by which germs enter the body, by inducing immunity
to diseases through inoculation, and by reducing the mortality of diseases,
once contracted, through the use of drugs and proper hospital care.

A classic example of the application of the principles of immunology
has been inoculation against smallpox, which was practiced irregularly

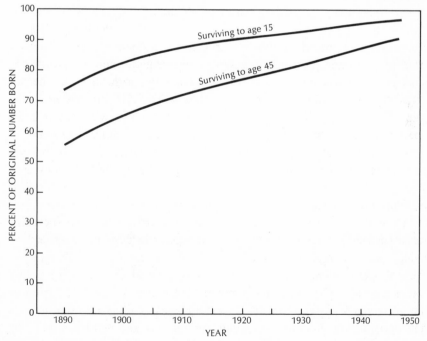

Figure 2. Percentage of white females in the United States who survive to and through
the fertile period.

long before the time of Pasteur. Prior to the introduction of vaccination, few people in Europe escaped having smallpox—and usually 1 out of 12 infected persons died. Today, by contrast, smallpox is a medical curiosity in the Western World. Following Pasteur's work, the principles of immunology have been extended to the point where we have today, in addition to smallpox vaccination, highly effective and preventive serums for a diversity of diseases, including typhoid fever, tetanus, rabies, scarlet fever, and diphtheria.

The most dramatic changes in mortality patterns during the past half-century have been connected with the control of infections in children. The pasteurization of milk alone has been largely responsible for the drop in frequency of diarrheal diseases in children under 5 years of age—a drop which has resulted in a decrease from 40 deaths per thousand children from this cause alone to a negligible number. During the early part of this century diarrhea and enteritis ranked as the chief causes of death of children under 1 year of age. Today these diseases rank fifth in importance as causes of death.

Death rates due to other diseases of childhood have likewise declined steadily through the years—some rapidly, others more gradually. The introduction of diphtheria antitoxin treatment in 1895 has led to a reduction of deaths resulting from that disease to a negligible proportion. Deaths resulting from scarlet fever, measles, and whooping cough have likewise decreased to levels which are low compared to those which existed at the turn of the century. We have now reached the point at which death rates among infants are determined, in the main, by causes other than infection—premature births, congenital malformations, and injury at birth. But the main causes of death during the second year of life are still diseases over which we have some, but not complete, control—bronchitis, pneumonia, measles, whooping cough, diarrhea, and enteritis.

In the Western World there is a clear relationship between mortality rates for the diseases of childhood, and economic class or "standard of living." For example, the infant death rate in England resulting from bronchitis and pneumonia in families of the poorest economic group was found recently to be seven times greater than that in families belonging to the professional class. Similarly, the ratio of deaths resulting from measles and whooping cough in the two groups were in the ratio of 15 to 1 and 7 to 1 respectively.

It seems likely that with further increased general medical care and fur-

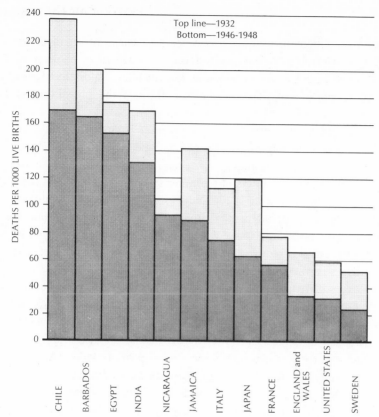

Figure 3. Deaths of infants under one year of age.

ther elevations of standards of living, death rates among children will be reduced to even lower levels than those which prevail today. Whereas at the present time we can expect approximately 96 per cent of the girls who are born to survive to the age of 15, it is not unlikely that two or three decades from now 98 per cent of the girls who are born will reach maturity. With further advances in the techniques of caring for prematurely born infants, a 99-per-cent survival to the age of 15 might be possible. Further reductions of infant and child mortality will be difficult, however, because of the limits imposed by congenital malformations and by congenital debility.

The principal reductions in mortality during the years from age 15 to age 40 have likewise been brought about by the control of infectious diseases. Perhaps the most outstanding achievement in this connection has been the virtual elimination of typhoid fever as a cause of death in the United States. Mortality from typhoid fever was highest in adolescence and early adult life, and its elimination has therefore substantially increased the proportion of persons who live through the breeding period.

During the latter part of the last century deaths from typhoid fever in Chicago were approximately 50 to 100 per year per 100,000 inhabitants. During occasional major outbreaks, mortality rose to even higher levels. Following the installation of filters in the water system in 1906, the inauguration of water chlorination in 1913, and the introduction of pasteurized milk, the number of typhoid deaths dropped precipitously to extremely low levels. In the United States as a whole, the further protection given by typhoid inoculations has reduced the annual mortality from the disease to less than 1 death per 200,000 persons.

Tuberculosis still remains one of the greatest of all threats to the lives of young adults, yet the decrease in mortality during the last 50 years has been dramatic. In the United States in 1900 nearly 200 out of every 100,000 persons were killed each year by the disease. With the spread of increased facilities for treating the disease, and improved methods of early diagnosis, mortality has been lowered to one-sixth the former number.

It is likely that mortality from tuberculosis will be decreased still further in the future, for we know that the death rate depends greatly upon the environment. Recently, for example, the tuberculosis mortality rate in the poorest class in England was found to be greater than twice the mortality rate in the wealthiest class.

It seems likely that with continued improvement of living conditions, coupled with continued increase in the general availability of adequate nutrition and medical care, death rates resulting from diseases such as tuberculosis, bronchial and lobar pneumonia, and rheumatic fever will be decreased to levels much lower than those which exist today, even if no really specific cures for the diseases are found. When this point is reached, the main barriers to further decreases in mortality will be deaths from such phenomena as childbirth, accidents, virus diseases such as influenza, . . . cancer, and "degenerative" diseases such as hypertensive vascular disease. It is quite possible that further research on the nature of virus diseases will disclose more effective controls than those which exist today. Further, it seems likely that death rates resulting from childbirth will be reduced to a level considerably lower than that now prevailing. In addition, growing awareness of the considerable incidence of accidental death has resulted in the establishment of accident-prevention programs of increasing scope and effectiveness.

When we take all of these factors into consideration, it is probable that the adult mortality curve of a century from now will be determined in the main by such diseases as cancer, nephritis, heart disease, cerebral hemorrhage, and diseases of the arteries. When that time arrives, we can expect approximately 96 per cent of all girls born to reach their forty-fifth birthdays.

Beyond the age of 45 a high percentage of death results from degenerative diseases. The human body, like other highly organized living structures, will apparently serve for only a limited period of time before certain processes start which we are helpless to combat—at least at the present time. A part of our helplessness results from our lack of understanding of the nature and the causes of the processes associated with aging. Nevertheless, a good case can be made for the view that although medical science is making it possible for ever-increasing numbers of people to live out their natural life span, the ultimate "limit" of the human life span is not being increased appreciably.

It seems likely that every human being is genetically endowed at conception with a certain "life potential"—a natural life span which could be fulfilled in the absence of physical or biological accidents, and which seems to vary greatly from individual to individual. At one end of the scale are those babies who are born with biological weaknesses that terminate their lives within a few minutes or hours. At the other end of the scale are those relatively few individuals who live to pass the century mark. The bodies of most individuals are of intermediate stability and appear to be sufficiently well constructed to permit them to function for at least 75 years (barring physical or biological accidents) before degenerative processes bring about death.

The record of decreasing mortality during the last half-century attests to the difficulty of increasing the life expectancy of the aged. Since 1900 we have lowered the mortality rates of infants, children, and young adults to one-fifth the previous number, but our success in reducing mortality rates in older age groups has been less spectacular. The probability of an 80-year-old woman dying during the course of a year is only 20 per cent less today than it was 50 years ago. In spite of our greatly increased medical knowledge and our improved facilities for the care of the aged, the decrease in mortality rate for 90-year-old persons is so slight as to be only barely observable.

It seems clear that the primary reductions in the mortality rates of older persons have resulted from the same developments which lowered the death rates of young people. But with older persons the probability of death due to degeneration and resultant stoppage of any one of the innumerable functioning components of the body is large compared with the probability of death due to infectious diseases. Consequently, although the deaths due to disease have been reduced considerably, the decreases have had but small effect upon the over-all death rates of older groups.

It is unlikely that the general situation with respect to the degenerative causes of death will change very rapidly in the future. Some progress has been made in the treatment of certain types of cancer and heart disease, but the over-all demographic effect has been small. When the body grows

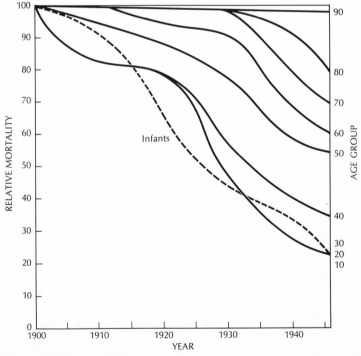

Figure 4. Relative mortality rates of white females in the United States (1900–1946). 1900 mortality = 100.

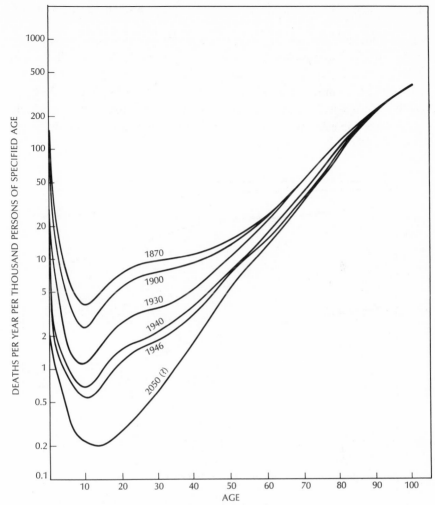

Figure 5. Mortality rates, United States white females.

old, there are many possibilities of failure. An older man might be saved one day from death from cancer, but he might die soon afterward of nephritis or heart failure.

Our knowledge of the processes of aging and degeneration must be considerably greater than it is today if the human life span is to be increased much beyond that which exists at present. And even when we understand the processes of aging, it may well turn out that there is little that can be done about it. However, in the unlikely event that new biochemical discoveries result in our attaining greatly increased life spans, the demographic consequences will be small when compared with the consequences of the biological discoveries that have already been made. Even if we are able at some future time to increase the average life expectancy to 150 years, the long-range consequences will be merely a doubling of Western population. When we compare this with the population increases which are made possible by our existing techniques, it appears that an increased

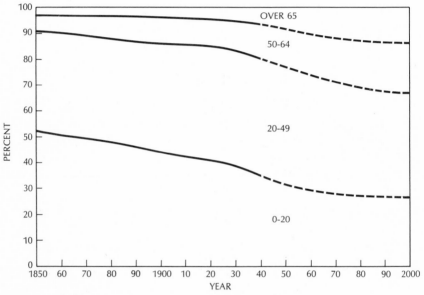

Figure 6. Changing age distribution in the United States since 1850.

natural life span would make a relatively unimportant contribution to future population changes.

The increased life expectancy that has been made possible by the technological developments of the past century has strongly affected two aspects of population growth. First, an increasingly large fraction of newborn girls survives to reach the breeding age. Second, and quite independent of birth pattern, the long life span has resulted in increased population solely because more people are living longer. The latter effect [combined with the declining birth rates have produced] . . . a marked change in the composition of the population.

One hundred years ago over 50 per cent of all persons living in the

United States were under the age of 20, a mere 2.6 per cent were over the
age of 65, and the median age of the population was only 18.8 years. By
1900 the median age had risen to 22.9. During the last 50 years the proportion of persons in the United States under 20 years of age has dropped
to 34 per cent, the proportion of persons over 65 has increased to approximately 7 per cent, and the median age of the population has risen to
30.1. These changes are still under way, and during the course of the next

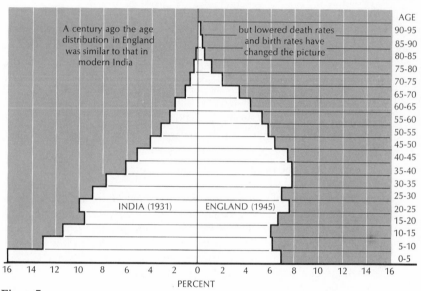

Figure 7.

few decades we can expect the proportion of persons over 65 years of age
to increase further and approach 15 per cent.

One hundred years ago the population age distribution in the United
States and in the rest of the Western World was very much the same as it
is in the Far East and in many other areas of the world today. Even in the
United States and in England we can expect further population increases,
solely on the basis of increasing the average life span, even if the net
reproduction rates should drop again to the neighborhood of unity and remain there. However, these expected increases are small when compared
with the increases that would result from this effect alone in India and
China if the mortality rates in those areas were lowered to the rates which

we now know are medically possible. Given adequate food and medical care, the populations of those countries would double even if birth rates were drastically lowered to the levels prevailing in the West.

In view of the fact that populations cannot increase without limit, the birth rate must eventually equal the death rate. All too often we lose sight of this fact, living as we do in a period of rapid population transition. But under what circumstances can we expect the two rates to become equal? Clearly equalization might take place in a variety of ways. We could have low birth rates and low death rates, or high birth rates and high death rates; or we could have any of the gradations between the two extremes.

If we extrapolate (i.e., calculate a future trend on the basis of past experience) the mortality rates prevailing in Western culture to the limits which might be achieved in the foreseeable future, the death rate for the population at equilibrium will be between 13 and 14 per 1000 persons. If intercourse took place freely in such a population, and if no protective measures were taken, the annual birth rate would be extremely high—over 40 per 1000. In order for it to be as low as 14 per 1000, the population must condone or urge one or more of several possible practices:

1. Restriction of sexual intercourse, either through postponement of marriage coupled with strong condemnation of intercourse prior to marriage, or through the establishment of culture patterns which severely restrict intercourse frequency after marriage. Included in this category would be restriction of intercourse resulting from reliance upon the "rhythm" or "safe-period" technique of family limitation.
2. Abortion.
3. Sterilization.
4. Fertility control, either through the practice of coitus interruptus or through the use of chemicals or devices designed to prevent conception.

In the absence of restraint, abortion, sterilization, coitus interruptus, or artificial fertility control, the resultant high birth rate would have to be matched at equilibrium by an equally high death rate. A major contribution to the high death rate could be infanticide, as has been the situation in cultures of the past. More likely, the high death rate would result from debility arising from insufficient food supply, poor living conditions, and inadequate medical care. If the population is limited primarily by food supply, medical care can never be adequate. No numbers of doctors and hospitals, or quantities of medicine, can lower mortality rates if there is insufficient food to support the population.

Food and Fertility

The Conflict Between Creeds and Needs
KARL SAX (1960)

A startling—though logical—proposal for control of population growth in these areas [underdeveloped] has been the suggestion that during the early stages of the Demographic Transition we *permit* rather than *control* high death rates. Gerald F. Winfield, who spent many years in China as a medical missionary, makes the following proposal:

> It is obvious that the first objective of the medical-health program must *not* be the simple, natural one of saving lives. Instead, it must be the development of means whereby the Chinese people will reduce their birth rate as rapidly as modern science can reduce the death rate. The proposition is made with an acute awareness of its radical nature. For one trained in public health it will seem rank heresy to propose that during the next twenty to thirty years not even severe epidemics in China should be attacked with every means available to modern medicine. I suggest that public health measures which can save millions of lives should not be practiced in China on a nation-wide scale until the stage is set for a concurrent reduction of the birth rate. . . . The future welfare of the Chinese people is more dependent on the prevention of births than on the prevention of deaths.[1]

A similar view is expressed by John D. Black:

> Another point of view is that of the pure unthinking sentimentalist who says that relieving hunger and disease is always good and that it is

1. Winfield, Gerald F. *China, the Land and the People.* New York: William Sloane Associates, 1948.

From Karl Sax, *Standing Room Only: The World's Exploding Population,* The Beacon Press, Boston. Copyright © 1955 by The Beacon Press. Preface to the New Edition Copyright © 1960 by Karl Sax. Reprinted by permission.

the moral obligation of other nations to do this just as it is of a doctor to help the sick. The answer is that, when whole populations are considered, prolonging a few lives this year is of no avail if this causes more misery and suffering in the years following. . . . Those who speak in this way are charged with being "hard-boiled" and non-humanitarian, but they are the true humanitarians.[2]

The Dangerous Doctor
WILLIAM VOGT (1948)

The modern medical profession, still framing its ethics on the dubious statements of an ignorant man who lived more than two thousand years ago—ignorant, that is, in terms of the modern world—continues to believe it has a duty to keep alive as many people as possible. In many parts of the world doctors apply their intelligence to one aspect of man's welfare—survival—and deny their moral right to apply it to the problem as a whole. Through medical care and improved sanitation they are responsible for more millions living more years in increasing misery. Their refusal to consider their responsibility in these matters does not seem to them to compromise their intellectual integrity. They have been primarily responsible for making Puerto Rico, for example, one of the most miserable areas on the face of the earth, by expanding the population beyond all possible bounds of decent subsistence, and their present efforts to correct the situation are not much more than tokens.[1] They set the stage for disaster; then, like Pilate, they wash their hands of the consequences.

Malthus and the Conscience of Mankind
RITCHIE CALDER (1962)

Nearly 160 years ago, the Rev. Thomas Malthus insisted that reproductive capacity encouraged population growth far in excess of the likely

2. Black, John D. "The Economics of Freedom from Want," *Chronica Botanica,* 1948.

[1. The population trend in Puerto Rico will be discussed in Part III, see pp. 284–301. Ed.]

increase in the means of subsistence. . . . There was nothing wrong with his mathematics nor can his basic thesis be disproved by showing that we have "got by". But, as the Hammonds pointed out in *The Town and Country Labourer,* "Malthus puts a cushion under the conscience of the upper classes." During the nineteenth century, all the social abuses—bad housing, bad sanitation, bad working conditions—could always be justified: if you did anything to improve the conditions of the poor, they would just have more children and, poor things, they would die of hunger!

There is a danger, obvious today, of Malthus "putting a cushion under the conscience" of the well-to-do, in this case the wealthy countries. When intelligent and humane men look at this problem in the abstract, without putting names and faces to people, they are led up dangerous alleys. Professor A. V. Hill, Nobel Prize winner for Medicine, as president of the British Association in 1952, expressed himself thus:

> "Had it been possible to foresee the enormous success of this application (of the benefits of science) would humane people have agreed that it could better have been held back, to keep in step with other parallel progress, so that development could be planned and orderly? Some might say yes, taking the purely biological view that if men will breed like rabbits they must be allowed to die like rabbits, until gradually improving education and the demand for a better standard of life teach them better. Most people will still say no. But suppose that it were now certain that increasing population, uncontrolled by disease, would lead not only to widespread exhaustion of the soil and of other capital resources, but also of continuing and increasing international tension and disorder making it hard for civilization itself to survive: would the majority of humane and reasonable people then change their minds? If ethical principles deny our right to do evil in order that good may come are we justified in doing good when the foreseeable consequences are evil?"

That was the rhetorical problem posed by a pre-eminently humane man. But consider the implications: they are nothing short of genocide. The ignorant, biologically improvident peoples of the backward races are to be denied the advances which science has made. All the humanitarian work which has gone on since the Second World War, offsetting so much that is squalid and cynical in world politics, has been "doing good when the foreseeable consequences are evil."

But putting the problem this way also ignores the essential truth, which takes no account of mathematics and scientific abstractions. The people who would thus be left in limbo are those of the emerging nations whose governments at their certain peril will deny them the benefits, the *known* benefits of modern science, because science which has deployed such benefits has also provided the means of communications which has made people aware of them. In Afghanistan I have seen illiterate tribes marching on Kabul to demand DDT, which would free them, as they knew it had freed their neighbours, from malaria, and typhus, and scratching. . . .

Democracy is a word which rumbles meaninglessly in empty bellies. Or, as [John Boyd Orr] put it to the statesmen of the West, "What you pretend to call 'Communism' in underdeveloped countries is hunger becoming articulate."

For hunger is a curious thing: at first it is with you all the time, waking and sleeping and in your dreams, and your belly cries out insistently, and there is a gnawing and a pain as if your very vitals were being devoured, and you must stop it at any cost, and you buy a moment's respite even while you know and fear the sequel. Then the pain is no longer sharp but dull, and this too is with you always, so that you think of food many times a day and each time a ter-

Constantin Joffe. Vogue.

Cas Oorthuys.

" . . . Nothing is real to us but hunger." Kakuzo Okakura.

rible sickness assails you, and because you know this you try to avoid the thought, but you cannot, it is with you. Then that too is gone, all pain, all desire, only a great emptiness is left, like the sky, like a well in drought, and it is now that the strength drains from your limbs, and you try to rise and find you cannot, or to swallow water and your throat is powerless, and both the swallow and the effort of retaining the liquid tax you to the uttermost.

Kamala Markandaya
Nectar in a Sieve

The need for more food is the most urgent problem facing the world today. More than half of the world's people do not get enough to eat. Hunger is an old story in human history. It is reflected in the Lord's Prayer, where the appeal for food takes priority over the appeal for forgiveness of sins. The same philosophy is expressed in the ancient Chinese proverb, "It is difficult to tell the difference between right and wrong when the stomach is empty." The wisdom of the Chinese is also reflected in their word for peace, *ho-ping,* which means literally "food for all." In more recent times, Gandhi observed that "to the millions who have to go without two meals a day, the only acceptable form in which God dare appear is food."

Karl Sax, *Standing Room Only:*
The World's Exploding Population

Editor's Note: *Many writers have attacked the Malthusian theory that population always presses upon the means of subsistence. One of the most interesting theories was proposed by Thomas Doubleday in 1853. This theory was recently revived and expanded by Josue De Castro.*

Fertile Is the Bed of Misery

JOSUE DE CASTRO (1952)

Growth of population is determined, in the final analysis, by the play between two basic factors: fertility and mortality. Everything that affects the

trend of a population does so by means of one or the other of these elements. Since starvation undeniably raises the death rate, it has always
been thought that it operated, like wars and plagues, to retard the growth
of population. It seems highly paradoxical, then, to say that hunger, far
from leading to *de*population, tends to bring about *over*population.

My statement, however, is based on a series of fully demonstrated facts.
First, it is a matter of common observation that, following periods of
calamity, famine and pestilence, populations always increase their rate of
growth. It is also clearly observable that the countries on the lowest nutritional level, where millions of people regularly and "normally" starve to
death, are also the areas of most violent increase in population: China,
India, Egypt, and various Central American countries. On the other hand,
the countries at the highest nutritional level show unmistakable evidence
of early population decline, with births barely equaling deaths. That is the
case in Australia, New Zealand and the United States.

That paradox is explained by the fact that while hunger as a social
phenomenon increases the death rate, it increases the birth rate even
more, so that the net effect is to speed up the rate of population increase.
It is commonly noted that the undernourished classes are the most fertile;
the ancient Romans had a word for those who, on a starvation diet, had
many offspring, or *proles*—"proletarians." There is a popular saying in
Latin America that "the table of the poor is meager, but fertile is the bed
of misery. . . ."

In spite of these significant commonplaces, however, speculation on the
question of population growth has generally followed the line that food
scarcity is associated with population decline, or reduced rate of growth,
while abundance of food has been held to determine more rapid growth.
That has been the established opinion, although toward the middle of the
last century there lived one philosopher and demographer who thought
otherwise. Thomas Doubleday, reacting against scientific conservatism,
undertook a systematic description of the manner in which lack of sufficient food increases the rate of population growth. In an essay which has
been completely forgotten, "The True Law of Population Shewn to Be
Connected with the Food of the People," he wrote, in 1853, these prophetic words:

> The GREAT GENERAL LAW then, which, as it seems, really regulates the
> increase or decrease both of vegetable and of animal life, is this, that
> whenever a *species* or *genus* is *endangered,* a corresponding effort is in-
> variably made by nature for its preservation and continuance, by an in-

crease of fecundity or fertility; and that this especially takes place whenever such danger arises from a diminution of proper nourishment or food, so that consequently the state of depletion, or the deplethoric state, is favorable to fertility; and on the other hand, the plethoric state, or state of repletion, is unfavorable to fertility, in the ratio of intensity of each state, and this probably throughout nature universally, in the vegetable as well as in the animal world; further, that as applied to mankind this law produces the following consequences, and acts thus:

There is in all societies a constant increase going on amongst that portion of it which is the worst supplied with food; in short, amongst the poorest.

Amongst those in the state of affluence, and well supplied with food and luxuries, a constant decrease goes on.[1]

Doubleday's theories, unfortunately, did not become widely known. Official circles rejected them for various reasons, of which the most powerful was, according to the canny observation of Raymond Pearl, that "he offended the sentimental susceptibilities and moral judgments of the early-Victorian middle and upper classes." And since Doubleday could not muster enough facts to prove his intuitive assertions, his whole theory was forgotten. This was another striking victory for the taboo that has made hunger a forbidden subject!

Today, however, the supporting facts are at hand, and we can risk a collision with Victorian prejudices and neo-Malthusian theories. It is high time to challenge a point of view which, inspired by economic or political interest, regards as a natural human condition what is in fact the result of social factors.

• • •

In its sexual effects, chronic hunger, whether specific or latent, operates quite diffierently from acute starvation. Starvation is known to diminish libido; groups of people subjected to persistent malnutrition, on the other hand, appear to be sexually stimulated. They show a definite increase in fertility over the less badly fed. This intensification of the reproductive capacities in chronically starved people develops through a complex process involving both physiological and psychological factors.

The psychological effect of chronic hunger is to make sex important enough to compensate emotionally for the shrunken nutritional appetite. Under normal conditions, it is universally agreed, the instincts toward re-

---

1. Thomas Doubleday, "The True Law of Population Shewn to be Connected with the Food of the People," London, 1853.

production and nutrition compete with each other, and when one retreats, the other advances. When chronic hunger, then, particularly hunger for proteins and certain vitamins, produces chronic lack of appetite and loss of interest in food, the sexual instinct becomes dominant. The chronic starveling, whose appetite for food is dulled and easily satisfied, turns his attention away from his weakened nutritional instincts. The biologically important and psychologically satisfactory activity which presents itself is sexual. Thus one primary need is emphasized to compensate for the diminution of the other.

The exaggerated sensuality of some societies or social classes who live in a state of chronic undernourishment is explained by this mechanism of compensation. Their high fertility index, however, is also due to an important physiological aspect of hunger.

Cattle raisers have long known that animals which get too fat may become sterile, and that reduced rations will re-establish fertility. This empirical evidence has caused no great stir in scientific circles. But there are today experimental data and systematic observations which explain the correlation between food and fertility. They make clear the way in which partial nutritional deficiencies work to accelerate the multiplication of a species.

Hunger for proteins, involving a deficit in certain important amino acids, increases significantly the fertility of animals. Proof of this is in the sensational experiments of J. R. Slonaker,[2] which have not yet had the recognition they should and must receive. Slonaker subjected groups of rats to diets which varied in protein content, and studied their reproductive indices for six generations. He found that diets rich in proteins, when proteins constituted more than 18 per cent of the total calorie intake, were unfavorable on all counts to the reproduction of the species: they increased sterility, retarded the epoch of fertilization of the females, and reduced the number of litters and the number of young in each litter.

Some of Slonaker's figures speak with such eloquence and discrimination that they merit presentation in detail. Slonaker observed that when male rats received a diet with only 10 per cent of its total calories in proteins, 5 per cent of them were sterile; when the protein content of the ration was increased to 18 per cent and 22 per cent, the sterility increased to 22 per cent and 40 per cent respectively. With females, the same in-

2. J. R. Slonaker, *American Journal of Physiology*, Nos. 71, 83, 96, 97 98, 123, 1925–1928.

crease of protein in the diet lifted the sterility rate from 6 per cent to 23 per cent and 38 per cent respectively. There were impressive differences in the average numbers of offspring of the various groups of rats. Eating 10 per cent protein, each rat produced an average of 23.3 offspring; with 18 per cent protein, 17.4; and with 22 per cent, only 13.8.

These figures clearly suggest that in proportion as the diet increases in protein content, reproductive capacity drops. It is also true, however, that the larger protein rations bring about a better resistance to disease in the young and an increase in the percentage of those that survive. It appears, then, that with a percentage of proteins high enough to guarantee a good survival index among the offspring, the number of these offspring falls off; and that when diets are inadequate in protein, nature multiplies the number of offspring so as to guarantee the continuation of the species.

With the human species, the case is the same. The groups with highest fertility are those who have the lowest percentage of complete proteins, animal proteins, in their regular diets. The highest birth rates in the world are registered by certain peoples of the Far East, Africa and Latin America, where the proportion of animal products in the habitual rations does not reach 5 per cent of the total food consumed. In contrast to this, the lowest birth rates exist among the peoples of western Europe, the United States, Australia and New Zealand, where the proportion of foods of animal origin in the ration reaches, respectively, 17 per cent (western Europe); 25 per cent (United States); and 36 per cent (Australia and New Zealand).

Geographically, the countries with high birth rates (above 30) are all tropical countries, whose geographic and economic conditions are ill adapted to either the production or the consumption of proteins of animal origin. The predominantly vegetable diet of these countries is certainly one of the decisive factors in their fertility. If we compare the birth rate with the consumption of animal proteins throughout the world, we find a frank correlation between the two factors, the fertility going down as the consumption of such proteins rises.

The table on page 71 is made up of countries with birth rates varying from the highest to the lowest. And while protein is not of course the exclusive controller of fertility, it does point up a significant correlation between fertility and protein consumption.

The exaggerated multiplication of humanity through excessive fertility, then, is ultimately a problem in specific hunger—one of the strangest aspects of the phenomenon of universal hunger. Hunger is responsible for the overproduction of human beings, excessive in number and inferior in quality, who are hurled blindly into the demographic metabolism of the world.

This manifestation of hunger is of primary importance to my study, since it provides a biological basis for my theory that specific hunger is the cause of overpopulation. . . .

The notion that lack of proteins stimulates fertility is not merely a hypothesis that happens to be borne out by the facts. Enough is known

Countries	Birth Rate	Daily Consumption of Animal Proteins, in Grams
Formosa	45.6	4.7
Malay States	39.7	7.5
India	33.0	8.7
Japan	27.0	9.7
Yugoslavia	25.9	11.2
Greece	23.5	15.2
Italy	23.4	15.2
Bulgaria	22.2	16.8
Germany	20.0	37.3
Ireland	19.1	46.7
Denmark	18.3	59.1
Australia	18.0	59.9
United States	17.9	61.4
Sweden	15.0	62.6

about protein metabolism so that we can trace the actual mechanism by which protein deficiency leads to increased fertility, while an abundance of protein has the opposite effect. A detailed explanation of this process is beyond the scope of this book, but I should like to outline its fundamental points in order to clarify the scientific basis of certain of my assertions.

Biologically, fertility depends on the functioning of organs whose action is regulated, in large part, by hormones, which are the secretions of certain ductless glands. Fecundation in women is closely related to the functioning of the ovaries, to the production of their hormones, particularly the estrogens, and to the quantity of these substances present in the blood and internal organs.

It is known that there is a direct connection between the functioning of the liver and the ovaries, the role of the liver being to inactivate the excess estrogens which the ovaries throw into the blood stream. Fatty degeneration of the liver and the tendency to cirrhosis are . . . among the characteristic results of protein deficiency, and are very common in the Far East and in certain tropical areas of other continents. When degeneration of the liver occurs it begins to operate less efficiently, and is less effective at its job of inactivating excess estrogens. The result is a marked increase in the woman's reproductive capacity.

The total reproductive capacity of an organism—its fertility—is the result of a series of physiological processes. In viviparous animals such as man, it depends on the production of the ovum by the ovary, on its fertilization and its development *in utero*. These processes, ovulation, fertilization and fetal development, are highly dependent on the functioning of the estrogenic hormones. Sexual appetite, the libido itself, which Raymond Pearl[3] includes among the factors determining the level of fertility, depends on the percentage of this hormone within the body.

It is no longer necessary, then, to imagine that by some obscure and mysterious process Mother Nature speeds up reproduction when the species seems threatened with extinction. The mechanism of animal metabolism which maintains this functional equilibrium is complex but not at all mysterious: protein deficiency leads to deficiency in the functions of the liver; this results in a reduction or loss of the liver's ability to inactivate estrogens; the excess of estrogens increases the woman's fertility. Then too, we have examined the psychological mechanism by which chronic hunger intensifies the sexual appetite at the same time that it lowers the appetite for food, and the assistance this process gives in maintaining a high birth rate among the hungry peoples of the world.

Comments on the De Castro Theory
KARL SAX (1960)

In view of the apparent acceptance of De Castro's theory by eminent people in various countries, and the apparent approval of his book by Sir John Boyd-Orr, former chairman of the Food and Agriculture Organiza-

3. Raymond Pearl, *The Natural History of Population*, London, 1939.

From Karl Sax, *Standing Room Only: The World's Exploding Population*, The Beacon Press, Boston. Copyright © 1955 by The Beacon Press. Preface to the New Edition copyright © 1960 by Karl Sax. Reprinted by permission.

tion of the United Nations, his theory should be examined in some detail. De Castro compares J. R. Slonaker's conclusions from experiments with rats with the relationship between human diet and birth rates in selected countries of the world. Slonaker fed rats with food varying in protein content from 10 to 26 per cent. (The protein from animal sources varied from about 5 to 23 per cent.) His experiment showed that a total protein content of 14 per cent gave the highest degree of fertility. With higher protein consumption, there was less fertility; rats on a 25-per-cent protein diet produced only one-fourth as many offspring as those on a 14-per-cent protein diet. A high-protein diet reduced not only fertility, but also viability, growth rate, activity, time of maturity, and longevity. Obviously, this particular high-protein diet was deleterious in every respect.

However, in an earlier experiment (not mentioned by De Castro), Slonaker and Card [1] had found that rats fed on a diet restricted to corn and vegetables were so sterile that by the third generation the family became extinct. (When 2 or 3 grams of meat scraps were added to the corn and vegetable diet, fecundity was more than doubled.) Sherman and Campbell [2] found that one part of dried milk added to five parts of wheat provided a better diet than wheat alone.[3] More recently, Davis [4] found that well-fed city rats were not only larger than their poorly fed country cousins but more than twice as fertile.

All of these experiments show that the well-fed rats and ones that consumed a moderate amount of animal protein grew larger, matured earlier, lived longer, were more active, and proved more fertile than rats that ate only plant products. It is true that Slonaker's high-protein diet reduced fertility; but it also reduced size, longevity, and activity—factors not found in well-fed populations such as ours. Excessive overweight does reduce fertility in livestock and presumably in man; but this is not an important factor among the great majority of couples during the most fertile years.

1. Slonaker, J. R., and Card, T. A. "The Effect of Restricted Diet," *American Journal of Physiology*, 1923.
2. Sherman, H. C., and Campbell, H. L. "Growth and Reproduction upon Simplified Food Supply," *Journal of Biological Chemistry*, 1924.
3. When the milk was increased to two parts dried milk, the diet was further improved. Rats receiving two parts milk in the diet grew larger, matured earlier, had a much longer reproductive span, lived longer, and were three times as fertile as the rats receiving only one part milk plus five parts wheat in their diet.
4. Davis, D. E. "A Comparison of Reproductive Potential of Two Rat Populations," *Ecology*, 1951.

De Castro presents a list of countries to show that people who live largely on a carbohydrate diet have high birth rates, and that those who get much of their food from animal sources have low birth rates. In general, birth rates are high in the countries with poor diets and low in the countries with good diets.

It can be shown that, in the demographic Group I countries of the world, the average animal protein consumption per person per day is 1.6 ounces; in Group II countries, 0.9; and in Group III countries, 0.3. The

Table 1
The Relation Between Animal–Protein Consumption and Birth Rates

	Protein consumption (grams per day per person)	1950 birth rates
Venezuela	23	43.0
Mexico	16	43.7
Ceylon	6	40.2
New Zealand	65	25.9
Greece	18	26.1
Japan	8	25.6
Ireland	50	21.0
France	40	20.4
Italy	20	19.6
Sweden	58	16.4
Belgium	36	16.5
Austria	27	15.6

Data from United Nations, *World Social Situation* (1952); and from *Population Index,* July 1952. The Japanese birth rate is given for 1951.

birth rates for the three demographic areas are about 20, 30, and 40 respectively. However, there is no evidence that there is any causal relationship between protein intake and fertility. There is also a high negative correlation between birth rates and the number of motor vehicles, literacy, and telephones per thousand of population.[5] It would be just as logical to assume that people who spend much of their time riding, talking, or reading have low birth rates because they have so little time for reproduction.

5. Spengler, J. J. "Economic Factors in the Development of Densely Populated Areas," *Proceedings of the American Philosophical Society,* 1951.

We find no significant causal relationship between animal protein consumption and human birth rates. Countries that vary greatly in per-capita consumption of animal proteins often have very similar birth rates (Table 1). The people of Venezuela consume nearly four times as much protein as the people of Ceylon; yet birth rates are high in both countries. The Venezuelans consume little more meat than the Italians; but their birth rate is more than twice as high. The New Zealanders consume eight times as much meat as the Japanese; yet their birth rates are similar.[6]

In the United States meat consumption happens to show, statistically, a positive correlation with birth rates. During the period from 1900 to 1950, meat consumption reached its peak in 1908, with a per-capita consumption of 163 pounds; the birth rate in 1909 was 27. The consumption of meat in 1935 reached its lowest level with a per-capita consumption of 116 pounds; in the following year the birth rate was 17 per thousand. With the return of more prosperous times, the per-capita meat consumption reached 153 pounds in 1946, and the birth rate increased to nearly 26 per thousand in 1947.

This does not, however, indicate a causal relationship between meat consumption and fertility. In 1908 the practice of contraception was not as prevalent as it became in later years. In the depression year of 1935, people could not afford to eat as much meat or to have as many children. In 1946—with the return of the servicemen, more prosperous times, and high marriage rates—both meat consumption and pregnancy increased substantially.

There is no evidence to support De Castro's conclusion that high birth rates in man are caused by diets deficient in animal proteins. . . .

There is, in fact, no evidence that the low birth rates of Western nations are due either to evolutionary trends, to education *per se,* or to ample food. If modern civilization, education, and ample diets were responsible for low birth rates, it would seen strange that Americans spend at least $250,000,000 per year for contraceptives.

---

6. The Eskimos consume more protein than any other ethnic group, 45 per cent of their food being in the form of animal proteins; yet their birth rate of 47 is among the highest in the world, according to a U.S. Census survey of selected villages. Hrdlička, in a survey of twelve Eskimo villages, found that 68.8 per cent of the women either were pregnant or had borne a child during the year. Hrdlička, A. "Fecundity of Eskimo Women," *American Journal of Physical Anthropology,* 1936.

Starvation and Fertility

MARSTON BATES (1955)

There is every shade in the spectrum of opinion about this population problem, and the most widely different views can be held with great tenacity and defended with ferocity. . . .

De Castro deals with the relationship between nutrition and reproduction at what might be called a physiological level; whereas I think that in man the cultural factors overwhelm any likely physiological effects. One may be able to show a relation between diet and litter size in rats, and there may well be a direct relation between the kind of food eaten and fertility in man. But when one examines actual situations, like Ireland, the explanation of changed fertility in man always seems to lie in things like marriage rates, birth control practices, infanticide, or such-like social factors, rather than in relative or absolute amounts of protein or vitamins or other things in the diet.

As far as I can see, most of the evidence from physiological studies indicates that malnutrition and famine tend to reduce fertility in man, so that the high reproductive rates in the Orient persist in spite of malnutrition rather than because of it.

One of the most interesting, and certainly the most thorough, of studies of the effects of starvation on man was carried out by Ancel Keys and a group of collaborators at the University of Minnesota, during World War II, using a group of volunteers from among "conscientious objectors." Their studies were written up and published in two huge volumes, which contain not only the results of their own observations, but also the results of combing through a vast literature.

One of the first effects of starvation on the men in the Minnesota group was a loss of all interest in sex. Their thoughts and dreams turned on food, not women; and their normal pattern of sexual activity . . . was broken.

> The diminution of the strength of the sex drive was so dramatic that the subjects were struck by the change and used colorful language to de-

From Marston Bates, *The Prevalence of People,* Charles Scribner's Sons, New York. Copyright © 1955 by Marston Bates. Reprinted by permission.

scribe it. As one of them put it, "I have no more sexual feeling than a sick oyster. . . ." In the rehabilitation period, sexual impulses, needs and interests were very slow in regaining their pre-experimental intensity; they were still low at the end of the 12th week of rehabilitation.[1]

Keys made all sorts of physiological measurements on his starvation subjects, including measurements of semen volume and sperm count. From these it appears that the men would probably have been sterile even if they had had the drive and opportunity for sex. Recovery was slow, and the semen did not become normal until more than 20 weeks after rehabilitation had started.

The female reproductive system is surely also affected by starvation. The most direct evidence is the frequency of amenorrhea, or interruption of regular menstruation, under internment camp conditions. Keys quotes one observation, however, of a physician who noted that menstruation continued to be regular among emaciated Chinese women, suggesting an "adaptation to chronic starvation."

Direct evidence on fertility under actual famine conditions is hard to come by, because the conditions that lead to famine are not conducive to orderly statistical studies. Such evidence as there is, however, all tends to indicate greatly lowered fertility. For instance, during the severe famine in Madras in 1877, there were only 39 births in the relief camps, although more than 100,000 people were being cared for over a period of some months. The birth rate dropped early in the famine, probably as a consequence of the preceding near-famine conditions, and continued low for a considerable time. Nine months after the worst food shortage the birth rate was four to five per 1,000, as compared to a usual rate of 29 per 1,000 in the same districts.

Statistical services were maintained in the Netherlands all through World War II, and the record of births there is consequently one of the few available for famine conditions. In Rotterdam, for instance, there was no significant change in the birth rate from 1939 through 1944. Food was moderately restricted from the middle of 1940; but serious failure of food supply did not occur until September, 1944, with a low point in availability of food from January to April, 1945. The birth rate started to fall in July, 1945, ten months after the failure of food the previous September. By October, 1945, births were less than half of normal (averaging 84 per

1. Ancel Keys, J. Brozek, A. Henschel, O. Michelsen and H. L. Taylor, *The Biology of Human Starvation*. University of Minnesota Press, Minneapolis, 1950.

week as compared with 210 to 245 per week in 1944). The birth rate in Rotterdam all through this period thus reflected neatly the food conditions prevailing nine or ten months previously.

Yet the half-starved millions of the Orient continue to reproduce themselves at very high rates. Perhaps there is an adaptation to chronic hunger. Certainly life goes on, even though it may seem to be painful and miserable. But I cannot believe that the reproduction is caused by the hunger; or that the reproduction will slow up just because the hunger is eased. The hunger is, while present, the primary thing to be dealt with; and perhaps under conditions of less stress, when people do not need to think about their hunger, they learn to think more carefully about the future and are thus less apt, blindly and miserably, to reproduce themselves, careless of how these new generations will find the means of subsistence. But this sort of relationship between hunger and ideas is cultural, not physiological.

Birth Control

Beginning of the Birth Control Movement
JAMES ALFRED FIELD (1931)

Malthus had confined himself to the recommendation of late marriage and of continence during the preliminary years of privation. For those who were once married he ventured no counsel of restraint.[1] Any physical device for limiting the family he vigorously denounced.[2] Continuance of continence in the marriage relation he may have thought it improper to advocate: he certainly did not expect it, as appears in his judging the propriety of marriage according to "the prospect of being able to support a wife and six children"[3]—a criterion which we must agreee with Weyland[4] in thinking ridiculous. Malthus avoided any direct clash with traditional morality, as might have been expected of one who had taken orders in the Church of England. This course may have been most conducive to the acceptance of his teachings, quite apart from the motives of his own conscience and belief.[5] But to more radical thinkers, it makes his book,

1. *Essay on Population,* (2nd ed.; 1803), p. 595.
2. *Essay on Population,* Appendix, (5th ed., 1817), p. 393; and sixth edition, 1826, 11, 479.
3. *Essay on Population,* (4th ed.; 1807), p. 410.
4. John Weyland, "The Principles of Population and Production, as They Are Affected by the Progress of Society; with a View to Moral and Political Consequences," (London, 1816), p. 415.
5. Francis Place, "Illustrations and Proofs of the Principle of Population: including an examination of the proposed remedies of Mr. Malthus, and a reply to the objections of Mr. Godwin and others," (London, 1822), p. 173.

From James Alfred Field, *Essays on Population,* The University of Chicago Press. Copyright 1931 by The University of Chicago Press. Reprinted by permission.

utilitarianism tempered by authority, seem to serve two masters. Meyerhof ("Hans Ferdy"), the German Neo-Malthusian, thinks that the logical outcome of the *Essay* was prevented by the intrusion of this spirit of deference to tradition—"a mythological cuckoo's egg in the nest of exact science!" [6] His is the view of one looking backward, however, out of a period with very much altered opinions. For a long time Malthus' formulation of the proper check was accepted. A long list of writers thought of the preventive check as essentially a postponement of marriage. . . . In fact, the discussion in England seems not to have contemplated any other form of preventive check as desirable until after 1820. Then, rather abruptly, it was proposed to carry the practice of restraint into the marriage relation, and a propaganda developed in favor of physical artifices to prevent conception.

For the observance by the married of what might still be called moral restraint the great advocate among English economists is John Stuart Mill. "That it is possible to delay marriage," he observes, "and to live in abstinence while unmarried, most people are willing to allow: but when persons are once married, the idea, in this country, never seems to enter any one's mind that having or not having a family, or the number of which it shall consist, is amenable to their own control." [7] In a footnote he adds: "Little improvement can be expected in morality until the producing of large families is regarded with the same feelings as drunkenness or any other physical excess"; and there is further instruction in his approving quotation from [S. de] Sismondi [8] of a passage which insists that the married should submit to the same restraint that is practiced by the unmarried.

But physical restraint, in the somewhat special sense in which the term has been applied, was contemplated almost without exception by those who made preventive checks invade the marriage relation. John Stuart Mill stands almost or quite alone in the less radical position, and even he doubtless had no intention of excluding physical means of prevention. Rumor had it that in his earlier years he had been sought by the police because he had distributed leaflets of the propagandists. At least his father was clearly in sympathy with the movement. James Mill, in his *Elements of Political*

6. *Sittliche Selbtsbeschränkung der Kinderzahl,* p. 10.
7. John Stuart Mill, *Principles of Political Economy,* (5th ed., London, 1862), Book 11, chap. xiii, par. 1.
8. For a statement of [S. de] Sismondi's position, see his article on "Political Economy" in the *Edinburgh Encyclopedia,* (Philadelphia, 1832), XVI, 71–77.

Economy, had written of ". . . . prudence; by which either marriages are sparingly contracted, or care is taken that children beyond a certain number, shall not be the fruit." [9] When one recalls that the elder Mill, in spite of the slender means of his earlier years, had a family of nine children— "conduct than which nothing could be more opposed," as his son remarked, "to the opinions which, at least at a later period of his life, he strenuously upheld" [10]—one feels no surprise at his expression, or at his conclusion that "the grand practical problem . . . . is, to find the means of limiting the number of births." [11] More importance, in the history of this school of thought, has been assigned to an *obiter dictum* of the same author which occurs in the article "Colony" in the *Encyclopædia Britannica Supplement* of 1824 and has reference to "the best means of checking the progress of population." There he writes, with the caution one would expect of a contributor to such a work:

> And yet, if the superstitions of the nursery were discarded, and the principle of utility kept steadily in view, a solution might not be very difficult to be found; and the means of drying up one of the most copious sources of human evil . . . . might be seen to be neither doubtful nor difficult to be applied.[12]

Radical declarations in favor of physical restriction made their appearance in the years following 1821. Between the dates of James Mill's *Elements* and his "Colony" article the outspoken propaganda in England had been started. The first unequivocal advocacy of this form of check appears to have been that contained in Francis Place's *Illustrations and Proofs of the Principle of Population,* the introduction to which is dated February 1, 1822. Place's book was one of the many contributions to the literature of population called forth by Godwin's *Enquiry* of 1820; but it was by no means a mere "refutation" of the familiar type. After passing in review various possible sources of improvement in the condition of the people Place comes to this notable utterance:

> If, above all, it were once clearly understood, that it was not disreputable for married persons to avail themselves of such precautionary means as would, without being injurious to health, or destructive of female delicacy, prevent conception, a sufficient check might at once be

9. First ed. (1821), p. 34.
10. J. S. Mill, *Autobiography* (London, 1873), p. 3.
11. *Op. cit.,* p. 51.
12. III, 261.

given to the increase of population beyond the means of subsistence; vice and misery, to a prodigious extent, might be removed from society, and the object of Mr. Malthus, Mr. Godwin, and of every philanthropic person, be promoted, by the increase of comfort, of intelligence; and of moral conduct, in the mass of the population.

And he adds prophetically: "The course recommended will, I am fully persuaded, at some period be pursued by the people, even if left to themselves." [13]

• • •

But the people were not left to themselves. By the following year an active propaganda had already begun.

One evening in July, 1823, a mysterious parcel was handed to Mr. Taylor, editor of the *Manchester Guardian*, with a note asking that he be so kind as to see that it was delivered to Mrs. Mary Fildes—known for her interest in the welfare of the working classes. With this request Mr. Taylor complied. When Mrs. Fildes opened the package she found a number of copies of what was subsequently called "the diabolical hand bill": a small leaflet, unobtrusively and almost elegantly printed, addressed *To the Married of Both Sexes,* setting forth the economic burden of an excessively large family, and describing with frank simplicity means of preventing conception. With the leaflets was an anonymous note which ran as follows:

London July 8th 1823

To Mrs. Fildes
    Madam
        The Bills enclosed with this note are sent to you, as to an experienced, sensible, discreet woman, having much influence in her neighbourhood, to one, who has shewn herself the ardent friend of the working people. You Madam must be well aware, that numberless evils are produced by too large a family, not only as it makes the working man & his wife poor, but breaks their spirits, & qualifies them to be ill used & trampled upon by those who are richer.—If you will give one of the Bills to each of such married women as in your opinion may be usefull you will confer on them a great benefit. The method recommended is getting fast into use amongst the working people in London, & will in a very few years produce the happiest consequences . . . . . Mr. Carliles people know nothing of the contents of the parcel, but should you be pleased to notice it, have the goodness to direct to Mr. James at Mr. Carliles No. 5

13. P. 165.

Water Lane Fleet Street London the letter will be called for, any number of bills you may desire to have shall be sent to you

by a sincere well wisher
to the working Classes.[14]

It is stated that Mrs. Fildes ultimately became an advocate of the practice thus suddenly brought to her notice.[15] At first however, outraged and indignant, and unable to fix the responsibility on Mr. Taylor,[16] she reported the happening to the Attorney General. Six weeks later, having received no answer, she addressed herself to Richard Carlile, who, for his zealous efforts to establish the freedom of the press, was at that time in Dorchester Gaol, in his characteristic state of imprisonment. Her letter, which begins with a brief narrative of the episode of the handbills, and an outcry against the indignity she had suffered, concludes thus:

> . . . I feel indignant at the insult which has been offered me; Is it possible that this infamous hand Bill has issued from the encouragers of the doctrines of the cold blooded Malthus or [his] servile supporter the detestable Lawyer Scarlett?
>
> I have no redress but what is afforded me through the medium of a free press; I submit this infamous transaction to you under a hope that you will give it that consideration which (I think) so flagrant an attack upon the morals of the community demands; hoping that you will expose the propagators of this infamous hand Bill
>
> I am Sir
yours very Respfy
Mary Fildes [17]

The story of the handbills was given publicity through Wooler's paper *The Black Dwarf*. Wooler did not approve the principle of the handbill; but inasmuch as he conceived that it was his function to insure the open discussion of topics which were in danger of being suppressed, he published Mrs. Fildes' letter and also reprinted the contents of the handbill itself,

14. Letter from Mary Fildes to "Mr. Richard Carlile, Dorchester Gaol . . . . ," Place Papers, British Museum (Hendon), Vol. LXVIII. [Place's "guard-books," containing for the most part newpaper clippings, are kept at the Hendon storage building of the British Museum newspaper room. Reference to these volumes in subsequent notes of this article will be made in abbreviated form: e.g. "Vol. LXVIII, Hendon".]
15. G. J. Holyoake, *Sixty Years of an Agitator's Life*, I, 130; and *The Republican*, XI, 561.
16. Cf. *Black Dwarf*, XI, 461–64; J. E. Taylor, *To the Public* (1823).
17. Letter to Carlile, as cited above.

with the anonymous note which Mrs. Fildes had found in the package.[18]

The authorship of these strange leaflets naturally became a matter of curious speculation. A pamphlet on *The History of the Diabolical Hand Bill* was issued in Manchester, championing the cause of Mrs. Fildes,[19] and presenting a circumstantial narrative of the facts in the case with more or less obvious bias of hostility to Mr. Taylor. He, however, had succeeded in disclaiming responsibility in a letter to the *Black Dwarf,*[20] which he subsequently republished, together with other correspondence, in a leaflet addressed *To the Public.*[21] Far more important, therefore, were allegations which ascribed the handbill to Robert Owen, the philanthropist-reformer of New Lanark.

The first public reference to Owen in this connection occurs in the *Black Dwarf* of October 1, 1823, to which one James Macphail communicated the following extract from an anonymous letter which had been received by the editor of the *Labourer's Friend:*

> You, I am sure, will give that truly benevolent man, Mr. Robert Owen, credit for good intentions, whatever opinion you may entertain of me, as an unknown correspondent. I will therefore relate an anecdote respecting him. It was objected to his plan that the number of children which would be produced in his communities would be so great, and the deaths from vices, misery, and bad management, so few, that the period of doubling the number of people would be very short, and that consequently in no very long period his whole plan would become abortive. Mr. Owen felt the force of this objection, and sought the means of averting the consequences. He heard of the small number of children in French families compared with English families. He knew from authentic sources that the peasantry in the South of France limited the number of their progeny. He knew that while our unfortunate countrymen were reduced to pauperism, and to six shillings a week wages, the peasants in the South of France received 2s. 6d. a day, which in their fine climate, and with their abstemious habits, enabled them to live in the most comfortable manner. He knew that these people were cleanly, simple and well provided with everything desirable in abundance, and he knew also that they married young. Mr. Owen resolved to ascertain the means by which this desirable state was produced and maintained. He went to

18. *Black Dwarf,* XI, 404–11; September 17, 1823. For Wooler's attitude, cf. Taylor, *To the Public.*
19. *The History of the Diabolical Hand Bill, for checking Population; With the various Correspondence which has taken place, on this subject with Mrs. Fildes, Mr. J. E. Taylor, The Attorney General, Mr. Wooler, and Mr. Carlile, With an interesting Statement from the latter respecting Mr. R. Owen, the Lanark philanthropist!! With observations by A. Clark* (Manchester: published and sold by T. Crabtree, 1823).
20. XI, 461–64.
21. "Printed at the Guardian Office, Manchester," and dated October 8, 1823.

France, discovered the means which prevents too rapid a population, and he brought back with him several [specimens of the contrivance there in use], two of which he gave to his friend who had been the cause of this inquiry. Mr. Owen no longer feared a too rapid increase of the people in his communities; he saw at once what to him was most desirable, the means of marrying all his people at an early age, and limiting their progeny to any desirable extent. Ask him, and he will acknowledge what is here asserted. Do not then condemn this virtuous man to punishment here and hereafter, because he entertains opinions which you call abominable. What Mr. Owen saw would be the greatest of all evils in his communities, is the greatest of all evils in the great community of this nation; and is tenfold increased in the community which composes the Irish people.

The source of this surprising statement is hardly less interesting than its unequivocal character. Almost certainly it emanated from no less an authority than Francis Place. . . .

The so-called "diabolical handbills," were the cause of first an outcry and then a more serious discussion. They attained, apparently, a considerable circulation; and they were instrumental in bringing forth a more substantial pamphlet literature, of which Richard Carlile's *Every Woman's Book* and Robert Dale Owen's *Moral Physiology* may be mentioned as the most important items. These two tracts attempted to deal with the physiological facts of reproduction as well as with the economics of overpopulation; and very naturally they prepared the way for the entrance of physicians into the neo-Malthusian discussion.

The first noteworthy contribution from a medical man was the pamphlet entitled *Fruits of Philosophy,* written in this country by Dr. Charles Knowlton, of Massachusetts, and published in 1833. Dr. Knowlton appears to have been not only an eccentric, but a sexual hypochondriac, whom years of worry and depression had led to take an interest in the general question of sex. When he learned of the neo-Malthusian arguments and read Robert Dale Owen's statement of the case for birth-control instead of sexual repression, he was led to put forth his own views, and in particular to devote a chapter to the prevention of conception. His book was reprinted in England and for forty years was more or less known to working-class radicals and free-thinkers. Then, in 1876, it furnished the ground for a prosecution which gave it a great though accidental notoriety.

Meantime another and intrinsically more remarkable book had appeared. This work, later called *The Elements of Social Science,* had at first the more striking title, *Physical, Sexual and Natural Religion.* The anonymous author, Dr. George Drysdale, was a physician of high intellectual ability; and his book, radical and even fantastic as it was, was none the less in its way a brilliant performance for a student hardly out of his medical school training. The book, first published in 1854, strove to show that the physical functions of man are of equal importance and dignity with the mental functions, and equally worthy of cultivation and exercise. To this rule the sexual function was held to be certainly no exception. Accordingly Dr. Drysdale ventured to revolutionize the code of sexual ethics. Recognizing, as did Dr. Knowlton, the kinship between some of his doctrines and those of the neo-Malthusians, Dr. Drysdale turned his attention more and more to Malthus and the economic explanation of poverty through overpopulation. *The Elements of Social Science,* in its elaborated form, was a literary crusade against what its author regarded as the three great and interrelated evils of poverty, prostitution, and celibacy. Only by the prevention of conception could society escape all three evils.

In 1876 a bookseller of Bristol, England, who had been selling indecently illustrated copies of Dr. Knowlton's *Fruits of Philosophy,* was arrested, tried, and convicted of selling an obscene book. The authorities turned their attention next to the publisher of the pamphlet, whom they persuaded to repudiate the work. This publisher was at that time the publisher also of much of the tract literature of the English secularists. His recantation seemed to some of the free-thinkers equivalent to an abandonment of the right of free discussion; and accordingly the leaders of the free-thought movement, Charles Bradlaugh and Mrs. Annie Besant, wishing to test the right of publication, deliberately brought out a new edition of the Knowlton pamphlet, in 1877, and challenged the police to arrest them. They were presently arraigned and brought to trial in the Court of Queen's Bench, before the Lord Chief Justice and a special jury. The Solicitor-General appeared against them: Bradlaugh and Mrs. Besant conducted their own able and dramatic defense. The case attracted inordinate attention; and by the time it had led to a half-hearted verdict of guilty, which was subsequently set aside on technical grounds, both judge and prosecutor were agreed that the trial had accomplished just what the prosecution had desired to prevent. The plea for neo-Malthusianism had been proclaimed to all England; and, if Mrs. Besant's figures may be taken as correct, three months' sales of *Fruits of Philosophy* had disposed of as many copies as would at the old rate have lasted for one hundred and eighty years.

The Bradlaugh-Besant trial brought into prominence the Malthusian League. This organization, which owed its origin to Bradlaugh and Dr. George Drysdale, and which had nominally existed for over fifteen years, was now revived, and, under the presidency of Dr. Charles R. Drysdale, brother of Dr. George Drysdale, became influential in organizing and diffusing neo-Malthusian opinion not only in England but in some of the countries of continental Europe. The Dutch society of similar name which has done so much to further the birth-control movement in Holland was suggested by the English league. In many other countries the example has been followed.

Organized or unorganized, the movement is becoming practically world-wide. One cannot of course contend that the notoriety of the Bradlaugh-Besant trial, or of similar trials elsewhere, is the primary cause of our present-day falling birth-rate. No doubt deep-lying influences more or less inherent in modern social conditions have led civilized peoples to extend their power of control over nature until they now exert a voluntary control over human propagation itself. But one can hardly venture to deny that the agitation of the seventies must have done much to hasten the effects of these social and economic motives. It is, to say the least, a very striking coincidence that the English birth-rate began so abruptly to fall about 1878; that the vigorous increase of population in New South Wales slackened simultaneously with the circulation and legal vindication there of neo-Malthusian leaflets; or that the decade of the eighties was marked by an unmistakable decline of the birth-rate in virtually every country where reliable records were kept.

Two general facts stand out prominently in this brief chapter of history. First, the more the movement for birth-control has been opposed, the more it has flourished. Attempts to suppress it have again and again given it fresh notoriety, and have aroused its partisans to new enthusiasm. One community after another has tried prosecution and concluded to drop it. Our own federal authorities appear to be the latest to learn discretion from the irony of this experience.

Beginning of the Movement in the United States
MARSTON BATES (1955)

There was nothing in the United States corresponding to the English Malthusian League until 1917, when the National Birth Control League was

From Marston Bates, *The Prevalence of People,* Charles Scribner's Sons, New York. Copyright © 1955 by Marston Bates. Reprinted by permission.

founded. There was, however, plenty of interest in the matter earlier, and a considerable volume of publication, both popular and medical. The first American book on birth control was published in 1830, *Moral Physiology* by Robert Dale Owen. The second (in 1832) was Knowlton's *The Fruits of Philosophy,* which caused so much trouble when imported into England.

The early writers on birth control in America also encountered legal difficulties; and in 1873 a federal statute was passed, the so-called Comstock law, prohibiting the distribution of contraceptive information through the mails. Dr. Edward Foote was indicted under this law in 1876 for mailing a copy of a pamphlet called *Words in Pearl.* He was found guilty and fined $3,000 with costs of some $5,000. This law long continued to be rigidly interpreted, creating a situation in the United States quite different from that in England, where the Bradlaugh-Besant trial of 1877 went far toward making legal the general, free distribution of contraceptive knowledge.

Birth control knowledge certainly continued to spread in the United States, legal or not, and Norman Himes has analyzed a considerable volume of American publication in his book on the history of the subject. The chief effect of the law was probably to delay the spread of information to the poorest economic classes, where the need would have been the greatest. The process of "democratization" of birth control in the United States made little headway until Margaret Sanger injected her personality into the movement in 1912. Her work as a nurse in the poor quarters of the lower East Side in New York convinced her that something ought to be done about bringing contraceptive information to poor mothers.

My Fight for Birth Control
MARGARET SANGER (1931)

Awakening and Revolt

Early in the year 1912 I came to a sudden realization that my work as a nurse and my activities in social service were entirely palliative and conse-

From Margaret Sanger, *My Fight for Birth Control,* Farrar & Rinehart, New York. Copyright 1935 by Margaret Sanger. © renewed 1959 by Grant Sanger and Stuart Sanger. Reprinted by permission.

quently futile and useless to relieve the misery I saw all about me. . . .

Were it possible for me to depict the revolting conditions existing in the homes of some of the women I attended in that one year, one would find it hard to believe. There was at that time, and doubtless is still today, a substratum of men and women whose lives are absolutely untouched by social agencies.

The way they live is almost beyond belief. They hate and fear any prying into their homes or into their lives. They resent being talked to. The women slink in and out of their homes on their way to market like rats from their holes. The men beat their wives sometimes black and blue, but no one interferes. The children are cuffed, kicked and chased about, but woe to the child who dares to tell tales out of the home! Crime or drink is often the source of this secret aloofness; usually there is something to hide, a skeleton in the closet somewhere. The men are sullen, unskilled workers, picking up odd jobs now and then, unemployed usually, sauntering in and out of the house at all hours of the day and night.

The women keep apart from other women in the neighborhood. Often they are suspected of picking a pocket or "lifting" an article when occasion arises. Pregnancy is an almost chronic condition amongst them. I knew one woman who had given birth to eight children with no professional care whatever. The last one was born in the kitchen, witnessed by a son of ten years who, under his mother's direction, cleaned the bed, wrapped the placenta and soiled articles in paper, and threw them out of the window into the court below.

They reject help of any kind and want you to "mind your own business." Birth and death they consider their own affairs. They survive as best they can, suspicious of everyone, deathly afraid of police and officials of every kind. . . .

In this atmosphere abortions and birth become the main theme of conversation. On Saturday nights I have seen groups of fifty to one hundred women going into questionable offices well known in the community for cheap abortions. I asked several women what took place there, and they all gave the same reply: a quick examination, a probe inserted into the uterus and turned a few times to disturb the fertilized ovum, and then the woman was sent home. Usually the flow began the next day and often continued four or five weeks. Sometimes an ambulance carried the victim to the hospital for a curetage, and if she returned home at all she was looked upon as a lucky woman.

This state of things became a nightmare with me. There seemed no sense to it at all, no reason for such waste of mother life, no right to exhaust women's vitality and to throw them on the scrap-heap before the age of thirty-five.

Everywhere I looked, misery and fear stalked—men fearful of losing their jobs, women fearful that even worse conditions might come upon them. The menace of another pregnancy hung like a sword over the head of every poor woman I came in contact with that year. The question which met me was always the same: What can I do to keep from it? or, What can I do to get out of this? Sometimes they talked among themselves bitterly.

"It's the rich that know the tricks," they'd say, "while we have all the kids." Then, if the women were Roman Catholics, they talked about "Yankee tricks," and asked me if I knew what the Protestants did to keep their families down. When I said that I didn't believe that the rich knew much more than they did I was laughed at and suspected of holding back information for money. They would nudge each other and say something about paying me before I left the case if I would reveal the "secret."

It all sickened me. It was heartbreaking to witness the rapt, anxious, eager expression on their pale, worried faces as I told them necessary details concerning cleanliness and hygiene of their sex organs. It was appalling how little they knew of the terms I was using, yet how familiar they were with those organs and their functions and how unafraid to try anything, no matter what the results.

I heard over and over again of their desperate efforts at bringing themselves "around"—drinking various herb-teas, taking drops of turpentine on sugar, steaming over a chamber of boiling coffee or of turpentine water, rolling down stairs, and finally inserting slippery-elm sticks, or knitting needles, or shoe hooks into the uterus. I used to shudder with horror as I heard the details and, worse yet, learned of the conditions *behind the reason* for such desperate actions. Day after day these stories were poured into my ears. I knew hundreds of these women personally, and knew much of their hopeless, barren, dreary lives. . . .

Finally the thing began to shape itself, to become accumulative during the three weeks I spent in the home of a desperately sick woman living on Grand Street, a lower section of New York's East Side.

Mrs. Sacks was only twenty-eight years old; her husband, an unskilled worker, thirty-two. Three children, aged five, three and one, were none too strong nor sturdy, and it took all the earnings of the father and the ingenuity of the mother to keep them clean, provide them with air and proper food, and give them a chance to grow into decent manhood and woman-hood.

Both parents were devoted to these children and to each other. The woman had become pregnant and had taken various drugs and purgatives, as advised by her neighbors. Then, in desperation, she had used some in-strument lent to her by a friend. She was found prostrate on the floor amidst the crying children when her husband returned from work. Neigh-bors advised against the ambulance, and a friendly doctor was called. The husband would not hear of her going to a hospital, and as a little money had been saved in the bank a nurse was called and the battle for that pre-cious life began.

It was in the middle of July. The three-room apartment was turned into a hospital for that dying patient. Never had I worked so fast, never so con-centratedly as I did to keep alive that little mother. Neighbor women came and went during the day doing the odds and ends necessary for our com-fort. The children were sent to friends and relatives and the doctor and I settled ourselves to outdo the force and power of an outraged nature.

Never had I known such conditions could exist. July's sultry days and nights were melted into a torpid inferno. Day after day, night after night, I slept only in brief snatches, ever too anxious about the condition of that feeble heart bravely carrying on, to stay long from the bedside of the pa-tient. With but one toilet for the building and that on the floor below, everything had to be carried down for disposal, while ice, food and other necessities had to be carried three flights up. It was one of those old air-shaft buildings of which there were several thousands then standing in New York City.

At the end of two weeks recovery was in sight, and at the end of three weeks I was preparing to leave the fragile patient to take up the ordinary duties of her life, including those of wifehood and motherhood. Everyone was congratulating her on her recovery. All the kindness of sympathetic and understanding neighbors poured in upon her in the shape of convales-cent dishes, soups, custards, and drinks. Still she appeared to be despond-ent and worried. She seemed to sit apart in her thoughts as if she had no part in these congratulatory messages and endearing welcomes. I thought at first that she still retained some of her unconscious memories and dwelt upon them in her silences.

But as the hour for my departure came nearer, her anxiety increased, and finally with trembling voice she said: "Another baby will finish me, I suppose."

"It's too early to talk about that," I said, and resolved that I would turn the question over to the doctor for his advice. When he came I said: "Mrs. Sacks is worried about having another baby."

"She well might be," replied the doctor, and then he stood before her and said: "Any more such capers, young woman, and there will be no need to call me."

"Yes, yes—I know, Doctor," said the patient with trembling voice, "but," and she hesitated as if it took all of her courage to say it, *"what* can I do to prevent getting that way again?"

"Oh ho!" laughed the doctor good naturedly, "You want your cake while you eat it too, do you? Well, it can't be done." Then, familiarly slapping her on the back and picking up his hat and bag to depart, he said: "I'll tell you the only sure thing to do. Tell Jake to sleep on the roof!"

With those words he closed the door and went down the stairs, leaving us both petrified and stunned.

Tears sprang to my eyes, and a lump came in my throat as I looked at that face before me. It was stamped with sheer horror. I thought for a moment she might have gone insane, but she conquered her feelings, whatever they may have been, and turning to me in desperation said: "He can't understand, can he?—he's a man after all—but you do, don't you? You're a woman and you'll tell me the secret and I'll never tell it to a soul."

She clasped her hands as if in prayer, she leaned over and looked straight into my eyes and beseechingly implored me to tell her something —something *I really did not know*. It was like being on a rack and tortured for a crime one had not committed. To plead guilty would stop the agony; otherwise the rack kept turning.

I had to turn away from that imploring face. I could not answer her then. I quieted her as best I could. She saw that I was moved by the tears in my eyes. I promised that I would come back in a few days and tell her what she wanted to know. The few simple means of limiting the family like *coitus interruptus* or the condom were laughed at by the neighboring women when told these were the means used by men in the well-to-do families. That was not believed, and I knew such an answer would be swept aside as useless were I to tell her this at such a time.

A little later when she slept I left the house, and made up my mind that I'd keep away from those cases in the future. I felt helpless to do anything at all. I seemed chained hand and foot, and longed for an earthquake or a volcano to shake the world out of its lethargy into facing these monstrous atrocities.

The intelligent reasoning of the young mother—how to *prevent* getting that way again—how sensible, how just she had been—yes, I promised myself I'd go back and have a long talk with her and tell her more, and perhaps she would not laugh but would believe that those methods were all that were really known.

But time flew past, and weeks rolled into months. That wistful, appealing face haunted me day and night. I could not banish from my mind memories of that trembling voice begging so humbly for knowledge she had a right to have. I was about to retire one night three months later when the telephone rang and an agitated man's voice begged me to come at once to help his wife who was sick again. It was the husband of Mrs. Sacks, and I intuitively knew before I left the telephone that it was almost useless to go.

I dreaded to face that woman. I was tempted to send someone else in my place. I longed for an accident on the subway, or on the street—anything to prevent my going into that home. But on I went just the same. I arrived a few minutes after the doctor, the same one who had given her such noble advice. The woman was dying. She was unconscious. She died within ten minutes after my arrival. It was the same result, the same story told a thousand times before—death from abortion. She had become pregnant, had used drugs, had then consulted a five-dollar professional abortionist, and death followed.

The doctor shook his head as he rose from listening for the heart beat. I knew she had already passed on; without a groan, a sigh or recognition of our belated presence she had gone into the Great Beyond as thousands of mothers go every year. I looked at that drawn face now stilled in death. I placed her thin hands across her breast and recalled how hard they had pleaded with me on that last memorable occasion of parting. The gentle woman, the devoted mother, the loving wife had passed on leaving behind her a frantic husband, helpless in his loneliness, bewildered in his helplessness as he paced up and down the room, hands clenching his head, moaning "My God! My God! My God!" . . .

[I resolved] I would never go back again to nurse women's ailing bodies while their miseries were as vast as the stars. I was now finished with superficial cures, with doctors and nurses and social workers who were brought face to face with this overwhelming truth of women's needs and yet turned to pass on the other side. They must be made to see these facts. I resolved that women should have knowledge of contraception. They have every right to know about their own bodies. I would strike out—I would scream from the housetops. I would tell the world what was going on in the lives of these poor women. I *would* be heard. No matter what it should cost. *I would be heard.*

Editor's Note: *Margaret Sanger searched the literature in this country for information about contraceptives and, finding very little, she went abroad to Scotland and France where she obtained more factual information. In 1914 she returned home and published a magazine* Woman Rebel. *Although the articles in this magazine adhered to the Comstock law in not offering contraceptive information, many of the issues were banned by the New York post office. Mrs. Sanger was indicted on nine counts of sending birth control information through the mails and was made liable to a prison term of 45 years. On the eve of the trial she fled to Europe where she spent two years, becoming active in the English Malthusian League and studying birth control methods in clinics in Holland.*

During her absence, Anthony Comstock, secretary of the New York Society for the Suppression of Vice, visited the Sanger home. Telling Mr. Sanger that he was a poor father in search of birth control information, he purchased a pamphlet written by Mrs. Sanger. For this sale Mr. Sanger served a month in jail.

Mrs. Sanger returned to this country again in 1916 and in October of that year opened a birth control clinic in Brooklyn with her sister, Mrs. Ethel Byrne. The clinic was raided by the police a few weeks later. Mrs. Sanger served 30 days in jail and her sister went on a hunger strike in Brooklyn's Raymond Street jail.

The following selection describing one of Margaret Sanger's battles with the police and the Roman Catholic hierarchy was typical of the picturesque struggles which marked her career and which served to bring the birth control movement to the attention of the American public.

My Fight for Birth Control (continued)

MARGARET SANGER (1931)

Town Hall

On Sunday, November 13 [1921], as a fitting conclusion to the first birth control conference in this country, a mass meeting was arranged at the

Town Hall in New York City. The subject chosen for discussion was "Birth Control; Is It Moral?" It was my intention to use this occasion not for agitation, but to sound the opinion of representative men and women of all professional classes. Opponents were invited to present their opinions openly.

The moral question of birth control was at that time constantly debated. Opponents hurled at us the statement that this knowledge would cause immorality among young people; that promiscuity, vice, prostitution would be the inevitable fruits of our efforts. This I did not believe. I knew that morality or immorality is not an external factor in human behavior; essentially it grows, emerges, and comes from within. If the young people of the war aftermath were slipping away from the old moral codes, it was not the fault of birth control knowledge any more than it was the fault of any other progressive or advanced idea of the modern day. Henry Ford's automobiles made transportation available for thousands of young people—morality or immorality as a consequence should not be placed at the door of Mr. Ford.

The moral question as a discussion had great possibilities. Thousands of people had applied for seats in the Town Hall auditorium on Sunday evening where the question was to be debated and the conference was to close. Mr. Cox and I had dined together at the home of Mrs. Juliet Rublee, and together we drove to the meeting place.

I shall never forget that night. Usually I had been able to visualize my audiences. But all day, try as I would to "tune in" to the evening's events, I could not do it. . . . I could not think *through* what I was going to say at that meeting. My brain seemed numb; I felt a strange lack of the worrying anticipation one usually feels previous to a large meeting.

When the car crept along West Forty-Third Street to the Town Hall, we found the thoroughfare swarming with thousands of people. Finally arriving in front of Town Hall, we pushed our way to the door. Two policemen stood before us. The doors were closed, and as Mr. Cox and I attempted to enter we were barred by the arm of the officer.

"You can't get into this place tonight," he announced brusquely.

"Why not?" I asked.

"There ain't going to be no meeting," he replied.

"But who has stopped this meeting?" I questioned. "I am one of the speakers, and this gentleman (Mr. Cox) is another. We wish to be allowed to go inside to find out about it."

"You can't go in, I tell you!" he repeated. "That's all I know about it."

I looked about and saw a cigar-store across the street, and quickly decided to telephone to Police Headquarters. This I did, and I received a reply that no such order to close the hall had been issued from there. Mystery! A meeting of self-respecting citizens stopped by the police, yet Police Headquarters had given no order to stop it.

Who then *did* give that order? I telephoned to the Mayor to ascertain what he knew about this; but before I could get a reply I noticed that people were coming out of Town Hall. Cautiously they were opening the doors, where two policemen still stood, to let people out, but at the same time they were violently pushing back the crowds vainly trying to get in. At the sight of that open door, I hung up the receiver and dashed across the street and wedged my way in and out of the crowd to the policemen. I waited for the door to open again and at once sprang forward, stooped down under that strong arm, and behold, I was within the hall! Then I hurried—yes, I fairly flew up the aisle to the stage.

Like naughty children being sent to bed, people were standing about reluctant to obey the orders to go home. They were grumbling, and seemed vague about it all. I looked up at the high stage and then at the steps on the side which led to the stage, but as I saw two official-looking men there on guard I decided not to go that way. A tall handsome man stood near me looking vacantly around and much perplexed. A small messenger boy with a large bouquet of pink roses also stood nearby. As I stood looking at that stage and wondering how on earth I could get upon it and call out to the audience to come back, I was suddenly caught up in the strong arms of the handsome man beside me and lifted—no, really flung over the footlights onto the stage. Before I could pick myself up and recapture my poise the same man grabbed the flowers from the messenger with the vacant stare, leaped upon the platform with the quickness and agility of an athlete, and placed the huge bouquet of roses into my arms and called out that I was present to address the meeting.

At that people in the aisles began to sit down and all over the house men and women resumed their seats. Then began such a thundering applause, as if it were the only relief for their angry, indignant, rebellious spirits. The fight was on, and every man and woman in that hall was there beside me to fight to the finish. I felt it in the air, in their voices, as they called out to me to speak. Mr. Cox was close behind me all the way along. I announced to the audience that the meeting would proceed as quickly as they took their seats and as soon as we could be heard.

While this was going on, I learned from Mrs. Anne Kennedy, our executive secretary, what had occurred. She said that at about seven-thirty, when the hall was half full of people, there appeared several policemen with Capt. Donohue of that district, attended by a man who stated that he was Monsignor Dineen, secretary of the then Archbishop, Patrick J. Hayes of the Roman Catholic Church. He stated that he had orders from the Archbishop to close the doors of that meeting; and Capt. Donohue then issued orders to his men to see that no more people entered.

Mrs. Kennedy, a capable, cool-headed woman of vast experience, calmly protested, but asked Monsignor Dineen to kindly put his order in writing so that she could read it from the platform to the early comers then occupying seats in the hall.

When I saw this statement, I grew hot with indignation. It was one thing to have halls closed by a mistaken or misguided ignorant police captain, but a very different thing to have a high dignitary of the Roman Catholic Church order me to stop talking. I knew the law of the city; I knew the rights of citizens guaranteed under the Constitution. I had been taught by my teachers in American history that the church and state were separate and apart; that we as citizens were guaranteed from interference by powerful church influence. At the thought of this official impertinence, this bullying, this arrogant dictatorship, this insolence of a Roman Catholic Archbishop, my resistance, my resolution became set. I would not close that meeting unless I was forced by arrest to do so. I knew our rights were being violated by the police captain. They must go the limit. Unless I stood my ground and got arrested, I could not take the case into the courts. I decided to stand firm; to hold my ground as long as I had strength in my body to stand upon that platform.

As I stepped to the front of the stage and began to speak, I was checked by another demonstration. Before I could continue, two policemen walked onto the stage, held me, and ordered me not to speak.

"Where's your warrant? What's the charge?" I asked. Confusion reigned.

In a few minutes, the stage was in a tumult. Several women began to address the audience, and as fast as one was silenced by the police another began to speak. Mr. Cox was pushed before the audience and was introduced to the crowd.

"I have come from across the Atlantic—" he began, but the rest of that sentence was lost when several minions of the law came between him and the audience.

The attitude of the police both on the platform and in the hall was as if they scarcely knew what it was all about. They seemed to be without official instructions. Back at the far end of the hall stood a medium-sized man in plain attire who seemed to be directing things from that side. Later on, he stood at the back of the platform, leaning against the wings, calmly directing the police by a casual nod of the head or a whisper to one of the men who acted as runner between him and the captain. This man was later identified as Monsignor Joseph P. Dineen, secretary to Archbishop Hayes.

No wonder Police Headquarters knew nothing of the order to close the hall! The Archbishop did not think it necessary to seek advice of the Chief of Police—nor to ascertain the legal rights of non-Catholic citizens and taxpayers of the City of New York.

Confusion and tumult continued for fully an hour. First one woman would attempt to speak; she would be silenced by two or three policemen; then the crowd would boo, roar, hiss, shout, catcall; as that wore down, someone else would attempt to speak only to be instantly silenced by the policemen on the platform. Mary Winsor, that brave and undaunted suffragist, insisted again and again on speaking; but finally, after continuous resistance and a show of determined effort never to give up the attempt to speak at that meeting, the police captain ordered my arrest and Miss Winsor's. By this time the crowd was in a belligerent and ugly mood—anything might happen.

People now excitedly jumped upon the platform to help me in case of trouble. Men from all classes and of all ages eagerly came forward to see that I was not improperly treated. I have never been afraid of the police, but it was a glorious feeling to see those men behind me with eager, determined faces with jaws set and eyes blazing with indignation—the faces of more than a hundred men citizens of this great metropolis who came forward to protect me.

With a policeman holding each arm, and the captain escorting us to the street, I was led out of the building. No speeches had been made; no laws had been broken except by the policemen who had taken orders from Captain Donohue.

Meanwhile, a call for reserves had been sent out, and the crowd was soon driven out by the police. Miss Winsor followed close behind me.

We were marched through the streets to the station-house, followed by a huge mob. When we reached our destination, the street was blocked by a great crowd of singing humanity. The reserves returned from the hall and tried to clear the street, but they had no success until after we had been

driven to Night Court in a patrol wagon. Then the crowd, still singing, boo-
ing, and jeering the police, fell into line and marched behind us up Broad-
way.

The case was put over until the following morning. The next morning I
was discharged by Magistrate Corrigan. Police Captain Donohue could not
be found.

In the investigation that immediately followed, it was proved by Monsignor Dineen's statement to the press that the raid had been ordered by
Cardinal Hayes. A complaint was made to headquarters at the Cardinal's
direction some time previous to the meeting, and Monsignor Joseph P.
Dineen, his secretary, went to the Town Hall to meet Captain Thomas
Donohue before the hour for the meeting. Captain Donohue, it was later
disclosed, did not know why he had been sent to the Town Hall until he
met the Monsignor there.

Faced with public censure and challenged by a protest sent to the mayor
by a group of prominent citizens, the Monsignor hedged, and attempted to
stake new claims of justification.

"I was present from the start. The Archbishop had received an invitation
from Mrs. Margaret Sanger to attend the meeting and I went as his representative. The Archbishop is delighted and pleased at the action of the police, as am I, because it was no meeting to be held publicly and without
restrictions." Such was the feeble explanation Monsignor Dineen offered in
the *Times* of November 15.

"I need not tell you what the attitude of the Catholic Church is toward
so-called birth control," he went on. "What particularly aroused me, when
I entered the hall, was the presence there of four children. I think any one
will admit that a meeting of that character is no place for growing children.
Decent and clean-minded people would not discuss a subject such as birth
control in public before children or at all," he went on. "The police had
been informed in advance of the character of the meeting. They were told
that this subject—this plan which attacks the very foundations of human
society—was again being dragged before the public in a public hall. The
presence of these four children at least was a reason for police action."

The humorous side of the situation, if such a flagrant violation of the
principle of freedom of expression can be said to have a humorous aspect,
was the fact that these "four children," these immature youngsters who
provoked the appearance of two hundred policemen, a patrol wagon, and a
front page news story, were four mature Barnard College students with

bobbed hair. They were students of Professor Raymond Moley in sociology.

The boomerang effect of this performance was indicated by the reverberation in the press. The idea of birth control was advertised, dramatized, given column after column of free and favorable publicity. Only a small section of the public had been aware of the first American Birth Control Conference, and even fewer knew of the proposed meeting in the Town Hall. The clumsy and illegal tactics of our religious opponents broadcast to the whole country what we were doing. Even the most conservative American newspapers were placed in the trying position of defending birth control advocates or endorsing a violation of the principle of freedom of speech.

The Pill

JOHN ROCK (1963; revised 1967)

Life has a way now and then of mocking man's more questionable designs. It must have amused some citizens of the Commonwealth of Massachusetts, with its rigid law against birth control, to discover that the first breakthrough in contraceptive technology in seventy-five years suffered and survived its labor pains in the environs of Worcester and Boston. Similarly, those who tend to see the drama of human fertility through one-dimensional viewers must still be confused by the fact that the new birth-control pills may turn out to be a useful therapeutic agent in the prevention of repetitive miscarriages, usually diagnosed as "habitual abortion," that have made many couples childless.

This seeming contradiction is a significant event in the history of the pill and helps to make it a classic illustration of the inclusiveness of research in human reproduction: Any investigation aimed at new methods of fertility control is at the same time research in the whole conceptive process. The converse is also true. When reproduction fails, we try to discover where there is a break in the chain of events associated with its normal functioning. When this is found, we try to repair it, to weld the chain together, for women who want to conceive. The facilitation of contraception poses just

From John Rock, *The Time Has Come*, Alfred A. Knopf, New York. Copyright © 1963 by John Rock. Reprinted by permission of Alfred A. Knopf, and Longmans, Green & Co. Ltd.

the reverse problem: To find harmless ways of creating such a break for wives who should not conceive. In the development of the oral pill, those of us who were working on welding the chain together joined with investigators seeking a way to sever it to bring forth a medication of great value for both objectives.

To comprehend how a single agent can accomplish such disparate purposes requires an understanding of how, in a woman's reproductive cycle, the female sex hormone, progesterone works. This chemical is secreted mainly after ovulation by a special tissue, called the *corpus luteum,* which is freshly formed from the wall of the follicle, or sac, from which the ovum is discharged. One of the major functions of the hormone is to prepare the lining of the womb, the endometrium, so that it may meet the needs of the egg if it becomes fertilized by a sperm. After the endometrium receives progesterone secreted in the ovary, it thickens and becomes a firmer matrix. Within this, progesterone also develops blood vessels needed to give easily accessible nourishment to the new organism, the conceptus, which becomes implanted in the uterine wall for the gestation period. If the egg is not fertilized, the supply of progesterone tapers off toward the end of the menstrual cycle; the endometrium begins to regress, even, in part, to disintegrate, and menstruation takes place. This is but the discharge of some escaping blood along with the disintegrated material from the lining of the uterus. If the egg is fertilized, however, the supply of progesterone must not diminish, for this would cause the endometrium to fail in its functioning and the conceptus would be subjected to miscarriage. Accordingly, nature has arranged for this indispensable hormone to be secreted in sufficient supply through the nine months of normal pregnancy, first by the *corpus luteum* and later by the placenta, or afterbirth.

Progesterone has one other major function in each monthly cycle as well as during all of pregnancy: After ovulation, it prevents the thalamo-pituitary complex, now thought to be the master control center of the reproductional endocrine system, from secreting more of those hormones that would cause an ovary to discharge another fertilizable egg. Postponing the entry of another ovum is necessary in order to eliminate the possibility of a contemporaneous second pregnancy which would submit the existing fetus to possibly lethal competition for the mother's resources during the gestation period. Although adjustments are not uncommon, it is clear that woman's physiology is typically geared to producing one child at a time.

The ovulation-suppressing effect of the follicular secretion had been referred to as early as 1897 and established in the early 1900's, and scientists in many countries had attempted to identify it. After other reproductive hormones were successfully defined in the 1920's, German and American investigators were able, in 1934, to isolate and determine the structure of progesterone. By 1937, A. W. Makepeace and his co-workers had conducted a series of classical experiments demonstrating ovulation-suppression in the rabbit by the pure hormone.

But there were problems. To administer the hormone to women in effective amounts required injection; treatment had to be frequent and, furthermore, painful. If it was given orally, such massive dosages were required as to render the supplies available for testing quite inadequate. Thus were clinicians misled into thinking that by mouth the hormone was inactivated; and although the physiological action of progesterone had been described and understood, it did not have much practical clinical use for more than a decade.

In 1951, Drs. Gregory Pincus and M. C. Chang, of the Worcester Foundation for Experimental Biology in Shrewsbury, received a small grant from the Planned Parenthood Federation of America to explore the potentialities of artificially synthesized progesterone for conception control. Their work confirmed the earlier findings that progesterone, when given to rabbits or to rats, would suppress ovulation. Since a female who does not ovulate cannot conceive, progesterone seemed to have contraceptive possibilities. Drs. Pincus and Chang were now ready to see if it would have the same effect in women as in animals.

Already we had started to use progesterone in some of the very baffling infertility cases at the Reproductive Study Center in Brookline. We had been unable to determine why the women under study were unable to bear children; all of the usual tests indicated that all factors were normal. Yet many of these people had been childless for years. We suspected that the cause might be in their Fallopian tubes and wombs, which perhaps were not sufficiently developed to permit successful conception and pregnancy. We knew that during a normal pregnancy, the tubes and uterus expand and that there is a concurrent increase in the two female sex hormones, progesterone and estrogen. Since the two phenomena were thought to be causally related, it was also thought that perhaps the administration of these hormones for a short period would stimulate growth in the tubes and wombs and thus facilitate pregnancy.

Eighty childless patients agreed to try treatment with added natural hormones, known to be harmless. Daily for three months they took massive doses of them. The women had some of the signs and symptoms of a genuine pregnancy. For instance, they did not menstruate during the months of treatment nor was ovulation detectable; the breasts and, in some cases, the uterus seemed to become larger. After treatment was discontinued, menstruation recurred, and within four months, thirteen of the women became pregnant. This was quite encouraging, for one could hardly have expected 16 per cent of the patients, with long-standing infertility of unknown cause, to conceive, all within four months of the same treatment.

Thus, both Dr. Pincus and I were investigating the same hormones, only from different approaches. As a result of our discussions, I instituted certain changes in our second series of twenty-seven women. Only progesterone was administered this time, and on the suggestion of Dr. Pincus the regimen was changed from one of continuity to successive cycles of 20 days of medication. This intermittent method produced intervening monthly menstruation. Promptly after the treatment was discontinued, four of the women became pregnant. All had continued their cyclic menstruation. Again, the number of pregnancies seemed higher than one would expect. We are still wondering if perhaps our theory of the possible improvement in function of tubes and uterus by administered sex hormone is not really valid. Possibly the ovaries or the other reproductive organs had simply benefited from several months of rest. Unquestionably, however, we had obtained confirmation that oral progesterone, given alone or with estrogen, could temporarily inhibit ovulation in humans as well as in animals.

Since very large doses of pure progesterone were required to obtain this result, our attention turned to other synthetic compounds somewhat similar to progesterone in molecular structure, for these might have the same effect as progesterone and possibly be more feasible for clinical use. From more than 200 substances chemically related to progesterone which had been screened by Dr. Pincus and his co-workers, three were selected as offering the greatest potential. These are steroid compounds derived from the roots of a wild Mexican yam. Varying only slightly from progesterone in molecular constituents, they are, nevertheless, many times more potent than this hormone and thus effective in much smaller dosages.

After the animal studies at the Worcester Foundation for Experimental Biology had indicated that these three were indeed the most promising compounds for our purposes, and withal quite harmless, we initiated the first tests with humans in December 1954. One or the other compound was administered to each of fifty childless patients of the clinical center in Brookline who volunteered for the study. The drugs, which are called progestins because of their close chemical relation to progesterone, were given in daily doses of 10 to 40 milligrams for 20 successive days of each menstrual cycle. With this regimen, we found that during the 20 days virtually 100 per cent postponement of ovulation resulted. Within five months after the end of the treatments, moreover, seven of the patients, 14 per cent, became pregnant. As with the earlier and smaller group, all non-pregnant patients were menstruating normally.

Our sizable extension of these early studies of the three progestins, supplemented by those conducted by other investigators, proved sufficient for approval of the compounds for therapeutic use by the Food and Drug Administration. Beginning in 1957, the steroids were marketed for the treatment of various menstrual disorders and for the prevention of miscarriage. The compounds are perhaps effective in dealing with this latter exigency possibly because, by amplifying the influence on the uterus of intrinsic, secreted progesterone, which in such cases may be inadequate, they help to maintain the endometrium in a condition more serviceable to the fetus.

To determine the usefulness for fertility control of their delaying effect on ovulation, however, the early studies had to be extended to include observation of a much larger number of women. This was begun in April 1956 in the Río Piedras section of San Juan, Puerto Rico, with the indispensable co-operation of Drs. Pincus and Celso-Ramón García, from the United States, and Edris Rice-Wray and, later, Manuel Paniagua, of the Family Planning Association of Puerto Rico. Similar field trials subsequently were initiated by Dr. Pincus and Dr. García in Haiti, and by others in San Antonio, Los Angeles, New York, and elsewhere. In all, several thousand women have volunteered as subjects for this work. The results are remarkable, particularly since pregnancy had been virtually an annual event for many of them. No woman who is known to have taken the pills faithfully for 20 successive days each month in an approved dosage has become pregnant. The postponement of ovulation by a progesterone-like compound has been fully confirmed.

Careful studies were made, as the trial progressed, to determine whether the pills had any harmful effects. Vaginal cells by which cancer could be detected were microscopically examined, as were specimens of endometrium. Other tests diagnostic of conditions in other important organ systems—blood, kidney, liver, etc.—were made periodically. There was no evidence of harm from the pills. Some women experienced moderately unpleasant but easily controllable side effects, such as nausea; but these were not serious. After consideration of the mass of data from these studies, the Food and Drug Administration approved the marketing for contraception of the first steroid, Enovid, in May 1960, and the second, Ortho-Novum, in February 1962. In 1966 the F.D.A. found that the same steroid combination presented in much lower concentrations was also acceptable. This is true also of Ovulen, containing a closely similar but more potent progestin that is equally effective in only one-fifth the strength of the original Enovid. Dr. Alan F. Guttmacher, then the director of obstetrics and gynecology at New York's Mt. Sinai Hospital, summed up the superiority of the progestins to other forms of fertility control with the observation that the clinical trials of the pills show "a record of effectiveness which no other contraceptive has matched." [1]

Today, more than one million women of many countries are taking the pills, not simply because of their great effectiveness but also because they provide a natural means of fertility control such as nature uses after ovulation and during pregnancy. Since they also dispense with the impediments to the coital act of other contraceptive techniques, they are favored by many couples. The pills are also used for a variety of other clinical purposes, including regulation of menstrual cycles; relief of pre-menstrual tension, improvement of troublesome menstrual flow, and relief of discomfort from endometriosis (growth outside the uterus of tissue such as normally lines the uterine cavity), and enhancement of fertility which sometimes follows after a few months of treatment. . . .

Sensational press reports during the summer of 1962 distorted the significance of what must be regarded, medically, as a relative handful of cases of thromboembolism—a blood clot in a vein—among women taking Enovid. Unfortunately these articles created doubts in the minds of some as to the drug's safety. I would reiterate here my own conviction which has been amply confirmed by a federal investigation that the pills are in no way the causal agent in these cases. Thromboembolism itself, as well as deaths from it, occurs in women who are taking no drugs at all, and many cases could certainly have been expected in as large a population sample as the million women taking Enovid. In fact, the epidemiological evidence we

1. A. F. Guttmacher, *The Complete Book of Birth Control,* Ballantine Books, 1961, p. 54.

have suggests strongly that instead of 150 cases, reported at this writing, one could expect something of the order of 700 or more cases. This and other data have led the Food and Drug Administration, as well as the American Medical Association, to agree that no causal connection has been proved between Enovid and the reported cases of thromboembolic disease; the F.D.A. could find no reason to alter its clearance of Enovid for marketing for fertility control.

The steroid compounds are the first *physiologic* means of contraception; that is, they prevent reproduction by modifying the time sequences in the body's own functions, rather than by use of an extraneous device or by a wholly artificial chemical action.

II ECONOMIC AND POLITICAL FACTORS

Introduction

Although the physical resources of space and food supply set an upper limit on population growth, man is also influenced by factors which are purely human. As the size of the human family comes more under conscious control, it is increasingly significant to consider the various factors which motivate family planning. The image of the ideal family size changes from time to time and from culture to culture. It is constantly being molded by pressures from many different sources: the teachings of religious prophets, the speeches of political leaders, the attitudes expressed in the press, as well as the customs and opinions of friends and neighbors.

The Readings in Part II explore the various types of economic and political pressures to which people are subjected. In the very private realm of family planning are people really influenced by public philosophies? By political ideologies? Will they have more children to improve their country's military might or to bolster the national economy? Or are they motivated principally by the desire to improve their own and their children's status in the society?

During the past century, changes in the economic structure of Western nations have had an important impact on the number of children people want. In the primitive agricultural communities, children were an economic asset. The expense of supporting them was more than compensated by the labor they provided. Then, with the changing way of life produced by urbanization and advancing technology, the raising of children became a financial burden. Malthus recognized this fact when he suggested that people would exercise "moral restraint" when they became aware of the economic burden which was the inevitable result of a large family. Mussolini also saw (and deplored) the trend toward lower birth rates in large industrial cities like Milan, Turin, and Genoa. This explained, he said, why he was opposed to the phenomenon of urbanism and believed that Italy should concentrate her energies on a "back to the land" movement.[1] When he studied the results of his slum clearance projects, he discovered that families living in buildings where electricity had been installed had a lower birth rate than those occupying buildings without this convenience, and he ordered the electric power removed from the buildings. But his attempts to turn the clock back were unsuccessful. People will not so easily relinquish the comforts which technology has made available.

Slightly more sophisticated approaches to the problem of encouraging higher birth rates were also instituted in Italy and Germany, as well as several other European countries. Higher wages were paid to fathers, the payment escalating with the size of the family. Extra taxes were imposed on bachelors and childless couples. However, these attempts to make large families more economically advantageous met with a surprisingly small degree of success. For many families these financial measures were not adequate to compensate for the extra expense of additional children. Perhaps, also, the financial burden of raising a large family was not the only reason for declining birth rates in industrial centers.

Ironically, both Hitler and Mussolini were doing everything possible to increase the population of their countries at the same time that they were telling the world they needed more *Lebensraum*. A large population, they believed, would assure their nations of greater military might and political power. How correct were they in making this assumption?

The authors in Part II present various points of view about the relation between population and power. They point out that the total population of a country is not in itself a reliable index of political power, otherwise China and India would be the most powerful nations. On the other hand, it does seem to be true that nations with a small population have little chance of achieving world power. France declined in political prestige during the period when her population was increasing much more slowly than the populations of Germany, Italy, and Russia.

Organski and Davis suggest that national income is the best single indi-

1. See *The New York Times,* May 27, 1927.

cator of political power. But national income is dependent on the state of economic development, and a high birth rate hinders the process of industrialization. John Boyd Orr suggests that the association of power with wealth may be one reason (although a subconscious one) why the white man is not doing more to relieve poverty throughout the world.

Because population growth has been associated with political power, suspicion and resentment are often aroused when a powerful and wealthy country takes it upon herself to help another nation reduce her birth rate. Historically, the degree of success has been greater when the initiative was taken by indigeneous leaders. During the occupation of Japan, General MacArthur made it his policy to take no official position on the matter of population control, in spite of the alarmingly high rate of population growth in Japan after the war. "Such matter does not fall within the prescribed scope of the Occupation," he said, ". . . decisions thereon rest entirely with the Japanese themselves. . . . Birth control is, in the final analysis, for individual decision." [2] Japanese people themselves waged a very successful campaign to reduce their birth rate. The number of births per thousand dropped from over 34 to about 17 in twelve years (see page 121). No other modern nation has achieved so rapid a drop in so short a time.

In passing through this demographic transition Japan followed the same pattern as the industrial nations of Western Europe. This pattern of declining birth rates has led to the optimistic belief that the population problem will be solved when the countries which are still largely agricultural become industrialized. But there are some fallacies in this line of reasoning, as the authors in these readings point out. A very high rate of national increase impedes industrialization and reduces per capita income in such a way that industrialization becomes progressively more difficult.

Furthermore, birth rates do not invariably decline as a country becomes more industrialized. For instance, the birth rate in the United States continued to rise during the 1950's in a period of increasing technological advance. In these years the United States reached a higher rate of natural increase than India! It is interesting to speculate whether this high birth rate was related to the philosophy of an expanding economy that has been so frequently expounded in the press in the last few decades. "More babies make more business," we read almost every day in popular magazines and newspapers. Again, this philosophy is shown to be an oversimplification by

2. *Nippon Times,* July 2, 1949.

the authors of these readings. Although it is true that a reasonable rate of growth in an advanced economy with plenty of savings will stimulate business expansion and new outlets for investment capital, a very rapid increase will create an unemployment problem and place too great a demand upon the natural resources.

It is reassuring to notice that since 1960 the birth rate in the United States has decreased in spite of a growing population and a steadily rising economy (see page 312). Perhaps, as Thomas Jefferson believed, the people demonstrate a collective wisdom which is greater than the wisdom of any single theoretician or political leader. The middle road, as Aristotle suggested two thousand years ago, may offer the best road to prosperity and power. "Experience shows," he said, "that a very populous city can rarely, if ever, be well governed . . . To the size of states there is a limit, as there is to other things, plants, animals, implements; for none of these retain their natural power when they are too large or too small." [3]

3. Aristotle, *Politics, II,* 6.

Population and Prosperity

Man is the only culture-building animal on the face of the earth. He not only adapts to environment but creates environment to which to adapt. In developing his culture and precipitating the technological, industrial, and scientific revolutions, man has profoundly altered the rhythm of his own reproduction. He has destroyed the equilibrium between the birth rate and the death rate which existed for most of the millennia he has been on this globe.

Philip Hauser
"Man and More Men"

Children Become an Economic Liability
A.F.K. AND KATHERINE ORGANSKI (1961)

The wonders of industry have not, as one might expect, produced a higher birth rate. Had the old peasant values favoring large families remained, this might well have happened, for surely, being richer, mankind can afford more children. But peasant values went the way of the peasants, and falling birth rates followed on the heels of industrialization. (Figure 1).

The decrease in fertility requires more explanation than does that in the death rate. Death, after all, is man's oldest enemy, and the desire to com-

From Philip Hauser, "Man and More Men: The Population Prospects," *Population: The Vital Revolution* edited by Ronald Freedman. Doubleday & Company, 1965.

From A.F.K. and Katherine Organski, *Population and World Power*, Alfred A. Knopf, New York. Copyright © 1961 by Alfred A. Knopf, Inc. Reprinted by permission.

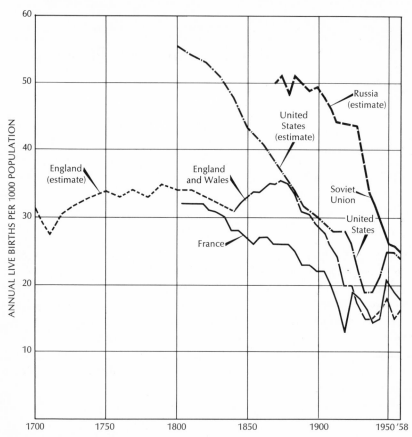

Figure 1. Changing birth rates.

bat hunger and disease is as old as human history. It is to be expected that improved technology would be used to lengthen life, but it is more difficult to explain its use to cut family size. It is by no means easy to find clear "causes" for anything as complex as a change in human values, which is what we are dealing with here. Looking backward, it is relatively easy to provide plausible explanations for what has happened in the past; but we do not know which factors were the key ones or what minor changes might have produced a different result.[1] Some of the reasons for the declining rate of human reproduction can be suggested, however.

1. Recent studies suggest that the relationship of lower fertility to industrialization and urbanization may not be as automatic as was previously assumed. See Frank Lorimer: *Culture and Human Fertility* (Zurich: UNESCO; 1954), Ch. vi; also John Durand: "Some Remarks on the Population Statistics of Ancient China and the Outlines of Chinese Population History," unpublished paper.

Consider the cost of raising children in the modern way compared to what it costs a landed peasant family. Except in times of famine or where the shortage of land is acute, peasant children put little economic strain upon their parents; indeed, they might almost be considered an economic asset. Six-year-old boys can tend goats and fetch wood and water; eight-year-old girls can serve as full-time nursemaids; twelve-year-olds can sweep and mend. Their usefulness increases with years. In many preindustrial societies grown sons stay home and work the land of their fathers, bringing home their wives to live and do the most unpleasant chores.

Compared to their peasant ancestors, modern children are an expensive if highly attractive luxury. They do not work: they play and go to school. Their full support—and full it is—must be provided until they reach maturity. At that point, sheltered, groomed, ready to give as well as to receive, they leave home and make their contribution elsewhere. Families with eight or ten children were not uncommon in the past, but who can afford such families today?

The social cost of a large family has also changed. In a peasant society a man's position is determined by his birth. Childlessness may bring him pity and derision, a large family, universal congratulation; but his social standing remains about the same. Not so for modern man: in an industrial society the family's standing depends heavily upon the occupation of the head of the household and upon the standard of living of the whole family as evidenced by the material goods it can display. A family with eight children cannot live in as good a neighborhood as a family with two; it cannot dress as well, drive as new a car, have as many conveniences and luxuries, or travel as much. The children will not receive as expensive an education, and this is particularly important in determining their social status when they become adults. False values? Perhaps modern men should feel, as do Indian peasants, that the family with eight children is richer than that with two—richer by six children. But that is not the way men count their wealth today or measure out esteem.

Industrial society, moreover, has invented new roles for women, holding out the lure of money and importance for work that takes them far from home. The training and education of women today directs them toward new goals. The current American pattern, for example, tends to minimize the differences between boys and girls in the early years and to provide a glamor pattern for young women. As a result, the role of aging mother-wife and housekeeper—"only a housewife," the phrase goes—is not as attractive as it used to be. Oddly enough, the Soviet pattern works in the same direction, although glamor is not the goal. The Russians put tremendous emphasis on careers for women because of the national shortage of labor. Be she capitalist or communist, modern woman finds herself faced with a choice of jobs that did not exist for her grandmother; and children, particularly if they are numerous, would bar her way to a career.

For all these reasons, and for many subtler ones as well, modern man for all his wealth has cut his birth rate. Planning his life, his work, his world, he has also begun to plan his family.

In their transition from the peasant world to the world of industry, Western nations have experienced falling birth rates, falling death rates, and a gap between them that has produced the largest population growth in history. Russia has followed such a pattern at a somewhat later date, and so has Japan, the only Asiatic land thus far to industrialize.

Experts have reasoned that if these population changes always accompany industrialization, similar changes may be in store for the rest of the world in the not-too-distant future.

Population

KINGSLEY DAVIS (1963)

. . . The first step in the demographic evolution of modern nations—a decline in the death rate—began in northwestern Europe long before it started elsewhere. As a result, although population growth is now slower in this area than in the rest of the world, it was here that the unprecedented upsurge in human numbers began. Being most advanced in demographic development, northwestern Europe is a good place to start in our analysis of modern population dynamics.

In the late medieval period the average life expectancy in England, according to life tables compiled by the historian J. C. Russell, was about 27 years. At the end of the 17th century and duirng most of the 18th it was about 31 in England, France and Sweden, and in the first half of the 19th century it advanced to 41.

The old but reliable vital statistics from Denmark, Norway and Sweden

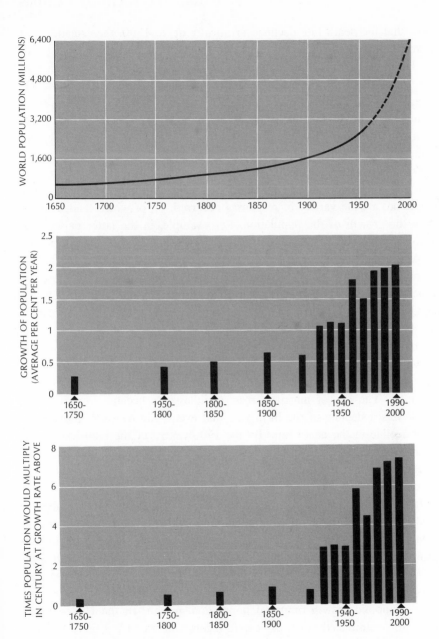

Figure 1. Population growth of world from 1650 to 1960 is shown by curve at top, which is projected to the year 2000. The middle chart shows the rate of growth, and the bottom chart the number of times the population would multiply in 100 years at that growth rate for various periods.

show that the death rate declined erratically up to 1790, then steadily and more rapidly. Meanwhile the birth rate remained remarkably stable (until the latter part of the 19th century). The result was a marked increase in the excess of births over deaths, or what demographers call "natural increase." In the century from about 1815 until World War I the average annual increase in the three Scandinavian countries was 11.8 per 1,000 —nearly five times what it had been in the middle of the 18th century, and sufficient to triple the population in 100 years.

For a long time the population of northwestern Europe showed little reaction to this rapid natural increase. But when it came, the reaction was emphatic; a wide variety of responses occurred, all of which tended to reduce the growth of the population. For example, in the latter part of the 19th century people began to emigrate from Europe by the millions, mainly to America, Australia and South Africa. Between 1846 and 1932 an estimated 27 million people emigrated overseas from Europe's 10 most advanced countries. The three Scandinavian countries alone sent out 2.4 million, so that in 1915 their combined population was 11.1 million instead of the 14.2 million it would otherwise have been.

In addition to this unprecedented exodus there were other responses, all of which tended to reduce the birth rate. In spite of opposition from church and state, agitation for birth control began and induced abortions became common. The age of marriage rose. Childlessness became frequent. The result was a decline in the birth rate that eventually overtook the continuing decline in the death rate. By the 1930's most of the industrial European countries had age-specific fertility rates so low that, if the rates had continued at that level, the population would eventually have ceased to replace itself.

In explaining this vigorous reaction one gets little help from two popular clichés. One of these—that population growth is good for business— would hardly explain why Europeans were so bent on stopping population growth. The other—that numerical limitation comes from the threat of poverty because "population always presses on the means of subsistence" —is factually untrue. In every one of the industrializing countries of Europe economic growth outpaced population growth. In the United Kingdom, for example, the real per capita income increased 2.3 times between the periods 1855–1859 and 1910–1914. In Denmark from 1770 to 1914 the rise of the net domestic product in constant prices was two and a half times the natural increase rate; in Norway and Sweden from the 1860's to

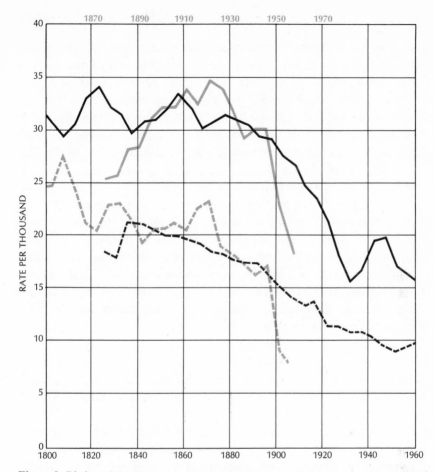

Figure 2. Birth and death rates for Denmark, Norway, and Sweden combined (*black lines and dates*) are compared with Japanese rates (*gray lines and dates*) of 50 years later. Japan has been passing through a population change similar to that which occurred earlier in Scandinavia. Area between respective birth-rate curves (*solid lines*) and death-rate curves (*broken lines*) shows natural increase, or population growth that would have occurred without migration. In past few years both Japanese rates have dropped extremely rapidly.

1914 it was respectively 1.4 and 2.7 times the natural increase rate. Clearly the strenuous efforts to lessen population growth were due to some stimulus other than poverty.

The stimulus, in my view, arose from the clash between new opportunities on the one hand and larger families on the other. The modernizing society of northwestern Europe necessarily offered new opportunities to people of all classes: new ways of gaining wealth, new means of rising socially, new symbols of status. In order to take advantage of those opportunities, however, the individual and his children required education, special skills, capital and mobility—none of which was facilitated by an improvident marriage or a large family. Yet because mortality was being reduced (and reduced more successfully in the childhood than in the adult ages) the size of families had become potentially larger than before. In Sweden, for instance, the mortality of the period 1755–1775 allowed only 6.1 out of every 10 children born to reach the age of 10, whereas the mortality of 1901–1910 allowed 8.5 to survive to that age. In order to avoid the threat of a large family to his own and his children's socioeconomic position, the individual tended to postpone or avoid marriage and to limit reproduction within marriage by every means available. Urban residents had to contend particularly with the cost and inconvenience of young children in the city. Rural families had to adjust to the lack of enough land to provide for new marriages when the children reached marriageable age. Land had become less available not only because of the plethora of families with numerous youths but also because, with modernization, more capital was needed per farm and because the old folks, living longer, held on to the property. As a result farm youths postponed marriage, flocked to the cities or went overseas.

In such terms we can account for the paradox that, as the progressive European nations became richer, their population growth slowed down. The process of conomic development itself provided the motives for curtailment of reproduction, as the British sociologist J. A. Banks has made clear in his book *Prosperity and Parenthood*. We can see now that in all modern nations the long-run trend is one of low mortality, a relatively modest rate of reproduction and slow population growth. This is an efficient demographic system that allows such countries, in spite of their "maturity," to continue to advance economically at an impressive speed.

Naturally the countries of northwestern Europe did not all follow an identical pattern. Their stages differed somewhat in timing and in the pattern of preference among the various means of population control. France, for example, never attained as high a natural increase as Britain or Scandinavia did. This was not due solely to an earlier decline in the birth rate, as is often assumed, but also to a slower decline in the death rate. If we historically substitute the Swedish death rate for the French, we revise the natural increase upward by almost the same amount as we do by substituting the Swedish birth rate. In accounting for the early and easy drop in French fertility one recalls that France, already crowded in the 18th century and in the van of intellectual radicalism and sophistication, was likely to have a low threshold for the adoption of abortion and contraception. The death rate, however, remained comparatively high because France did not keep economic pace with her more rapidly industrializing neighbors. As a result the relatively small gap between births and deaths gave France a slower growth in population and a lesser rate of emigration.

. . . The emphasis in Ireland's escape from human inflation was on emigration, late marriage and permanent celibacy. . . .

The Irish preferences among the means of population limitation seem to come from the island's position as a rural region participating only indirectly in the industrial revolution. For most of the Irish, land remained the basis for respectable matrimony. As land became inaccessible to young people they postponed marriage. . . . Marriage was also discouraged by the ban on divorce and by the lowest participation of married women in the labor force to be found in Europe. The country's failure to industrialize meant that the normal exodus from farms to cities was at the same time an exodus from Ireland itself.

Ireland and France illustrate contrasting variations on a common theme. Throughout northwestern Europe the population upsurge resulting from the fall in death rates brought about a multiphasic reaction that eventually reduced the population growth to a modest pace. The main force behind this response was not poverty or hunger but the desire of the people involved to preserve or improve their social standing by grasping the opportunities offered by the newly emerging industrial society.

Is this an interpretation applicable to the history of any industrialized country, regardless of traditional culture? According to the evidence the answer is yes. We might expect it to be true, as it currently is, of the countries of southern and eastern Europe that are finally industrializing. The crucial test is offered by the only nation outside the European tradition to become industrialized: Japan. How closely does Japan's demographic evolution parallel that of northwestern Europe?

If we superpose Japan's vital-rate curves on those of Scandinavia half a century earlier [see Figure 2], we see a basically similar, although more rapid, development. The reported statistics, questionable up to 1920 but good after that, show a rapidly declining death rate as industrialization took hold after World War I. The rate of natural increase during the period from 1900 to 1940 was almost exactly the same as Scandinavia's between 1850 and 1920, averaging 12.1 per 1,000 population per year compared with Scandinavia's 12.3. And Japan's birth rate, like Europe's began to dip until it was falling faster than the death rate, as it did in Europe. After the usual baby boom following World War II the decline in births was precipitous, amounting to 50 per cent from 1948 to 1960—perhaps the swiftest drop in reproduction that has ever occurred in an entire nation. The rates of child-bearing for women in various ages are so low that, if they continued indefinitely, they would not enable the Japanese population to replace itself.

In thus slowing their population growth have the Japanese used the same means as the peoples of northwestern Europe did? Again, yes. Taboo-ridden Westerners have given disproportionate attention to two features of the change—the active role played by the Japanese government and the widespread resort to abortion—but neither of these disproves the similarity. It is true that since the war the Japanese government has pursued a birth-control policy more energetically than any government ever has before. It is also clear, however, that the Japanese people would have reduced their childbearing of their own accord. A marked decline in the reproduction rate had already set in by 1920, long before there was a government policy favoring this trend.

As for abortion, the Japanese are unusual only in admitting its extent. Less superstitious than Europeans about this subject, they keep reasonably good records of abortions, whereas most of the other countries have no accurate data. According to the Japanese records, registered abortions rose from 11.8 per 1,000 women of childbearing age in 1949 to a peak of 50.2 per 1,000 in 1955. We have no reliable historical information from Western countries, but we do know from many indirect indications that induced abortion played a tremendous role in the reduction of the birth rate in western Europe from 1900 to 1940, and that it still plays a considerable role. Furthermore, Christopher Tietze of the National Committee for Maternal Health has assembled records that show that in five eastern European countries where abortion has been legal for some time [1] the rate has shot up recently in a manner strikingly similar to Japan's experience. In 1960–1961 there were 139 abortions for every 100 births in Hungary, 58 per 100 births in Bulgaria, 54 in Czechoslovakia and 34 in Poland. The

[1. See p. 142 for reversal of this policy in Romania. Ed.]

countries of eastern Europe are in a developmental stage comparable to that of northwestern Europe earlier in the century.

Abortion is by no means the sole factor in the decline of Japan's birth rate. Surveys made since 1950 show the use of contraception before that date, and increasing use thereafter. There is also a rising frequency of sterilization. Furthermore, as in Europe earlier, the Japanese are postponing marriage. The proportion of girls under 20 who have ever married fell from 17.7 per cent in 1920 to 1.8 per cent in 1955. In 1959 only about 5 per cent of the Japanese girls marrying for the first time were under 20, whereas in the U.S. almost half the new brides (48.5 per cent in the registration area) were that young.

Finally, Japan went through the same experience as western Europe in another respect—massive emigration. Up to World War II Japan sent millions of emigrants to various regions of Asia, Oceania and the Americas.

In short, in response to a high rate of natural increase brought by declining mortality, Japan reacted in the same ways as the countries of northwestern Europe did at a similar stage. Like the Europeans, the Japanese limited their population growth in their own private interest and that of their children in a developing society, rather than from any fear of absolute privation or any concern with overpopulation in their homeland. The nation's average 5.4 per cent annual growth in industrial output from 1913 to 1958 exceeded the performance of European countries at a similar stage.

As our final class of industrialized countries we must now consider the frontier group—the U.S., Canada, Australia, New Zealand, South Africa and Russia. These countries are distinguished from those of northwestern Europe and Japan by their vast wealth of natural resources in relation to their populations; they are the genuinely affluent nations. They might be expected to show a demographic history somewhat different from that of Europe. In certan particulars they do, yet the general pattern is still much the same.

One of the differences is that the riches offered by their untapped resources invited immigration. All the frontier industrial countries except Russia received massive waves of emigrants from Europe. They therefore had a more rapid population growth than their industrializing predecessors had experienced. As frontier countries with great room for expansion, however, they were also characterized by considerable internal migration and continuing new opportunities. As a result their birth rates remained comparatively high. In the decade from 1950 to 1960, with continued immigration, these countries grew in population at an average rate of 2.13 per cent a year, compared with 1.76 per cent for the rest of the world. It was the four countries with the sparsest settlement (Canada, Australia, New Zealand and South Africa), however, that accounted for this high rate; in the U.S. and the U.S.S.R. the growth rate was lower—1.67 per cent per year.

Apparently, then, in pioneer industrial countries with an abundance of resources, population growth holds up at a higher level than in Japan or northwestern Europe because the average individual feels it is easier for himself and his children to achieve a respectable place in the social scale. The immigrants attracted by the various opportunities normally begin at a low level and thus make the status of natives relatively better. People marry earlier and have slightly larger families. But this departure from the general pattern for industrial countries appears to be only temporary.

In the advanced frontier nations, as in northwestern Europe, the birth rate began to fall sharply after 1880, and during the depression of the 1930's it was only about 10 per cent higher than in Europe. Although the postwar baby boom has lasted longer than in other advanced countries, it is evidently starting to subside now,[2] and the rate of immigration has diminished. There are factors at work in these affluent nations that will likely limit their population growth. They are among the most urbanized countries in the world, in spite of their low average population density. Their birth rates are extremely sensitive to business fluctuations and social changes. Furthermore, having in general the world's highest living standards, their demand for resources, already staggering, will become fantastic if both population and per capita consumption continue to rise rapidly, and their privileged position in the world may become less tolerated.

Let us shift now to the other side of the population picture: the nonindustrial, or underdeveloped, countries.

As a class the nonindustrial nations since 1930 have been growing in population about twice as fast as the industrial ones. This fact is so familiar and so taken for granted that its irony tends to escape us. When we think of it, it is astonishing that the world's most impoverished nations, many of them already overcrowded by any standard, should be generating additions to the population at the highest rate.

The underdeveloped countries have about 69 per cent of the earth's adults—and some 80 per cent of the world's children. Hence the demo-

[2. See Figure 1, p. 312. Ed.]

graphic situation itself tends to make the world constantly more underdeveloped, or impoverished, a fact that makes economic growth doubly difficult.

How can we account for the paradox that the world's poorest regions are producing the most people? One is tempted to believe that the underdeveloped countries are simply repeating history: that they are in the same phase of rapid growth the West experienced when it began to industrialize and its death rates fell. If that is so, then sooner or later the developing areas will limit their population growth as the West did.

It is possible that this may prove to be true in the long run. But before we accept the comforting thought we should take a close look at the facts as they are.

In actuality the demography of the nonindustrial countries today differs in essential respects from the early history of the present industrial nations. Most striking is the fact that their rate of human multiplication is far higher than the West's ever was. The peak of the industrial nations' natural increase rarely rose above 15 per 1,000 population per year; the highest rate in Scandinavia was 13, in England and Wales 14, and even in Japan it was slightly less than 15. True, the U.S. may have hit a figure of 30 per 1,000 in the early 19th century, but if so it was with the help of heavy immigration of young people (who swelled the births but not the deaths) and with the encouragement of an empty continent waiting for exploitation.

In contrast, in the present underdeveloped but often crowded countries the natural increase per 1,000 population is everywhere extreme. In the decade from 1950 to 1960 it averaged 31.4 per year in Taiwan, 26.8 in Ceylon, 32.1 in Malaya, 26.7 in Mauritius, 27.7 in Albania, 31.8 in Mexico, 33.9 in El Salvador and 37.3 in Costa Rica. These are not birth rates; they are the *excess* of births over deaths! At an annual natural increase of 30 per 1,000 a population will double itself in 23 years.

The population upsurge in the backward nations is apparently taking place at an earlier stage of development—or perhaps we should say *undevelopment*—than it did in the now industrialized nations. In Britain, for instance, the peak of human multiplication came when the country was already highly industrialized and urbanized, with only a fifth of its working males in agriculture. Comparing four industrial countries at the peak of their natural increase in the 19th century (14.1 per 1,000 per year) with five nonindustrial countries during their rapid growth in the 1950's (32.2 per 1,000 per year), I find that the industrial countries were 38.5 per cent urbanized and had 27.9 per cent of their labor force in manufacturing, whereas now the nonindustrial countries are 29.4 per cent urbanized and have only 15.1 per cent of their people in manufacturing. In short, today's nonindustrial populations are growing faster and at an earlier stage than was the case in the demographic cycle that accompanied industrialization in the 19th century.

As in the industrial nations, the main generator of the population upsurge in the underdeveloped countries has been a fall in the death rate. But their resulting excess of births over deaths has proceeded faster and farther, as a comparison of Ceylon in recent decades with Sweden in the 1800's shows [see Figure 3].

In most of the underdeveloped nations the death rate has dropped with record speed. For example, the sugar-growing island of Mauritius in the Indian Ocean within an eight-year period after the war raised its average life expectancy from 33 to 51—a gain that took Sweden 130 years to achieve. Taiwan within two decades has increased its life expectancy from 43 to 63; it took the U.S. some 80 years to make this improvement for its white population. According to the records in 18 underdeveloped countries, the crude death rate has dropped substantially in each decade since 1930; it fell some 6 per cent in the 1930's and nearly 20 per cent in the 1950's, and according to the most recent available figures the decline in deaths is still accelerating.

The reasons for this sharp drop in mortality are in much dispute. There are two opposing theories. Many give the credit to modern medicine and public health measures. On the other hand, the public health spokesmen, rejecting the accusation of complicity in the world's population crisis, belittle their own role and maintain that the chief factor in the improvement of the death rate has been economic progress.

Those in the latter camp point out that the decline in the death rate in northwestern Europe followed a steadily rising standard of living. Improvements in diet, clothing, housing and working conditions raised the population's resistance to disease. As a result many dangerous ailments disappeared or subsided without specific medical attack. The same process, say the public health people, is now at work in the developing countries.

On the other side, most demographers and economists believe that economic conditions are no longer as important as they once were in strengthening a community's health. The development of medical science has provided lifesaving techniques and medicines that can be transported overnight

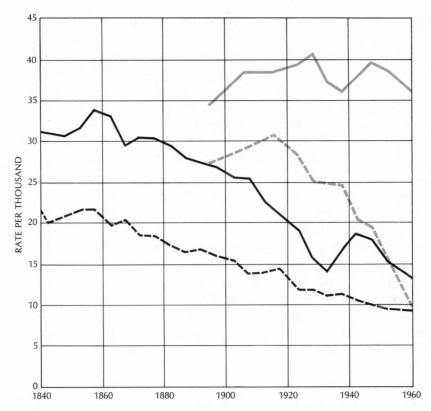

Figure 3. New demographic pattern is appearing in the nonindustrial nations. The birth rate (*solid line*) has not been falling significantly, whereas the death rate (*broken line*) has dropped precipitously, as illustrated by Ceylon (*gray*). The spread between the two rates has widened. In nations such as Sweden (*black*), however, the birth rate dropped during development long before the death rate was as low as in most underdeveloped countries today.

to the most backward areas. A Stone Age people can be endowed with a low 20th-century death rate within a few years, without waiting for the slow process of economic development or social change. International agencies and the governments of the affluent nations have been delighted to act as good Samaritans and send out public health missionaries to push disease-fighting programs for the less developed countries.

The debate between the two views is hard to settle. Such evidence as we have indicates that there is truth on both sides. Certainly the newly evolving countries have made economic progress. Their economic advance, however, is not nearly rapid enough to account for the very swift decline in

127

their death rates, nor do they show any clear correlation between economic growth and improvement in life expectancy. For example, in Mauritius during the five-year period from 1953 to 1958 the per capita income fell by 13 per cent, yet notwithstanding this there was a 36 per cent drop in the death rate. On the other hand, in the period between 1945 and 1960 Costa Rica had a 64 per cent increase in the per capita gross national product and a 55 per cent decline in the death rate. There seems to be no consistency—no significant correlation between the two trends when we look at the figures country by country. In 15 underdeveloped countries for which such figures are available we find that the decline in death rate in the 1950's was strikingly uniform (about 4 per cent per year), although the nations varied greatly in economic progress—from no improvement to a 6 per cent annual growth in per capita income.

Our tentative conclusion must be, therefore, that the public health people are more efficient than they admit. The billions of dollars spent in public health work for underdeveloped areas has brought down death rates, irrespective of local economic conditions in these areas. The programs instituted by outsiders to control cholera, malaria, plague and other diseases in these countries have succeeded. This does not mean that death control in underdeveloped countries has become wholly or permanently independent of economic development but that it has become temporarily so to an amazing degree.

Accordingly the unprecedented population growth in these countries bears little relation to their economic condition. The British economist Colin G. Clark has contended that rapid population growth stimulates economic progress. This idea acquires plausibility from the association between human increase and industrialization in the past and from the fact that in advanced countries today the birth rate (but not the death rate) tends to fluctuate with business conditions. In today's underdeveloped countries, however, there seems to be little or no visible connection between economics and demography.

In these countries neither births nor deaths have been particularly responsive to economic change. Some of the highest rates of population growth ever known are occurring in areas that show no commensurate economic advance. In 34 such countries for which we have data, the correlation between population growth and economic gain during the 1950's was negligible, and the slight edge was on the negative side: —.2. In 20 Latin-American countries during the period from 1954 to 1959, while the annual

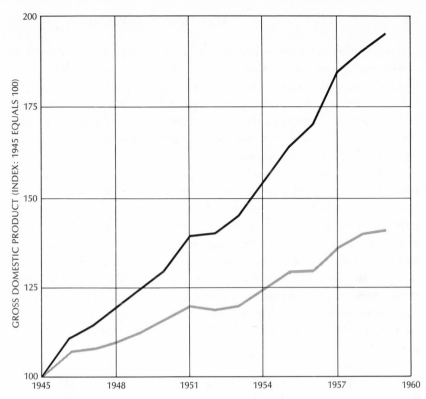

Figure 4. Gross domestic product of Latin America doubled between 1945 and 1959 (*black line*) but population growth held down the increase in per capita product (*gray line*).

gain in per capita gross domestic product fell from an average of 2 per cent to 1.3 per cent, the population growth rate *rose* from 2.5 to 2.7 per cent per year.

All the evidence indicates that the population upsurge in the under-developed countries is not helping them to advance economically. On the contrary, it may well be interfering with their economic growth. A surplus of labor on the farms holds back the mechanization of agriculture. A rapid rise in the number of people to be maintained uses up income that might otherwise be utilized for long-term investment in education, equipment and other capital needs. To put it in concrete terms, it is difficult to give a child the basic education he needs to become an engineer when he is one of eight children of an illiterate farmer who must support the family with the pro-duce of two acres of ground.

By definition economic advance means an increase in the amount of product per unit of human labor. This calls for investment in technology, in improvement of the skills of the labor force and in administrative organization and planning. An economy that must spend a disproportionate share of its income in supporting the consumption needs of a growing population—and at a low level of consumption at that—finds growth difficult because it lacks capital for improvements.

A further complication lies in the process of urbanization. The shifts from villages and farmsteads to cities is seemingly an unavoidable and at best a painful part of economic development. It is most painful when the total population is skyrocketing; then the cities are bursting both from their own multiplication and from the stream of migrants from the villages. The latter do not move to cities because of the opportunities there. The opportunities are few and unemployment is prevalent. The migrants come, rather, because they are impelled by the lack of opportunity in the crowded rural areas. In the cities they hope to get something—a menial job, government relief, charities of the rich. I have recently estimated that if the population of India increases at the rate projected for it by the UN, the net number of migrants to cities between 1960 and 2000 will be of the order of 99 to 201 million, and in 2000 the largest city will contain between 36 and 66 million inhabitants. One of the greatest problems now facing the governments of underdeveloped countries is what to do with these millions of penniless refugees from the excessively populated countryside.

Economic growth is not easy to achieve. So far, in spite of all the talk and the earnest efforts of underdeveloped nations, only one country outside the northwestern European tradition has done so: Japan. The others are struggling with the handicap of a population growth greater than any industrializing country had to contend with in the past. A number of them now realize that this is a primary problem, and their governments are pursuing or contemplating large-scale programs of birth-limitation. They are receiving little help in this matter, however, from the industrial nations, which have so willingly helped them to lower their death rates.

The Christian nations withhold this help because of their official taboos against some of the means of birth-limitation (although their own people privately use all these means). The Communist nations withhold it because limitation of population growth conflicts with official Marxist dogma (but Soviet citizens control births just as capitalist citizens do, and China is officially pursuing policies calculated to reduce the birth rate).

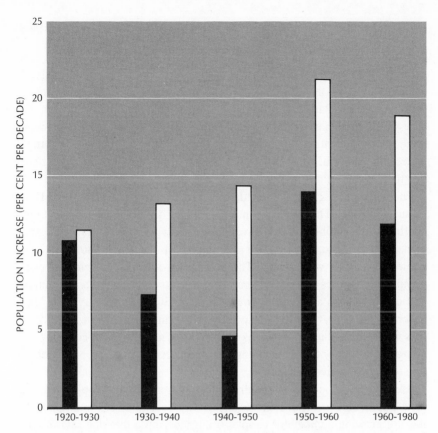

Figure 5. Differential population growth in underdeveloped regions (*white bars*) and developed regions (*black bars*) is plotted. The 1960–80 projections may turn out to be low.

The West's preoccupation with the technology of contraception seems unjustified in view of its own history. The peoples of northwestern Europe utilized all the available means of birth limitation once they had strong motives for such limitation. The main question, then, is whether or not the peoples of the present underdeveloped countries are likely to acquire such motivation in the near future. There are signs that they will. Surveys in India, Jamaica and certain other areas give evidence of a growing desire among the people to reduce the size of their families. Furthermore, circumstances in the underdeveloped nations today are working more strongly in this direction than they did in northwestern Europe in the 19th century.

As in that earlier day, poverty and deprivation alone are not likely to generate a slowdown of the birth rate. But personal aspirations are. The agrarian peoples of the backward countries now look to the industrialized, affluent fourth of the world. They nourish aspirations that come directly from New York, Paris and Moscow. No more inclined to be satisfied with a bare subsistence than their wealthier fellows would be, they are demanding more goods, education, opportunity and influence. And they are beginning to see that many of their desires are incompatible with the enlarged families that low mortality and customary reproduction are giving them.

They live amid a population density far greater than existed in 19th-century Europe. They have no place to which to emigrate, no beckoning continents to colonize. They have rich utopias to look at and industrial models to emulate, whereas the Europeans of the early 1800's did not know where they were going. The peoples of the underdeveloped, over-populated countries therefore seem likely to start soon a multiphasic limitation of births such as began to sweep through Europe a century ago. Their governments appear ready to help them. Government policy in these countries is not quibbling over means or confining itself to birth-control technology; its primary task is to strengthen and accelerate the peoples' motivation for reproductive restraint.

Meanwhile the industrial countries also seem destined to apply brakes to their population growth. The steadily rising level of living, multiplied by the still growing numbers of people, is engendering a dizzying rate of consumption. It is beginning to produce painful scarcities of space, of clean water, of clean air and of quietness. All of this may prompt more demographic moderation than these countries have already exercised.

Population Increase and Economic Development
EUGENE R. BLACK (1962)

There are movements in the less developed countries which vitiate all efforts to raise world living standards. One of the most massive of these obstacles is the tremendous rise in the populations of already crowded countries. . . .

Some people argue that a big population implies a good market for the businessman's product: he can use mass production techniques and charge low prices. They insist, too, that with a growing population, the business-man constantly finds demand exceeding his estimates. Optimism and pro-duction run high; new products win ready acceptance, while obsolete indus-tries die painlessly; the incentive to invest is strong; and social mobility and change are encouraged. The burden of social costs is spread widely. By contrast, they suggest, a declining or even stationary population brings pessimism and economic stagnation; there is insufficient reward for private enterprise, and the state is thereby forced to intervene increasingly in fields better left to the private citizen.

This body of theory may conceivably be true in the circumstances of a rich country with resources to spare. But it is wildly irrelevant to the prob-lems of most developing countries today.

It is, of course, a fact that some of the poorer countries do not have do-mestic markets big enough to support mass-production industries. But it is clearly ridiculous to suggest that inadequate population is holding back the development of, say, India, which packs more than twice the population of the United States into less than half the space. Where most people go bare-foot for lack of shoes, industry is not failing to grow because its products are not wanted. Where the agricultural laborer can find work to occupy him for only half the year, no further pressure is needed to make him wish for a different occupation. Where two thirds of every dollar of income must be spent on food, where manufacturing industry is almost nonexistent, one need not worry that excessive saving will lead to underemployment of re-sources. The lash of further poverty is not required to drive these people to action. The developing countries need many things—not only capital, but the skills and health to make good use of it. By no means do all of them need population growth.

But need it or not, they have it. They should ask themselves if they can afford it. In Asia, in the Middle East, in Latin America, in Africa, the population of most countries is growing at the rate of 2 percent annually —and sometimes 3½ percent or more. In some parts of Latin America and Africa there is fortunately room for the extra people. In the long run, although not now, there should also be adequate resources available to feed, clothe, and house them. But in many parts of Asia and the Middle East, resources are few, and there is not nearly enough room. Agricultural land which once sufficed to support a stationary and much smaller popula-tion has already been divided and subdivided beyond the limits of effective cultivation. Cities are crowded to bursting, and are still getting bigger.

Population growth on this scale would be a serious challenge to a country with adequate living standards. Where incomes are very low, and economic development is a desperate need, such growth can be a crippling handicap.

The speed at which a country develops depends largely upon its ability to direct its growing resources to investment rather than consumption, to uses which will raise tomorrow's output rather than satisfy today's demands. A poor society finds it difficult to save at all, and will be doing well if it can set aside 10 percent of its income. At this rate, if its population is growing, it will be investing barely enough to stay where it is. Yet the likelihood must be that it will invest not more than 10 percent, but less: a growing population with a high proportion of dependent children will find it increasingly difficult to spare any of its income.

Unless foreign aid can be increased, a country in this position is faced with a stark alternative. It must reduce its savings, or lower its living standards—although both are already inadequate.

The industrialized countries have shown their willingness to help. Common humanity and self-interest alike impel them to do so. All the evidence points to a greater flow of aid in the coming years. But I find myself increasingly doubtful whether domestic savings and foreign aid together will be sufficient to allow real progress, if present rates of population growth continue for long.

Figures are hard to come by in this field. But it may be possible to indicate some orders of magnitude.

Some calculations have been made about the cost of providing houses in India during the next generation if the population continues to grow at its present rate of about 2 percent a year. If you disregard the cost of rural housing, on the somewhat optimistic assumption that it can be carried out entirely with local materials and labor, then you still have to pay for the homes of nearly 200 million extra people who, it is expected, will be living in India's cities twenty-five years hence. Making full allowance for the fact that many of the extra persons will be children needing not new houses, but simply more space in existing households, a sober estimate of the cost suggests that in the thirty years between 1956 and 1986 a total investment in housing on the order of 118 billion rupees, or roughly $25 billion, will be needed. If you find a figure like that difficult to grasp, I may say that it is well over four times the total lent by the World Bank in all countries since it started business fifteen years ago. Put another way, it is more than thirty times the initial resources of the International Development Association—and those resources are supposed to cover IDA's first five years of operations.

My cost estimate takes no account of the need to improve existing housing in such cities as Calcutta. It leaves out the cost of roads, sewage systems, water supplies, and other services. Yet the problems of urban growth form only a small part of the challenge presented when economic development is attempted in the context of a vast expansion in population.

In the social field, many more new hospitals and clinics will be needed, simply to maintain present standards—standards which by common consent are sadly inadequate. Far more must be spent on education. Here look again at India, not because its problems are unusual, but because they are well documented. In 1956 about 31 million Indian children were getting an education—less than 40 percent of those of school age. It is mathematically certain that if the population grows as expected, a three- or fourfold increase in educational investment will be needed if all children are to be receiving an education by 1976. When you come to productive investment, the story is similar. Enormous investments will be needed. But population growth does not only tend to reduce the flow of investment funds. It also means that the capital invested in industry must be spread increasingly thin over the labor force: each pair of hands is backed by fewer dollars of capital. Productivity suffers, and the gap in living standards between the developing and the industrialized countries widens, instead of narrows.

I must be blunt. Population growth threatens to nullify all our efforts to raise living standards in many of the poorer countries. We are coming to a situation in which the optimist will be the man who thinks that present living standards can be maintained. The pessimist will not look even for that. Unless population growth can be restrained, we may have to abandon for this generation our hopes of economic progress in the crowded lands of Asia and the Middle East.

Effect of Density

ANSLEY J. COALE (1963)

The question of population density tends to be the dominant concept in most casual thought about the population problems of underdeveloped

From Ansley J. Coale, "Population and Economic Development," *The Population Dilemma,* edited by Philip Hauser, Prentice-Hall, Englewood Cliffs. Copyright © 1963 by The American Assembly, Columbia University. Reprinted by permission.

areas. The notion of excessive density is certainly implicit in the term "overpopulation." The underlying idea is that when there are too many workers relative to the available resources, per capita output is smaller than it would be with a smaller number of workers. Given gross enough differences in the numbers of workers being compared, it is certainly possible in principle to establish that overpopulation in this sense exists. . . .

There are, however, two reasons for doubting the immediate usefulness of the concept of density in considering population problems of underdeveloped areas. The first is that in this period of human history few countries have any genuine freedom of choice of policy that would have an important effect on population density (or, more specifically, on the density of the labor force) in the short run. There are few areas where realistic alternatives of promoting or retarding international migration would have an important effect upon density. It is unlikely, and I would argue strongly undesirable, that an underdeveloped country should contemplate a deliberate restraint on its public health programs in order to retard the decline of mortality and thus prevent an increase of population density. As is shown in Figure 1, a reduction in fertility does not have an important effect on density for a long time in the future. The difference in the size of the labor force is less than ten per cent thirty years after a rapid and extensive decline in fertility begins. After thirty years, however, the difference in density between sustained and reduced fertility rapidly mounts, reaching a factor of two in about sixty years, a factor of three in seventy-five years, and a factor of eighteen after 150 years. In other words, so far as acceptable and attainable policies are concerned, only in the relatively distant future can the density of the labor force relative to resources be affected. In the meantime the policy that would have a long-run effect on density, namely one that reduces fertility, would through changes in dependency and differences in the annual rate of growth of the labor force have produced major economic effects.

A second reservation about the relevance of density is that it is of clearcut importance only in a closed economy—i.e., one that does not trade extensively—or in an economy where the principal industry is extractive. Only in extractive industries—mining, agriculture, and forestry—are resources as related to numbers of workers a dominant element in productivity. For example, if India were compelled to continue to employ seventy per cent of its labor force in agriculture, increasing density would inevitably mean smaller average holdings. The average holding today is only about two

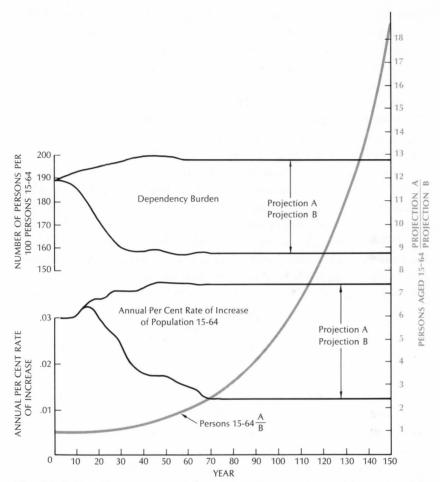

Figure 1. Dependency burden (total number of persons 15 to 64); relative size of the population 15 to 64; and annual rate of increase of population 15 to 64 in two model projections (Projection A, Fertility unchanged; Projection B, Fertility reduced linearly by 50 per cent in 25 years, thereafter constant). Office of Population Research, Princeton University.

acres per person aged fifteen to sixty-four dependent on agriculture, and the possibility of bringing new areas under cultivation is limited.

In non-extractive industries international trade can greatly reduce the effect of limited resources. In all industries, extractive or otherwise, productivity is determined to a large degree by the stock of capital per worker.

137

The underdeveloped areas have in common a small endowment of productive equipment per worker relative to the industrialized countries; in other words, the underdeveloped countries all have a "high density" of workers relative to capital, whether the country appears to be sparsely or densely settled relative to land and other resources.

Two examples indicate the dubious relevance of the concept of overpopulation where non-extractive industries are dominant and a large volume of trade is possible. One is the narrow strip of territory extending from Boston to Washington along the east coast of the United States. There is a 400 mile long line of contiguous counties with an aggregate area of about 14,000 square miles and an aggregate population in 1960 of about 28,000,000, or a population density of more than 2,000 per square mile. There are few if any areas of similar extent in the world with a higher density. The median family income of this strip is $6,660, just a thousand dollars more than the median for the United States as a whole. Is it overpopulated? It would certainly be difficult to demonstrate that per capita output would be greater if the population density were less. Of course this area belongs to a large market—the United States and its territories—where trade is unrestricted. Extractive industries play a trivial role in the output of this area. It can readily import the raw materials and semi-finished products that it requires in exchange for the finished goods and services it produces.

The second example, Hong Kong, shows that the possibility of importing raw materials and semi-finished goods in exchange for finished goods and services is not limited to a region within a country. Hong Kong has a population of 3.1 million on a land area of 398 square miles, with a resultant density of 12,700 persons per square mile. Land for new buildings on Victoria Island is dredged from the harbor. After the war Hong Kong had a very low per capita income, and its density was inflated by an influx of refugees. Nevertheless Hong Kong has achieved increases in national produce of seven to ten per cent per year and has probably doubled its real output in a decade. It obtains its needed imports (including food) on the world market. Mainland China has receded to a minor position in Hong Kong's pattern of trade, providing only seventeen per cent of Hong Kong's imports in 1961. Hong Kong has very important special advantages, especially in terms of human capital, as data from the 1961 census show. The refugees that swarmed into Hong Kong were not illiterate peasants but had an average educational attainment well above what must characterize China as a whole. Among the immigrants were experienced entrepreneurs from Shanghai. In short, Hong Kong was endowed with an energetic, literate and partially trained labor force and had no scarcity of organizational and entrepreneurial skills. It nevertheless remains a fact that an extraordinarily high density of population relative to resources has not prevented an extraordinarily rapid increase in per capita income. . . .

In very sparsely settled countries the adverse effect upon the possible reduction of density relative to capital of rapid growth of the labor force may be partially offset by an increasingly advantageous relationship between numbers and land area and other resources. A larger population may, when original density is unusually low, permit the use of more efficient large-scale operations. This possibility does not imply, however, that the more rapid the rate of growth the better. Additional capital for the additional labor force is still essential, and rapid growth prevents an increase in the capital/worker rates. Moreover, from a strictly economic point of view the most advantageous way to attain a larger labor force is through immigration, because it is possible by this means to obtain additional labor without incurring the expense of childhood dependency.

A reduction in fertility has the immediate effect (during the first generation after the decline begins) of reducing the burden of child dependency without any major effect on the size of the labor force. After twenty or twenty-five years the decline in fertility begins to effect a major reduction in the rate of growth of the labor force. In the more remote future, beginning after forty or fifty years and with increasing importance with the further passage of time, reduced fertility produces a population of lower density —with a smaller labor force relative to the available resources. The age distribution effect of reduced fertility operates to produce during the first generation a larger total national product than would result if fertility had not been reduced. The greater rise in total output results from the fact that the same number of producers—the same number of persons eligible for participation in the labor force—is accompanied by a smaller number of consumers. The smaller number of consumers decreases the fraction of national output that must be allocated to current consumption, and thus promotes the mobilization of resources for economic growth. Both private savings and the ability of the government to raise funds for development are increased.

The American Fertility Cult

LINCOLN H. AND ALICE TAYLOR DAY (1964)

Given the attitudes and values of Americans concerning population limitation in the United States, it is not surprising that, to date, the case for population stability has failed to receive the hearing accorded its opposite: the
case for population growth. In fact, arguments in favor of continued population increase predominate to such an extent that they suggest the existence of an "American Fertility Cult." Enthusiastically endorsing our
abundant growth, the apologists for further population increase in the
United States ignore all evidence of its detrimental consequences, and in
some instances even go so far as to claim that our prosperity and very survival depend upon maintaining growth at its present high level. . . . With
a spirit reminiscent of the Couéism of 1923—whose followers went about
proclaiming, "Day by day in every way I am getting better and better" [1]
—a self-styled "public service" advertisement in the New York subways
informs us: "Your future is great in a growing America. Every day 11,000
babies are born in America. This means new business, new jobs, new opportunities." In the same vein, a 1958 issue of *Life* greeted its one million
subscribers with a cover picture of three dozen children and the title:
"Kids: Built-in Recession Cure—How 4,000,000 a Year Make Millions in
Business." Inside, it was "Rocketing Births: Business Bonanza." . . .

We have the "deepest" canyon, the "tallest" building, the "largest" sta-
dium. The folder of souvenir snapshots tells us that the statue of the Iwo
Jima flag-raising ceremony is "the biggest ever cast in bronze." After every
census dozens of mayors and Chambers of Commerce take vehement issue
with census takers over the number of people enumerated in their home
towns. The mastheads of newspapers and signs on the outskirts of small
towns urge all and sundry to "watch us grow!"

"Bigger and better" is not just a handy alliteration. It is part of the very
fabric of our society. Growth stands for youth; the cessation of growth for
old age. A population that has ceased to grow is considered weak, unpro-

1. Frederick Lewis Allen, *Only Yesterday,* Bantam Books, New York, 1952, p. 74.

gressive, lacking in vigor; even, somehow, impotent or sterile. The "cult of youth" is an important part of American culture.[2] Not only are Americans as individuals reluctant to grow old, they seem reluctant also to think of their country as growing old. It may never be expressed in these terms, but we suggest that the feeling that they will retain their youth as a nation so long as they manage to keep growing is important to much of the support Americans give to continued population increase.

Another source of support comes from the vested interest. Among the most active propagators of the "benefits" of population growth is a magazine with one of the nation's largest circulations. Since in this country any profits to be had from operation of the various media of mass communication will come from advertising revenues and not subscriptions, these media have a vested interest in fostering a general attitude of optimistic boosterism. In the case of population growth, it takes a form such as this: More people means more consumption; more consumption means the advertisers had better get into gear and put their messages across to the consuming public; the more "messages," the more revenue for the media.

Publishing is not the only business that stands to realize a short-run gain from population growth; housing construction and real estate are two other examples. House-buying is widespread in our sociey; so is changing houses, whether because of a change in jobs or a desire for something "better." [3] For the average person, buying a house is the only financial speculation he makes in a lifetime. He wants not only to preserve his equity, but also to make a profit. With such an attitude, he is already primed for an argument in favor of poulation growth as a means to keeping up the demand for housing. It sounds reasonable—and the cost is never mentioned. Many of the great American fortunes were acquired in precisely this something-for-nothing way. Why should not the little fellow share in the bounty of capitalism?

The construction business can also anticipate gains from the greater demand for schools, roads, dams, etc. that population growth makes necessary. The textile and food processing industries have similar vested interests.

Most arguments for population increase were formulated during the 1930's as antidotes to the sharp declines in birth rates that the western in-

2. See Talcott Parsons, "Age and Sex in the Social Structure," in Talcott Parsons, *Essays in Sociological Theory Pure and Applied,* Glencoe, Ill., Free Press, 1949.
3. See, for example, Detroit Area Study, *A Social Profile of Detroit: 1956,* University of Michigan Press, Ann Arbor 1957, Chapter 2.

dustrialized countries were then experiencing. Yet, their influence, despite the substantially different circumstances, seems at its height today.

Editor's Note: *The following selections describe attempts to raise the declining birth rates during the 1920's and 1930's by economic sanctions and incentives. The reasons for wanting to raise the birth rates were largely nationalistic and military. There may also have been a psychological element. As Robert C. Cook, in his book* Human Fertility, *has said: "Declining birth rates have a way of making nations panicky."*

In retrospect, we see that panic was unjustified. Although the specific fertility rates declined for a few years, the total populations of these countries have increased. However, the thinking which led to these economic measures is still influential today, as we can see from an Associated Press release of early January 1967:

Reds Impose Childless Couple Tax

BELGRADE, YUGOSLAVIA (AP)—Communist Romania has introduced additional income taxes for childless couples and all those over 25 who are unmarried, the Yugoslav news agency Tanjug reported from Bucharest.

The agency said the decree of the state council went into force Jan. 1. A decree in October made divorces difficult to obtain and banned abortions.

Families with more than three children have special allowances.

All these measures came after an alarming decrease in births in Romania, the agency said. According to statistics, in the last 10 years births decreased from 14 to 6 per 1,000.   (*Chicago Daily News,* Jan. 12, 1967)

The Province of Quebec on March 16, 1967, announced a new baby bonus to encourage larger families:

OTTAWA, ONT., March 17—A provincial baby bonus, the first in any province, which will be in addition to the federal baby bonus, will start on April 1, and will cost 88 million dollars in the first full year.

More than 800,000 mothers in Quebec will receive bonuses for more than 2 million children up to the age of 16, at an ascending rate as they have more children.

Falling Birth Rate

Quebec will pay $30 a year for the first child, an additional $35 for the second, $40 for the third, $50 for the fourth, $60 for the fifth, and $70 a year for the sixth and each additional child. French Canadians have been worried about a falling birth rate in Quebec in recent years.

Canada's federal baby bonus program, started in 1945, and now costing the country 600 million dollars a year, goes to all mothers, needy or not, at rates of $6 a month for children under 10 years old, $8 for children from 10 to 16, and $10 a month for children 17 years old if they are in school.

Most mothers use baby bonus checks as extra spending money, and some have formed investment clubs to gamble on the stock market.

(Chicago Tribune, March 17, 1967)

Attempts to Raise the Birth-Rate

A. M. CARR-SAUNDERS (1936)

In this article we shall be concerned with the efforts which have been made in certain countries to raise the birth-rate. We may begin with Italy and Germany because in those countries measures have been put into force with the direct object of increasing population; then we may pay attention to some legislation in certain other countries which was initiated primarily for reasons unconnected with the population problem, but which has been supported and expanded largely with the hope that it would also stimulate the birth-rate. These attempts to raise the birth-rate have recently been described and analysed in a most valuable book by Mr. Glass,[1] and in this article his work is closely followed.

Ever since the establishment of the Fascist régime in Italy the declining birth-rate has been a matter for comment and a subject for anxiety. Certain measures were taken in the early days of the régime; but it was not until 1927, after a speech by Mussolini on the 26th May of that year,[2] that legislative and administrative action was initiated on a large scale. Action has been both repressive, that is designed to discourage celibacy and childlessness, and positive, that is designed to favour large families. As examples of the former there are taxes on bachelors, first introduced in 1926 and doubled in 1928, and extra rates of income tax on bachelors and childless couples. But the burdens imposed are not heavy; the tax on bachelors aged 35 to 50 years is 100 lire a year, and this is said to be less than the cost of a dog licence. More important is the preference given to married candidates with children for posts in government service and for state sub-

1. D. V. Glass, *The Struggle for Population,* 1936.
[2. See p. 170. Ed.]

From A. M. Carr-Saunders, *World Population,* Oxford at the Clarendon Press, 1936. Reprinted by permission.

sidized houses and flats; men with families are also preferred in private industry. The most important positive measures have taken the form of reducing or abolishing taxes falling on 'large families'; thus the income tax is graduated so as to fall lightly on 'large families' which are also entirely exempted from taxes levied for education and from certain communal contributions. But a family must be really 'large' in order to qualify for favours; state employees must have seven children, and other employees must either have ten children, or have had twelve of whom six remain to be provided for. Mr. Glass calculated that about 15 per cent of the population of Italy benefits under the measures which were introduced in 1928.

In addition to these schemes, the sole object of which is to raise the birthrate, there are others which have this as one of their objects. Thus family allowances or cost of living bonuses in proportion to the number of children have been paid to state employees since 1929. In 1934 family allowances were extended to industrial workers; they are paid out of a fund to which both employers and employees contribute. The social services for mothers and children have been much expanded since 1925. Finally, an attempt has been made to counteract the tendency towards urbanization partly on account of the fact that the birth-rate is lower in the towns than in the country. It must also be remembered that, apart from material help for large families, every effort has been made to represent parents of large families as those most worthy of honour and esteem.

It is not easy to attempt to trace the influence of these measures owing to the lack of the necessary statistical data. Taking marriage first we notice a decline in the annual number of marriages from 1921 to 1928, a slight rise in 1929 and 1930, a fall to an unprecedentedly low level in 1931 and 1932 followed by a marked rise in 1933 and 1934. We may perhaps recognize the effects of penalizing bachelors in the events of 1929 and 1930. The subsequent events, a decrease of marriage in the early years of the depression and an increase in the last year or so, can be paralleled in countries, such as the United States, where there are no measures against bachelors in force. It is thus doubtful whether any noteworthy result has followed from the action which has been taken to encourage marriage. As to the birth-rate we find that it fell steadily to 1929, rose in 1930, and has fallen ever since.[2] The total number of live births, however, was larger in

[2. More recent statistics since this article was written show a continued downward trend. From 1935 to 1939 the birth rate per thousand in Italy averaged 23.2; in 1940–44 it averaged 20.7; in 1945–49 it rose slightly to 21.1; and in 1950–54 it dropped again to 18.3. Ed.]

1933 than in 1932, and larger in 1934 than in 1932, though not as large as in 1933. The increase over 1932 was small and, since the population was increasing, it was not enough to raise or even to maintain the birth-rate. It seems likely that this increase was due to the greater number of marriages, and that the latter was due to the contraction of marriages which were postponed at the onset of the depression. Figures prepared by Professor Mortara and quoted by Mr. Glass show that, when 1921–5 is compared

Table 1

Marriages and Births in Italy: 1921 to 1934

Year	No. of marriages	No. of marriages per 1,000 total population	No. of live births	No. of live births per 1,000 total population
1921	438,535	11.0	1,163,213	29.2
1922	365,460	9.6	1,175,872	30.8
1923	334,306	8.7	1,155,177	30.0
1924	306,830	7.9	1,124,470	29.0
1925	295,769	7.6	1,109,761	28.4
1926	295,566	7.5	1,094,589	27.7
1927	302,564	7.6	1,093,772	27.5
1928	285,248	7.1	1,072,316	26.7
1929	287,800	7.1	1,037,700	25.6
1930	303,214	7.4	1,092,678	26.7
1931	276,035	6.7	1,026,197	24.9
1932	267,771	6.4	990,995	23.8
1933	289,915	6.9	995,979	23.7
1934	312,662	7.4	992,975	23.4

with 1930, legitimate live births per 1,000 married women aged 15 to 45 have fallen for all Italy from 248 to 212, and also for every province with the doubtful exception of Sicily. It would therefore seem that the utmost which can be claimed for these measures is that, if they had not been taken, the Italian birth-rate would have fallen still more rapidly.

Measures to stimulate marriage and the birth-rate were not taken in Germany until after the National Socialist party had come into power. Since that time efforts have been made in many directions; of these one is important and the others much less so. To illustrate the latter, mention may be made of modifications in the law of inheritance in favour of large families, preference to heads of large families when men are selected for employment, a system of sponsoring third and subsequent children which has been adopted by several large towns, and minor matters such as privileges in railway trains for expectant mothers and mothers with young children. Attention, however, may be confined to the Act for the provision of marriage loans which came into force in August 1933. The aim of the Act is not only to encourage marriage, but also to withdraw women from the labour market. It is therefore laid down that the loans are payable only to couples where the woman concerned has been employed for at least nine months during the two preceding years. There is no income limit; but those who want loans must show that they could not otherwise afford to furnish a home. Loans may be of any amount up to 1,000 marks, and the average loan has been just over 600 marks. The loans take the form of the provision of coupons which may be exchanged for household goods. They bear no interest but are repayable at the rate of 1 per cent per month; a quarter of the original loan is remitted on the birth of each child. To finance the scheme a sum of 150 million marks is set aside each year.

The scheme has been put into force with vigour; in 1933 141,559 loans were granted and the percentage of couples receiving loans was 22.4, while in 1934 the corresponding figures were 224,619 and 30.7. What has been the effect? Let us examine the data given in Table 2. They show some dramatic changes; marriages have jumped up and so has the birth-rate. But care must be exercised before we conclude that these changes are wholly due to the system of loans, and that the figures support all that we may be inclined to infer at first sight. To begin with marriages, we notice that they increased substantially in the second quarter of 1933, that is before marriage loans became available. We know that in several other countries marriages, which were postponed at the onset of the depression, were contracted later, causing an increase in the number of marriages, and it is clear that the rise in the second quarter of 1933 came about in this way. It is further certain that a proportion of the increase in marriages during the remaining quarter of 1933 and during 1934 would have occurred in any case. Evidence in favour of this view is provided by some figures from Württemberg, quoted by Mr. Glass, which show that the rise in marriage was exhibited by members of all economic classes and not only by those which benefited from the loans; indeed, the rise was greater among those employed on their own account, and therefore not eligible for loans, than among wage earners. On the other hand, there is no reason to doubt that in the absence of loans the increase would not have been as great as it has been; the loans are substantial and provide precisely the help and stimulus which are needed. But we can make no kind of estimate of the number of marriages which have been made possible by them.

The object of the German scheme, however, is to stimulate births; if it raises marriages but not births, it will be a failure. When we turn to the

Table 2

Marriages and Births in Germany: 1932 to 1934

	No. of marriages	Marriage-rates per 1,000 total population	Index (same quarter of previous year = 100)	No. of live births	Live birth-rates per 1,000 total population	Index (same quarter of previous year = 100)
1933						
1st quarter	94,686	5.8	93.5	246,915	15.2	95
2nd "	157,906	9.7	116.9	243,425	14.9	97
3rd "	157,715	9.7	131.1	237,720	14.6	100
4th "	220,519	13.5	142.2	228,855	14.0	99.3
Average for year	630,826	9.7	122.8	956,915	14.7	97.3
1934						
1st quarter	138,438	8.5	146.6	281,024	17.2	113.3
2nd "	196,129	12.0	123.7	295,819	18.1	121.5
3rd "	178,638	10.9	112.4	299,667	18.3	125.4
4th "	213,223	13.3	98.5	304,669	18.6	132.8
Average for year	731,431	11.1	114.4	1,181,179	18.0	122.4
Year 1932	509,591	7.9	—	978,161	15.1	—

figures for births we find that they have risen immensely; there were 978,210 births in 1932, 956,915 in 1933, and 1,181,179 in 1934. The rise in births is reflected in the birth-rate which increased from 14.7 per 1,000 in 1933 to 18.0 in 1934. . . . It is noteworthy that the number of abortions has greatly decreased. . . . In Berlin in 1929 the proportion of abortions to live births was 103.4 to 100; in April 1935 it was 14.3 to 100. This gives an indication of what has apparently happened. There has been an increase in the number of recently married couples, and many of them, who under former conditions would have postponed the arrival of the first child, have not taken steps to do so. In other words, there has been an increase in the proportion of the recently married who have had a child within a year or so of marriage; that is to say, that the effect has not only been to stimulate marriage and with it what was formerly the normal proportion of first births per 100 marriages in a year, but also to raise the proportion of first births within a year or so of marriage.

It would not be reasonable to expect a greater result from the scheme in so short a time. But it is very necessary to understand that what has so far happened may not ultimately in the least affect the trend of population in Germany. For the trend of population depends upon fertility, and apparently all that has so far happened is that an unusually large number of first births has been crowded into a year. The question is whether the families now being founded will be larger than the families founded earlier. If they do not prove to be so, then the trend will remain as before.[3] . . .

We come next to a consideration of family allowance schemes and may take the position in France first, since it was there that they were originally put into force. Family allowances may be defined as payments in cash, apart from and in addition to wages, to employees in proportion to the number of their dependent children. They are advocated as a measure of social justice; the argument in their favour is that, since wages have no relation to family responsibilities, the man with dependent children is penalized; moreover it is not only the man who is penalized but also in many cases the children, since the family income, however judiciously spent, may not be sufficient to buy the requisite food and clothing. But, as we shall see, support for family allowances is now largely based upon the belief that they may tend to check the declining birth-rate.

Family allowances were introduced by an engineering firm at Grenoble during the War; they were soon extended to central and local government employees. Prices were rising, and employers, instead of, or in addition to, raising wages, began to pay allowances to men with dependent children. In France the allowances have always been paid in this way out of the employer's pocket without any contributions from the employees or the State; but since until recently the spread of the system has taken place while prices were rising, it is possible that no extra burden has been placed upon employers. The extension of the system was continuous; it was taken up by an increasing number of employers who were encouraged to fall into line

[3. In 1936 the birth rate per thousand in Germany was 18.8; in 1937 it was 19.7; and 14.8 in 1938. *World Almanac,* 1940. Ed.]

when, under the laws of 1922 and 1923, local authorities were empowered
to require that firms contracting with them should pay allowances. In order
that there might be no reason for discriminating against married men seeking employment, the employers set up equalization pools into which they
paid their contributions and out of which the allowances were allocated.
Since the contributions of an employer are in proportion to the number of
his employees and bear no relation to the number of dependents of these
employees, there is no incentive for him to engage childless workers.

The system grew until it covered a considerable proportion of all wage
earners in France. Then in 1932 a law was passed which made the payment of allowances compulsory to all employees, wage earning or salaried;
the provisions were to come into force by stages, and the first administrative order was promulgated in October 1933. But the system has not as
yet been applied to all industries; agriculture, though it will be brought
within its scope, at present remains outside. Under this law allowances are
payable to all children under the age of 14, and to those over 14 and under
16 who remain at school. The contributions of employers amount to about
2 per cent of the wages bill. There is a minimum allowance which must be
paid which varies in each Department. The allowances increase for the
later children in the family; thus the minimum in the department with the
lowest rates is 15 francs per month for one child, 30 francs for two children, 45 for three, 65 for four, and so on. If, after the payment of the minimum allowances, a surplus remains in the pool, it can be used either to
augment the cash allowances or to provide services in kind such as medical
attention. It is not easy to generalize concerning the extent to which the
allowances cover the cost of caring for children. But, according to the calculations made by Mr. Glass, it would seem that, even when the allowances
are highest, they do not cover more than fifty per cent of the cost of maintaining a child, and that on the average they do not amount to more than
25 per cent of the cost.

The reason originally advanced for initiating allowances was, as stated
above, that they helped to remove the injustice of the wage system which
took no account of family responsibilities. No doubt employers were also
induced to adopt them in the hope that they would reduce industrial fric-
tion. But long before the War the declining birth-rate was the subject of
public discussion and the cause of much anxiety in France; the Alliance
Nationale pour l'Accroisement de la Population, for instance, was founded
in 1896. When those who wanted something done in order to check the

fall, but had not been able to propose any remedy, became aware of the family allowance system, they soon saw that it might provide the mechanism which they sought. We find, in fact, that the population aspect of the allowance system was being discussed as early as 1919; and the powerful sentiment in favour of a higher birth-rate was soon enlisted in support of the extension of allowances. We can see the influence of the population motive in that characteristic of the system which has already been mentioned—namely that allowances become larger with successive children. Thus in the case mentioned, where 15 francs are payable for the first child, we saw that the rate rises to 20 francs for each child from the third onwards. In some schemes, in that prevailing in the Haut-Rhin department, for example, the grading is more marked; the allowances are 25 francs for the first child, 37.5 francs for the second, 50 francs for the third and fourth, 62.5 francs for the fifth, 75 francs for the sixth—a total of 300 francs per month for six children. If the object was merely to provide for the cost of maintaining a child, in part or in whole, there could be no sense in such a grading of allowances; evidently the intention is also to encourage large families. Indeed, large families are encouraged in France as in Italy by prizes, presentations, and acclamation in the press.

It is therefore appropriate to inquire whether it is possible to detect in French vital statistics any influence of the family allowance system. But, before we do so, some description may be given of the system as it has developed and now exists in Belgium; for an analysis can also be made of Belgian experience, and it is convenient to undertake the analysis of French and Belgian experiences at the same time. The family allowance system began later, but has developed more rapidly, in Belgium than in France. The first equalization fund was established at Verviers in 1921; as in France, prices were rising, and it seemed that the payment of allowances was preferable to a general rise in wages. An additional motive was provided by the fact that the payment of allowances in France was attracting Belgian workers across the frontier. The system spread rapidly; the central government and local authorities began to require that firms, with which they made contracts, should pay allowances. Proposals that the system should be made compulsory were advanced as early as 1924, and in 1930 an Act was passed which laid down that allowances were to be paid to all workers, whatever their income, in respect of dependent children. As in France allowances are graded and rise for later born children; thus the minimum scale is 9 francs per month for one child and 308 francs per month for six children. As regards details there are many differences between the Belgian and the French system. Under the former, employers pay a fixed contribution to the equalization fund for each employee, whereas under the latter the contribution is calculated as a percentage of the wage bill and adjusted from time to time so as to produce the amount required to enable the allowances to be paid. The rigidity of the Belgian system has caused some difficulties. Again, in Belgium there is a super-equalization fund. But in one important respect the two systems are alike; the allowances represent only a fraction of the cost of maintaining a dependent child. Indeed, in Belgium the allowances represent a smaller fraction of this cost than in France; this is partly due to the fact that it is permissible for the funds, after the minimum cash allowances have been paid, to distribute what remains in the form of social services.

In Belgium the falling birth-rate was not a cause for public anxiety until after the War. It then began to rouse discussion, and in 1920 the Ligue des Familles Nombreuses was formed which has now more than a million members. Those concerned with this problem soon saw that the family allowance system might be an instrument wherewith to fight the declining birth-rate and they enthusiastically supported proposals for its extension. In fact it would seem that the desire to raise the birth-rate has played a more prominent part in Belgium than in France in bringing into being a universal compulsory system. M. Heyman, the Belgian Minister of Labour, when introducing the Bill in 1929 which became law in 1930, said: "above all the bill aims at encouraging births and large families." It is also significant that under the Act of 1930 a Family Allowance Committee was set up which includes two representatives of the Ligue des Familles Nombreuses.

When we ask what effect these schemes have had, it is surprising, in view of the extent to which the desire to raise the birth-rate has been important in bringing about the extension and finally the compulsory generalization of the schemes, to discover how little the results have been analysed either in France or in Belgium. There are certain widely quoted figures, but an examination of these shows that they prove little or nothing. In the case of Belgium the inadequacy of official statistics is a serious impediment to any research into the matter, but in France, where official data are more adequate, little useful work has been done with them. Let us, however, briefly survey the situation.

We may begin by taking note of the course of the birth-rate since the War. No obvious influence of the allowance system can be detected; the rates trend downwards to the present day. But it must be remembered that the Acts generalizing the system over all workers are of very recent date, and that they have not even yet been put fully into operation; it would therefore be fair to object that, so far as the rate for the whole of each country is concerned, it is too early to judge, or at least too early to see more than part of what will be the ultimate effect.[4] Again, as we have often had occasion to observe, crude birth-rates may be misleading; we might hope to overcome this difficulty by the use of more refined data. In Belgium such data are not available, but for France we have official figures

Table 3
Birth-rates in Belgium and France: 1921 to 1931

| Year | Births per 1,000 total population | |
	Belgium	France
1921	21.8	20.7
1922	20.4	19.3
1923	20.4	19.1
1924	19.9	18.7
1925	19.8	19.0
1926	19.0	18.8
1927	18.3	18.2
1928	18.4	18.3
1929	18.1	17.7
1930	18.7	18.0
1931	18.2	17.5

for standardized fertility of women aged 15 to 49, figures, that is to say, in which changes due to altered age composition are eliminated. They are given in Table 4 up to 1931, the last year for which they are available. It will be seen that they show a check to the fall in fertility between 1929 and 1931; but since the number of births in France has fallen considerably since 1931, it may be taken as certain that the standardized fertility has not been stabilized at the level of 1931 but has fallen farther. . . .

The most that can be said about the results of the attempts to raise the birth-rate in France, Belgium, and Italy up to date is that the rate may have fallen less fast than it would otherwise have done. In Germany the rate has been raised, but it remains to be seen whether this has been achieved by

[4. In Belgium and France the minimum birth rates occurred in 1938. See *Determinants and Consequences of Population Trends,* United Nations, New York, 1953, p. 83. Ed.]

raising fertility or merely by stimulating the appearance of a large number
of first-born children in a short period of time.

One other feature of the campaigns to raise the birth-rate deserves attention. They have usually been accompanied by attempts to suppress birth-
control. In Germany alone, among the countries which we have discussed,

Table 4

Standardized Fertility Rates in France: 1926 to 1931

Year	Number of births per 1,000 females aged 15 to 49 years in a standard population
1926	735
1928	716
1929	678
1930	696
1931	679

is this not so; but it is understood that action is contemplated. Under a law
passed in Italy in 1926 propaganda in favour of birth-control is punishable by imprisonment for a year, while a woman may be imprisoned for
four years for abortion; in 1932 it was made illegal to stock or list contraceptive appliances. It is not clear how rigorously these laws are enforced.
In France under a law of 1920 abortion is punishable by imprisonment,
while action in favour of birth-control is subject to a similar penalty. But
the sale of contraceptive appliances is apparently not held to come under
the head of the latter, and so far as contraception is concerned the only
effect seems to have been to interfere with open propaganda. A Belgian law
of 1923 punishes birth-control propaganda, the sale of abortifacients, and
the exhibition of contraceptive appliances; but apparently the sale of the
latter is not forbidden.

Economic Incentives in Sweden

ROBERT C. COOK (1951)

During the 1920s and the 1930s several other European countries hatched
schemes designed to encourage—or force—a higher birth rate. These pro-

From Robert C. Cook, *Human Fertility: The Modern Dilemma*, William Sloane
Associates. Copyright © 1951 by Robert C. Cook. Reprinted by permission.

grams were not marked by much finesse or any great originality. Birth control was usually outlawed, and heavy penalties were prescribed for abortion. Baby bonuses and marriage loans—fractionally cancelled on the birth of children—were offered to encourage larger families.

Programs to increase birth rates which have their roots in withholding knowledge and offering trivial bribes are rarely very successful, but Hitler's baby-boosting campaign combining propaganda, marriage loans, and baby bonuses was—at least for a time—an exception; it actually raised the German birth rate in the mid-thirties.[1] Mussolini's experience, however, was more typical. Since Italy could not afford a decent level of living for its existing population, it is to the eternal credit of the Italian people that during all the years of Mussolini's frantic efforts to increase procreation, the birth rate slowly declined. Unfortunately the decline never was great enough to bring births into balance with deaths, so Italy remains one of the population danger points of the world.

Josef Stalin has followed the same pattern to keep the Soviet birth rate high. The liberalized birth-control and abortion laws of the early years of communism have been repealed. A sliding scale of baby bonuses is now in effect. Mothers of a dozen children are given an annual sum of five thousand roubles for five years, and are honored as "Heroes of the Soviet Union," with a personal greeting from Stalin himself.[2] How greatly these measures have affected the Russian birth rate is not known, but there is little doubt that during the 1940s the population of the Soviet Union increased very rapidly.

Sweden's population crisis arose because of a different set of circumstances. The Swedes had no imperialistic ambitions, so a growing population was not an issue. They had assumed that slowly declining birth and death rates would eventually achieve a balance. But in the early 1930s demographers sounded the alarm: A rapid decline in numbers was in prospect. Their small country had an unusually homogeneous population, and a high level of education. Few people were very rich, and few were very poor; in earlier times industry had been organized on a guild or family basis, and a majority of the population were farmers. Children were thus an economic asset to their parents at an early age.

1. Osborn gives the details of Hitler's program for increasing the population of Germany. Frederick Osborn, *Preface to Eugenics,* New York, Harper and Brothers, 1940.
2. Lorimer describes the Soviet plan for boosting births by cash plus accolades. Frank Lorimer, "The Population of the Soviet Union: History and Prospects." Geneva, League of Nations, 1946. (Publications, 1946, 2, A, 3.)

But under modern urban and industrial conditions, the bearing and rearing of children requires an increasing cash outlay—especially for housing, food, and medical care—over at least sixteen years; even longer when children go to college. In Sweden, as elsewhere, couples living in the middle-income bracket found the rearing of several children an almost unbearable economic burden and a serious threat to the family standard of living.

This increasingly heavy burden of rearing children had reached a critical point in Sweden by 1930. As in the United States, most couples with a sense of responsibility for the welfare of their children had sharply limited their families. But in Sweden the great mass of the people now began to follow this same pattern so enthusiastically that too few babies were being born to keep numbers in balance.[3]

In 1934, a brilliant book entitled *Kris i Befolkningsfrågan* (*Crisis in the Population Question*), by Alva and Gunnar Myrdal, analyzed the predicament. It was widely read and created a sensation. The following year the Swedish government appointed a Commission on Population, composed of leaders in the fields of economics, vital statistics, genetics, and medicine, and members of Parliament, to survey the population problem and to develop a program designed to bring the birth rate up to a point of balanced replacement. The Commission's broad and imaginative view of the problem is reflected in its series of voluminous reports. All these were widely read and discussed by the Swedish people.

Many of the Commission's recommendations were enacted into law in 1937 in a session that has since been called the "Mothers' and Children's Parliament." The program represented the boldest experiment in social invention ever undertaken by any government. Many people in America heard of it for the first time when they visited the Swedish Pavilion at the New York World Fair in 1939. That the war delayed the timetable for the implementation of the program in no way diminishes its social significance. In 1941 the actions taken four years earlier were reconsidered and important changes were made then; further changes were made in 1947 and 1948.[4]

The Parliament accepted the philosophy of the Population Commission

3. See Osborn, *op. cit.*, and Myrdal for a description of the Swedish population problem. Alva Myrdal, *Nation and Family; the Swedish Experiment in Democratic Family and Population Policy,* New York, Harper and Brothers, 1941.
4. For information about developments since 1940, I am indebted to Dr. Karen Kock, Director of the Swedish Statistical Institute, who made available advance proofs of the forthcoming book *Socialstyrilsen,* Swedish Statistical Institute, 1951.

that an appeal to ignorance and cupidity was not in the interest of the nation; that a healthy balance of births could be maintained in a spirit of affirmation rather than of compulsion or bribery; that people with a strong conviction that life in their country is good will want and have fine children to carry on after them.

Though faced with the crisis of a population decline, the Swedes did not let the emergency eclipse the question of quality. To place the responsibility of procreation increasingly on those citizens living in leached-out, depressed rural areas was neither socially nor biologically in the national interest. Out of this philosophy grew a program designed to encourage balanced reproduction throughout the population by easing the burden of parenthood for those couples who earnestly desired to have children.

As originally set up, the plan called for aid to parents in services and kind, rather than in the payment of direct cash subsidies. The initial plan proposed to make most of the benefits available to all citizens, without regard to financial status. Revisions of the original plan have modified both these policies. Legislation was enacted to eliminate, so far as was possible, involuntary parenthood by reason of ignorance or poverty. Existing laws limiting the dissemination of contraceptive information were repealed. Provision was made to establish clinics throughout the country where supplies and information were available to all.

Those who wanted children were assisted in sundry ways to bear and rear them. Since 1948, the Swedish government has paid an annual allowance of 260 kroner to all children under sixteen, regardless of the financial status of the parents. Parliament shifted to the national budget the entire cost of prenatal care, hospitalization, and delivery of all Swedish babies. Any Swedish woman, married or not, rich or poor, can have a baby with no other expenses than paying a kroner a day—about twenty-seven cents—for food while she is in the hospital. The government pays the rest.

After the baby comes into the world, the nation shares some of the cost of rearing it. Health centers for mothers and infants are being made available to all citizens, but these are free only for citizens who are unable to pay. Recreation facilities are provided so that mothers of small children can have enough time away from home to rest from the responsibilities of motherhood. Nurseries have been established to care for the children of mothers with jobs. "Social home helpers" stand ready to take over in the home in case of illness or emergency. This service is free to poor families, though a fee is charged those who can afford to pay.

The nutrition of the children is considered a major concern of the state. School textbooks are provided free to all children, just as in most areas of the United States, and on the same basis all children are furnished lunches at school. Essential food elements, like vitamins and trace-elements, are offered to low-income families. The ultimate plan envisions kindergartens for all pre-school children, and day nurseries for those not yet ready for kindergarten. . . .

The government recognized that one of the most serious checks on its program for a balanced reproduction pattern was housing; adequate housing for larger families was costly and scarce. To overcome this, a plan was devised to permit growing families to occupy larger houses at no additional cost. Low-income families are eligible for housing rebates amounting, for each child after the first, to 20 per cent of the annual capital charges on the property—but not over 175 kroner per child per year.

In spite of this help by the government, housing conditions are still very bad in Sweden. One recent visitor described the problem of housing in Sweden as one of "slums without a slum psychology." Of 227,000 rural communities or farm establishments listed, only 66,000 had water in the kitchen. In 1947, 30,000 substandard dwellings which should be condemned as health risks were listed. At least 200,000 town and city dwellings are rated by the Swedes as grossly inadequate. But by 1950 the collapse of the private housing industry during the war was being met by a comprehensive government housing program.

It is probable that the emergency which the Myrdal book anticipated in 1934 was a little exaggerated. The replacement index of the demographers means that if the ratio remains below 1000 for a generation at least, the population will *eventually* decline, and once such decline sets in, it can be quite rapid. Actually the Swedish population has recorded a net gain of births over deaths every year during the "critical" 1930s, even though the replacement index was down to 730 in 1935. It had risen to parity (1000) in 1942; in 1945 it was up to 1150, and the threatened disappearance of the Swedish nation was indefinitely delayed. That this has been done through an extension of liberty instead of by repression and compulsion vindicates the confidence which the government placed in the people.

Since the Swedish government embarked on a comprehensive population program in 1935 the original plan has been considerably changed. The emphasis on qualitative aspects has been somewhat modified. Some of the services offered to reduce the cost of rearing children are still extended to all citizens. The maternal, pregnancy, and childbirth cash benefits, the child allowances, and the school services are the most important of these. Other state services available without cost to low-income families must be paid for by citizens who are financially able. Balancing these mainly qualitative encouragements to reproduction is the unique state marriage loan program, where young couples "who show evidence of thrift" may set up housekeeping with the aid of a substantial loan. These loans are often applied for in order to legalize premarital relations resulting in pregnancy. But the practical-minded Swedes are not going to be forced into accepting all comers on this basis; ten Advisory Bureaus which are separately administered adjuncts of the maternal welfare services provide a means for making confidential arrangements for abortions deemed to be socially and economically desirable.

To allege that the Swedes have "solved" the problem of population in its qualitative and quantitative aspects would be an exaggeration. They have made a notable contribution by recognizing that the problem exists, and that it cannot be answered by hysteria or hush-hush. They have attempted to approach the subject at a practical level of social dynamics rather than in a cloud of abstractions and philosophical principles. In such an approach lies the hope of the future.

Population and Policy

Policies designed to increase or maintain fertility are flattering to the people who are urged to perpetuate themselves. But government policy which seeks the rapid reduction of fertility in the village populations is difficult both in adoption and implementation. . . . It is here that internal political forces become the greatest deterrent to population policy.

Frederick Osborn, "Population:
An International Dilemma"

Issues of Population Policy

FRANK LORIMER (1963)

Racial and Nationalistic Aspects of Population Policy

If this paper were being written a few years ago, it would be necessary to examine at some length the possible risks incurred in any expression of interest in the control of fertility elsewhere in the world by American or European officials, or even by private scholars or philanthropic organizations in Western countries. The question still requires some attention, but most of its dynamite has been detonated.

There was a considerable flurry of books and articles, a quarter-century

From Frederick Osborn, *On Population: Three Essays,* Princeton University Press, 1958. Copyright © 1958 by The Population Council. Reprinted by permission.

From Frank Lorimer, "Issues of Population Policy," *The Population Dilemma,* edited by Philip Hauser, Prentice-Hall, Englewood Cliffs, N.J. Copyright © 1963 by The American Assembly, Columbia University, New York. Reprinted by permission.

ago, about "The Rising Tide of Color," "Death of the White Peoples," "Passing of the Great Race" and so forth. The sentiments expressed in these writings were, of course, obnoxious to Asians and Africans. Presumably they have not been forgotten by some of their leaders. Moreover, this theme was played up in Communist polemics. "Neo-Malthusianism" was linked with "neo-colonialism" and "racial imperialism." It was possible to portray Western concern about the increase of population in Asia as snobbery, and to treat propaganda for its limitation as a plot to check the ascendancy of Asia and Africa in order to maintain white supremacy.

Today, one can hardly accuse Nehru of promoting birth control in India in order to support the British Raj. Nor can one plausibly argue that the Asian and African sponsors of the resolution recently passed by the Assembly of the United Nations were motivated by a desire to perpetuate white supremacy. Now the shoe is on the other foot. Asians and Africans want to act in this matter, but encounter resistance in doing so from some European governments because important elements in their population insist that the proposals advanced by these statesmen are immoral and will jeopardize the vitality and integrity of their nations.

Americans must continue to exercise restraint and to act circumspectly in dealing with this subject. Any attempt to coerce other governments as, for example, by making aid contingent on the adoption of a family limitation program (as has been rashly suggested by some enthusiasts), would obviously be resented. No responsible statesman endorses any such idea. The major question which our government now faces in this context is the extent to which it is willing to cooperate with other governments at their request in the development of projects and programs dealing with the problems of population.

The concern of some European nations about promoting their aggrandizement or security through pro-natalist policies is much less intense today than in the inter-war period, but has not entirely ceased. . . .

Communist Indifference

Again, this aspect of the questions under consideration appears in a quite different light today than it did a few years ago. This is now evident. So long as criticism of "neo-Malthusianism" served to inflame suspicion about the motives of "imperialist" and "neo-imperialist" statesmen in the minds of "oppressed" people, and to foster dissension in the non-Communist world, the Communist party played on this theme. Now that the indigenous leaders of non-European nations are engaging in programs to check mounting population growth, this theme has lost its punch and is being soft-pedalled. Moreover, in their more realistic approach to economic and social issues, the Communist governments in Eastern Europe have officially established abortion clinics and are freely promoting contraception.[1]

The action of the Communist Bloc in abstaining from the vote on the United Nations resolution concerning population problems is perfectly logical. Communists, as such, are necessarily indifferent to all attempts to improve social conditions gradually under "capitalist" auspices.

•   •   •

Obstacles to Objective Analysis

Much of the discussion on population questions is channeled through well-worn grooves to antagonistic positions. Each of the positions is characterized by over-simplification. The proponents of each position reinforce one another in their arguments and stimulate counter-attack by their opponents. This hampers objective analysis and a fresh approach to policy formation.

The confusion is, in part, a heritage of the century-and-a-half old Malthusian controversy. . . . [Malthus] did not comprehend the potentialities of science and technology, and his followers have persisted in minimizing their importance. They also minimize the importance of changes in social structure, culture and economic institutions. And, incidentally, they fix attention on absolute ratios of population to resources, as contrasted with the dynamic interrelation between demographic and economic changes, which may be more important over a considerable period than the absolute ratios.

Reactions to Malthusian dogma by proponents of changes in social institutions and by those concerned with the advancement of agriculture, the control of disease, etc., often lead them to an equally dogmatic denial of the economic and social effects of population trends.

A classic anti-Malthusian dogma was formulated by Karl Marx. The phenomenon described by Malthus as "over-population" is interpreted by Marxists as a "relative surplus" of labor. This is said to be an essential characteristic of capitalism, but non-existent in other types of society. The

[1. This policy was recently reversed in Romania, as noted on p. 142. Ed.]

relation is stated as follows by T. V. Ryabushkin in "Social Aspects of Population Structure and Movement," United Nations: *World Population Conference,* 1954 (Volume 5, meeting 28):

> Every social system has its own concrete laws of population. . . . In conditions of capitalistic mode of production a certain part of the population systematically becomes relatively superfluous. . . . In socialist society . . . the problem of excessive population no longer arises (pp. 1032–33). Thus the Malthusian theory is completely wrong and fruitless to explain historical facts. But maybe it has some sense for population policy in the future? Maybe it makes some sense to reduce rate of increase of population in any economically backward country in order to increase to some extent the level of well-being of population in the nearest future? To these questions we also give a sharp negative answer. *The Malthusian theory is harmful because it distracts attention from really scientific ways of increase of the working people's well-being.* (p. 1038, italics added.)

These dogmas present a false antithesis. They imply that the control of population and advances in economic productivity, health and education are *alternative* solutions to the problem of mass poverty. Most modern scientists, on the contrary, agree that they are essentially *complementary* and, in fact, mutually dependent.

There is considerable evidence that in the communist world anti-Malthusianism is more important as an ideological weapon than in actual conduct. Lenin, prior to the Russian revolution, had opposed the idea of a "birthstrike" against intolerable conditions of life in Germany as an expression of defeatism. However, he promoted contraception and abortion in the Soviet Union, allegedly on humanitarian grounds. This drastically reduced the economic burden of juvenile dependency in the early stages of socialist construction. (There were ten million fewer children in the USSR at the time of World War II than there would have been if fertility had remained at its early 1920 level.) It is unlikely that Lenin was completely indifferent to such effects. His program with respect to the control of births was reversed during the periods of forced collectivization and war when deaths exceeded births. It has subsequently been reestablished in the Soviet Union and in Eastern Europe. A similar ambivalence has been characteristic of Chinese policy in this field.

Opposition from other sources to concern about population trends often stems from a similar fear that attention to this topic may distract attention from other goals, such as the struggle against colonialism, the construction of giant industries, the improvement of a nation's health, reform of land tenure, or what not.

So the sterile controversy between Malthus and anti-Malthus goes on, fed and confused by extraneous issues. Liberals who demand freedom in personal affairs, social workers seeking to relieve the burdens of the poor, and isolationists who oppose American aid to impoverished nations all seek support from neo-Malthusian theory. Opponents of contraception on religious grounds, radical politicians with Marxist leanings, and conservative statesmen, especially in the Latin countries of Western Europe, who view increase of population as a contribution to national power and prestige, ridicule "Anglo-Saxon Malthusianism."

Progressive Production of a Relative Surplus-Population or Industrial Reserve Army

KARL MARX (1883)

. . . The labouring population therefore produces, along with the accumulation of capital produced by it, the means by which itself is made relatively superfluous, is turned into a relative surplus population; and it does this to an always increasing extent.[1] This is a law of population peculiar to

1. The law of the progressive decrease of the relative size of the variable capital, and of its effects on the condition of the wage-working class, has been more intuitively felt than actually comprehended by some excellent economists of the classic school. The greatest honor in this respect is due to John Barton, although he, like all the others, jumbles together the constant with the fixed capital and the circulating with the variable capital. He says: "The demand for labour depends on the increase of circulating, and not of fixed capital. Were it true that the proportion between these two sorts of capital is the same at all times, and in all circumstances, then, indeed, it follows that the number of labourers employed is in proportion to the wealth of the state. But such a proposition has not the semblance of probability. As arts are cultivated, and civilization is extended, fixed capital bears a larger and larger proportion to circulating capital. The amount of fixed capital employed in the production of a piece of British muslin is at least a hundred, probably a thousand times greater than that employed in a similar piece of Indian muslin. And the proportion of circulating capital is a hundred or thousand times less . . . the whole of the annual savings, added to the fixed capital, would have no effect in increasing the demand for labour." (John Barton. "Observations on the Circumstances which Influence the Condition of the Labouring Classes of Society." London, 1817, pp. 16, 17.) "The same cause which may increase the net revenue of the country may at the same time render the popula-

From Karl Marx, *Capital,* Charles H. Kerr & Company, Chicago, a critique of political economy, translated from the third German edition by Samuel Moore and Edward Aveling, and edited by Frederick Engels, 1906.

the capitalist mode of production; and in fact every special historic mode of production has its own special laws of population, historically valid within its limits alone. An abstract law of population exists for plants and animals only, and only in so far as man has not interfered with them.

But if a surplus labouring population is a necessary product of accumulation or of the development of wealth on a capitalist basis, this surplus population becomes, conversely, the lever of capitalistic accumulation, nay, a condition of existence of the capitalist mode of production. It forms a disposable industrial reserve army, that belongs to capital quite as absolutely as if the latter had bred it at its own cost. Independently of the limits of the actual increase of population, it creates, for the changing needs of the self-expansion of capital, a mass of human material always ready for exploitation. With accumulation, and the development of the productiveness of labour that accompanies it, the power of sudden expansion of capital grows also; it grows, not merely because the elasticity of the capital already functioning increases, not merely because the absolute wealth of society expands, of which capital only forms an elastic part, not merely because credit, under every special stimulus, at once places an unusual part of this wealth at the disposal of production in the form of additional capital; it grows, also, because the technical conditions of the process of production themselves—machinery, means of transport, &c.—now admit of the rapidest transformation of masses of surplus product into additional means of production. The mass of social wealth, overflowing with the advance of accumulation, and transformable into additional capital, thrusts itself frantically into old branches of production, whose market suddenly expands, or into newly formed branches, such as railways, &c., the need for which grows out of the development of the old ones. In all such cases, there must be the possibility of throwing great masses of men suddenly on the decisive points without injury to the scale of production in other spheres. Over-population supplies these masses. The course characteristic

tion redundant, and deterioriate the condition of the labourer." (Ricardo, l. c., p. 469.) With increase of capital, "the demand [for labour] will be in a diminishing ratio." (ibid. p. 480, Note.) "The amount of capital devoted to the maintenance of labour may vary, independently of any changes in the whole amount of capital. . . . Great fluctuations in the amount of employment, and great suffering may become more frequent as capital itself becomes more plentiful." (Richard Jones. "An Introductory Lecture on Pol. Econ., Lond. 1833," p. 13.) "Demand [for labour] will rise . . . not in proportion to the accumulation of the general capital. . . . Every augmentation, therefore, in the national stock destined for reproduction, comes, in the progress of society, to have less and less influence upon the condition of the labourer." (Ramsay, l. c., pp. 90, 91.)

of modern industry, viz., a decennial cycle (interrupted by smaller oscillations), of periods of average activity, production at high pressure, crisis
and stagnation, depends on the constant formation, the greater or less ab-
sorption, and the re-formation of the industrial reserve army of surplus
population. In their turn, the varying phases of the industrial cycle recruit
the surplus population, and become one of the most energetic agents of its
reproduction. This peculiar course of modern industry, which occurs in no
earlier period of human history, was also impossible in the childhood of
capitalist production. The composition of capital changed but very slowly.
With its accumulation, therefore, there kept pace, on the whole, a corresponding growth in the demand for labour. Slow as was the advance of accumulation compared with that of more modern times, it found a check in
the natural limits of the exploitable labouring population, limits which
could only be got rid of by forcible means . . . The expansion by fits and
starts of the scale of production is the preliminary to its equally sudden
contraction; the latter again evokes the former, but the former is impossible without disposable human material, without an increase in the number
of labourers independently of the absolute growth of the population. This
increase is effected by the simple process that constantly "sets free" a part
of the labourers; by methods which lessen the number of labourers employed in proportion to the increased production. The whole form of the
movement of modern industry depends, therefore, upon the constant transformation of a part of the labouring population into unemployed or half-
employed hands. The superficiality of Political Economy shows itself in the
fact that it looks upon the expansion and contraction of credit, which is a
mere symptom of the periodic changes of the industrial cycle, as their
cause. As the heavenly bodies, once thrown into a certain definite motion,
always repeat this, so is it with social production as soon as it is once
thrown into this movement of alternate expansion and contraction. Effects,
in their turn, become causes, and the varying accidents of the whole process, which always reproduces its own conditions, take on the form of
periodicity. When this periodicity is once consolidated, even Political
Economy then sees that the production of a relative surplus population—
i.e., surplus with regard to the average needs of the self-expansion of
capital—is a necessary condition of modern industry.

"Suppose," says H. Marivale, formerly Professor of Political Economy
at Oxford, subsequently employed in the English Colonial Office, "suppose
that, on the occasion of some of these crises, the nation were to rouse itself

to the effort of getting rid by emigration of some hundreds of thousands of superfluous arms, what would be the consequence? That, at the first returning demand for labour, there would be a deficiency. However rapid reproduction may be, it takes, at all events, the space of a generation to replace the loss of adult labour. Now, the profits of our manufacturers depend mainly on the power of making use of the prosperous moment when demand is brisk, and thus compensating themselves for the interval during which it is slack. This power is secured to them only by the command of machinery and of manual labour. They must have hands ready by them, they must be able to increase the activity of their operations when required, and to slacken it again, according to the state of the market, or they cannot possibly maintain the pre-eminence in the race of competition on which the wealth of the country is founded." [2] Even Malthus recognises over-population as a necessity of modern industry, though, after his narrow fashion, he explains it by the absolute over-growth of the labouring population, not by their becoming relatively supernumerary. He says: "Prudential habits with regard to marriage, carried to a considerable extent among the labouring class of a country mainly depending upon manufactures and commerce, might injure it. . . . From the nature of a population, an increase of labourers cannot be brought into market in consequence of a particular demand till after the lapse of 16 or 18 years, and the conversion of revenue into capital, by saving, may take place much more rapidly; a country is always liable to an increase in the quantity of the funds for the maintenance of labour faster than the increase of population." [3] After Political Economy has thus demonstrated the constant production of a relative surplus-population of labourers to be a necessity of capitalistic accumulation, she very aptly, in the guise of an old maid, puts in the mouth of her "beau ideal" of a capitalist the following words addressed to those supernumeraries thrown on the streets by their own creation of additional capital:—
"We manufacturers do what we can for you, whilst we are increasing that capital on which you must subsist, and you must do the rest by accommodating your numbers to the means of subsistence." [4]

Capitalist production can by no means content itself with the quantity of

2. H. Marivale: Lectures on Colonization and Colonies, 1841." Vol. I., p. 146.
3. Malthus. "Principles of Political Economy," pp. 254, 319, 320. In this work, Malthus finally discovers, with the help of Sismondi, the beautiful Trinity of capitalistic production: over-production, over-population, over-consumption—three very delicate monsters, indeed. Cf. F. Engels. "Umrisse zu einer Kritik der National-Oekonomie," 1. c., p. 107, et seq.
4. Harriet Martineau. "The Manchester Strike," 1842, p. 101.

disposable labour-power which the natural increase of population yields. It requires for its free play an industrial reserve army independent of these natural limits.

Up to this point it has been assumed that the increase or diminution of the variable capital corresponds rigidly with the increase or diminution of the number of labourers employed.

The number of labourers commanded by capital may remain the same, or even fall, while the variable capital increases. This is the case if the individual labourer yields more labour, and therefore his wages increase and this although the price of labour remains the same or even falls, only more slowly than the mass of labour rises. Increase of variable capital, in this case, becomes an index of more labour, but not of more labourers employed. It is the absolute interest of every capitalist to press a given quantity of labour out of a smaller, rather than a greater number of labourers, if the cost is about the same. In the latter case, the outlay of constant capital increases in proportion to the mass of labour set in action; in the former that increase is much smaller. The more extended the scale of production, the stronger this motive. Its force increases with the accumulation of capital.

We have seen that the development of the capitalist mode of production and of the productive power of labour—at once the cause and effect of accumulation—enables the capitalist, with the same outlay of variable capital, to set in action more labour by greater exploitation (extensive or intensive) of each individual labour-power. We have further seen that the capitalist buys with the same capital a greater mass of labour-power, as he progressively replaces skilled labourers by less skilled, mature labour-power by immature, male by female, that of adults by that of young persons or children.

On the one hand, therefore, with the progress of accumulation, a larger variable capital sets more labour in action without enlisting more labourers; on the other, a variable capital of the same magnitude sets in action more labour with the same mass of labour-power; and, finally, a greater number of inferior labour-power by displacement of higher.

The production of a relative surplus-population, or the setting free of labourers, goes on therefore yet more rapidly than the technical revolution of the process of production that accompanies, and is accelerated by, the advances of accumulation; and more rapidly than the corresponding diminution of the variable part of capital as compared with the constant. If

the means of production, as they increase in extent and effective power, become to a less extent means of employment of labourers, this state of
things is again modified by the fact that in proportion as the productiveness
of labour increases, capital increases its supply of labour more quickly than
its demand for labourers. The over-work of the employed part of the working class swells the ranks of the reserve, whilst conversely the greater pressure that the latter by its competiton exerts on the former, forces these to
submit to over-work and to subjugation under the dictates of capital. The
condemnation of one part of the working-class to enforced idleness by the
over-work of the other part, and the converse, becomes a means of enrich-
ing the individual capitalists,[5] and accelerates at the same time the production of the industrial reserve army on a scale corresponding with the
advance of social accumulation. How important is this element in the formation of the relative surplus-population, is shown by the example of England. Her technical means for saving labour are colossal. Nevertheless, if
tomorrow morning labour generally were reduced to a rational amount, and
porportioned to the different sections of the working-class according to age
and sex, the working population to hand would be absolutely insufficient
for the carrying on of national production on its present scale. The great
majority of the labourers now "unproductive" would have to be turned into
"productive" ones.

5. Even in the cotton famine of 1863 we find, in a pamphlet of the operative cotton-
spinners of Blackburn, fierce denunciations of overwork, which, in consequence of the
Factory Acts, of course only affected adult male labourers. "The adult operatives at
this mill have been asked to work from 12 to 13 hours per day, while there are hundreds who are compelled to be idle who would willingly work partial time, in order to
maintain their families and save their brethren from a premature grave through being
overworked . . . We," it goes on to say, "would ask if the practice of working overtime by a number of hands, is likely to create a good feeling between masters and
servants. Those who worked overtime feel the injustice equally with those who
are condemned to forced idleness. There is in the district almost sufficient work to
give to all partial employment if fairly distributed. We are only asking what is right
in requesting the masters generally to pursue a system of short hours, particularly until a better state of things begins to dawn upon us, rather than to work a portion of
the hands overtime, while others, for want of work, are compelled to exist upon charity." (Reports of Insp. of Fact., Oct. 31, 1863, p. 8.) The author of the "Essay on
Trade and Commerce" grasps the effect of a relative surplus-population on the employed labourers with his usual unerring bourgeois instinct. "Another cause of idleness
in this kingdom is the want of a sufficient number of labouring hands. . . . Whenever from an extraordinary demand for manufacturers, labour grows scarce, the labourers feel their own consequence, and will make their masters feel it likewise—it
is amazing; but so depraved are the dispositions of these people, that in such cases a
set of workmen have combined to distress the employer, by idling a whole day together." (Essay, &c., pp. 27, 28.) The fellows in fact were hankering after a rise in
wages.

Communist and Other Misconceptions
FREDERICK OSBORN (1958)

As late as 1954 "birth control" was anathema to Communist governments. But by 1955 and 1956 the leaders of Communist China found that their plans for industrialization and the increase of the food supply could not be successful unless a limit were put on the growth of population. An active campaign to reduce the number of births is now being carried on by the Chinese government. The conversion of the Communist leadership to the necessity of limiting family size came about through the process of deduction from planning for other things, but has been wisely publicized as a health and welfare measure. The Chinese government has thus placed itself on the side of those who seek to improve the quality of family life.

In addition to bringing the need of family limitation to leaders through such processes as we have indicated, it is desirable to correct a number of erroneous ideas which are very generally held. Many Europeans and a number of American leaders undoubtedly still believe that gross population is an index of national power, and this false idea is probably widely held in other countries. The idea is false because if population is out of balance with resources and productivity, the extra population can be a serious handicap. And in so far as population growth exceeds the growth of production, growth is an index of national weakness, not of power.

Nor is a high proportion of large families a sign of biological vigor, as so often asserted by Hitler and others. There is no evidence of differences in capacity to breed between different races of peoples. Differences in average size of family between large groups are determined by social and psychological influences. After mortality has been reduced, a high birth rate is too often the concomitant of ignorance and low levels of living, rather than a sign of vitality or progress.

From Frederick Osborn, "Population: An International Dilemma," *On Population: Three Essays,* Princeton University Press, 1958. Copyright © 1958 by The Population Council. Reprinted by   permission.

Population and Power

To count for something in the world, Italy must have a population of at least 60 millions when she reaches the threshold of the second half of this century. . . . It is a fact that the fate of nations is bound up with their demographic power. . . . Let us be frank with ourselves: what are 40 million Italians compared with 90 million Germans and 200 million Slavs?

Benito Mussolini
Speech, May 26, 1927

Population and World Politics
PHILIP HAUSER (1958)

. . . A pro-natalist policy designed to accelerate population growth, or social policies which have a pro-natalist effect intended or not, or, for that matter, even great reductions in the death rate—all these may affect the position of a nation in its foreign relations. Population changes are often barely perceptible by human conception of time; yet they may profoundly affect the course of events. Especially may this be the case when nations of about the same cultural and economic level undergo, over time, great relative changes in size.

In Europe in 1800, for example, France with a population of some twenty-seven million conducted her foreign relations vis-à-vis a less devel-

From Philip Hauser, *Population and World Politics,* Free Press of Glencoe, 1958. Copyright © 1958 by The Free Press, a Corporation. Reprinted by permission.

oped Russia of some thirty-seven million persons, a Germany of less than twenty-five millions, an Italy of eighteen millions, a United Kingdom of some sixteen millions. The United States at the time had little more than five million inhabitants. By 1910, however, a France of less than forty million faced a Germany of sixty-five million; Russia had a population of 140 million, the United Kindom forty-five million, Italy thirty-five million. The United States in 1910 had grown to ninety-two million. Were balance-of-power considerations and the international positions of these nations affected by the changes in their populations? The answer to this question points to a continuing way in which population is, in the long run, related to the course of world politics.

Nations and Numbers

A.F.K. AND KATHERINE ORGANSKI (1961)

Power has many sources, but a large and healthy population is surely one of them. It is no mere coincidence that every great power in the world today has a population of at least 45 million, while the two most powerful nations are both far larger.

Population is, indeed, a nation's greatest resource, though like other resources it may be squandered or misused. What greater asset can a nation have than a multitude of able-bodied citizens, ready to stoke its furnaces, work its mines, run its machinery, harvest its crops, build its cities, raise its children, produce its art, and provide the vast array of goods and services that make a nation prosperous and content? On the other hand, what greater liability can a nation have than a mass of surplus people, living in hunger and poverty, scratching at tiny plots of land whose produce will not feed them all, swarming into cities where there are no more jobs, living in huts or dying in the street, sitting in apathy or smouldering with discontent, and ever begetting more children to share their misery? The relationship between numbers and wealth and power is not simple, but surely it is significant. . . .

Military Manpower

That some connection exists between a nation's size and its power is obvious at a glance. No matter how efficient or how troublesome, no nation of small or even moderate size can push its way into the ranks of the great powers today. Admission to this ever shrinking circle requires a population of at least 45 million; tomorrow the minimum may well be 200 million, for size becomes more important as the years go by. To be a great power, a nation needs many millions of citizens to serve as cannon foddder, labor force, world market and—most important of all—as taxpayers. But let us begin with the obvious contribution of manpower to military strength.

Ever since citizen recruits displaced professional soldiers in major wars, it has been necessary to have a large population in order to have a large armed force, and armies are still a major source of strength. The nation possessed of mighty armies commands not only the power to attack and to defend, to threaten and to scoff at the threats of others, but also the power to lend its protection to others—a significant reward—or to withhold it— an effective punishment. America courts the favor of her former enemies in Western Germany not only because they are prosperous, industrious, and able, but because they make up the largest population on the European continent, and because they alone have the potential of a military force that might be capable of holding Western Europe against a communist assault. In Asia the United States has risked a great deal to force a military treaty on Japan because, outside of neutral India, Japan is the largest non-communist nation in the Far East. . . .

Push-Button Warfare

It is often argued that population size is no longer so important in the age of the bomb and the missile. It is contended that the rapidly changing technology of modern warfare is making the foot soldier obsolete, and the pilot, too, and that new weapons have made unnecessary the possession of vast armed forces.

Perhaps—but missiles require launching teams and tracking stations and communication networks even though they need no pilots. And defense against missiles requires widespread and elaborate installations manned around the clock. Hydrogen bombs require mighty industries to manufacture them and teams of scientists, technicians, and laborers to perfect the latest models in a constant race with obsolescence. The nature of military work is changing, as the nature of peaceful work has changed before it; but the need for manpower remains, in war as well as peace.

Perhaps the age of automation, on the edge of which we stand, will retire the combat soldier from attack, though many will find employment in making, transporting, and servicing the super-weapons that take his place; but who can replace him after the initial attack? Who will occupy the ruins, police the survivors? And who will fight the small wars that are typical of a century in which great nations hesitate to unloose total horror? We learned, or should have learned, in Korea and in Indochina that even peasant soldiers can put up a good fight against modern weapons. One cannot use a jet plane to stop a coolie carrying explosives on his back. One cannot use atomic bombs on every haystack that may hide a tank.

This is the second great military advantage of a large population: wars do not end with the winning of battles; the land must be held and the vanquished controlled. The twentieth century has taught us old methods of foiling new conquerors. The peasant guerrilla who takes to the mountains, the bomb-throwing terrorist who hides in the crowd, the army that melts in the daylight, all are a part of the total war that takes new forms. A large population can mock its conquerors, who may spread their thin net of control along the highways and across the major cities but sit like trapped birds in their own net while the country heaves beneath them. . . .

The argument that modern weapons will soon cancel the advantages of a large population is invalid for yet another reason. Atomic bombs require more than knowledge for their manufacture. America's war machine is manufactured by a long list of her greatest industries. Only a great and populous nation has the kind of industrial installations required to turn out modern weapons of mass destruction. Their cost is staggering: one intercontinental ballistics missile alone costs 35 million dollars; an atomic submarine costs from 50 million to 150 million dollars. No private source can possibly afford the capital investment required to make such weapons; furthermore, once made, they are almost immediately out of date. Only a national government can afford such outlays, and only a national government with millions of taxpayers and billions of dollars at its disposal. Even Britain has given up her missile program as too expensive and has decided to rely on American missiles to protect her.

The simple fact is that, far from reducing the power of large nations with great armies, modern weapons have increased the power of large nations with large military budgets. The advancing technology of warfare has already become so frighteningly expensive that *only* giant nations can afford it. Few shifts are more striking than the concentration of power in the hands of a few giant nations that has marked the first half of the twentieth century. The second half will see this concentration continue. . . .

Confidence and Fear

A population of great size inspires confidence at home and fear and respect abroad; this in itself may be a source of power, for power in part becomes what people think it is. There are self-fulfilling and self-defeating prophecies: the nation sure of its future power works with a will to bring that power to pass; the nation that foresees a hopeless struggle gives up at the start, thus guaranteeing defeat. There is strength in numbers, satisfaction in the knowledge that one's small effort is multiplied by millions, consolation for private frustration in identification with a mighty nation. A nation the size of China feels certain it can work miracles.

> Rip holes in the sky—we'll patch them!
> Crack the earth's crust—we'll mend it!
> For we can tame oceans,
> We can move mountains.

So goes a Chinese marching song, and 700 million strong, the Chinese think they can.

The possession of a vast population does not in itself confer power to conquer or to buy, but all the world knows that it is one of the prerequisites of power and treats with respect the nation so blessed. Poor, battered China—laid low by Japan, racked with dissension, shot through with corruption, so weak that the state fell apart within four years—was nevertheless formally accorded the status of one of the Big Five when the United Nations was created, for the great powers saw her potential. India today has little power in military or economic terms, but her voice is heeded throughout Asia and throughout the world because her great size betokens great power tomorrow. It is with an eye to the future that East and West contend for the friendship of India today, but their very contention increases India's present ability to influence the actions of other nations. Size confers power not only by its material consequences but also through its effect upon the minds of men.

The Determinants of Power

That population is not the only determinant of power we may be certain. A handful of Englishmen ruled the subcontinent of India with all its millions, as tiny Belgium ruled the Congo. There are three major determinants of national power: the size of a nation's population, the level of its economic development, and the skill and efficiency of its government.[1] High standing in one respect may compensate to some degree for lack in another, but no nation can attain first rank without all three. Canada possesses a modern economy and an efficient government and has in addition rich resources, extensive territory, and high morale; but her population of less than 20 million relegates her forever to second rank. India has a giant population and a government of considerable efficiency; but until she succeeds in modernizing her economy she will have trouble even in defending her own frontiers.

To assess with accuracy the relative power of nations, one ought to have some way of taking into account the state of these three determinants. Kingsley Davis [2] suggested an index of national power based upon two of these qualities and reflecting the third to at least a limited extent. He would use national income, properly speaking a better measure of a nation's wealth than of its power. National income, however, is a product both of the size of the work force and of the level of economic efficiency. It also reflects, less clearly, the ability of the government to organize its resources effectively. Thus in a rough way a nation's income may be used as an indication of its power, for even though the two are not the same, the size of both is determined by so many of the same factors that one may be used to indicate the other.

The index is deficient in several respects. First of all, the size of the national income gives only a very indirect suggestion of the efficiency of political organization. It is true that a high degree of economic development assumes that political modernization cannot be far behind, but national income does not reflect at all the increase in power that comes when a backward nation reforms its political structure before it modernizes its economy. The power of Communist China, for example, increased immensely

1. See Organski: *World Politics,* Chs. vi, vii, and viii.
2. Kingsley Davis: "The Demographic Foundations of National Power," in M. Berger, T. Abel, and C. H. Page (eds.): *Freedom and Control in Modern Society* (New York: Van Nostrand; 1954), pp. 206–43.

between 1949 and 1952, as the Korean War clearly indicated, primarily because the communists built a political organization that reached down to the villages and welded the mass of Chinese into a unit, mobilizing them into the service of the state; and yet the national income of China would not have registered this change.

The problem is serious, for China is not alone in modernizing her government in advance of industrialization. Unlike the nations of Europe that industrialized for the most part within the framework of older political forms and modernized their governments last of all, the new nations of Asia and Africa are overhauling their governments first. This will have the effect of speeding their economic development and increasing their power considerably more rapidly than national income figures alone would indicate.

Other drawbacks in the use of national income are that it underestimates the power of nonindustrial nations, where much of the wealth is never translated into money but is consumed directly by those who make it; and that it tends to inflate the image of power of nations industrially mature, where nearly all that is produced and exchanged has monetary value and finds its way into the national income even though some of it may not add

Table 1

Ten Most Powerful Nations by National Income, 1952–54 [a]

	National Income (millions of U.S. dollars)
United States	298,530
Soviet Union [b]	110,000
United Kingdom	39,480
France	31,720
West Germany	24,990
China [c]	————
India	22,320
Canada	19,360
Japan	16,470
Italy	14,740

[a] United Nations, Statistical Office; *Per Capita National Product of Fifty-five Countries: 1952–1954* (New York: United Nations; 1957), pp. 8–9. The Statistical Office defined net national product as identical to national income.
[b] 1954 only. Figures on the Soviet Union are not included in the United Nations study but have been estimated independently.
[c] No data for 1952–4. Rank estimated on the basis of 1949 rank.

to the nation's power in proportion to its price. Changes in national income provide a superb indication of the dramatic increase in power that accompanies the early industrialization of a nation, the increase that comes with the initial shift from a peasant economy to a modern industrial system. Later additions of wealth, however, do not add as much to the power of a nation.

With full admission of all these shortcomings, we still insist that national income is the best general index of national power currently known. The alternative is to count weapons and bases, and to fall back on general impressions which may be highly accurate with the benefit of hindsight, but which have led serious scholars and statesmen badly astray in their past looks into what was then the future.

The United Nations has unfortunately ceased its publication of comparative national income figures, but its latest list, for 1952–54 is recent enough to give some indication of the comparative standing of nations. The top ten at that date are shown in Table 1.

Listed by national income today, the ten top nations would probably remain the same, though the order might well have shifted and the gap between the United States and Russia would probably have narrowed. Our guess at the order of nations today in national income, and in power, is:

> United States
> Soviet Union
> United Kingdom
> China
> West Germany
> France
> India
> Japan
> Canada
> Italy

Future years will see further changes in the list.

Population and Shifts in Power

Population size will play an important part in determining future shifts in power, usurping to large extent the crucial role now played by the level of economic advance. . . . Once the entire world is industrialized, it will have entered a new age, quite different from the peasant past when no nation was industrial, and quite different from the present era in which industrialization has bestowed its favors so unevenly. Shifts in the relative power of nations in the near future will be greatly influenced by rates of economic advance; but once the whole world has achieved industrial status and shares the same technology, population size will become the major determinant of power.

There are three nations with populations larger than that of the United States. Each has the potential to surpass America in power, if only it can equal her economic advancement. Each has the potential to dominate the world.

The first of these giant rivals to industrialize has been the Soviet Union, whose rapid economic development, still incomplete, has shaken the Western World. Russian power—military, economic, and ideological—continues to grow. In the last twenty years the Soviet Union has passed Japan, Germany, France, and England to attain second place behind the United States. Russian leaders boast almost daily that they have no intention of remaining in second place. Indeed, if modern Russia has a single goal, it is to surpass the United States in economic production, in living standards, and in power.

Theoretically, Russia has the potential to do this. She has the people, the land, the resources, the organization, the technology, and the will. The United States, on the other hand, has a commanding head start, many allies, and the heritage of Western power. This heritage unites with America even those nations that complain bitterly of how the West has treated them in the past. Russia and the United States do not start together from scratch, competing for the favor of a neutral world. Much of the world today is dependent upon America militarily and economically and tied to her ideologically. Russia can win world domination only if she breaks such ties and takes the world away from the United States. Alone, Russia might succeed in equalling American power but would have difficulty surpassing it, for the world is stacked against her. But Russia is not alone.

Communist China, a nation of some 700 million people, has started to industrialize. With a degree of effort and humorless dedication rarely equalled in human history, China, long a great power by courtesy, has set out to become a great power in fact. By taking the communnist road to industrialization, China has placed herself on the path that led the Soviet

Union to its present position of strength. China's power potential is enormous—far greater than Russia's, greater even than that of the United States. Her population is almost four times as large as America's. In economic terms this giant population contains the world's largest labor force—producing today at a very low per capita level, it is true, but even minimum modernization has increased Chinese productivity greatly. With only one quarter of America's efficiency China could equal total American production; with full modernization she could outproduce the United States dramatically.

In military terms China can field an armed force of staggering size. She has a military manpower pool of more than 100 million men, and under the new communal system virtually all of China's peasant population, male and female, will receive some military training. At present a backward economy limits China's ability to equip a large force with modern weapons, but the Korean War showed that even with borrowed and inadequate equipment peasant soldiers are an effective enemy. China today is the greatest military power in Asia, and she has only scratched the surface of her military potential.

Communist China also has great assets in any ideological battle with the West. There is scarcely an underdeveloped area on earth that does not seek rapid economic development. Impatient and deeply ashamed of their backwardness, such nations dream of leaping into the modern world in a span of years far shorter than the West believes possible. If China succeeds in making such a leap, her example will far outweigh the Western admonition that the price of such progress is slavery.

The threat posed by Soviet Russia to the Western World and its way of life is so real, so pressing, so unremitting that Americans are understandably reluctant to face up to other dangers. Cassandras warning of doom from other quarters are likely to be sternly hushed or wearily ignored (thus faring no better than the original Cassandra, who was, we so often forget, correct). In its preoccupation with Russian rivalry, America dares not overlook Red China, potentially the greatest threat of all.

India, too, is potentially a nation of greater power than either the United States or Russia. When she finally solves her population problem and gathers enough momentum to change her economic life to accord with the brave hopes and promises of her leaders, the second place in world power should be hers. If India completes her modernization within a Western-oriented, democratic framework, she should eventually become the leading noncommunist nation on earth; but if, as seems more likely, the competition of her giant neighbor to the north forces her to jettison her democracy and turn to communism to speed the pace of industrialization, the loss to the West will be incalculable.

• • •

Political Consequences

It is fortunate for the West that the demographic transition has not run its course. Were the Western peoples declining as the new industrial communist nations expand, the shift in power from West to East would be proceeding even more rapidly than it is.

The West owes its position of world leadership to the fact that industrialization came early to the West. Once the secrets of industry are known to all—and, indeed, they are no longer secrets—industrial status alone will no longer guarantee superior power. Population size will then assume more importance as a determinant of national power. Tiny industrial England ruled a quarter of the world, including some 300 million unindustrialized Indians. Japan subdued and terrorized the bulk of preindustrial China. The United States dominates her neighbors to the south despite the fact that they outnumber her. But once the whole world is industrialized, population size will matter more. The West can be glad that its population is growing. Its slender chances of maintaining world leadership are thereby improved.

Demographic Factors in National Efficiency
KINGSLEY DAVIS (1954)

Although the case for population as a factor in power has been put strongly, the truth still remains that it is not the only factor. After all, despite the influence of the United States and Russia, the four most populous nations in the world are not the four most powerful. In fact, the two with the most people, China and India, can be regarded as weaker than Britain

From Kingsley Davis, "The Demographic Foundations of National Power," *Freedom and Control in Modern Society,* edited by M. Berger, T. Abel, and C. H. Page, Van Nostrand Company, New York. Copyright 1954 by M. Berger, T. Abel, and C. H. Page. Reprinted by permission.

at the moment, and in a few years they may once again be weaker than Japan and Germany. Nor can it be said that all the less populous countries are powerless. Australia, with only eight million inhabitants (far below the mean for independent countries and barely above the median) is the most conspicuous example of the powerful but demographically small country. Other examples are Canada, Argentina, the Netherlands, and the Scandinavian countries. Clearly there must be other determinants of national power in addition to total population.

Mention has already been made of the fact that per capita productivity or income is a rough index of the other factors. Although it is obtained by dividing the national income by the population, this is a purely formal relationship. Per capita income varies independently of total population. A country with a big population may have a high per capita income (for example, the United States) or a low one (India); and the same is true of a country with a small population. What per capita income really measures is (a) the adequacy of the resources and (b) the efficiency with which these resources are combined with technology, economic organization, social structure, and population. Two countries with the same efficiency may have a differing real income per head because of different resources; or two countries with the same resources may differ in real income per person because of differences in such things as their technical efficiency, their economic organization, or their population balance. For our purposes the main point to bear in mind is that demographic factors are involved in efficiency (which is partly measured by per capita income), and that this is a channel of influence on a nation's power different from that of sheer total population. The latter measures the sheer strength of the human material that a country has at its command—the raw manpower, so to speak— whereas the demographic factors in efficiency concern the ways in which this human material is produced, trained, and utilized in relation to resources and the social order. . . .

Not only does national income cease at some theoretical point to grow in proportion to the rise in population, but the ways in which the income is produced and distributed are altered—and they are altered in such a way as to weaken the nation. That a population must have subsistence is axiomatic. The arts of war, propaganda, and diplomatic negotiation, however, require something beyond subsistence. Insofar as a national economic system, because of the density and rapid increase of numbers, must devote most of its economic effort to gaining mere subsistence for its people, it is in no condition to enjoy a high degree of industrial production for purposes of foreign trade, military might, and assistance to allies. It has the manpower but cannot put it to effective use. As war has grown more dependent upon intricate weapons produced by advanced industry, the capitalization of each soldier has increased tremendously. A country bogged down by excessive manpower in relation to both its natural resources and its existing technology cannot secure the necessary capitalization. Nor can it afford the nonmilitary avenues to foreign influence; propaganda by short-wave radio in foreign languages is expensive, as is the dissemination of literature overseas or the maintenance of economic and military missions on foreign soil. A country with a huge population, or even a large national income, may therefore be forced by its overpopulation into a defensive position in international affairs. It may tend to become the object of propaganda rather than the disseminator of it; it may focus its military force on defense rather than offense; it may receive rather than give aid. It may thus be forced into a secondary role which, with a more appropriate population, it could eschew.

An excessive population in relation to productive factors has other disadvantages. One is that an equitable distribution of the national product, if it should occur, would mean virtually no opportunity for capital development. Funds would be invested in immediate necessities rather than productive enterprise. By a sort of functional adaptation, therefore, most of the societies with excess numbers have evolved a rigid social stratification whereby a small but wealthy elite runs the government and the economy, the bulk of the population being in great poverty. The elite has surplus funds to invest; it does the investing and the managing, the rest of the population doing the hard physical work. While such an arrangement worked well enough in the antique world, it has a hard time surviving now. The state is today faced with the necessity of instituting basic reforms (thereby offending the rich and the powerful) or of doing nothing (thereby risking the pent-up and explosive resentment of the gradually awakening masses). Few states in heavily overpopulated agrarian countries have shown themselves capable of steering smoothly and firmly past the two horns of this dilemma. The usual history has been one of vacillation in the face of mounting domestic problems, which has of course weakened the nation in international affairs.

There are other disadvantages accruing from a redundant population. . . . The main point to be stressed for the moment is that a country with a large population in relation to its resources is worse off, from an international point of view, than one with the same resources but with fewer people. It does not follow, then, that the bigger the population, the more powerful the nation. Whether or not a nation has too many people is independent of the absolute size of its total population, but depends rather on the relationship of population to resources and existing economic efficiency. Some small countries are overpopulated, some big ones are not. Our view is that India would have a much better chance to be one of the great powers if it had 100 million fewer citizens than it has. Egypt, Japan, Italy, China, Pakistan, Mexico, Haiti, Ceylon, and Israel would also be more powerful with fewer people.

. . . there is a widespread belief that an ever greater pool of manpower is a military and economic asset to a nation. It therefore comes as a shock to many people to hear it maintained that one of the demographic factors weakening a nation's power is a high birth rate. No one can maintain that a pre-industrial birth rate is always and in every way disadvantageous. In certain instances it may be an asset. But an analysis of the effect of birth rates on a nation's efficiency will show that in most cases today the advantage lies with a low rather than a high rate. . . .

In sum, a birth rate of 30 or more per 1000 inhabitants is a drag on any nation. It is certainly a drag from a short-run military point of view, because it loads the age structure with children who increase nonmilitary costs; it withdraws women from the industrial labor force; it increases ill-health and mortality; and it places a great burden on educational and other facilities which must be either expanded or allowed to deteriorate. Accordingly, both Hitler and Mussolini were mistaken in their policy of trying to increase the birth rate. Both of them knew that they would shortly be at war. They should have known that the main task of a nation at war is to win the war. Had their population policies succeeded as they hoped, the flood of births would have made their chances of winning even less than they were. As it turned out, Mussolini did not succeed in raising the birth rate at all in Italy, and Hitler succeeded only in getting a normal post-depression rise earlier than usual. Eventually other countries, which had no pro-natalist policy at all, such as the United States, had a greater rise in the birth rate than did the Third Reich. As it turned out, therefore, the pro-natalist policies of the Fascist nations did not interfere with their war effort because they did not succeed. The kind of birth rate that really impedes a war effort is the kind that an urban-industrial nation has never succeeded in inducing by any policy yet developed. It is the kind of birth rate which Russia had during all her wars and which was one of the factors making her a weaker nation than her total population and her resources would have otherwise made her. It is the kind of birth rate that peasant-agricultural nations always have.

The Widening Gap
HARRISON BROWN (1967)

The United States Government has now been in the business of providing technical and economic assistance to a number of the poorer nations of the world for about twenty years. It seems likely that had we not become involved with assistance programs, certain countries would be worse off economically than they actually are. And the Agency for International Development points with pride to Taiwan as an example of a country in which our efforts have been so successful that it is no longer necessary for us to continue them. Yet when we look at the plight of the poorer countries today we find that from certain points of view they are worse off today than they were twenty years ago. In particular during the last ten years the situation has been deteriorating at an alarming rate.

Although the economies of both the richer and poorer countries have grown at about the same rate during the past decade—about 4 per cent per year, the economic well-being of the average individual in the poorer countries has not improved very much. The reason for this is the relative rates of population growth. Although rates of population growth in the richer countries have dropped to an average of about 1.1 per cent per year, those in the poorer countries have risen to an average of about 2.5 per cent per year and are still growing. Indeed, in some regions rates of population growth are approaching 4 per cent annually. Thus, while on the average the economic well-being of persons in the richer countries is improving at the rate of nearly 3 per cent per year, that of persons in the poorer countries improves at a rate of but 1.5 per cent per year—a rate too small to raise the hope of the individual. The ratio of annual per capita incomes in the richer countries to those in the poorer ones, which stands at about 15 to 1

From Harrison Brown, "The Combustibility of Humans," *Saturday Review,* June 24, 1967. Reprinted by permission.

today, is increasing at the rate of about 1.5 per cent annually, giving rise to what Patrick Blackett, the president of the Royal Society, calls "the ever-widening gap." . . .

Unfortunately, our knowledge of how to develop a poor country into a less-poor one is not very good. We can learn some basic lessons by examining the economic, social, and political histories of countries which have recently made the transition, such as the United States, the U.S.S.R., and Japan. We can learn more by examining success and failures in countries which are now attempting to transform themselves. From these experiences we know that large quantities of capital are required. There must be a resource base which can be utilized. There must be a transfer of technology enabling effective utilization of the resource base. There must be education, the development of technical and administrative skills, the evolution of technical, economic, and social "problem-solving capacities" (i.e., local research and development capabilities). And ever-present is the question of social organizations—old ones must be changed and new ones must be created.

No one today knows enough about the development process to say just what the most effective "mix" of these ingredients should be for a given country. But certain conclusions can be drawn.

First, a great deal of time is required for the transition. Thus far, at least, there is no such thing as "instant development." We must think in terms of many decades rather than of years.

Second, most of the poorer countries appear to have reached the point where they simply cannot, without help, extricate themselvs from the vicious circle in which they now find themselves. Population growth rates have grown too high, per-capita food production has fallen too low, and the crushing problems of urbanization and industrialization have become too great. Certainly few, if any, of the poorer countries are in a position to develop by themselves at rates which are sufficiently rapid so that the economic and social well-being of the average individual improves visibly during his lifetime.

It seems clear that in the absence of truly substantial help from the outside, the poorer nations are headed squarely toward famine, pestilence, revolution, and bloodshed on a massive scale—with consequences for the rest of the world which are difficult to foresee. But in addition to being substantial the help must be sustained. And if it is to be effective it must be balanced. Thus far, development efforts in the world have not been large enough, nor have they been sustained, nor have they been adequately balanced.

The White Man's Dilemma
JOHN BOYD ORR AND DAVID LUBBOCK (1953)

There is a reason, though it is largely subconscious, for the reluctance of those in power to co-operate in abolishing hunger and poverty. The power of money depends not so much on the absolute amount a man has, as on the relative amount to other men. If all men were wealthy, a wealthy man would have no more power than anybody else. If, however, a few men are wealthy, and the rest are so poor that they are dependent on the wealthy for getting work to earn the price of food, then the wealthy can obtain both service and, at least, the outward show of submission. So soon as the poor are assured of food and the other physical essentials of life, they have taken the first and by far the most important step to liberty. The power of money over their lives is broken. They no longer need to cringe to live. As an American writer put it, "when you clean up the slums the servant problem gets tough." The same problem has arisen in the "welfare state" of the United Kingdom. This does not mean that people are no longer willing to work. Everyone wants more than merely the physical necessities of life. It is the people above the poverty level who work hardest. But if assured of the necessities of life they can work with the "glorious feeling of being independent" of another human being for the right to live.

This applies to the two-thirds of the population of the world who lack food and other physical necessities of life. A world development authority which would provide sufficient food for everybody would inevitably eliminate preventable disease, improve housing, and spread education. The natives of Asia, Africa, and Latin America, whose average expectation of life at birth is only thirty to forty years, would then enjoy the environmental conditions which the common people of Western Europe have won since the early part of the nineteenth century, when their average length of life was also only about forty years, but who now attain an average of sixty-five

From John Boyd Orr and David Lubbock, *The White Man's Dilemma*, George Allen & Unwin Ltd., London, and Barnes and Noble, New York, 1953. Reprinted by permission.

to seventy years. Under these favourable conditions the Asians, the Africans, and the Latin Americans would have gained the "right to life, liberty, and the pursuit of happiness." The American fathers were wise to put life first, because the man who suffers premature death for lack of the necessities of life has little interest in political liberty and little chance of catching happiness, however hard he pursues it. Economic freedom is the first freedom for poverty-stricken people.

But if all the people in the world had environmental conditions which would enable them to attain their full inherited capacity for physical and mental ability there would be little, if any, difference between the ability of men of different races. The natives of Asia, Africa, and Latin America would become the equals of the white man, and as these continents became industrialized the Europeans and their descendants, the Americans, would lose the control of the world they gained in their 300 years of conquest from the seventeenth to the nineteenth centuries. This, then, is the white man's dilemma. He can attempt by force to maintain military and economic supremacy, in which case he will be involved in an almost world-wide disastrous war, worse than Korea, the final outcome of which will be the downfall of Western civilization. On the other hand, he can, as Stringfellow Barr puts it, join the human family and use his present industrial supremacy to develop the resources of the earth to put an end to hunger and poverty, with resulting world-wide economic prosperity—in which case he would lose his superior power. This is a hard decision to make. To give up power goes against the grain, and all the patriotism and pride of race which has been dinned into him revolt at the suggestion of the equality of races.

The sacrifice of the power of individuals in the white races, however, is not so great as would appear. Equality would not be reached until long after those who now hold power are dead and when equality, with equal opportunity for all, were attained, the men of outstanding ability would secure leadership. Whatever the form of world society, there must be leaders who are given power and authority. In a democratic society that kind of power which is combined with real respect is for mature minds more satisfying and more dignified than power over the lives of men secured by military force or money.

Some will be impatient with the idea of applying modern science to develop the vast potential resources of the earth because they think the first task is to destroy Communism (or from the other point of view to destroy Capitalism) and in the meantime science should be applied to building up more powerful weapons of war. Those who believe that their side in the present conflict is so right and so good and the other side so wrong and so evil that they are prepared to go to war to destroy the opposing side might well ponder the Biblical injunction, "Be not overwise and be not overrighteous: why shouldst thou destroy thyself?" Others might say we should be prepared to help fulfil the promise of the Atlantic Charter—freedom from want for all men in all lands—but that the other side will not co-operate. A firm offer has never been made. If either the USA or the USSR, with their satellites or allies according to the point of view, made a definite offer to co-operate through an international authority representing the interests of all nations and to give it 10 or even 5% of the money being spent on armaments, provided all others willing to join would make the same percentage contribution, that country would convince the world that it was sincere in its declared objective of promoting human welfare and not acting from purely selfish motives. Any power which refused to join could then rightly be labelled as a warmonger and an aggressor against human society. If none of the Great Powers is willing to make such an offer, then there is some reason to believe that the ideological conflict is merely a smokescreen for the old game of power politics, in which the common people of different countries—who have no quarrel with each other—are sacrificed to the lust for power of those who control their destiny.

The United States and the United Kingdom might argue that by giving technical assistance through the Colombo Plan and President Truman's Point 4 they are making their contribution to the abolition of poverty in the underdeveloped countries. The technical assistance, though helpful, is hopelessly inadequate. Further, it is given not in the interests of the people, but to stop the spread of Communism in the interests of the Western powers. An American has said that 600 million dollars could save India from going Communist. To bring India within the sphere of influence of the United States at a cost of a dollar and a half per head of its population would be a good bargain if it could be carried through. But India, proud of its independence, could not be bought by all the wealth of the United States, and that goes for all the resurgent nations. The Western powers, while willing to pool their military resources under one organization for war, are unwilling to make one organization of the British Colombo Plan and the American plan for technical assistance, or to co-operate through the United Nations organizations such as FAO for an out and out war on want. This gives some justification for the propaganda of the Russians that the Western imperialistic countries, by their mutual competition for their own selfish ends, will lead to the disintegration of the forces opposing Communism.

The Western Powers are faced with the rising waves of revolt of Asia, Africa, and Latin America against poverty. They can try to resist it by force or buy it off by the offer of technical assistance and trifling loans with political strings attached to them, which will break on the first strain. In that case they will ultimately be destroyed or submerged. On the other hand, either with or without the co-operation of the USSR, they could recognize the inevitable and use their overwhelming industrial superiority to create a new world of plenty. In so doing they would gain a new power and prestige by assuming leadership in the march of the human family to the new age of peace and prosperity and the common brotherhood of man, which modern science has made the only alternative to the decline and fall of the Western civilization.

III   RELIGIOUS AND SOCIAL FACTORS

Introduction

The world population crisis is often blamed on organized religious resistance to the use of birth control, but a survey of the teachings of the world religions on procreation and marriage does not support this stereotype. The countries of Western Europe passed successfully through the demographic transition in spite of the fact that none of their churches sanctioned birth control during the major part of this transition. The Protestant churches have just within the past fifty years changed their policy on contraceptives. The first decisive action permitting their use was taken by the Bishops of the Anglican Church in the Lambeth Conference of 1930 (see p. 231), reversing the position taken in a similar conference ten years earlier. Furthermore, as we have seen in the story of Margaret Sanger and in the Bradlaugh-Besant trial, organized resistance by either Church or State has often served to publicize the question and bring the whole matter to the attention of the mass of the population.

"The handiest scapegoat," says Catholic doctor John Rock, ". . . is the Catholic Church. But my Church has not deserved all the opprobrium for the impasse in public activity. Historically there have been numerous obstructive forces at work—not all of them conscious or blameworthy. The oldest force, I think, might be called the 'force of habit': During all but the last dozen or so of the roughly 30,000 generations of man, assiduous procreation was the primary guarantee of family and group survival. It is not easy for the intellect alone to modify such an age-old response." [1]

1. From John Rock, *The Time Has Come.*

As the readings in this part show, the Roman Catholic Church is now passing through a period of re-examination of policy and further clarification may be expected in the near future. But even a drastic change in its policy can hardly be expected to solve the population problem, because formal religious doctrine is only one of many factors that influence the fertility of a people. The most important ones seem to lie in the broad, nebulous area where religious beliefs and social traditions meet and delineate a way of life. The *macho* of the Puerto Rican, the ancestor worship of the Chinese, the child marriages of India, the harems of the Arab peoples— these customs are ancient and resistant to change. In some societies even when birth control information has been made available and there has been no organized resistance from Church or State, the patterns of family life have been very slow to change, particularly where women have been subjugated and men must prove their virility by the procreation of many sons. It is not easy, as John Rock says, for the intellect alone to modify these age-old responses.

In the documents and reports of the various religious groups which have made a study of the birth control question, we find the concept of responsible parenthood emerging as the central recommendation. Responsible parenthood, as defined in these documents, involves a recognition of the total needs of the society, a consciousness of the future and of the effect that each individual couple's decisions will have on the quality of life, not only for themselves but for their children and grandchildren. This is an enlightened concept but unfortunately it has not always been clear what policies on family planning are in the best interests of society. In these readings we find many conflicting interpretations of the concept of social duty with respect to procreation and parenthood. Does it refer primarily to the nation, the ethnic, or racial group, or to the whole community of man?

Hitler and Mussolini told the German and Italian people that it was their "social duty" to have large families in order to increase their nation's power, to conquer the world, to breed a master race. Much more recently one of India's top holy men, Jagatguru Shankaracharya of Puri told his people to ignore family planning and launch a "baby race" with the Moslem minority. Moslems with four wives each, he said, could have so many babies that in ten or fifteen years they could claim all India.[2]

During the 1940's and early '50's many books and articles appeared in America and the Western European countries telling the more intelligent

2. Associated Press Release, Bombay, May 23, 1967 (*Chicago Daily News*).

and well-to-do people that it was their social duty to have large families in order to counteract the eugenic degeneration of the human species.[3] The practice of family limitation by the best-educated sectors of Western society had resulted in smaller families among the best endowed while the poor and ignorant continued to breed at very close to the biological limit. It was feared that this differential reproduction would cause a decline in the average intelligence of each succeding generation. American college students who were having their families in the late 1940's and throughout the '50's had been well indoctrinated with this philosophy. Perhaps this influence was as important as the economic prosperity of those years in producing birth rates that continued to be high long after the postwar baby boom was over in other countries. Statistics show that couples of high socio-economic class were having larger families during this period (see pp. 307–309) and that the rise in fertility in the United States was caused primarily by the preference for more children among those who consciously planned their families.

We do not have the space in these readings to present the various sides of the eugenic problem. The concern on this issue has been somewhat eased in recent years by the fact that no conclusive proof has been found that the average I.Q. is declining. Furthermore, studies do indicate a gradual shift in this differential birth rate as birth control is becoming more available to the less privileged.[4]

One of the difficulties with any attempt to encourage the best educated to have the most children is that these people set the styles in family size, as well as in other things, and these styles are emulated by the rest of the population. The intellectual leaders react first to changing concepts of social duty and there is inevitably a time lag before this change can be reflected in the attitudes of the bulk of the population.

Indeed the whole matter of how people respond to changing concepts in matters of family size raises many interesting questions. Is it easier to convince people that they should have more children because this is flattering to their egos? Or is it easier to convince them that they should have fewer children because this requires less personal effort and hardship? How long does it take to effect changes in attitudes toward family planning? For instance, if one generation has been convinced that it is their social duty to

3. See, for instance, Charles G. Darwin, *The Next Million Years,* and Robert C. Cook, *Human Fertility: The Modern Dilemma.*
4. See *Determinants and Consequences of Population Trends,* United Nations, Department of Social Affairs, Population Division, New York, 1953, pp. 85–97.

have many children can they be re-educated during their child-bearing years to accept the opposite premise? In attempting to change attitudes that are deeply rooted in the cultural pattern is it necessary to alter the total pattern? Sweeping changes in customs relating to marriage and family life are occurring in Communist China and it will be interesting to see what effect they have on the rate of acceptance of family planning.

One impression that emerges very strongly from a perusal of the literature on population over the past half-century is the wide variety of opinions about the consequences of voluntary parenthood. They vary all the way from the panic of the 1930's that man was not adequately reproducing himself and would soon die out, to the belief often voiced today that man has become the cancer of our planet and cannot stop his own uncontrolled reproduction. It seems fair to say that no one really knows what would happen if all families became completely voluntary in the sense that each child was wanted before it was conceived. Our experience with this kind of parenthood has been very limited and has yielded conflicting evidence. In the past fifty years the families of Western industrial nations have been voluntary to a larger extent that at any other time in history, and the net reproductive rate in these countries has varied from .78 during the 1930's to 1.70 in the 1950's. Either one of these extremes would result in serious population problems if maintained over several generations.

It is reasonable to suppose that there would be differences in the size of voluntary families from culture to culture, depending on social values and traditions. People want children for many different reasons. As Ruth Benedict says:

> In most countries people have children because there must be someone to till the piece of land in the village where the family has lived for centuries, there must be an heir to inherit the Hof, or there must be a son to perform the ancestral rites. In our atomistic American families these motivations seldom arise. We have children, not because our parents are sitting in judgment, not because of the necessity of having an heir, but because we personally want them—whether as company in the home or to show our friends we can have them.[5]

While we all recognize the existence of this desire for children, it is a factor whose strength cannot be measured. It may well vary from epoch to epoch as well as from culture to culture. The most universal reason for

5. Ruth Benedict, "Are Families Passé?", *Saturday Review of Literature,* 31 (52), 25 December, 1948.

having children is more often expressed by poets or artists than by demographers. The wish to pass life on is an affirmation of human experience, an emotional response to the presence of beauty and vitality as experienced at a particular moment in time. As James Thurber so succinctly expresses it, the resurgence of love that causes the ebb and flow of human populations may depend upon the existence of that last flower.

Religious Beliefs on Parenthood and Marriage

As Mankind Thinketh
WILLIAM VOGT (1948)

In China, the idea that it is necessary to be an ancestor is a cardinal belief, despite the obvious fact that descendants are becoming more wretched with every generation. In starving India, the country is overrun by millions of cattle that cannot be used to satisfy human hunger because they are "sacred"; nor can they be killed and prevented from drawing from the land energy supplies desperately needed for human beings. The *idea* is dominant over the peristalsis of starving stomachs.

When mankind began the massive development of its forebrain, which is its greatest glory, it also began to lay up trouble for itself on the earth. The shackles of instinct, protectors of the amoeba and the ape, were largely discarded, and Plato became a possibility, and Moses, Aristotle, and Beethoven, and Darwin and Freud. Man was now on his own; he had the freedom to mold his own destiny. Unfortunately, the freedom did not always have its counterpart in wisdom. For this reason, ancient civilizations fell —and our own is tottering.

It has been the fashion, especially of modern years, to emphasize what man has done in the way of material accomplishments. But there has been a strong tendency to neglect what he has thought. For a nation whose founders left the blood of their bare feet in the snow at Valley Forge, we Americans are strangely blind to the power of ideas. . . .

The *idea* of the milpa farmer may be far more difficult to change than is the direction of the gullies through his land. To limit the desire of the Chinese for sons may be a problem more formidable than the provision of at least limited food for them. A slogan may twist the arm of Peace as dangerously as a new weapon. Faith in ancient precepts may be a more effective eroder of soil than two inches of rain in an hour.

Behind nearly every human act lies an "emotion" that sets the act going; and behind the "emotion" lies a "thought" or an "idea." If such survival-emotions as the desire for conservation are to become part of our daily existence, they must be based on knowledge and the thought that stems from it. If we are to make peace with the forces of the earth, that peace must begin in our minds—and we must seek, and accept, many new ideas. We must reject many old ones.

Parenthood and World Religions

RICHARD M. FAGLEY (1960)

Anything as fundamental, mysterious, and awesome as the birth of new life is inescapably related to man's religious instinct. The miracle of birth links the living with the dynamic, the creative in the universe. Fertility in the natural world is essential to individual survival, and human fertility is essential to social survival. Thus it is understandable that anthropologists should find fertility rites common in primitive religion in all parts of the world.[1] The uncertainties of the flock and the harvest, and the uncertainties of high mortality surrounding the family, made propitiation of the fertility gods important for daily bread and progeny. In some societies ignorance of the physiology of generation made parenthood doubly mysterious, and where the relationship between sexual intercourse and procreation was dimly understood, there were still the baffling questions of successful pregnancy, of safe childbirth, of healthy babies, of sons. The fertility cult was a normal fact in primitive society.

Apparently, the major religions of today had to struggle in their infancy

1. The various rites connected particularly with food and vegetation were compiled impressively by Sir James Frazer in *The Golden Bough,* Macmillan, New York and London, 1936.

From Richard M. Fagley, *The Population Explosion and Christian Responsibility.* Copyright © 1960 by Oxford University Press, Inc. Reprinted by permission.

in varying degrees against such cults and the sex mores related to them. Hinduism, in its characteristic syncretistic fashion, absorbed a fertility cult in the worship of Shiva, who among other things is the god of reproduction.[2] Buddhism is an ascetic revolt against the passions of this life, yet in the Buddhist literature can be found the imprint of older pro-fertility patterns.[3] Judaism had a struggle to oust the local fertility gods, the *baals*. Early Christianity was concerned with the corrupting influence of Greco-Roman license, in which the worship of Venus was a factor. And Islam came onto the scene in this field as a reform movement, elevating somewhat the low status of women and curbing somewhat the unrestricted polygamy in the Arab culture of the time.

At the same time the major religions, except perhaps Buddhism, preserved the nearly universal concern for fertility in their doctrines and practices, and Buddhism offered a compromise way for the married laity. In addition to Hindu syncretism, there is the strong fertility element in Judaism, which continued in the Old Testament heritage of Christianity. And the moral and marital reforms of Mohammed stopped far short of any hostility to fertility. The persistence of pro-fertility attitudes may represent to some extent the impact of the vanquished faiths, or the compromises contributing to victory. In either case, the mystery of new life is a basic question for all religion, and since for most of man's history the struggle for life has been waged against heavy natural odds, a generally strong pro-fertility emphasis in the major religious traditions is wholly comprehensible.

Our concern, however, is primarily the contemporary bearing of the main religions on the question of responsible parenthood, particularly as they affect attitudes and policies in the underdeveloped world, rather than the historical evolution of their teachings. . . .

Hinduism

The attitude toward parenthood in Hinduism, which counts a total community of perhaps 300 million souls and is the predominant faith in the most densely populated large region on earth, is obviously important if a limitation of fertility is to restore a balance between population and available re-

2. The current fertility cult associated with Shiva, the "left hand" *shaktism* of the *Tantras*, "is obviously a survival and a recrudescence of a phase of original Indian religion." J. C. Archer, *The Faiths Men Live By*, Nelson, New York, 1934, p. 203.
3. In the tale of the Ogress Kālī attributed to "the Master," for example, the mother whose daughter-in-law is barren exclaims, "A sonless family falls into ruin, the line of its succession lost; let me seek out another maiden." *The Heart of Buddhism*, ed. by K. J. Saunders, Association, Calcutta, 1915.

sources. Hinduism is such a conglomeration of different religious beliefs and folkways that the answer is complex. The amoral behavior of the Hindu pantheon, reminiscent of the Greek deities, gives little or no ethical guidance, and the wide range of cults existing side by side offer quite divergent norms for conduct.

There are strong pro-fertility elements in Hinduism beyond the rites associated with Shiva and his consorts, with the *lingams* or phallic symbols, Nautch girls, and all that. The male-centered view of life, combined with the belief in reincarnation, makes sons important to pray for their ancestors and deliver them from hell, and tends to relegate woman chiefly to her childbearing function. The "seed and soil" concept of procreation seems to be common in the Hindu tradition and, with the *ahimsa* or noninjury doctrine, would appear to indicate a predisposition against any form of contraception.

On the other hand, there is a strong ascetic element in Hinduism. Kenneth Saunders has pointed out in *The Ideals of East and West* that the early thinkers held out as "the ideal man the *muni,* or wandering friar, who has 'risen above the desire for sons, for wealth and for domination.'" Later the religious ideal is the *yogi:* "aloof, benevolent, detached, severe in mystic contemplation." This ideal was diluted for the layman in the favorite book of devotion, the *Bhagavad Gita,* but it offers some counterweight to the erotic and fertility elements in Hinduism. Probably more important, in regard to present-day issues of contraception, is the fact that the Hindu approach places more emphasis on spiritual attitudes than on ethical rules. The head of the Ramakrishna Mission in New Delhi wrote a friend in Chicago, stating that the Mission had "no official opinion on social problems like birth control," having faith in enlightened social opinion:

> Swami Vivekananda held the view that social evils are like diseases in the body politic whose radical cure is through purifying and strengthening the life blood of the body through fundamental spiritual education of man; social reforms remove only the surface symptoms; this is also important and necessary; but he desired his movement to concentrate on the first while saying godspeed to all well-meaning social reformers.

The problem of special population pressures in India is comparatively recent.[4] One factor was high rates of infant mortality. Carr-Saunders in

4. "Prior to 1921 the growth of population and cultivation were nearly in balance. Population increase was fitful and slow, and increase in cultivation managed to keep pace with it. After 1921, however, population growth has been rapid and uninterrupted, while increase in cultivation, even where it has occurred, has been small and proportionately much less than the increase in population"—*Census of India,* 1951, vol. I, part IB, p. 1.

World Population points to three other factors. One was maternal mortality: the census of 1931 showed that the average Indian mother had four children born alive and slightly less than three survive; the partial explanation is that many mothers died before reaching the end of the reproductive period. A second factor was child marriages, with 181 per thousand married "women" under the age of 15 in 1931. Carr-Saunders points out that intercourse shortly after puberty is "inimical both to health and fecundity." The third factor was the Hindu ban on the remarriage of widows. The health programs have since reduced infant and maternal mortality and the reform spirit of modern India has reduced the number of child marriages and relaxed the prohibition on remarriage. Another antifertility factor was the various and numerous ritual restrictions on sexual intercourse. It seems probable that this factor, too, has been modified in the growth of secularism in the new India.

Thus both the natural and unintended religious and social restrictions on fertility have been reduced during the past generation, inexorably raising the question of other means to keep the birth rate in check. I say "inexorably," though it is evident that Gandhi's opposition to birth control, apart from complete abstinence, considerably delayed a more realistic approach to the problem. Gandhi regarded contraception as morally equivalent to prostitution, and, as Father de Lestapis has recorded, told Mrs. Sanger that he regarded periodic continence in the same category. But his successors have felt compelled to initiate birth control measures, starting rather gingerly with the promotion of contraception in the First Five Year Plan, and stressing more energetically both contraception and sterilization in the Second. At the Third All India Conference on Family Planning in January 1957, a government spokesman declared the intention to equip 2,000 rural planned parenthood clinics. The desperate character of the situation is indictated by the fact that in at least one state bounties are now offered to parents who undertake sterilization after the third or fourth child.[5]

[5. In the fourth 5-year plan (1966–71) the government has allocated 306 million dollars for family planning, an increase of nearly 10 times over the allocation in the third 5-year plan. Govind Narian, secretary of state for family planning in the ministry of health, said that a total of 800,000 intra-uterine devices were inserted in 1965–66 and he estimated that 900,000 would be inserted in 1966–67. In the voluntary sterilization program 542,000 operations were performed in 1965–66 (90 per cent on men), and it was estimated that 800,000 would be performed in 1966–67. Sterilization is recommended only after the couple has three children and written consent of both husband and wife is required. A mass education program has been organized using all methods of communication, including a direct mailing to 250,000 literate villagers. 4,569 primary health centers have been established and the plan calls for 41,122 subcenters by 1971. Ed.]

While the statement that "all the great Hindu social reformers" in recent years have been in favor of family limitation may give too optimistic a picture, it seems true that Hinduism presents no sharply defined doctrinal obstacle to curbs on parenthood. The fundamental doctrine is on a different level. Moreover, Indian opinion is moving toward support of family limitation. A poll in several communities in the states of Mysore and Uttar Pradesh indicated that from 60 to 78 per cent of the parents expressed the desire to limit progeny. Yet this does not mean that the cultural obstacles, partly rooted in religious belief and custom, are no longer formidable. Nor does it mean, especially in view of the lack of suitable and readily available methods of contraception, that social inertia is not still a major obstacle to India's most critical problem.

Buddhism

Buddhism like Hinduism . . . appears rather "passive" in regard to efforts to control fertility. "Passive" seems particularly appropriate for the faith that counts from 300 to 350 million Asians, for Buddhism appears to have very little doctrine of parenthood in the sense used in this review. The whole point of view seems calculated to discourage fertility.

A central tenet of Buddhist doctrine is that the origin of suffering is desire. In his final words under the *sala* tree, the Buddha said:

> Consider your body; think of its impurity; how can you indulge its cravings as you see that both its pain and its delight are alike causes of suffering? . . . You must break the bonds of worldly passions and get rid of them as you would a viper.

Buddhist literature abounds with references to renunciation of earthly love for the free mind and spirit. A man, for example, sees his fair wife approaching, his son upon her arm; but he sees in her "a subtle snare"—such bonds have lost their hold, because his mind is free.[6] Passions accumulate the *karma* or just reward of further troubles in later reincarnations. This asceticism applies to love of children as well. In the tale of Prince Wessantara, whose vow of self-abnegation is tested, the Prince gives his children away "that I may have perfect insight," whereupon legions of gods exclaim: "Wondrous is he whose mind is unshaken even at the loss of

---

6. *The Heart of Buddhism*, p. 43. This works both ways: another verse describes how a wife is a "liberated bride," freed from mortar, butter churn, and "crooked hunchback lord," and now "freedom from birth and death's assured" (ibid.). There is considerable sexual equality in Buddhism.

both his children!" The hierarchy of values is indicated in this teaching, the last point bringing us back to the primacy of individual salvation:

> One should forget himself for the sake of his family;
> one should forget his family for the sake of his village;
> one should forget his village for the sake of his country;
> one should forget all the world for the sake of enlightenment.

Under Buddhism, the married man is definitely a second-class citizen, tied down by worldly desires and cares, who may ultimately achieve enlightenment—by leaving his family to become a "homeless brother." In the meantime, he should learn to live with wife and child in harmony, train and provide for his children, and follow the rules of detachment so far as possible. The family should work as "busy as bees"—partly to support the "homeless brother," the ascetic beside whom the benedict is a "common man." In all this there is precious little sanction either for marital relations and procreation or against family limitation. Parenthood seems to begin after the children are born.

There is in Buddhism a strong compassion for all sentient life, one of the points in the "noble eightfold path" being to harm no living creature. This presumably constitutes a ban on abortion as well as infanticide.[7] In the tale of Kālī there is a reference to the use of an abortifacient given by the barren wife to the pregnant wife, but the point of the tale is the evil of hatred rather than the immorality of abortion. Thus far I have found no evidence that the "seed" is regarded as a living creature, and the legislative situation in predominantly Buddhist countries, mentioned below, supports the view that it is not so regarded.

From the point of view of actual practice, it appears that Buddhist belief gives a certain spiritual tone to the culture of its adherents, rather than any kind of detailed ethical system. Referring to the Buddhist ideal of compassion and awareness of common creaturehood, Professor Philip Ashby of Princeton wrote in an unpublished paper:

> While it cannot be denied that the precepts did succeed to some degree in furthering this ideal, yet the moral patterns which predominate among the masses of the people in Buddhist areas are more to be identified with the indigenous pre-Buddhist cultures and general custom morality of the specific area than with a system of ethics or morals which are peculiarly Buddhist.

7. Thomas Burch, however, states that, in regard to Japan, "neither Shinto nor Buddhism, the two largest creeds in Japan, categorically oppose abortion." Thomas K. Burch, "Induced Abortion in Japan," *Eugenics Quarterly,* vol. 2, no. 3, September 1955.

Islam

The followers of Mohammed, who constitute the largest religious group in the underdeveloped world, with a total of 350 to 400 million persons, form an obviously key sector not only in Asia but also in northern Africa. Two of the gravest population problems are found in Egypt and Indonesia, or, more accurately, Java. The Population Reference Bureau estimated in 1958, on the basis of admittedly inadequate statistics, that the population of the Middle East was growing at the rate of 2½ to 3 per cent a year, a rate of growth exceeded only by that of tropical South America. While the Muslim world is not growing proportionately as rapidly as it did in those astounding decades of the 7th century, it is no doubt growing more rapidly today in terms of numbers. The cradle is proving more potent than the sword.

Islam has important roots in the Old Testament, but in regard to parenthood, they grow chiefly in the soil of patriarchal history. In contrast with the unrestricted marital opportunities for Arab males in his time, Mohammed limited his masculine followers to four wives at a time, an austerity tempered by permission to supplement the quota with such slaves as they could afford. Also wives that did not suit could be replaced at the cost of the *mahr* or marriage settlement. "Consecutive polygamy" consequently has been a common pattern.[8] One of the conveniences of the Mohammedan heaven is that a righteous man may have his favorite wives with him, or opt for the "large-eyed maidens" if he did not fare too well on earth.

Actually, this is not the full picture. Mohammed recognized some reciprocal marriage rights and urged men to "admonish your wives with kindness, because women were created from the crooked bone of the side." He tolerated rather than approved divorce: "the thing which is lawful but is disliked by God is divorce." Also, impartial treatment of wives was a moral obligation: "When a man has two wives and does not treat them equally he will come on the day of resurrection with half of his body fallen off." [9] Contemporary Muslim reformers argue from this that the Prophet was bas-

8. "It has probably always been true that by far the largest part of Moslem men have had but one wife at a time." George Foot Moore, *History of Religions,* Scribner's, New York, 1932, II, p. 492.
9. Cf. L. T. Hobhouse, *Morals in Evolution,* Holt, New York, 1915, p. 200f. for additional examples.

ically opposed to polygamy, since it is obviously impossible for a man to treat two wives equally.[10]

In regard to parenthood, the ethos of Islam might be generally described as procreation unlimited. The Koran echoes Genesis 1:28 in the injunction, "marry and generate," and "marry a woman who holds her husband extremely dear, and who is richly fruitful." The description of family conditions in Egypt appended to the Warren Report, *The Family in Contemporary Society* indicates some additional pro-fertility factors that operate and have operated in the past in other Muslim countries as well as in Egypt. Children are employed on the land at an early age, and hence are economically useful. Muslim (as well as Christian) opinion attaches high prestige to the parents of large families. Further encouragement to the large family is given by the Muslim law of inheritance.

Despite the generally strong pro-fertility pattern in Islam, there is some evidence that efforts may have been made to limit conception in sexual relations with slave girls. Norman Himes notes, for example, that the *Encyclopedia of Islam speaks* of *'azl* or *coitus interruptus* being frequently used with slave girls." [11] The purpose in such practices probably lies in the following from Professor George Foot Moore:

> If such a slave bears a son who is acknowledged by her master, she becomes a "mother of a child"; thereafter her master cannot sell her, and at his death she becomes free without further formality. A son thus acknowledged is free and shares in his father's inheritance with the sons of the wedded wives.

Dr. Himes also cites the varied contraceptive knowledge held by Al-Rāzī of Persia in the late 9th century, the "greatest physician of the Middle Ages"; Avicenna in West Africa in the early 11th century; and Al-Jurjānī in 12th century Persia. The "rational element" in their knowledge, he points out, was remarkable for the period, and far ahead of European knowledge. How widespread was such knowledge is hard to guess. In any

10. In one place the Koran appears to regard monogamy as a means to family limitation. If a man fears he may not be fair, he is to take one wife—not counting slaves—"that is more likely to secure that ye be not over-burdened with children" (4:3). This phrase is an alternate reading for "that ye be not partial." *The Qur'ān*, trans. by Richard Bell, Clark, Edinburgh, 1939.

11. Himes also says, "In Islam the fetus is not considered a human being until it has reached a distinctly human form; hence abortion is not forbidden." The references to abortion I have seen have all been strongly condemnatory, except in regard to therapeutic necessity. Himes, Norman E., *Medical History of Contraception*, William Wood, Baltimore, 1936, p. 136.

case, it does not answer the question of a religious sanction. All it suggests is that there was no clear ban on contraception in the Koran; in the Sunna or tradition somewhat comparable to the Talmud in Judaism; or in the Ijma, the Islamic consensus which defines the authoritative.

With the explosive population pressures of the past decades, Islamic scholars have been making a fresh search of their traditions to find clues favorable to a doctrine of voluntary family limitation. They find a reference by a companion of the Prophet to the need to watch out for too many children; they are difficult to raise. Another reference suggests that birth control may be permitted when a woman is too feeble, a man too poor, or a woman fears the loss of her beauty. Such arguments are supplemented by demographic and nationalistic reasons.[12] In March 1953, the Fatwa Committee of Azhar University in Cairo, an influential group of scholars on Muslim "canon law," stated in response to a query:

> The use of medicine to prevent pregnancy temporarily is not forbidden by religion, especially if repeated pregnancies weaken the woman due to insufficient intervals for her to rest and regain her health. The Koran says, "Allah desireth for you ease; He desireth not hardship for you" (2/185); "And hath not laid upon you in religion any hardship" (22/78). But the use of medicine to prevent pregnancy absolutely and permanently is forbidden by religion.

This statement indicates, I think, that there is little specific sanction for contraception in the tradition of Islam, and also that the contemporary leaders are determined not to let that fact impede the current efforts for voluntary family planning. The Minister of Social Services in Egypt spoke of birth control as a social necessity. The Minister of Food and Agriculture in Pakistan said: "The senseless race between increase of food and increase of population must not continue any longer." The governments of both countries have established a number of family planning clinics. Despite the pro-fertility elements in Islamic culture, the leaders of some Muslim countries, at least, do not find serious doctrinal obstacles in the way of a necessary population policy.

• • •

12. Father de Lestapis also cites an opinion by the Grand Mufti of Egypt in January 1937, concerning a kind of oral tradition supporting 'azl; it had been used by the ancient Arabs, had not been banned by the Koran, and had been discussed by other interpreters; consequently, it was "not absolutely illicit" by the precepts of Islam (p. 45). de Lestapis (S.J.), Stanislas, La Limitation des Naissances, SPES, Paris, 1959. p. 42f.

The Old Testament, Judaism, and Parenthood

The story of Israel's life and beliefs, under the impact of God's progressive revelation of His righteous will, is important in a consideration of the question of responsible parenthood. The Old Testament record is significant as the formative influence on the ethos of the Jewish people. Historically, it has wider significance in its influence on the shaping of the Christian ethos. Consequently, we now turn to a brief examination of Old Testament doctrine which bears on the issue of responsible parenthood. . . .

As in many early societies, there were strong reasons in the environment for a major concern in fertility. No other concern affecting the family appears so often in Biblical literature. Both economic insecurity and international insecurity served to elevate the value of large families and large flocks. The challenge to survival for the tribes of Israel was seen as a call to growth and expansion. Underpopulation, rather than overpopulation, was the dominant reality.

It is true that the followers of Yahweh waged a victorious struggle against the fertility cults, the worship of the Baalim (cf. Num. 25:1–3; Deut. 4:3; 23:17).[13] But it was a long and hard struggle and continued into the time of Josiah, who "broke down the houses of the cult prostitutes which were in the house of the Lord" (2 Kings 23:7). The persistence of the fertility cults indicates, it can be argued, popular concern with fruitfulness.

The indignation of the prophets against the fertility cults, it should be noted, was directed against their idolatry and licentious rites rather than their preoccupation with fertility. . . .

Part of the prophetic indignation over the worship of the Baalim stems, no doubt, from the conviction that Yahweh is the true author of fruitfulness. His injunction, "be fruitful and multiply," to Adam (Gen. 1:28), repeated to Noah (Gen. 9:1,7) and to Jacob (Gen. 35:11), is also seen as a divine promise and blessing. . . . The dream might be called the abundant society: one in which a man is able to surround himself with many children to comfort him in his old age, and to tend the growing flocks and fields; one in which the tribe advances toward a pre-eminent position by

13. Biblical references, except where noted, are from the Revised Standard Version, by permission.

reason of its numbers and prosperity; one in which the whole people of God become a great nation, strong and secure.

The distinguishing feature of Old Testament thought in this matter, however, is insistence on the ethical and religious preconditions for human expansion, for the fulfillment of God's promises. The requirement is stated thus: "if you obey the voice of the Lord your God, keeping all his commandments which I command you this day, and doing what is right in the sight of the Lord your God" (Deut. 13:18). Then, and then only, "Blessed shall be the fruit of your body, and the fruit of your ground, and the fruit of your beasts, the increase of your cattle, and the young of your flock" (Deut. 28:1–4). If you had "hearkened to my commandments," said Isaiah, then "your offspring would have been like the sand" (Isa. 48:18–19).

In addition to the dream of the abundant society, the Hebraic concern for posterity has another major source; the concern for preservation of the family name, for what might be called social immortality. Personal survival after death did not loom very large in Jewish tradition. One reason for this was no doubt the view of man as a unity of flesh and spirit, without the dualism characteristic of Greek thought. A great prophet like Elijah might be transported bodily by a whirlwind into heaven (2 Kings 2:11). But this obviously did not happen to the general run of men. For them there was Sheol, a rather dreary and Stygian underworld, the world of the grave. Existence in Sheol was shadowy, indistinct, diluted. The survival that really mattered was in this world, in posterity. The intense sense of belonging to a community, of group solidarity, so attenuated in modern man, must be appreciated to grasp the satisfactions found in this social immortality.

Preservation of the family name before the Lord was the way this concept was expressed. . . . If a man died without progeny, it was his brother's duty to marry the widow and beget children to carry on the name of the deceased. The denouement of the story of Ruth hinges on whether the next of kin will "do the part of the next of kin" or assign his obligations to Boaz. The next of kin decides that a levirate marriage might impair his own inheritance and Boaz takes over, "to perpetuate the name of the dead in his inheritance, that the name of the dead may not be cut off from among his brethren and from the gate of his native place" (Ruth 4:5, 10). Onan, in a similar situation, decided he did not want to give offspring to his dead brother, and when he went in to the widow, Tamar, "he spilled the semen on the ground" (Gen. 38.8–10). Deuteronomy describes the levirate duty: to provide a son to succeed to the name of the deceased brother, "that his name may not be blotted out of Israel." The procedure to be followed when the duty is spurned suggests that evasion was a common problem (Deut. 25:5–10).

The special evasive action of Onan has been generally interpreted as signifying *coitus interruptus,* although onanism has also been given broader connotations. The case of Onan is the one clear example of an act with contraceptive intent in the Old Testament, and it is understandable that it should involve *coitus interruptus,* undoubtedly the most universal and commonly practiced method of averting conception down the ages. It is also understandable that much subsequent attention and debate should have been focused on this example, because of its singularity. Efforts at family limitation were hardly in keeping with the ethos of Israel.

Was the sin of Onan, for which the Lord "slew him," his refusal to honor his levirate duty—his unbrotherly and selfish attitude—as the proponents of birth control tend to argue; or was it spilling his seed intentionally, as the opponents contend? . . .

While the principal motif in the Biblical record is the concern for procreation, for building up the family and society, so that parenthood, and particularly the wife—or wives—is seen rather as a means to an end, the concern here for man and wife as an end in themselves under God is a secondary theme which helps to elevate the whole ethos. Despite the tradition and environment of polygamy and the other customs which put the woman in an inferior role, the concept of companionship worked as a leaven in Israel, disturbing the conscience over marital injustices and directing the hearts of men toward a higher view of marriage. The Old Testament provides considerable evidence of a greater appreciation of woman as a person and as a mate, and not solely as a mother, than obtained in other ancient societies. . . .

Post-Canonical Judaism

Thus far we have been considering the Judaic heritage common to Judaism and Christianity. . . .

The pro-fertility orientation of the Old Testament is continued in Judaism. "Be fruitful and multiply" is the first of the 613 *Mitzvoth*—precepts or commandments. . . . The *Jewish Encyclopedia,* however, indicates that as Judaism became urbanized the injunction regarding procreation was modified. Two children might meet the requirements of the *mitzvah.* Rabbi Kertzer gives a summary formula: "According to Jewish law, every man and wife have a solemn obligation to bring at least two children into the world."

On the obligation to marry and procreate, Judaism is agreed. Celibacy, says Rabbi Hertz, is "contrary to nature." The differences come in regard to limiting the size of families, the Orthodox tending to restrict severely both the reasons and the means, the Reformed and Conservative taking a less strict position. There is also considerable variety of interpretation among the Talmudic teachers. . . .

The composite picture is one of a tradition which permits, if it does not encourage, certain measures of family limitation at least after the second child. From the Orthodox viewpoint, according to Willy Hofmann, "Jewish tradition and viewpoint cannot consider planned parenthood for social or economic reasons." The Conservative and Reformed Rabbis do consider such reasons.[14] The resolutions of 1929 and 1930 of the Central Conference of American Rabbis, the Reformed group in the United States, "urge the recognition of the importance of the control of parenthood as one of the methods of coping with social problems," and support "intelligent birth regulation." "We are aware," said the Conference, "of the many serious evils caused by the lack of birth control." The Rabbinical Assembly, the Conservative body in the United States, stated in 1935:

> Careful study and observation have convinced us that birth control is a valuable method for overcoming some of the obstacles that prevent the proper functioning of the family under present conditions. . . . Proper education in contraception and birth control will not destroy, but rather enhance, the spiritual values inherent in the family and will make for the advancement of human happiness and welfare.

It should be added that the practice of the Jewish laity has outstripped the debate among the Rabbis. As Moses Jung has stated in *Judaism in a Changing World* (ed. Leo Jung), "the practice of birth control seems to

14. On contemporary Jewish views, cf. also Marc. H. Tanenbaum's article "Religion" in *The American Jewish Yearbook,* American Jewish Committee, New York, 1959 edition.

have become almost universal among the Jews." This is borne out by census statistics, indicating the low birth rate of Jewish groups in Western countries. One is reminded of the fact that polygamy was not finally outlawed until the 11th century although monogamy, favored in the oral tradition, had established itself as the norm much earlier.

We find in Judaism, despite the legalism which has played such a large part in Jewish thought, the continuing ferment produced by the leaven of the "one flesh" concept. "Named 'covenant' in the Bible," writes Professor Jung in the symposium cited, "marriage became in the Talmud '*kiddushin,*' sanctification—the hallowing of two human beings to life's noblest purpose." A similar concept is expressed by Sidney Goldstein in *The Meaning of Marriage and Foundations of the Family:* "The sanctity of marriage does not depend upon conception or contraception but upon the spirit of consecration with which men and women enter the marriage bond." A good conclusion is provided by Rabbi Eugene Mihaly in *Marriage and Family Life* (ed. A. B. Shoulson):

> Procreation is undoubtedly a fulfillment in marriage, but the love and companionship is no less a primary purpose. Eve was created to be a "helpmate" to Adam since "it is not good for man to be alone" and only later were they commanded "to be fruitful and multiply."

The Interests of Catholic Christianity

FRANK LORIMER (1963)

In view of the importance of Catholic interest in marriage and the family, we must try to understand and appreciate its position.

We can then examine the possibility of establishing a reasonable *modus vivendi* among conflicting interests in this field in a pluralistic society—in particular the United States—and in the pluralistic world order represented in the United Nations.

In origin, Catholic doctrine on sexual relations reflects the conflict that men have often experienced between intellectual and religious interests and more elemental impulses and pleasures—frequently called "the war between the spirit and the flesh." The early Christian community in the

From Frank Lorimer, "Issues of Population Policy," *The Population Dilemma,* edited by Philip Hauser, Prentice-Hall, Englewood Cliffs, N.J. Copyright © 1963 by The American Assembly, Columbia University, New York. Reprinted by permission.

ancient world was much concerned with this issue and it influenced many theological controversies. St. Paul viewed chastity as a supreme value, though he approved of marriage. It came gradually to be assumed that the essential reason for marriage and the sexual union of spouses was the procreation of children and, as a secondary end, the "relief of concupiscence" ("It is better to marry than to burn.") St. Augustine explicitly condemned any attempt to regulate births except through abstinence. (The principal means of avoiding births in his day were *coitus interruptus* and abortion. However, he also condemned periodic avoidance of coitus at times when conception was most likely to occur, then assumed to be soon after menstruation. Some subsequent teachers took a different position on this point.[1] It was not a major issue, prior to recent scientific discoveries concerning ovulation. Catholic tradition was, for a long time, ambivalent on this point.) The idealization of chastity is, of course, not peculiar to Catholic tradition. It has been a recurrent theme in many Christian and non-Christian religious communities. . . .

In line with this ideal, some modern Catholic writers attribute great psychological and religious value to the practice of periodic continence. They maintain that it promotes self-discipline in all aspects of life, reinforces the mutual respect of husbands and wives, deepens their affectional life, and brings a constant sense of obedience to, and dependence on, divine guidance.[2]

The unique position of the Catholic Church as distinct from these more general ideals is grounded in the theological-metaphysical and moral doctrine of the great scholastic teacher, Thomas Aquinas, who re-worked Aristotelean philosophy in the light of Christian tradition. According to this doctrine each organic element in nature, each kind of natural action, and each divinely established institution has a final end (*finis operis*) intrinsic to its structure, as distinct from mere human intention (*finis operantis*). Catholicism seeks to bring human wills into conformity with the divine will, of which the order of nature is a partial expression. However, though intentions are taken into account, it treats the conformity of *acts* to "natural law" and to ecclesiastical law as the primary criterion of

---

[1. See selection starting on p. 397. Ed.]

2. Rev. de Lestapis is particularly eloquent on this subject. However, in the opinion of some Catholic scholars, as well as secular scientists, he makes serious errors in his attempt to present an empirical analysis of the psychological effects of contraception and related social and demographic matters. See his *Family Planning and Modern Problems: A Catholic Analysis,* 1961.

morality. Thus according to Catholic teaching, a couple may, for serious reasons, plan to avoid pregnancy though continuing to have sexual inter-course, and may try to achieve their intent by timing their sexual acts in the light of modern knowledge about the ovulatory cycle, but it is deemed immoral for them to modify the act itself to achieve this aim.

The metaphysical structure of Catholic ethics and Catholic faith in the timeless validity of its sacred tradition enforces a strong conservatism. This is illustrated in another field by the adherence through successive centuries to the doctrine, prescribed by the fifth century and more fully developed by Aquinas, that the acceptance of interest (usury) on financial loans is contrary to principles of justice and to the law of nature. A papal decree in 1830 finally gave authoritative tolerance to the acceptance of in-terest, within limits set by civil law, but concluded with the statement that the whole subject requires further consideration and precise formulation. According to an article in the *Dictionnaire de Droit Canonique* published in Paris in 1953, the church still maintains a reserve on this question. "It does not consider it useful at present to define precisely the conditions under which it is legitimate to draw income from one's money."

There have been significant developments in Catholic doctrine on mar-riage and procreation during the twentieth century. The definitive endorse-ment of periodic continence as a method of regulating births, subject only to the condition that it be for serious reasons, was an important advance. There have also been profound though subtle shifts toward increased em-phasis on personal and social values in marriage. The "education" of chil-dren is firmly linked with "procreation" in defining the primary end of marriage. There are also more positive expressions of appreciation of the values of mutual respect and love in marital life. At the same time, the differentiation between the "primary" and "secondary" ends of marriage, with insistence that the latter are essentially subordinate to the former, has been reaffirmed with clarity and rigor.

There will be continuing development of Catholic doctrine in this, as in other fields. . . .

The primary interest of the Catholic community in the furtherance of ethical principles firmly grounded in its tradition has at times been con-fused with extraneous "pro-natalist" motives. Some hostile critics have as-sumed that the whole structure of Catholic doctrine in this field is a scheme to increase the population of Catholic countries and the numbers of Catholics in other countries. This notion reveals a misconception of the origin and nature of Catholic doctrine, but it finds some confirmation in the writings and activities of some churchmen.

Prolific families are held in high esteem in many traditional societies. The present writer has elsewhere suggested that this is especially so in societies with unilineal kinship systems and in societies that stress military values (*Culture and Human Fertility,* UNESCO, 1954). For example, the Ashanti of central Ghana ceremonially honor a mother on the birth of her tenth child. The glory of numerous offspring is emphasized in Islamic culture, where it is associated with polygyny. There was also an idealization of prolificacy among the ancient Hebrews, a people of pastoral origin living in a fertile land surrounded by hostile nations. This ideal is reflected in many passages in the Old Testament.

This was not, however, a major theme in Western Christianity prior to the rise of modern nationalism—though in all societies there is general respect for vigorous and cohesive large families. . . .

The official position of the Catholic Church is still somewhat ambiguous with respect to the idealization of prolificacy without respect to conditions or motives. Catholic prelates in some countries seem to endorse indiscriminate glorification of large families. Leading Catholic ethicists, however, generally repudiate this position. They advocate rational and conscientious decisions by individual couples concerning their responsibilities in procreation. This seems to be the central position of the Catholic Church, but further official clarification of this subject may be expected.

Contrary to a fairly prevalent notion, the familial attitudes and behavior of Catholics in the United States are strongly influenced by the teachings of their church—though, of course, the conformity of individuals to religious instruction on this or any other subject is usually quite imperfect. According to the Scripps-Michigan study,[3] we find that among fecund Catholic couples eighty-three per cent (as compared with ninety-three per cent of the Protestant couples) have tried in some way to regulate births. Among all Catholic couples, married ten years or more who have tried to regulate their births, sixty-two per cent had, at some time, practiced periodic continence, and forty-four per cent had relied exclusively on this approved method. Thus, apparently about one-half of all fecund Catholic couples in this country, married ten years or more, have conformed to the teachings of their church, either by accepting pregnancies as they occurred

3. Ronald Freedman, Pascal K. Whelpton, and Arthur A. Campbell: *Family Planning, Sterility and Population Growth in the United States,* 1959.

without any effort to regulate fertility or by relying exclusively on the rhythm method.

Among Catholics, as among Protestants, the proportion of couples who purposively regulate their births is greater at the higher than at the lower educational levels. Moreover, among Catholics who attempt to regulate births, the proportion relying on periodic continence is positively associ-· ated with education. According to the Scripps-Michigan study, among Catholic couples who had tried in any way to regulate fertility, one-third of those with wives who had completed college, one-half of those who had completed high school, but about two-thirds of those with less schooling, resorted to contraceptive methods other than periodic continence. Effective use of rhythm (1) requires calculation of intervals, (2) is dependent to an important degree on regularity of the menstrual cycle to permit accurate records on this subject over a considerable period, and (3) requires a high degree of discipline in sexual life. These conditions seriously limit its application in populations with inferior health conditions, frequent pregnancies at short intervals and widespread illiteracy, or lack of discipline in sexual relations (as indicated by instability of marriages or high frequencies of illegitimate births).

The information reviewed above may be deemed encouraging in many respects to Catholic leaders. However, it also shows that the Catholic Church faces difficult problems in this field—particularly in attempts to enforce Catholic ideals of responsible parenthood in some of the less developed countries.

The situation in Latin America, which contains one-third of all adherents to the Catholic faith, is particularly acute. Large segments of the population in this region are impoverished and illiterate. Moreover, there is great instability of conjugal unions, frequent concubinage and desertion, and illegitimate procreation in many Latin American countries. Among seventeen countries in this region for which such statistics are available, there are nine in which more than half of all births are illegitimate.

It seems reasonable to hope that the major emphasis of Catholic endeavor in Latin America in the future with respect to family relations may be directed toward promoting the legalization and stability of conjugal relations and reduction of concubinage, desertion, and "instinctual fertility," instead of placing major emphasis on the avoidance of contraception—until conditions can be established that are more conducive to adherence to the highest Catholic standards. This is, at least, a possibility to which some Catholic leaders will undoubtedly give serious consideration. Although Catholics are cautious in drawing distinctions between "greater" and "lesser" evils, they do take such distinctions into account.

The interests of the Catholic community are, of course, less *directly* involved in population trends and policies in most Asian countries, though there is strong Catholic interest in many parts of tropical Africa as well as in Latin America. The interpretation by Catholic leaders of their interests and responsibilities in this field have led them both to resist emphasis in international councils on the problematic aspects of population trends, and to resist the development of family limitation programs in any country, whether or not it is predominantly Catholic in culture.

The Catholic church can not roll back "the waves of family planning" in the modern world. It can, however, continue to apply brakes to the actions of international agencies in this field and it can delay, through indefinite periods, trends toward the purposive regulation of births in some critical areas. Continued achievement along these lines may, however, cause increasing strains in relations between governments that do and those that do not conform to Catholic policy in this respect, and within the political life of many countries.

The Accommodation of Religious Interests in a Pluralistic Society

The problem with which we are concerned arises from the divergence between Catholic interests on the one hand and other religious and secular interests on the other with respect to population and parenthood. We must face this issue squarely. The Catholic Church is bound by its faith to guide its communicants in accordance with the tradition that it has received. Moreover, it is bound to try to persuade all men to act in accordance with its principles. These rights and obligations of the Catholic community are entitled to respect in a pluralistic society, committed to the principle of religious toleration—just as, for example, we must respect the right and moral obligation of Quakers to protest the maintenance of our military establishment and the expenditure of public funds for armaments.

The Catholic Church is not bound by its doctrine to try to compel other men to act in accordance with its teachings, or to exert *undue pressure* on political processes in an attempt to bring legislation and other public affairs into conformity with its teachings. Any such attempt is properly resisted by those who have conflicting rights and interests. We have purposely used the elastic term "undue pressure," because there is a rather wide and undefined area between proper and improper influence on political processes in any society. Action within this area is guided by the political philosophy, judgment and conscience of the persons concerned. One related principle can, however, be stated more categorically. Though public officials must avoid unnecessary scandal or offense to any group in the nation, they must respect the rights of individuals as *persons*. They can not properly try to compel persons to conform to the precepts of any church, including that to which they adhere, or refuse on this ground to serve their legitimate rights. For example, states that maintain liquor dispensaries can not properly refuse to sell liquor to Methodists.

These are basic principles of American society. Fortunately, they are clearly recognized by the most competent exponents of Catholic doctrine—though they are sometimes neglected in practice by Catholic prelates and by enthusiastic lay organizations:

> Human law is not obliged to forbid all the immoral acts from which virtuous people abstain, but only the most heinous, those from which the majority of men are able to abstain, and especially those which harm other people and the suppression of which is seen to be indispensable if a human society is to be preserved (Thomas Aquinas).
>
> The obligation of repressing moral and religious offenses cannot be an ultimate norm of action. It must be subordinated to higher and more generous norms which, in certain circumstances, allow and even perhaps make it obvious that it is better not to prevent error in order to bring about a great good. (Pope Pius XII) [4]

There has been a notable trend away from religious bigotry in the United States in recent decades. All men of good will hope that progress along this line can be carried forward. Contraception is approved and practiced by an overwhelming majority of American citizens. The proportion approving contraception must be at least as high as the proportion that approves of divorce. Both of these practices are contrary to Catholic ethics. Yet the Catholic Church acquiesces in the existence of statutes in most states which permit divorce, and Catholic judges preside over divorce proceedings. The Catholic Church tolerates these conditions, because in line with the principles stated by Aquinas and Pius XII, its leaders in America recognize that violent protest against the legalization of divorce

4. de Lestapis, *op. cit.*, p. 258.

would serve no useful purpose, and would engender unnecessary animosity. It is not unreasonable to assume that within the near future the Catholic Church may apply the same principles with respect to official and quasi-official actions relating to the regulation of fertility. This would be a change in tactics, but it would not involve any repudiation of principles —much less a change in doctrine.

Mater et Magister, Encyclical Letter

HIS HOLINESS POPE JOHN XXIII (1961)

Population Increase and Economic Development

More recently, the question often is raised how economic organization and the means of subsistence can be balanced with population increase, whether in the world as a whole or within the needy nations.

Imbalance Between Population and Means of Subsistence

As regards the world as a whole, some, consequent to statistical reasoning, observe that within a matter of decades mankind will become very numerous, whereas economic growth will proceed much more slowly. From this some conclude that unless procreation is kept within limits, there subsequently will develop an even greater imbalance between the number of inhabitants and the necessities of life.

It is clearly evident from statistical records of less developed countries that, because recent advances in public health and in medicine are there widely diffused, the citizens have a longer life expectancy consequent to lowered rates of infant mortality. The birth rate, where it has traditionally been high, tends to remain at such levels, at least for the immediate future. Thus the birth rate in a given year exceeds the death rate. Meanwhile the productive systems in such countries do not expand as rapidly as the number of inhabitants. Hence, in poorer countries of this sort, the standard of living does not advance and may even deteriorate. Wherefore, lest

From Pope John XXIII, *Mater et Magister,* Paulist Press, New York, 1961. Translated by William J. Gibbons, S. J., assisted by a Committee of Catholic Scholars. Reprinted by permission.

a serious crisis occur, some are of the opinion that the conception or birth of humans should be avoided or curbed by every possible means.

The Terms of the Problem

Now to tell the truth, the interrelationships on a global scale between the number of births and available resources are such that we can infer grave difficulties in this matter do not arise at present, nor will in the immediate future. The arguments advanced in this connection are so inconclusive and controversial that nothing certain can be drawn from them.

Besides, God in His goodness and wisdom has, on the one hand, provided nature with almost inexhaustible productive capacity; and, on the other hand, has endowed man with such ingenuity that, by using suitable means, he can apply nature's resources to the needs and requirements of existence. Accordingly, that the question posed may be clearly resolved, a course of action is not indeed to be followed whereby, contrary to the moral law laid down by God, procreative function also is violated. Rather, man should, by the use of his skills and science of every kind, acquire an intimate knowledge of the forces of nature and control them ever more extensively. Moreover, the advances hitherto made in science and technology give almost limitless promise for the future in this matter.

When it comes to questions of this kind, we are not unaware that in certain locales and also in poorer countries, it is often argued that in such an economic and social order, difficulties arise because citizens, each year more numerous, are unable to acquire sufficient food or sustenance where they live, and peoples do not show amicable cooperation to the extent they should.

But whatever be the situation, we clearly affirm these problems should be posed and resolved in such a way that man does not have recourse to methods and means contrary to his dignity, which are proposed by those persons who think of man and his life solely in material terms.

We judge that this question can be resolved only if economic and social advances preserve and augment the genuine welfare of individual citizens and of human society as a whole. Indeed, in a matter of this kind, first place must be accorded everything that pertains to the dignity of man as such, or to the life of individual men, than which nothing can be more precious. Moreover, in this matter, international cooperation is necessary, so that, conformably with the welfare of all, information, capital, and men themselves may move about among the peoples in orderly fashion.

Respect for the Laws of Life

In this connection, we strongly affirm that human life is transmitted and propagated through the instrumentality of the family which rests on marriage, one and indissoluble, and, so far as Christians are concerned, elevated to the dignity of a sacrament. Because the life of man is passed on to other men deliberately and knowingly, it therefore follows that this should be done in accord with the most sacred, permanent, inviolate prescriptions of God. Everyone without exception is bound to recognize and observe these laws. Wherefore, in this matter, no one is permitted to use methods and procedures which may indeed be permissible to check the life of plants and animals.

Indeed, all must regard the life of man as sacred, since from its inception, it requires the action of God the Creator. Those who depart from this plan of God not only offend His divine majesty and dishonor themselves and the human race, but they also weaken the inner fibre of the commonwealth.

Education Toward a Sense of Responsibility

In these matters it is of great importance that new offspring, in addition to being very carefully educated in human culture and religion—which indeed is the right and duty of parents—should also show themselves very conscious of their duties in every action of life. This is especially true when it is a question of establishing a family and of procreating and educating children. Such children should be imbued not only with a firm confidence in the providence of God, but also with a strong and ready will to bear the labors and inconveniences which cannot be lawfully avoided by anyone who undertakes the worthy and serious obligation of associating his own activity with God in transmitting life and in educating offspring. In this most important matter certainly nothing is more relevant than the teachings and supernatural aids provided by the Church. We refer to the Church whose right of freely carrying out her function must be recognized also in this connection.

Creation for Man's Benefit

When God, as we read in the book of Genesis, imparted human nature to our first parents, He assigned them two tasks, one of which complements the other. For He first directed: "Be fruitful and multiply," [1] and then immediately added: "Fill the earth and subdue it." [2]

The second of these tasks, far from anticipating a destruction of goods, rather assigns them to the service of human life.

Accordingly, with great sadness we note two conflicting trends: on the one hand, the scarcity of goods is vaguely described as such that the life of men reportedly is in danger of perishing from misery and hunger; on the other hand, the recent discoveries of science, technical advances, and economic productivity are transformed into means whereby the human race is led toward ruin and a horrible death.

Now the provident God has bestowed upon humanity sufficient goods wherewith to bear with dignity the burdens associated with procreation of children. But this task will be difficult or even impossible if men, straying from the right road and with a perverse outlook, use the means mentioned above in a manner contrary to human reason or to their social nature, and hence, contrary to the directives of God Himself.

Editor's Note: *A Papal Study Commission on Birth Control presented majority and minority reports to Pope Paul VI on June 26, 1966. These reports were not made public by the Vatican. On April 16, 1967* The National Catholic Reporter, *an independent weekly published by laymen in Kansas City, printed a text said to be from these reports (in unofficial translation from the Latin).*

Excerpts from Majority and Minority Reports of Papal Panel on Birth Control (1967)

Majority Report

In fulfillment of its mission, the church must propose obligatory norms of human and Christian life from the deposit of faith in an open dialogue with the world. But since moral obligations can never be detailed in all their concrete particularities, the personal responsibility of each individual

1. Gen., 1, 28.
2. *Ibid.*

From *The New York Times,* excerpts from Majority and Minority Reports of Papal Panel on Birth Control, as published by *The National Catholic Reporter,* April 17, 1967.

must always be called into play. This is even clearer today because of the complexity of modern life; the concrete moral norms to be followed must not be pushed to the extreme.

THE FUNDAMENTAL VALUES OF MARRIAGE

A couple ought to be considered above all a community of persons which has in itself the beginning of new human life. Therefore those things that strengthen and make more profound the union of persons within this community must never be separated from the procreative finality which specifies the conjugal community.

God created man male and female so that, joined together in the bonds of life, they might perfect one another through a mutual, corporal and spiritual giving and that they might carefully prepare their children, the fruit of this love, for a truly human life.

RESPONSIBLE PARENTHOOD AND THE REGULATION OF CONCEPTION

Responsible parenthood (that is, generous and prudent parenthood) will make a judgment in conscience before God about the number of children to have and educate according to the objective criteria indicated by Vatican Council II.

Responsible parenthood—through which married persons intend to observe and cultivate the essential values of matrimony with a view to the good of persons (the good of the child to be educated, of the couples themselves and of the whole of human society)—is one of the conditions and expressions of a true conjugal chastity. For genuine love, rooted in faith, hope and charity, ought to inform the whole life and action of a couple. By the strength of this chastity the couple tend to the actuation of that true love precisely inasmuch as it is conjugal and fruitful. They accept generously and prudently their task with all its values, combining them in the best way possible according to the particular circumstances and of their life and in spite of difficulties.

The regulation of conception appears necessary to many couples who wish to achieve a responsible, open and reasonable parenthood in today's circumstances. If they are to observe and cultivate all the essential values of marriage, married people need decent and human means for the regulation of conception. They should be able to expect the collaboration of all, especially from men of learning and science, in order that they can have at their disposal means agreeable and worthy of man in the fulfilling of his responsible parenthood.

The morality of sexual acts between married people takes its meaning first of all and specifically from the ordering of their actions in a fruitful married life, that is one which is practiced with responsible, generous and prudent parenthood. It does not depend upon the direct fecundity of each and every particular act.

ON THE CONTINUITY OF DOCTRINE AND ITS DEEPER UNDERSTANDING

The tradition of the church that is concerned with the morality of conjugal relations began with the beginning of the church. This tradition always, albeit with various words, intended to protect two fundamental values: the good of procreation and the rectitude of marital intercourse. Moreover the church always taught another truth equally fundamental, although hidden in mystery, namely original sin. This had wounded man in his various faculties, including sexuality. Man could only be healed of this wound by the grace of savior. This is one of the reasons why Christ took marriage and raised it to a sacrament of the new law.

An egotistical, hedonistic and contraceptive way that turns the practice of married life in an arbitrary fashion from its ordination to a human, generous and prudent fecundity is always against the nature of man and can never be justified.

The large amount of knowledge and facts that throw light on today's world suggest that it is not to contradict the genuine sense of this tradition and the purpose of the previous doctrinal condemnations if we speak of the regulation of conception by using means, human and decent, ordered to favoring fecundity in the totality of married life.

Then must be considered the sense of the faithful: According to it, condemnation of a couple to a long and often heroic abstinence as the means to regulate conception cannot be founded on the truth.

The acceptance of a lawful application of the calculated sterile periods of the woman—that the application is legitimate presupposes right motives—make a separation between the sexual act which is explicitly intended and its reproductive effect which is intentionally excluded.

The tradition has always rejected seeking this separation with a contraceptive intention for motives spoiled by egoism and hedonism, and such seeking can never be admitted. The true opposition is not to be sought between some material conformity to the psychological processes of nature and some artificial intervention. For it is natural to man to use his skill in order to put under human control what is given by physical nature.

The opposition is really to be sought between one way of acting which is contraceptive and opposed to a prudent and generous fruitfulness, and another way which is in an ordered relationship to responsible fruitfulness and which has a concern for education and all the essential, human and Christian values.

THE OBJECTIVE CRITERIA OF MORALITY

The question comes up which many men rightly think to be of great importance, at least practically: What are the objective criteria by which to choose a method of reconciling the needs of marital life with a right ordering of this life to fruitfulness in the procreation and education of offspring?

It is obvious that the method is not to be left to purely arbitrary decision.

The objective criteria are the various values and needs duly and harmoniously evaluated. These objective criteria are to be applied by the couples, acting from a rightly formed conscience and according to their concrete situation. They will thoughtfully take into account both their own welfare and that of their children, those already born and those which may be foreseen. Finally they will consult the interests of the family community, of temporal society and of the church herself.

Likewise, these are objective criteria as to the means to be chosen of responsibly determining the size of the family: If they are rightly applied, the couples themselves will find and determine the way of proceeding.

In grave language, Vatican Council II has reaffirmed that abortion is altogether to be excluded from the means of responsibly preventing birth. Sterilization, since it is a drastic and irreversible intervention in a matter of great importance, is generally to be excluded as a means of responsibly avoiding conceptions.

The natural law and reason illuminated by Christian faith dictate that a couple proceed in choosing means not arbitrarily but according to objective criteria. Among these criteria, this must be put first: The action must correspond to the nature of the person and of his acts so that the whole meaning of the mutual giving and of human procreation is kept in a context of true love. The means which are chosen should have an effectiveness proportionate to the degree of right or necessity of averting a new conception temporarily or permanently.

Therefore not arbitrarily, but as the law of nature and of God commands, let couples form a judgment which is objectively founded, with all the criteria considered. This they may do without major difficulty, and with peace of mind, if they take common and prudent counsel before God.

THE TASK AND FUNDAMENTAL CONDITIONS OF EDUCATIONAL RENEWAL

Couples who might think they find in the doctrine as it has just been proposed an open door to laxity or easy solution make a grave mistake, of which they will be the first victims. The conscientious decision to be made by spouses about the number of children is not a matter of small importance. On the contrary to impose a more conscientious fulfilling of their vocation to fruitfulness of a whole complex of values which are involved here.

APPLICATION OF THE DOCTRINE OF MATRIMONY TO DIFFERENT PARTS
OF THE WORLD

It seems very necessary to establish some pontifical institute or secretariate for the study of the sciences connected with married doctrine of matrimony should be applied to different parts of the world.

There are many reforms and initiatives that are needed to open the way to decent and joyful living for all families. Together with all men of goodwill, Christians must approach this great work of human development, without which the elevation of families can never become actual. It cannot be that anyone would wish to elevate his own family without at the same time actively dedicating himself to opening a way for similar elevation for all families in all parts of the world.

DEMOGRAPHIC FACT AND POLICY

The church is not ignorant of the immense difficulties and profound transformations which have arisen from the conditions of contemporary life throughout the world and especially in certain regions where there has been a rapid rise in population.

The church, by her doctrine and by her supernatural aids, intends to help all families so that they might find the way in undertaking their generous and prudent responsibility. Governments that have the care of the common good should look with great concern on subhuman conditions of families and "beware of solutions contradicting the moral law, solutions which have been promoted publicly or privately, and sometimes actually imposed." These solutions have contradicted the moral law in particular by propagating abortion or sterilization.

Political demography can be called human only if the rights of parents with regard to the procreation and education of children are respected and conditions of life are fostered with all vigor so that parents are enabled to exercise their responsibilities before God and society.

THE INAUGURATION AND FURTHER DEVELOPMENT OF MEANS FOR EDUCATION OF COUPLES AND YOUTH

Couples are burdened by multiple responsibilities throughout the whole of life; they seek light and aid. With the favor of God there will develop in many regions what has already been initiated often by the married couples themselves, to sustain families in their building and continual development.

Maximum help is to be given to parents in their educational task. Therefore it is fitting everywhere to work out many better means to remote and immediate preparation of youth for marriage. This requires the collaboration of everyone. Married people who are already well educated will have a great and indispensable part in this work. In these tasks of providing help to spouses and to the young who are peparing to build a conjugal and family community, priests and the religious will cooperate closely with the families.

Minority Report

Contraception is understood by the church as any use of the marriage right in the exercise of which the act is deprived of its natural power for the procreation of life through the industry of man. Contraceptive sterilization may be defined theologically as any physical intervention in the generative process (opus naturae) which, before or after the proper placing of generative acts (opus hominis), cause these acts to be deprived of their natural power for the procreation of life by the industry of man.

Always evil. Something which can never be justified by any motive or any circumstances is always evil because it is intrinsically evil. It is wrong not because of a precept of positive law; but of reason of the natural law. It is not evil because it is prohibited, but it is prohibited because it is evil.

A constant and perennial affirmative answer is found in the documents of the Magisterium and in the whole history of teaching on the question.

First of all, some more recent documents of the pontifical teaching authority may be cited, namely the encyclical "Casti Connubii" of Pius XI (1930); the "Allocution of Midwives" of Pius XII (1951); the encyclical "Mater et Magistra" of John XXIII (1961).

Pius XI, "Casti Connubii":

"But no reason, however grave, may be put forward by which anything intrinsically against nature may become conformable to nature and normally good. Since, therefore, the conjugal act is destined primarily by nature for the begetting of children, those who in exercising it deliberately frustrate its natural power and purpose, sin against nature and commit a deed that is shameful and intrinsically vicious.

"Any use whatsoever of matrimony exercised in such a way that the act is deliberately frustrated in its natural power to generate life is an offense against the law of God and of nature, and those who indulge in such are branded with the guilts of a grave sin.

"If any confessor or pastor of souls, which may God forbid, leads the faithful entrusted to him into these errors or should at least confirm them by approval or by guilty silence, let him be mindful of the fact that he must render a strict account to God, the Supreme Judge, for the betrayal of his sacred trust, and let him take to himself the words of Christ: 'They are blind and leaders of the blind: and if the blind lead the blind, both fall into the pit.' "

Pius XII, "Allocution to Midwives," 1951:

"Every attempt on the part of the married couple during the conjugal act or during the development of its natural consequences, to deprive it of its inherent power and to hinder the procreation of a new life is immoral. No 'indication' of need can change an action that is intrinsically immoral into an action that is moral and lawful.

"This prescription holds good today just as much as it did yesterday. It will hold tomorrow and always, for it is not a mere precept of human right but the expression of a natural and divine law.

"Direct sterilization, that which aims at making procreation impossible as both means and end, is a grave violation of the moral law, and therefore illicit. Even public authority has no right to permit it under the pretext of any 'indication' whatsoever, and still less to prescribe it or have it carried out to the harm of the innocent." . . .

The answer of the church in the present century is also illustrated by declarations of the bishops, either collectively speaking in a particular region or speaking individually in their own diocese.

It must be noted that the Holy See between 1816 and 1929, through the Roman Curia, answered questions in this matter 19 times. Since then it has spoken almost as many times. In the responses given, it was at least implicitly supposed that contraception was always seriously evil.

History provides fullest evidence that the answer of the church has always and everywhere been the same. The theological history of contraception is sufficiently simple, at least with regard to the central question: Is contraception always seriously evil? For in answer to this question there has never been any variation and scarcely any evolution in teaching. The ways of formulating and explaining this teaching have evolved, but not the doctrine itself.

Theologians have never said, "Homicide is always evil because God has said 'Increase and multiply,' but because He has said 'You may not kill the innocent.' "

Similarly they have not said that contraception is evil because God has said 'Increase and multiply,' but because they have considered it in some way analogous to homicide. In every age it is clearly evident that contraception essentially offends against the negative precept: "One may not deprive the conjugal act of its natural power for the procreation of new life."

Majority's Rebuttal

Today, no one holds that the solemn declaration of the encyclical "Casti Connubii" constitutes a true doctrinal definition. This is by no means an apostolic tradition or an attestation of faith, but merely the tradition of teaching formulated in diverse ways at divers times.

Little by little, the church has freed herself from this inadequate concept of nature and the natural law. The teaching of the Second Vatican Council affrmed the great importance of the expression of conjugal love through intercourse and especially the virtuous exercise of responsibility in determining the number of children.

The reason for seriously rethinking the traditional teaching on the illicit contraceptive intervention as regards each and every conjugal act is based on various things: the social change in marriage; in the family; in the position of woman; the diminution of infant mortality; advance in physiological, biological, psychological and sexological knowledge; a changed estimation of the meaning of sexuality and conjugal relations; but especially a better perception of the responsibility of man for humanizing the gifts of nature and using them to bring the life of man to greater perfection.

It is more and more evident today that in man sexual relations in marriage are raised to the expression of a mutual personal giving. Intercourse materially considered carries with it some orientation toward fecundation, but this finality must be rationally directed by man according to the measure and conditions of human love, size of family, educational need, etc. Fecundation must be a personal human act (deliberate, responsible for its effects, etc.). With the progress of knowledge, man can exercise this dominion and ought to exercise it with responsibility.

It is the duty of man to perfect nature (or to order it to the human good expressed in matrimony) but not to destroy it. When man intervenes in the procreative process, he does this with the intention of regulating, and not excluding, fertility.

The rhythm method is very deficient. Besides, only 60 per cent of women have a regular cycle. Intervention ought to be done in a way more conformed to the expression of love and to the respect for the dignity of the partner.

Editor's Note: *On March 28, 1967, the fifth encyclical of Pope Paul VI as made public by the Vatican in translation from the Latin, contained the following comment on the population problem:*

"Populorum Progressio" (1967)

Demography

It is true that too frequently an accelerated demographic increase adds its own difficulties to the problems of development: The size of the population increases more rapidly than available resources, and things are found to have reached apparently an impasse. From that moment the temptation

From Pope Paul VI, *Populorum Progressio,* translated from Latin, *The New York Times,* March 29, 1967.

is great to check the demographic increase by means of radical measures. It is certain that public authorities can intervene, within the limit of their competence, by favoring the availability of appropriate information and by adopting suitable measures, provided that these be in conformity with the moral law and that they respect the rightful freedom of married couples. Where the inalienable right to marriage and procreation is lacking, human dignity has ceased to exist. Finally, it is for the parents to decide, with full knowledge of the matter, on the number of their children, taking into account their responsibilities toward God, themselves, the children they have already brought into the world, and the community to which they belong. In all this they must follow the demands of their own conscience enlightened by God's law authentically interpreted, and sustained by confidence in him.

· · ·

Editor's Note: *Throughout the nineteenth century and the first part of the twentieth century the major organs of the Protestant churches officially condemned contraception. The first decisive action to the contrary was taken by the Bishops of the Anglican Church in the Lambeth Conference of 1930, reversing the stand taken in a similar conference ten years earlier. While agreeing that procreation is "the primary end of marriage" and that, where there is "a clearly felt obligation to limit or avoid parenthood," complete abstinence from sexual relations is the "primary and obvious method," nevertheless, they went on to adopt by a vote of 193 to 67 a resolution that if there be a morally sound reason for avoiding abstinence, "other methods may be used, provided that this is done in the light of Christian principles."*

A Protestant's View
THE RT. REV. JAMES A. PIKE (1962)

For many years Roman Catholics and most Protestants shared the view that the primary purpose of the sexual relationship was the procreation of children. According to this line of reasoning, any use of the sexual act which does not have at least the possibility of procreation within it is a perversion of that act. It is upon this premise that the present Roman Cath-

From James A. Pike, "A Protestant's View," *Our Crowded Planet: Essays on the Pressures of Population,* edited by Fairfield Osborn, Doubleday and Company, Garden City. Copyright © 1962 by Doubleday and Company. Reprinted by permission.

olic position on contraception is built, as was the previous position of many Protestant groups.

However, in recent years, Protestants have been reexamining the nature of the sexual relationship, particularly in the light of sacramental theology, and many Protestant theologians are no longer able to accept the premise that procreation is the only primary function of the sex act. One sometimes hears the statement that there are at least two "primary functions"—which, of course, is only an ungrammatical way of saying that there is no *primary* function. According to this view, the sex act is a sacramental means of expressing love between a man and a woman, in which "the twain become one flesh." Under certain circumstances this act may result in procreation, but even if it does not, the sacramental nature of marriage has been expressed therein. A sacrament is an outward and visible sign of an inward and spiritual grace. The sex act can be this and like other sacramental actions is both "symbol" (in this case, of the inward love and commitment already there) and a "means of grace" (that is, a means of strengthening and "refueling" the binding love). It should be noted that this position differs markedly from that of those who say that the sex act has only the two functions of procreation and "pleasure"; for pleasure—simply as such —is essentially a selfish aim. Surely the relationship which is consummated in the sex act is far too deep and meaningful to be summed up in the word "pleasure." This would be, at least, the position of many Protestant theologians today.

With this premise as a starting point, the Protestant theologian then is able to consider those circumstances under which the act should or should not result in procreation. He is able to bring to bear upon this problem the whole range of the Christian doctrine of vocation, i.e., responsibility, and finally to declare that a married couple has a Christian responsibility in this area as in many others, namely, that of doing the will of God as they understand it. Thus, it would be perfectly proper for a couple to decide, before God, that they should at a given time make every effort to increase their family, and their so doing would be responsible behavior— and their failing to do so would be irresponsible. But by the same token it would be possible for them to decide that, because of circumstances beyond their control, or because of a real conviction as to God's will for them, they should *not* be increasing their family at a certain time; and then it would become incumbent upon them, not only permissibly but as a positive duty, to take such steps as are necessary to avoid having children. Some theologians would go even further, and say that given a couple who have decided that according to their best insights they should not be having children, this couple would then be guilty of positive irresponsibility if they did *not* use the best methods available to prevent conception. If they were convinced that artificial contraceptives represented for them the best method available, they would actually have a religious imperative to use these devices.

It is hard for one to speak of a "Protestant position," and it would be only honest to say that the "Protestant position" as it exists in the mid-twentieth century extends all the way from a position indistinguishable from that of the Roman Catholic Church, through the position stated immediately above, to one simply of "liberty"—which is not the same as the view of responsibility stated above. I do think it accurate to say, however, that the main stream of Protestant theological thought is in the direction herein indicated and is expressed in a recent statement of the National Council of Churches and in previous declarations of principal churches.

It should also be reemphasized that, so far as I am able to ascertain, no Protestant thinker on this subject feels bound by any one solution to the population problem. I myself have been active in proposals that the Federal Government join in research aimed toward making more effective the so-called "rhythm system" which is acceptable to Roman Catholics. All of the methods have in common the drawback that they are exceedingly difficult to teach to a backward population; and it may be that, if it could be made more accurate, the rhythm system would be easiest of all to bring into widespread use—and also would eliminate in our own country the political barriers in the way of technical assistance to overpopulated countries desiring our help.

By the same token, every effort must be made in the fields of economics, agronomy, etc., to make the world habitable for a greater population. Even were the entire population of the world to accept the necessity for artificial limitation of population, we are well on our way toward that "infinite explosion" which scientists tell us will occur early in the twenty-first century. In other words, we are all aware that an enlightened view on the use of contraceptives cannot do the job alone, and that we are merely wasting time when we debate with one another the relative merits of the different systems. All possibilities must be considered and probably all of them must be brought into play if the real danger is to be met with any sort of responsibility.

Protestants generally, too, have felt quite strongly the responsibility which accrues to mankind in bringing about a solution to this problem, since man has himself to thank for the problem in the first place. Even a few generations ago the whole concept of a "Population Explosion" would have been ridiculous, for we were so far from approaching the maximum number which the earth could support. However, with no thought that we were disturbing the "natural order," we have taken tremendous strides in what might be called "death control." We have increased the life span of people all around the world, we have succeeded in wiping out many of the most pressing problems which have beset us and which, to some extent, helped to control the population, and we have done these things in the name of mercy and concern for others. These things should have been done. There was no excuse for the average life-span, e.g., of the Indian, which was less than thirty years. But by changing this, we have contributed to the population problem. We must now attack it with the same single-mindedness and the same effectiveness that we used earlier upon such problems as famine and disease.

Finally, the problem is one which depends for its solution upon a far wider measure of education than has yet been allowed for. None of us wants to see the Orwellian state of *1984,* in which government will be charged with telling each family how many children it can have. There will always be families without children and families with twelve or fourteen. However, as whole populations begin to see the problem for what it is, and begin to understand their responsibilities toward it, we may hope that an increased measure of responsibility will begin to make itself felt in various national birth rates. It may well be that some solution other than any we have thought of will present itself before the problem becomes finally critical, but the time is short; indeed, if our demographers can be trusted, it is running out. There is little more time for argument, and unless firm action is taken soon, it may well be too late to act at all.

Responsible Parenthood and the Population Problem
RICHARD M. FAGLEY (1960)

Report of an international study group on "Responsible Parenthood and the Population Problem," convened at the instance of officers of the World

Council of Churches and the International Missionary Council, which met at Mansfield College, Oxford, April 12–15, 1959.

Included in the study group were the following: Dr. Norman Goodall, London, Chairman; Dr. Thérèse Chausse, M.D., Geneva; Dean William G. Cole, Williamstown, Mass.; Dr. Egbert de Vries, The Hague; Canon G. R. Dunstan, London; Miss Freda H. Gwilliam, London; Dr. Irene Ighodaro, M.D., Ibadan, Nigeria; Prof. A. D. Mattson, Rock Island, Illinois; Mrs. Asuncion Perez, Cabanatuan City, Philippines; Dr. Heinz G. Renkewitz, Arnoldshain, Germany; The Rt. Rev. John Sadiq, Bishop of Nagpur, India; The Rev. Ingmar Stoltz, Stockholm; The Very Rev. Archimandrite E. Timiadis, Geneva; Prof. H. Van Oyen, Basel; Dr. Elizabeth J. Welford, M.B., D.R.C.O.G., London; Dr. Richard M. Fagley, New York, Secretary. Consultants included Dr. Harold Anderson, M.D.; Dr. Madeleine Barot; Dr. R. A. Dudley; Mr. Denys L. Munby; Mr. B. Ch. Sjollema.

The fourth section of the report, dealing with procedural recommendations to the officers of the parent bodies, is omitted here.

I. *The Contemporary Setting*

1. It has become a truism to speak of a world in crisis. The struggle for self-determination, for dignity and freedom of peoples round the globe, the economic and technological revolution and the emerging of a world-wide industrial society, these are a few of the facts with which we must learn to live.

2. The larger crisis of our time is reflected in families throughout the whole wide earth. Different regions and different nations produce varying problems, but nowhere is the family unaffected. It, too, is in crisis. The emancipation of women and the growing acceptance of partnership between men and women are revolutionizing the previously masculine-dominated social structures which now appear so patently unjust. Under pressures within and without, age-old patterns of family relations are disintegrating on every side. Out of the ruins of the old must be built the new, but built on foundations of respect and dignity and freedom, not of servitude, injustice and conflict.

3. The rapid improvement and extension of much-needed public health programmes in all continents are bringing dramatic reductions in death rates, particularly in areas where high fertility has hitherto been offset by a tragically high mortality. The world confronts a doubling of the present

number of people before the end of this century, and is presently experiencing an annual increase of 50 million persons. While the effects of the mounting population pressures are felt throughout the world, the main thrust is occurring in the economically less developed regions of the earth, and indeed may be intensified by the first stages of industrialization. The crisis here stems less from the size of the human increase in relation to potential resources, than from the rapidity of the increase in relation to the present and practicable rate of development of available resources.

4. The social, political, economic and even religious repercussions of this population explosion are vast and grave. Its shock waves buffet countless human families. Nor is there an easy or quick solution to this crisis. Indeed, it seems probable that only a wise combination of vigorous economic and social development aided by substantial technical and financial assistance, the easing of certain pressures by means of migration, the wide development of education, as well as the extension of "family planning" can hope to offer an acceptable answer.

5. Living in such a world and confronted with such problems the Church bears her continuing witness that God is at work, as He has been since the dawn of creation. The Church has survived past times of troubles and stands fast in faith toward the future. The concern of Christian faith for the family is not a new one, born out of the travails of the present. From the very beginning the Church has seen itself as the Family of families, and has known that the Christian witness is necessary and effective in the home, in the relationships between husband and wife, between parents and children. Throughout the centuries Christians have sought to relate the eternal truths of the Gospel to the problems and perils of their times. Yet it must be confessed that in the past Christian thought has, especially in the area of the family and its relationships, often clung to tradition without taking into account new knowledge. In the current age, God is calling upon us not to desert the eternal Christian truth, but to apply it to the changing circumstances of the modern world.

6. We recognize the wide dimensions of the challenge, social, political, economic, medical and educational, and we welcome the fact that various agencies, national and international, are devoting their attention to them. Responsible parenthood does not in itself provide a solution to all problems of social and economic development, including the certainty of rapidly increasing world population. The application of science and technical progress in agriculture and industry and the maintenance of peace and

international co-operation will have to play a major role. On the other hand, no acceptable solution seems in sight without responsibility taken by individual parents. In this short report, we attempt to offer what seem to us some fundamental Christian principles on which those who are in Christ many base their personal decisions in faith and not in fear. The family embodies the most intimate of all personal relations and has a rightful privacy of its own, but in these days of annihilated distances and common cause the Christian family must open itself to the wider claims of the world and learn to live responsibly in the love of God, the grace of our Lord Jesus Christ and the communion of the Holy Spirit.

II. Contributions Toward an Ecumenical Consensus

7. We have been impressed and encouraged by the evidence of a growing sense of responsibility for the family on the part of churches and councils in the ecumenical movement. Within the past decade there have been a number of important statements on Christian marriage and parenthood, and additional studies are being undertaken. A compendium of quotations from documents received is appended to this report.[1]

8. Particular reference should be made to the 1958 Lambeth Conference Report and related resolutions, on "The Family in Contemporary Society," and to the preparatory volume under the same title. The ecumenical movement as a whole is indebted to this undertaking for the serious way in which the problems of the family have been approached and for the substantive contribution made to a Christian response.

9. The degree of agreement found in the available statements of various communions is striking, and indeed significant in terms of a prospective consensus within the ecumenical movement. Yet we are also mindful of the partial character of the evidence so far received. Our information is incomplete and the known silence of important Christian bodies may have diverse meanings. We have in mind in this connection the Orthodox Church, the churches and councils in many parts of Asia, Africa and Latin America, churches in Communist countries, as well as some of the churches in the West. The action of the W.C.C. Central Committee at Galyatetö (1956) in recognizing the need for more serious ecumenical consideration and study of the population problem, and the related question of family planning, is still highly relevant.

1. Not included here.

10. These facts, however, do not minimize the import of the beginnings that have been made. The combined testimony of the churches that have spoken provides a thesis for future ecumenical study and action. It may be well to note briefly a few of the recurrent themes in the statements at hand, which indicate their common tenor.

> There is repeated stress on the spiritual character of true matrimony, expressed in physical union and transcending it. The "two become one" is part of God's grace, to be accepted as a mystery and lived in faith.

> The family likewise is surrounded by grace. Children are the gift of God, and procreation is sharing in God's creation.

> Christian marriage and family life are consequently described in terms of responsibility; the mutuality of husband and wife, the loving care of parents for children, the love and respect of children for parents, the duties of the family in the service of society, the obligations of all to God and His Church. There is repeated emphasis on the applicability of principles of stewardship to procreation within the marriage bond, and on the duty of the Church to inculcate such principles.

> True marriage and parenthood are seen at the same time to be part of the realm of Christian freedom. This means freedom from sensuality and selfishness which enslave. It also means considerable latitude of choice, when the motives are right, in regard to mutually acceptable and non-injurious means to avert or defer conception. Marital freedom, indeed, is the pre-condition of marital responsibility.

11. The principles embodied in the available statements provide significant material for further work by the churches, councils and agencies of the ecumenical movement. To aid that process, we advance considerations which, despite possible differences as to detail, and except as noted below,[2] find general assent among the members of this study group.

III. *The Meaning of Responsible Parenthood*

12. Marriage as a divine institution can be described in Biblical terms as a covenanted relationship within which man and woman receive the grace, security and joy promised by God to those who are faithful to it. Marriage

2. The historic and doctrinal position of the Orthodox Church necessitates, at certain important points, a different approach to this subject from that reflected in the general course of this statement. The Orthodox member of the group, while sharing the concern of the group and contributing fully to its deliberations, drew attention to "the different teaching and practice of the Orthodox Church, which holds that parents have not the right to prevent the creative process of matrimonial intercourse; also, that God entrusted to them this responsibility for childbearing, with full confidence that His Providence would take care of material and other needs."

is the "great mystery" which yet illumines for men the covenant or marriage of Yahweh with Israel (Hos. 2:19f.), and of Christ with His Bride, the Church (Eph. 5:23–33; Rev. 21:9, 22:17).[3]

13. The Christian marriage relationship is a covenant, entered into with sacrifice in the joyful giving of each to the other; it is confirmed by the exchange of vows to which God's promised blessing is attached; it has its own rules or commandments related by God's ordinance to the nature of man and woman and to the relationship between them. Like every other part of human life, it is redeemed by Christ, it is preserved by His forgiveness, it is enriched beyond human measure by the Holy Spirit dwelling in the husband and wife as members of the Body of Christ, the Church.

14. Thus the covenanted relationship of husband and wife within marriage, is, in the purpose of God, one of total commitment, a total giving of self and a total acceptance of the other, resulting in a union, spiritual and physical, described in the Bible as becoming "one flesh." The terms of this union are not those of a human contract. In the Biblical narration the ordinance of marriage is integrated with the very creation of man and woman as such; so its terms, as given by God, are proper to the nature of man and woman, and to the nature of their union. Companionship and parenthood are therefore established together as the purposes of marriage from the beginning, with sexual union as the ordained servant of both. Marriage has its fulness where both are attained (Gen. 2:18–25; Matt. 19:4ff.; 13ff.).

15. The social, cultural and economic circumstances surrounding marriage and family life vary widely from region to region and from age to age. The formation of the family, and of companionship within it, varies accordingly; so does the area of life open to personal decision. The gift of dominion to mankind, within the created order of which mankind is part (Gen. 1:28), reinforced by the command to man to love the Lord God with all his mind (Lk. 10:27), calls upon us to extend this area of decision in humble accordance with our knowledge. Knowledge is thus a liberating gift of God, to be used for the glory of God, in accordance with His will for men. Such use of improved medical knowledge has brought a drastic reduction of infant mortality, and this is to be accepted gratefully as coming from God; at the same time it affects deeply the size of the family and the rate of population growth, and has therefore created a new area for responsible decision.

16. Our concern is therefore with the responsible use of knowledge in

3. Biblical references are from the Revised Standard Version by permission.

family life, particularly in relation to the procreation and nurture of children. A knowledge of the relation of sexual love to the procreative process gives to a couple the power, and therefore the responsibility, to lift the begetting of children out of the realm of biological accident, or "fate," into the realm of personal decision—which is also the realm of grace, where man is free to wait upon God and consciously to respond to His will. Carried further, it enables husband and wife to decide, within the Providence of God, whether any one act of intercourse shall be for the enrichment or expression of their personal relationship only, or for the begetting of a child also.

17. That these two purposes of the act are thus separable, within the divine ordinance of the marriage covenant, is evident from the nature of the act itself, which is known to fulfil the first when it is incapable of fulfilling the second, either through sterility, or in times of periodic infertility and after the age of childbearing in woman. Sexual intercourse within marriage has in itself a goodness given by God, even when there is neither the possibility nor the immediate intention to beget children.

18. Given this responsibility of choice, founded upon knowledge, what considerations are to guide a Christian husband and wife in the exercise of it? They would surely begin with the general ordinance of God for the marriage covenant, integrating the power of parenthood with the expression of sexual love; so parenthood will be normal and right for them, unless there are specific and compelling indications against it, as, for example, a valid threat to the wife's life or health.

19. This obligation—or fulfilment—accepted, the questions may remain, "How many children?," "At what intervals?" Here the considerations involve:

a. *the integrity of the marriage:* every decision should be a joint one of husband and wife, made in faith and prayer and after deliberation in love.

b. *the claims of children as persons in their own right:* they are to be valued, not primarily as economic or social assets or even to assure the comfort of parents in old age or (as is believed in some Asian societies) their beatitude after death; but as persons with a right to parental care in infancy and youth and to a proper equipment from society to serve God fully in it themselves.

c. *the witness of a Christian family in society:* the Christian family, as a cell in the Body of Christ, has a unique vocation and power to exhibit the fruit of the Spirit, often in what are humanly regarded as the most adverse physical conditions—a witness especially needed in a non-Christian or sub-Christian society. To say this is in no way to deny the complementary witness of celibacy, to which the Christian life adds new power and significance in many societies.

d. *the needs of the social order of which the family forms part:* there are factors of special urgency in regions where rapid multiplication of population co-exists with poverty, insufficient supplies of food and other necessities of life, and a low potential for rapid economic development; responsible parenthood has to take account of these.

e. *Church tradition:* when deciding in conscience, Christians would have proper regard to the teaching or tradition, if any, of their own church, and then offer their own decision to God in faith.

20. What considerations should guide parents in the means they employ for the responsible exercise of their procreative power? Responsible parenthood begins with responsible marriage. Biological maturity alone is not the only criterion of readiness for marriage. Life in the Christian community ought to have prepared the young man and woman to raise their sexual relationship above the domination of mere biological impulse, and to have dominion over it. Further, in the life of grace, not only chastity before marriage but also periodic continence within it, when freely accepted by both the spouses, are virtues of positive worth attainable by Christian people.

21. But this is by no means the whole of the answer. The extremely high rates of abortion in many regions, Eastern and Western, with their toll of human suffering and violation of personality, testify to a tragic determination among parents to find some means, however bad, to prevent unwanted births. The Christian conscience cannot approve of abortion, involving as it does the destruction of human life—unless, of course, the termination of a pregnancy is necessary to save the life of the mother.

22. "Life," however, does not begin until the sperm has fertilized the ovum and conception has taken place. Knowing this, what means may Christians properly employ to prevent an individual act of intercourse from resulting in conception? Granted that the attempt may rightfully be made, there appears to be no moral distinction between the means now known and practiced, by the use whether of estimated periods of infertility, or of

artificial barriers to the meeting of sperm and ovum—or, indeed, of drugs which would, if made effective and safe, inhibit or control ovulation in a calculable way. It remains that the means employed be acceptable to both husband and wife and in Christian conscience, and that, on the best evidence available, they do neither physical nor emotional harm. Here we would quote some words of a Committee of the Lambeth Conference of the Bishops of the Anglican Communion of 1958:

> It must be emphasized once again that family planning ought to be the result of thoughtful and prayerful Christian decision. Where it is, Christian husbands and wives need feel no hesitation in offering their decision humbly to God and following it with a clear conscience. The *means* of family planning are in large measure matters of clinical and aesthetic choice, subject to the requirement that they be admissible to the Christian conscience. Scientific studies can rightly help, and do, in assessing the effects and the usefulness of any particular means; and Christians have every right to use the gifts of science for proper ends.

23. In conclusion we may quote also Resolution 115 of the same Conference, based on the report of this Committee:

> The Conference believes that the responsibility for deciding upon the number and frequency of children has been laid by God upon the consciences of parents everywhere: that this planning, in such ways as are mutually acceptable to husband and wife in Christian conscience, is a right and important factor in Christian family life and should be the result of positive choice before God. Such responsible parenthood, built on obedience to all the duties of marriage, requires a wise stewardship of the resources and abilities of the family as well as a thoughtful consideration of the varying population needs and problems of society and the claims of future generations.

24. It is to be observed that such deliberation, and such estimation of human, spiritual and social values, as has been outlined above, is well nigh impossible in some of the regions where they are most urgently required. Where there is grinding poverty, a high birth rate, high death rate and high infant mortality, a fatalistic attitude to birth as to death is almost inevitable, and a high valuation of human personality is difficult to attain. Christians in wealthier regions have a duty to ponder, and to act upon, this truth in order to help their fellows in less developed lands towards conditions in which they can enjoy the freedom to make personal decisions of this sort, and to exercise responsible parenthood for themselves. To secure this help, the Christian is led by his faith to consider such matters as the need for

capital investment and hence his opportunities as a citizen for political action. The command to love thy neighbour as thyself (Lev. 19:18; Lk. 10:27) is thus relevant at all points: it defines the duty of spouse to spouse; of parents to their children and of children to parents; of families to other families in society; of churches to churches; and of nations to nations.

Sex and the Meaning of Marriage

Comments on Sex

DONALD CULROSS PEATTIE (1935)

It is a startling bit of intelligence for the moralists, but the fact seems to be that sex is a force not necessarily concerned with reproduction; back in the primitive one-celled animals there are individuals that fuse without reproducing in consequence; the reproduction in those lowly states is but a simple fission of the cell, a self-division. It seems then that reproduction has, as it were, fastened itself on quite another force in the world; it has stolen a ride upon sex, which is a principle in its own right. . . .

A long survey of the ascent of sex has shown all who ever made it that the purpose of this awe-inspiring impulse is nothing more, nor less, than the enrichment of life. Reproduction purely considered gets on a great deal better without anything so chancy as mating. What sex contributes to it is the precious gift of variation, as a result of commingling. And as variety is the spice of life, it has come to be—thanks to the invitation of sex which creatures accept with such eagerness—one of life's chief characteristics. Thus sex is what the lover has always wished to believe, a worthy end in itself.

From Donald Culross Peattie, *An Almanac for Moderns*. G. P. Putnam's Sons, New York. George Allen & Unwin Ltd., London. Copyright 1935 by Putnam's & Coward-McCann. Reprinted by permission.

Sex and Reproduction

H. G. WELLS, J. HUXLEY, AND G. P. WELLS (1934)

If we trace very briefly its evolution, and show how it presents itself among the simpler forms of life, we shall discover a fact which to us vertebrates seems startling—that essentially sex is not reproductive. *It is a different thing from reproduction.*

In the bacteria there is no sex. There is simply sexless proliferation. The creatures divide and divide by binary fission, by tearing themselves into halves, and as far as we can see they get on perfectly well without any form of sexual union. Thus the simplest living things today; and thus, presumably, life began.

Among the microscopic single-celled animals and plants we see the beginnings of sexual union. We see it appearing as a new intrusive process, perfectly distinct from reproductive proliferation, interrupting and delaying the latter and in its essence antagonistic to it. In the simplest flagellates, for example, the organisms multiply by binary fission just as bacteria do, but their life-history is complicated by a contrary tendency. Occasionally, if we are watching the creatures through a microscope, two individuals may be seen to come together and to melt completely into one. It is, of course, a much rarer event than normal fission—otherwise the species would not increase—and the individuals taking part in conjugation, as this union is called, often come from different and not very closely related stocks. And it is as obviously unrelated to reproduction as are feeding or excretion.

In other kinds of protozoa the process is varied in divers ways. In the highly organized Ciliates, for example, two individuals come to lie side by side and then exchange bits of their nuclei. Here the fusion does not involve the whole organism, but, nevertheless, there is a definite mixing of material from different strains. Here also the process is anti-reproductive, because it occupies time which might be spent in the normal rhythm of growth and fission; actually the act of union takes about as long as would three generations of ordinary fission.

From H. G. Wells, J. Huxley, and G. P. Wells, *The Science of Life,* Doubleday and Company, New York, Cassell & Co., Ltd., London, 1934. Reprinted by permission of Professor G. P. Wells, Sir Julian Huxley, and the publishers.

In the simpler many-celled animals and plants—the slime-fungi, for example, or the seaweeds—the gradual entanglement of sex with reproduction can be seen. They reproduce by liberating clusters of tiny dancing flagellated cells whose business is to grow into new individuals. But before they do so these cells generally come together in pairs and melt into one. Here then the business of sexual conjugation is relegated to the reproductive cells. Their reproductive value is evidently diminished by this process which halves their number; but it has another compensating purpose, for the members of conjugating pairs are usually from different parents, and so it affords a method for the actual blending of living material from different stocks.

From these lowly plants we can trace a series of stages leading up to the state of affairs that is found in ourselves. In all the higher animals and plants the essence of the process is the same—the reproductive cells have to melt together before they can give rise to new individuals; they are called, therefore, *gametes,* or marrying cells. These gametes are usually of two kinds—active smaller male gametes or sperm-cells and passive larger female gametes or egg-cells. There is every gradation in this inequality. We may have quite equal cells conjugating or we may find very considerable inequality in the size of the conjugating cells. Thus, in the simplest phase of the sexual process there is neither male nor female; there is a sexual process without distinction of sex.

But as a further development of the appearance of the differentiation of the conjugating elements into larger and smaller there presently appears a differentiation of the parent bodies into those producing active and those producing larger conjugating cells. These are the incipient phases of sexual differentiation.

In plants, and in the lowest animals in which sex is thus entangled with reproduction, the sexual method exists, as an alternative to asexual, but in higher forms such as vertebrata reproduction is exclusively sex-ridden. Before we can produce new individuals there has to be this actual mixing of the substance of two parents. Even in our own species this is plainly an anti-reproductive thing, for if we could proliferate asexually it would take only one to do what now needs two, and we could multiply twice as fast. Thus, in the course of Evolution the two originally distinct and antagonistic processes have come together and become inseparably blended.

Evidently there is a riddle here, and one of very profound importance.

There must be something very important about this sexual process, this mixing of the stuff of different stocks.

. . .

In a word, sexual union is good in plants and animals alike, because it affords a method of variation. By shuffling about the mutations that appear, by combining them in various ways and presenting the results to Natural Selection, it lends efficiency and speed to the evolutionary process.

Sexual union is essentially the pooling of the mutation-experience of two lines of descent. A useful mutation is a precious event, not too frequent; the sex machinery keeps up a continual mixing and interweaving of germ-plasm strands so that these treasures can be preserved and combined to the best possible advantage.

Such seems to be the clue to our riddle. Sex is forced upon organisms because they reproduce so fast, because of that Malthusian population-pressure that compels them . . . to compete and seize every advantage. Moreover, it is precisely because mutation is a casual random process that the continual juggling machinery of sex is so important. It allows the race to get the most out of its mutations. That is why conjugation interrupts the normal proliferation of protozoa every now and then. That is why in large and elaborately organized individuals like ourselves, which reproduce themselves comparatively infrequently, sexual union is entangled with every reproductive act.

Marriage is essentially a new state to which God calls man, not for natural needs but for deeper needs. . . . Consequently, procreation is neither the purpose nor essential element of marriage. The children who ensue can add something, but marriage is fully sufficient without children, being given its spiritual purpose as its principal end.

Jacques Ellul

"We two form a multitude." Ovid.

"We two form a multitude." Ovid.

"We two form a multitude." Ovid.

"We two form a multitude." Ovid.

Social Customs as They Affect Fertility

Attitudes and Practices Affecting Fertility

FREDERICK OSBORN (1958)

European Experience

The traditional social structure, the culture, and the historical development of western Europe enabled its population to enter the era of rapid technical advance with (1) a lower initial ratio of population to resources than many Asian nations possess today, (2) lower initial fertility, (3) a social structure amenable to entrepreneurial activity and social change. It also promoted (4) an approach to personal relations between men and women that may have influenced later trends in the control of fertility.

The folk culture of medieval Europe included many elements that limited the operation of values favorable to high fertility. Social conditions did not require universal marriage, or impel men and women to have children as early as possible, or provide rewards for large families. On the contrary, there were very considerable impediments against a realization of the full reproductive capacity of the population.

The primary unit in the social organization of European villages was the nuclear family, formed through the marriage of a man and a woman and including, as dependents, only their own children, along with any relatives deprived of support. This kind of family unit is in contrast to the extended or joint family common in Asian cultures. The emphasis on the nuclear family in Europe was in line with the individualistic legal and religious principles of late Hellenistic, late Hebraic, and early Christian cultures.

Each man at marriage became responsible for the support of his wife and of any children that might be born to them. It was commonly assumed that a man could not properly marry until he was in a position to discharge these responsibilities. Neither his parental family nor any larger kinship group regarded his children as their children or shared full responsibility for their nurture.

There was, in fact, strong social pressure against "improvident marriages." Sons who were assured of inheriting a living on the land were not encouraged to take wives while they were still young. Those who entered military orders had to postpone marriage, and those who entered religious orders had to forego marriage altogether. At the lower end of the social scale, servants and retainers were expected to remain single; there were often rules against the marriage of domestics. Edicts against the marriage of paupers were issued in many of the German states during the sixteenth and seventeenth centuries.

The economic pressure operating through this social system in medieval times was the limitation of land resources. The use of a plot of land of at least minimum size was needed to provide a living for each peasant family; and new lands could be brought into use only by slow degrees. At a later time, this pressure of limited resources gradually gave way to a desire for better houses, better clothing, better food, and the satisfaction of new interests which equally contributed to the postponement of marriage.

The average age of brides at first marriage in France in the late eighteenth century was about 25 years, and this average figure has remained fairly constant up to the last few years. Even around 1930, 38 per cent of all women aged 25 to 29 years old were still unmarried in the Netherlands, 41 per cent in England, 48 per cent in Switzerland, and 52 per cent in Norway—in contrast to 1 per cent in Korea, 2 per cent in India, 4 per cent in Formosa, and 8.5 per cent in Japan. The comparable figure for Ireland, in 1941, was 63.5 per cent.

Birth rates in Europe in the eighteenth century, prior to the commercial and industrial revolutions and the marked decline of fertility under modern conditions, were significantly lower than in most other parts of the world —not much above 30 per thousand in the Scandinavian countries, and between 30 and 40 per thousand throughout western Europe. A difference of 5 or 10 points per thousand is not striking in comparison with the wide variation in birth rates now found among various nations and among various classes within a nation. But, as death rates decline, such a difference in fertility has an important effect on rates of natural increase (determined by the excess of births over deaths).

In contrast to Asian cultures where there is little provision for intimate association outside the family between men and women in work and play, young men and women in Europe (except in the upper classes where maidens were zealously chaperoned) worked together in the fields and joined in village festivals during the long years between puberty and marriage. Many of these men and women became deeply attached to one another. But European culture firmly discouraged maternity out of wedlock. Even where community sentiments were relatively lax, the unmarried mother embarrassed her family and forced them to assume an unwelcome burden.

Community sentiment expected men to respect the interests of women; the men usually must have had some concern to protect women whom they loved from shame. Thus through many centuries the European culture posed difficult problems in personal relations for couples deeply bound by emotional ties but unable to marry. They might at one extreme avoid all erotic association, or at the other ignore all inhibitions. Probably most chose some middle course. In this process it is possible that attempts to prevent conception became part of the European mores long before contraception was publicly advocated. The later acceptance of various forms of family limitation may thus have been made easier.

The emphasis in European culture on the nuclear family and the postponement of marriage for prudential reasons provided two possible approaches to a more drastic restriction of births, in response to new motivations. One possible approach was a tightening of the restraints on marriage. This approach was actually followed on a large scale in only one country: Ireland. The response was precipitated suddenly by the potato famine in 1845 and sustained by strong social and religious sentiments.

The alternative was the use of restrictive measures within marriage. This has been the preponderant response, beginning at different times, in all western European countries except Ireland. In the population of the United States contraceptive practices spread gradually, probably in advance of their spread through any country in Europe except France. Increase of contraceptive practice accompanied, step by step, the accelerated decline of fertility in the United States between 1890 and the 1930's.

Modern movements toward restriction of fertility in Europe were, in all cases, spontaneous personal responses under changing social conditions, wholly independent of governmental action. The support given to family limitation practices by organized institutions seems generally to have followed rather than to have initiated popular movements.

The family limitation movement in England was implemented at first mainly by an increased use within marriage of folk methods for preventing pregnancy. But we must not assume that family limitation could have gained the scope and force that it has attained in Europe, the United States, and some other regions, if the control of fertility had not been facilitated by new contraceptive techniques.

Eastern and Southern Asia

In most Asian cultures the traditional family is in principle if not in fact an extended or joint family. Inheritance is patrilineal, and there is a strong emphasis on the unity of the paternal line through successive generations. These cultures prescribe the procreation and nurture of a son who must eventually assume his father's prerogatives; this is often a religious obligation. But there is no moral or religious prescription of unlimited fertility in any of these societies.

A common characteristic of social life in most Asian nations is early marriage. In some South Asian cultures, girls are married about the time of puberty, and childbearing begins soon thereafter. It has been estimated that about 25 per cent of the potential reproductive capacity of women is eliminated by a prevention of pregnancies prior to twenty-five years of age. Thus the traditionally early marriage of women in South Asian societies has been conducive to high fertility.

Child Brides
RITCHIE CALDER (1962)

In Indian Bengal, I was very touched to see little girls carrying babies around and commented, to a Hindu doctor, on this concern for their brothers and sisters. He looked at me to see if I was joking and then realized that I was not.

From Ritchie Calder, *Common Sense About a Starving World,* The Macmillan Company, New York. Copyright © 1962 by Ritchie Calder. Reprinted by permission.

"Not brothers and sisters," he said. "These are their own babies." I then found that the average age for marriage for girls in this district was 12 years and that this was "a decided improvement," on the average a generation ago, when it was 10.

"But," I asked, "isn't there an Act which makes the minimum marriageable age 14?"

The doctor shrugged his shoulders. The Act depended on common informers, and since child marriage was so common there was no one to inform. If anyone had tried to enforce it, he said, it would only mean an increase in illegitimacy, because a girl was regarded as nubile at 10 or even younger. So the fertility rate here was 213 compared with about 50 in Britain. One child in five died before the age of one year and 7 per cent of the babies of teen-age mothers were still-born. The population of this area was 1,900 per square mile. The average age of the population was 23; half the school children were suffering from critical malnutrition and an eighth of the population was chronically ill. The mud houses were shockingly overcrowded and four out of every five families were in the hands of moneylenders.

In adjoining East Bengal (Pakistan), three babies are born every minute and every ninety seconds one dies. In a maternity ward, there were six mothers and during the day I was there, five of them died—including Fatima. "Fatima" one recalls was the favourite daughter of the Prophet Mohammed and this girl—this child—had been called after her. She was lying wide-eyed and expressionless waiting for her baby—for the birth which would kill both her and it. I asked the doctor how old she was. He asked her and bent over her to hear her failing whisper.

"She says 'three babies,' " he told me. "That is the nearest we ever get to their ages. That makes her perhaps 16 or 17."

Fatima died, worn out by child-bearing, at 17. She might not have died if she could have had a blood transfusion, but because *taboo* said that she could only have her husband's blood, and because he was unlikely to give it, and because it was almost certainly the wrong blood group and lethal with infection, she could not have it.

Because she had had three babies, because she had had anaemia due to malaria and malnutrition, and because modern science was not available, Fatima died and her baby died. If she had lived she would have gone on producing more babies, and if her baby had lived, it would have eventually married and produced more babies.

There are the two ruthless schools of thought: one which says that girls like Fatima should go on having children because it is "the will of God," and the other which says that "it is just as well that she and her baby died because they would have put further strains on the world's food supply."

I was scarcely less shocked the following day when I went to a Roman Catholic orphanage. Here were child-victims of communal upheaval—the parentless children of Hindus and Christian Indians. It was a delightful place, where the children were obviously happy—a sanctuary from the stark tragedy of their young lives. In a gala, put on for my benefit, girls of 12, 13 and 14, in the long white saris of puberty, danced and sang and performed *lushai,* that agile, rhythmic skipping with bamboo poles. As we watched them I asked the American nun in charge for what careers she trained the girls. She did not answer and I later repeated the question.

She looked at me disapprovingly and said, "I heard you the first time. It was an improper question. We of course train them for marriage. If we do not get them married by the age of 14 they may never get a husband."

She pointed to an attractive girl of 16.

"Until she was over 14 she was ailing and missed her chance. Now she will be lucky if she gets some old widower."

I found that every Sunday prospective bridegrooms and their parents came down to that orphanage and the girls paraded like mannequins, but it was the girls, not the dresses, which were being traded. Or it could be done by mail-order. I was shown a questionnaire by the nun: "Name of girl. . . . . Age. . . . . Complexion. . . . . Is she obedient? . . . . Is she fit for hard work? . . . . Has she full faith in the Roman Catholic Church? . . . . Is she basic Catholic or convert? . . . . If converted what caste did she belong to previously? . . . ."

When I expressed some natural surprise at a Christian institution condoning child marriage and contriving "blind dates" for matrimony, the nun was indignant and asked whether I expected the Church to go against the customs of the country. These girls matured much earlier than those "back home," and it was right that they should marry and bear children.

As a result, three babies are born every minute, one dies every ninety seconds and the 44,000,000 people of East Pakistan live in abject poverty and soul-destroying hunger.

The truth, and human decency, must lie somewhere between these two ruthless schools of thought, the "will of God" and the mathematicans.

Contrast the populations of Burma and India: Burma is an eighth of the size of India but its population is barely a twentieth. Some population control must be operating. I asked a social worker in Rangoon, How? She pointed out that the women of Burma had been emancipated even back in the times of the Burmese kings. Indeed, at one time there had been polyandry (polygamy, in which the woman chooses several husbands) and women have been basically career women—traders, property owners, lawyers and doctors. This meant that a considerable proportion married late by eastern standards, and thus cut off the earlier years of childbearing.

(Carl Mydans, LIFE Magazine © Time Inc.)

The Family in China: The Classical Form

FRANCIS L. K. HSU (1959)

China has been known as a land of large families where many generations live under the same roof. In reality, the average size of the family in China, as shown by a number of field investigations, consists of approximately five persons. This figure, though it is higher than that of the average United States family today, fails to justify the use of the term big family. Nevertheless, the matter is a more complicated one than a mere question of size. What distinguishes the family in China from that in the United States and some other countries is the pattern or patterns underlying the institution.

The Traditional Chinese Family

The backbone of the family in traditional China is the father-son relationship. Almost every phase of the family can be explained on the basis of, or at least referred to, the glorification of this relationship. The essence of the principle is expressed in a concept familiar to the West: filial piety. As originators of the sons' lives parents are regarded also as the originators of the children's social and financial achievements. While the parents are alive it is the sons' duty to support and obey them; after their death it is the sons' duty to continue the support and obedience by providing proper funerals and entering into ancestor worship.

In the name of filial piety no action is too harsh or too difficult. In the famous Twenty-four High Examples of Filial Piety, transmitted from historical times, we read of a son who lay bare-bodied on ice in deep winter for the purpose of melting the ice because his ailing father wanted to taste some fish; of another man who wept in a bamboo grove until nature responded to his tears so that there would be bamboo shoots for his father's dinner plate; of still another who found hidden treasure in a pit in which he

The author is grateful to Professor M. J. Herskovits for reading this chapter in its galley form and offering valuable suggestions.

attempted to bury his son because he could not afford to support both his aged father and his young son. Some Westerners and many Chinese may say that these stories are but legends which have not the slightest truth. This is beside the point. Even if they are legends they have been dear to the majority of Chinese and are still very much alive among them. . . .

Since the family consists not only of a father-son but also of a husband-wife relationship it is clear that filial piety, in the form we have just recounted, must have far-reaching consequences. In the West, even before the arrival of the Troubadours, marriage was in principle a matter of individual choice. In traditional China, on the other hand, marriage might be determined even before the prospective life partners were born. It began with no courtship but with an agreement between two pairs of parents. Not only was there no contact between the young couple during betrothal, but all public gestures of intimacy, as the West understands them, were regarded as indecent and immoral. Widely circulated in the last imperial dynasty was the report of a certain high official in the Hupei province and his wife who were famous for the mutual respect they publicly manifested toward each other. They lived in separate quarters; before going to his wife's side of the house the husband usually first sent a servant bearing his calling card. Their ceremonious conduct was analogous to that of host and guest.

That such a case was by no means typical is borne out by the fact that it became a subject of public interest and conversation. On the other hand, that such individuals, instead of being regarded as neurotics, were proclaimed as heroes, reveals that their behavior met with public approval. They merely carried to the logical extreme that which was inherent in the socially enjoined marital pattern.

A married woman's duty is first and above all toward her parents-in-law, just as a married man's is primarily toward his parents. Even marriage itself is couched in terms of securing a daughter-in-law and making an addition to the household. A man who suppressed his wife because of his father or mother, and a woman who neglected her husband because of her parents-in-law, would be equally praised; a husband who failed to favor his parents, and a wife her parents-in-law, because of his or her spouse would be condemned.

Observed from the aspect of filial piety, such a pattern of behavior between spouses is necessary. Filial piety calls for complete devotion to the man's parents. It prescribes the pattern of many generations under the same roof. Any behavior originating from romantic ideals tends obviously to hamper the smooth functioning of the father-son relationship as defined and is therefore incompatible with the family organization. Thus the glorification of the father-son relationship is to be achieved at the expense of the husband-wife relationship. This being the established premise, sex inequality in the form of concubinage, male-centered divorce laws, and certain sadistic practices against women such as compulsory widowhood, fall into their proper perspective. Relegated to a secondary role, women exist for the convenience of men. They have no right to immovable property. They are not entitled to school education because their activities are confined to the home. They are compelled to "follow their fathers before their marriage; their husbands after that; and their sons if and when their husbands pass away."

Contrary to the popular conception, however, the father-son relationship is not a unilateral matter in favor of the parents. From the point of view of the family lineage, the roles of the father and his son or sons are complementary to each other. At a given point of time one of them is the father and the other is the son. But in a long range view the father is a son and the son is also a father. The son owes his existence and all to his father, but the father stands in the same relationship, in turn, with the son's grandfather. This is why filial piety describes only part of the facts involved. The pattern underlying the father-son relationship must be approximated by the term father-son identification. For the continuity of the long family line has been of ultimate importance. The sons marry because their parents wish to have daughters-in-law and grandsons, but the older men also owe it to their fathers to see that their young ones are suitably married and in a position to continue the lineage. Not only do the sons owe their all to their fathers, but whatever the fathers possess also automatically belongs to their sons. This automatic sharing refers not only to property, on which no father can make a will in favor of anyone else except his sons, but also to personal qualities and social prestige. In this way the sons of the powerful tend to be automatically as powerful as their fathers, and those of the lowly tend automatically to share their fathers' humble state.

But the matter does not end here. Complete father-son identification means not only that the son's social station is determined by that of his father but also that the social station of the latter is equally determinable by the former. The difference consists only of a matter of time and is expressed fully and effectively by a well-known proverb, "During the first thirty years of a man's life, people look at the father and respect his son; thirty years later people look at the son and respect his father." The father-son relationship, from this point of view, instead of being an encumbrance on the young, provides an incentive for the latter to progress.

Ideal and Reality

If completely carried out, the two complementary patterns—glorification of the father-son relationship and estrangement of the sexes—would make the Chinese an unusual people. It may be possible to find human beings who can cling to their parents throughout life while disregarding their spouses, but the Chinese have not exemplified this system. The ideal picture given above has been modified at various points by compromises. The immediately observable symptom of a compromise is manifested in the size of the family. As pointed out at the beginning of this article, China has been reputed to be a country of large families, yet the average size of the Chinese family as revealed by field investigations all over the country is about 5.3 persons. This small average size cannot be accounted for by any changes which have come about in modern times because such changes are negligible among the vast majority of the peasantry. What then is the explanation?

One reason which may be taken as a point of departure is the close and direct correlation between the size of the farm and that of the household. J. L. Buck's surveys show that on the small farms the average number of persons per household is 4.4; on the medium-sized farms, 5.5; on the medium large farms, 6.9; on the large farms, 8.3; and the very large farms, 10.1.[1]

The prevailing explanation of the phenomenon, however, has been that it represents "a close adjustment between the amount of land and the number of people obtaining a living from it." That the pressure of population has been and is intense in China is not to be denied. But if we consider only this factor we shall be unable to explain why, in spite of the fact that the majority of Chinese farms are below what Buck regarded as the most economic unit for production, families continue to divide.

If we move away a little from the purely economic aspect and look at the phenomenon as a compromise between the social ideal and social reality, we arrive at a more plausible explanation. The social ideal is the glori-

1. J. L. Buck, *Land Utilization in China*, Chicago, 1937, p. 278.

fication of the father-son relationship. Within the confines of the family, its complementary pattern of estrangement between the sexes means the suppression of the husband-wife relationship. But the wealthy and the poor families live up to this social ideal to different degrees. As the author has stated elsewhere, "In the poor family the difficulty of living together is easily aggravated by poverty and often overshadows even the wisdom for continued economic cooperation, so that the more a family needs to keep the land intact the more it tends to divide. Here the husband-wife relationship has greater weight for the additional reason that, for the poor man, to secure a wife is a matter of immediate economic consequence. On the other hand, with the wealthier families the social ideal has more weight because that is the mark of prestige and status. Furthermore, men in such families have no concern about remarriage. When sons and brothers do not actively side with their wives the family can hold out together longer and the father-son relationship has a greater chance."

The differential adherence to the social ideal between rich and poor, not the pressure of population pure and simple, has been the decisive factor in shaping the family size. The differences in family size not only may be caused by differences in the number of children born and surviving but evidently are also affected by the number of collateral kinsmen and their wives and children.

The Family in China: The People's Republic
MORTON H. FRIED (1959)

In the previous article, Francis L. K. Hsu makes clear certain weaknesses in the assertion that the large family was a typical unit in Chinese society. Relying heavily on the monumental work of John Lossing Buck, Hsu notes that available statistics fail to support the common notion. . . .

There is a tendency to interpret the data of Buck . . . [and of other earlier] surveys as reflecting a new situation. According to this viewpoint, the traditional Chinese family *was* large and studies conducted in the twentieth century only show the decline attributable to pernicious Western influ-

From Morton H. Fried, "The Family in China: The People's Republic," *The Family: Its Function and Destiny*, rev. ed., edited by Ruth Nanda Anshen. Copyright 1949 by Harper & Row, Publishers, Incorporated. Copyright © 1959 by Ruth Nanda Anshen. Reprinted by permission.

ences. We are fortunate in attempting to solve this problem to be able to turn to Chinese census material that has been collected for almost two thousand years. This data reveals that average family size of five or six persons has been characteristic for the entire period for which records exist and is in no sense a novelty.[1] Many factors, such as the location of the family in one region of China rather than another, or the political and economic tranquility of the period, affect family size. One of the major variables has been the class status of the persons involved. Large families have been a reality in China but as a social phenomenon the large family has had its locus in a particular class—the gentry.[2] While this class has been relatively small, it has had power and influence entirely disproportionate to its size. A main aspect of this power and influence has been the virtual monopoly of the recording of Chinese history enjoyed by this class. Even in the absence of ulterior motives, there was a tendency for members of this class to assume that the customs and modes of behavior to which *they* were accustomed represented all, or at any rate the very best, of Chinese institutions; they reported accordingly.

The Marriage Law of 1950

Among the great tasks which the Communist government of the People's Republic of China has set itself has been the promulgation of laws and statutes which, at least in theory, will reweave the fabric of Chinese society. The formulation of a new set of ordinances governing marriage and family relations has been a primary part of the reform program; in the eyes of the People's Government this part of the program is equal to, if not of greater importance than, land reform. Seventeen months of study, discussion, and field research preceded the enactment of the Marriage Law of

1. See, for example, Hans Bielenstein, "The Census of China during the Period 2–742 A.D.," *Bulletin of the Museum of Far Eastern Antiquities,* Stockholm, 19 (1947), 125–163. According to this sinologist the average size of households at various points during the 740 years concerned was: 4.7 in 2 A.D. (p. 135); 5.1 in 140 A.D. (p. 139); 5.9 early in the seventh century (p. 145); and 5.8 in 742 A.D. (p. 149).
2. Cf. Fei Hsiao-tung, "Peasantry and Gentry in China," *American Journal of Sociology,* 52 (1946); Fei Hsiao-tung, *China's Gentry,* Chicago, University of Chicago Press, 1953. Some sinologues take exception to Fei's use of the term "gentry" and would restrict it to scholars and others who attained official rank. These sinologues believe that the term has no proper application in post-Imperial times. In that case, our remarks about family size would apply to the gentry, strictly defined, plus non-office-holding landlords of means and successful merchants. See Chang Chung-li, *The Chinese Gentry,* Seattle, University of Washington Press, 1955, especially the Introduction by Franz Michael.

1950. Public presentation was made on May 1st of that year, the date testifying to the symbolic importance of the new law. . . .

> The arbitrary and compulsory feudal marriage system, which is based upon the superiority of man over woman and which ignores the children's interests shall be abolished.
>
> The New Democratic marriage system, which is based on free choice of partners, on monogamy, on equal rights for both sexes, and protection of the lawful interests of women and children, shall be put into effect.[3]

With these words . . . it is made to appear that the reform of Chinese marital and familial practices awaited the triumph of the People's Liberation Army. It is quite true that in some particulars the Marriage Law of 1950 introduces revolutionary changes in marriage and the family. For the most part, however, the fundamental contents of the 1950 law are to be found in the Civil Code of the Republic of China (adopted 1931).[4] This is not to say that the Civil Code of 1931 was implemented in town and country with anything like the fervor with which the provisions of the Marriage Law of 1950 are being applied. The Nationalist Government deserves credit for having adopted the far-reaching provisions of its 1931 family law; in this area, as in the problem of restraining landlords and usurers in their exploitation of the peasantry, the Nationalist Government failed to carry out either the spirit or the letter of its legal provisions in the matter. On the other hand, the zeal of the People's Government in pressing the provisions of the 1950 law has been met, in some areas, with considerable resistance so that the gap between promise and fulfillment plagues the People's Government too, if for different reasons.

It is very difficult to make a précis of the contents of the Marriage Law of 1950 because of the compactness of the document; a mere 12 pages of pamphlet text gives it *in toto*. The major articles are these: bigamy, concubinage, child betrothal, and the exaction of gifts in connection with marriage are prohibited. Widows are encouraged to remarry. Marriage is completely voluntary; no third parties can interfere. Men must be 20 years of age, women 18, to contract marriage. Lineal relatives by blood, siblings, and half-siblings may not marry each other. Sexual impotence, venereal disease, mental disorder, leprosy, and other similar medical conditions ren-

3. *The Marriage Law of the People's Republic of China, op. cit.,* Art. 1, pp. 1–2. Henceforth referred to as MLPRC.
4. *The Civil Code of the Republic of China, Book IV, Family,* translated by C. L. Hsia, James L. E. Chow, Liu Chieh and Yukon Chang, Shanghai, Kelly & Walsh, 1931. Henceforth referred to as CCRC.

der a person unfit for marriage. Husband and wife are equals, sharing a home; they are duty bound to love and care for each other and engage in production. Each has free choice of occupation and may participate freely in social affairs. Each has equal share and voice in family property. Each can use his/her own family name. Parents are duty bound to rear and educate their children who, in turn, must support and assist their parents. Neither shall maltreat or desert the other. Infanticide is strictly prohibited. Children born out of wedlock have full and equal rights. If the natural father can be identified he is charged with support of the child until it attains 18 years of age. Divorces shall be granted when both parties consent. If one opposes, the case must go to mediation and reconciliation must be attempted. Men may not apply for divorce if their wives are pregnant; such suits may be brought only after the child is one year old.

Divorce does not terminate a parent's obligations to a child. Both must continue to provide, though only one is official guardian. Babies being breast-fed shall be given in custody to their mothers. After weaning, the man may seek custody. Provisions are made for sharing support of the child.

After divorce, a wife retains the property she held before marriage and the disposal of the household property is made by agreement, the people's court assisting if necessary. If one of the divorced couple remains unmarried and has difficulties in maintenance, an agreement on alimony should be reached.

National minorities may enact modifications of this law to accord with their own customs but such enactments must be ratified by the Government Administration Council.

The New and the Old Marriage Laws

It is impossible to make a full-scale contrast and comparison of the Marriage Law of 1950 and the relevant portions of the Civil Code of 1931 in the compass of a brief article. Something of a comparison in depth has recently been published by Marius H. Van der Valk,[5] a jurist who has been a student of Chinese family law for more than two decades. Another study of considerable value has been contributed by a sociologist, Mrs. Wen-hui C. Chen.[6] In the present chapter, I shall treat of some major similarities and certain equally significant departures.

5. *Conservatism in Modern Chinese Family Law,* Leiden, E. J. Brill, 1956, issued as vol. 4 of *Studia et Documenta ad Iura Orientis Antiqui Pertinentia.*
6. Wen-hui C. Chen, *The Family Revolution in Communist China,* Research Memo-

The Communists have raised the minimum age of marriage one year for each of the sexes. As we will see, the People's Government is rather unhappy about its minimums and urges its youth to marry at age 25 or later. On the subject of child betrothals the major difference between the two laws is in tone. The Civil Code of 1931 includes an article specifying that "An agreement to marry shall be made by the male and female parties of their own accord." [7] There was further protection against forced marriage in another article which said, "No demand may be made for the specific performance of an agreement to marry." [8] Against these articles is the clear evidence of the number of women who asked for divorce after the revolution and gave forced betrothal as their grounds.

The prohibition on bigamy is no novelty. While concubinage has been commonplace in wealthy families, concubines have always been sharply differentiated from wives in Chinese law.[9] Certainly bigamy was a crime in China as early as the T'ang Dynasty.[10] There is, however, no prohibition of concubinage, per se, in the Civil Code. At best and in the hands of a shrewd lawyer, there are certain articles which might be cited by a concubine as granting her minimal rights.[11] Against this stands the absolute prohibition of concubinage in the 1950 law.

Where the new law explicitly forbids interference with the remarriage of widows, the Nationalist Code was silent but certainly placed no impediments in their way. During the residence of the author in Ch'u Hsien, Anhwei, in 1947 and 1948, he knew several remarried widows, all of them peasant women or the keepers of small shops in the county seat. That there was considerable resistance to the remarriage of widows is again apparent in the number of trouble cases that have arisen from this source since 1949. It is also evident that the People's Government has taken special pains to inform widows of their free status. One of the main techniques has been the arrangement, by the government, of mass weddings for widows.[12]

randum No. 35, Human Resources Research Institute, Maxwell Air Force Base, Alabama, 1955.
7. CCRC, Art. 972, p. 5.
8. CCRC, Art. 975, p. 5.
9. Cf. *Conservatism in Modern Chinese Family Law, op. cit.,* p. 40 ff.
10. *Ibid.,* p. 40. One form of bigamy has given difficulties and still continues to occur, though rarely. I refer to *chien* (or *ch'eng*) *t'iao,* in which a man has inherited leadership in two distinct though related unilineal kin groups, each of which maintains a separate ancestral shrine and rites. Such men often married twice; once in each kinship personality, to give a separate heir to each of the groups he headed. *Ibid.,* p. 44 ff.
11. Cf. CCRC, Art. 1127, p. 44.
12. Wen-hui C. Chen, *op. cit.,* pp. 18–19.

Where the Civil Code continued to stress the patrilineal descent group, the Marriage Law of 1950 makes no acknowledgment of such a group. Several differences between the two codes establish this. Article 1131 of the Civil Code deals with the constitution of the family council, thereby automatically recognizing a body of larger dimensions than the nuclear family; the 1950 law confines all of its provisions to the nuclear family. Article 1131 further specifies that the first order of precedence in succession to the family council goes to lineal ascendants and "among those of the same degree of relationship, the relative of the paternal line comes first." [13] No such privilege or distinction appears in the 1950 law.

Another way in which the Civil Code accommodated the emphasis on patrilineal descent was in the special handling accorded the *chui-fu* (a man who marries with the understanding that he will move into his wife's father's house, take his wife's father's name, and raise his children as the heirs of his father-in-law). No reference to this institution appears in the Marriage Law of 1950

Perhaps the sharpest differences between the two codes occur in the area of relationships within the family. The Civil Code insists that each *chia* must have a head; though sex is not specified (and in Chinese the pronoun of the third person is ambiguous, though not necessarily so), the context strongly suggests that males normally hold the position.[14] The 1950 law states that husband and wife are companions of equal status.[15] Where the Civil Code is silent as to the rights of women, except with regard to their property rights in succession and divorce, the 1950 law devotes several articles to the subject.[16] The Civil Code makes the home of the husband the legal residence but the 1950 law makes no such provision. The Civil Code provided that the wife should prefix her husband's name to her own, "unless otherwise agreed upon." [17] This is somewhat ambiguous but seems generally similar to Article 11 in the 1950 law which gives each party the right to his/her own name.[18] Finally, the Civil Code obligated the couple

13. CCRC, Art. 1131, p. 45.
14. CCRC, Arts. 1123–1125, p. 43.
15. MLPRC, Art. 7, p. 4.
16. MLPRC, Arts. 8–12, pp. 4–5.
17. CCRC, Art. 1000, p. 12.
18. MLPRC, Art. 11, p. 5. The law is silent on the question of the name of the children. The use by married women of their maiden names has been commonplace in Chinese intellectual circles for some time. Married women with children have used their maiden names professionally but do not seem to have questioned the custom of transferring the surname of the father to their children.

to live together unless for good reason they could not. The 1950 law makes it a duty for the couple to love each other and join in production.

Official Communist commentators on the marriage law repeat in similar phrases the charge that under the Nationalist Government legal provision for divorce existed but was conditioned by so many qualifications that it hardly ever applied, particularly when suit was brought by the woman.[19] It may well be that the courts displayed a total lack of sympathy on the subject of divorce petitions filed by women, but the law itself contains little evidence of discrimination. Indeed, the Marriage Law of 1950 requires at least two attempts at reconciliation in contested divorce suits, but the Civil Code lacks such provisions. Both codes allow for uncontested divorces by mutual consent. The 1950 law gives no specific grounds for divorce, other than mutual consent and the violation of the marriage law in the arrangement of the marriage; the Civil Code listed ten grounds, including sexual intercourse with any person other than the lawful spouse (which provision could theoretically be used by a wife against a husband who wished to take a concubine), cruelty, desertion, etc. The only limitations on divorce in the Civil Code are, however, of such kind that they could be powerful weapons in the hands of shrewd or unprincipled counsel. These limitations concern the failure to act, within a specified period of time, upon the knowledge of actions which are grounds for divorce. Thus, in the case of extramarital dalliance, the offended party might not use this as grounds for divorce if he/she previously consented to the activities, had knowledge of them for six months without taking action, or if the events cited occurred more than two years before the petition.[20]

It can be seen from this brief review that the family law of Communist China is generally similar to the relevant provisions of the Republican Civil Code of 1931.

The Family in Communist China

The family still exists in China and there is every indication that it will continue to be a viable institution in the future. However prosaic this conclusion, it is somewhat at odds with that presented in some other essays on the Chinese family under Communism, essays which seek to prove that the

19. Chang Chih-chang, "A Much Needed Marriage Law," *Jen Min Jih Pao*, April 17, 1950. Translation appears in MLPRC, *op. cit.*, and also in Mme. Chou En-lai's article in MLPRC.
20. CCRC, Arts. 1053, 1054, p. 24.

Chinese Communist Party has already subverted the Chinese family and is presently in the process of extirpating its remnants. . . . Such essays seem no more reliable than the energetic but hopelessly biased pronouncements of the official propagandists of Communist China. . . .

Paradoxically, the end of the present process will probably see both marriage and the family in China resembling more closely than ever before the patterns of these institutions in Western nations. The institutions which the Communists are attacking are not family institutions in the narrow sense, but those that have to do with extensions of the nuclear sphere of the family. Certainly the institution of the *tsu* is under grave attack and has little legal protection. Concomitantly, the aspects of marriage and the particular sexual relationships which are undergoing stress are those which are most closely associated with the patrilineally extended kin group. Viewed from this angle, the shift of the locus of familial power from the oldest ascendant generation to the generation of young adults is the key move. Though it has revolutionary political implications, and breeds its own counter-revolutionary reaction, it is conspicuously in step with the evolution of familial organization under comparable circumstances elsewhere in the world.

Birth Control

Planned parenthood is a matter so close to the heart of family life and the Chinese population problem is such an enormous one that it is fitting to consider the topic of birth control under a separate rubric. Chinese demographers following the party line have, until recently, denied that China had any population problem. When the People's Government managed to rationally organize production and distribution, it was said, the problems associated in the bourgeois world with great populations would be automatically overcome. The Chinese Census of 1954 seems to have jolted all such thinkers to their very roots, for it showed that there were almost 600 million people in China. Today, discounting the people on Taiwan and the overseas Chinese who appear in that figure, it is likely that there are more than 600 million Chinese on the mainland—the reason is the rate of increase of the population which is between 2 and 2½ percent. Each year there is in China a net gain of about 12 or 15 million people.[21]

21. That is, the surplus of successful births over the death rate leaves an increment of 12 to 15 million.

The situation is viewed with alarm in official circles and the answer has been the development in the past two years of a full-scale campaign to spread knowledge of birth control and the mechanical means of achieving it. The campaign has many facets. One of these is the drive to discourage early marriage, discussed above. We may add that this campaign utilizes not only teachers and persons serving youth, but has involved leading medical personalities as well. Thus the quasi-official *Chung Kuo Fu-nu* (*China Women*) features such articles as one which appeared recently under the signature of the Chairman of the Department of Obstetrics and Gynecology of the China Union Medical College. This article deplores the romanticism that drives young people to marriage and goes on to reiterate many of the charges presented earlier in this paper. Added, however, are some clinical details on parturition. To counteract the desire of women to have their children before they are 25, which is based on the commonly held belief that the intensity of labor pains varies directly with the age of the mother, the article assures its readers that labor pains are mildest between the ages 22–29 but warns that they are hardest to bear before the age 20. The gynecologist concluded with the statement that 25 is the ideal age for marriage.[22]

The major birth control measures consist of education in contraception and the permitting of abortion. The latter method has led to a great furor. In August, 1956, the Ministry of Public Health began a drive to encourage the sale of contraceptive devices and issued a directive which favored abortion as a technique of population control. In May, 1957, the North China News Agency reported, however, that the Chinese Medical Association had sent a long letter to the Ministry of Public Health, denouncing the permissive attitude toward abortions. Subsequently, there has been considerable discussion of the issues involved but at the time of writing no final line has been established. The objections of the Chinese Medical Association are of interest. Abortions are assailed as a menace to health, as an ineffective means of population control, and as a violation of the principle of equality of the sexes, since abortion places great strain on a woman but has no physiological consequences for a man. Incidentally, in this letter there is implicit evidence of male resistance to the use of contraceptive devices.

The birth control campaign is beset with ideological difficulties. The classic Communist position on birth control assails it as a reformist diver-

---

22. Dr. Lin Ka-ti, "The Best Marriageable Age from the Physiological Point of View," *Chung Kuo Fu-nu,* April, 1957.

sion. Were production and distribution rationalized, it is argued, there would be no problem of poverty, hence no fear of overpopulation. The present stand of the Chinese Communist Party, favoring birth control and staging a full-scale drive,[23] is felt to contradict the theoreticians. The matter is treated in the usual way; a letter raises the question in an influential journal and the editor sets the line in his reply. In this case a Comrade Li Tung-sheng wrote to *Cheng-chih Hsüeh-hsi* (*Political Study*) in April, 1957, wanting to know in what respects, if any, the Chinese Communist Party position on birth control differed from that of Thomas Malthus. Malthus, replied the editor, was a reactionary, bourgeois economist whose position had nothing in common with the Chinese Communist Party line.[24] The birth control movement in China is necessary because even with the herculean progress made since liberation, the People's Government has been unable to overcome the initial handicap imposed on China by centuries of feudal and imperialistic restraints on her productivity. Birth control, it is said, is necessary to ensure a happy, healthy upbringing for the children of the country. It will also relieve the strain on the national resources and permit an easier transition to socialism. Finally, unplanned and anarchic population increase is incompatible with the general context of economic and social planning.

A Study in Fertility Control

BERNARD BERELSON AND RONALD FREEDMAN (1964)

. . . This article will describe an experiment designed to find out what can be done in one of the world's most densely populated places: the island of Taiwan off the coast of mainland China.

23. For examples note the following: "Harbin Municipal Health Bureau Studies and Develops Guidance on Contraception," SCMP, No. 1445, November 29, 1956; "Hunan Provincial Public Health Bureau Holds Talks on Birth Control," SCMP, No. 1445, December 8, 1956; "Shao-Li-tzu on Contraception at Hangchow," SCMP, No. 1458, December 21, 1956; "Hopei Completes Plan for Contraception in 1957," SCMP, No. 1480, January 24, 1957; etc.
24. Oddly enough, no mention is made in this article of the *I-yen* of Hung Liang-chi (1746–1809) who is sometimes called "the Malthus of China" for his independent statements about population pressure.

From Bernard Berelson and Ronald Freedman, "A Study in Fertility Control," *Scientific American,* May 1964. Copyright © 1964 by *Scientific American*. Reprinted by permission.

祖母說：「看！我的兒子和媳婦只有三
個子女，他們多麼健康幸福！」

➤ 請向附近的衛生所詢問 ◀

台灣省婦幼衛生研究所編印 。

Figure 1. Posters were used widely in an educational campaign throughout Taichung. The caption reads: "A wise grandmother says: 'Look! My son and his wife have only three children. How healthy and happy they are!' If you have any questions, go to the nearest health station."

Large-scale efforts to control fertility are, to be sure, not unknown. A number of governments have assumed the responsibility of providing their people with information and services on family planning, and some countries have organized major national programs. Lowering a birthrate is a novel objective for a government, however, and no country has yet managed to achieve widespread family limitation through a planned social effort. Current programs are therefore handicapped by a lack of information on attitudes toward fertility control and by a lack of experience with programs to implement family planning.

Since any change in birthrate depends on individual decisions by large numbers of husbands and wives, it is essential to know first of all how the people concerned feel about family size and limitation. Do they need to be motivated toward family planning? If they are so motivated, how can they best be helped to accomplish their aim? To investigate these questions the Taiwan study was inaugurated a year and a half ago under the sponsorship of the provincial health department of Taiwan with the support of the Population Council, a U.S. foundation that advances scientific training and study in population matters. The most significant preliminary finding is that the people do not need to be motivated. They want to plan their families, but they need to know how. Teaching them how—implementing a family-planning program—has proved to be feasible.

Taiwan has a population of about 12 million in an area of 14,000 square miles, and its population is increasing rapidly. In recent years mortality has fallen almost to Western levels: life expectancy is more than 60 years and the death rate is less than eight per 1,000 of population per year. The birthrate is about 37 per 1,000, so the rate of increase is almost 3 per cent per year, or enough to double the population in 25 years.[1] Nevertheless, compared with other parts of Asia, Taiwan provides a favorable situation for the diffusion of family planning. The island is relatively urbanized and industrialized, the farmers are oriented toward a market economy, literacy and popular education are fairly widespread, there is a good transportation and communication system and a solid network of medical facilities. The standard of living is high for a population of this size in Asia outside of Japan. The society is highly organized. Women are not sharply subordinated and there are few religious or ideological objections to contraception.

The birthrate in Taiwan has been falling slowly since 1958. When fertil-

1. For more recent statistics see Editor's Note on p. 284. Ed.

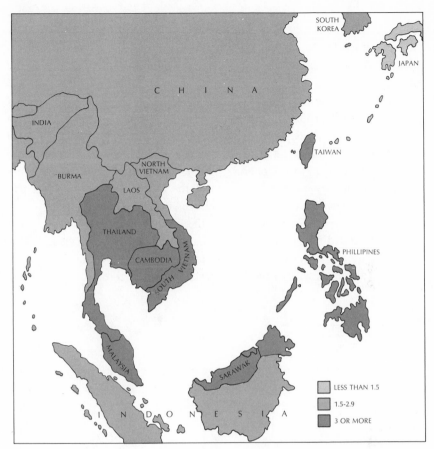

Figure 2. Population growth in eastern Asia is mapped above. The three shades indicate average yearly percentage increases, many of them rough estimates, from 1958 to 1961.

ity rates are analyzed by age group [*see* Figure 3], it becomes apparent that they have decreased first and most for the older women of the childbearing population. This is exactly what one would expect if many women wanted to have a moderate number of children, had them with low mortality by the age of 30 and then tried to limit the size of their families in some way. The same pattern was observed earlier in a number of Western countries at the beginning of the declines in fertility that have tended to follow declines in mortality.

Although the situation in Taiwan was quite favorable for family planning and the birthrate trend had been downward, this was not to say that it would be a simple matter to accelerate the decline in fertility. As a first step in that effort the Population Studies centers in Taiwan and at the University of Michigan undertook a survey that would serve as a base line and also as a guide for a program of action. Between October, 1962, and January, 1963, public health nurses interviewed nearly 2,500 married women of the city of Taichung in the prime reproductive age group (ages 20 to 39) as to their attitudes toward family planning, their information about it and what they did about it. The survey made it clear that these women as a group wanted to have a moderate number of children, were having more children than they wanted, approved of the idea of family limitation and were trying—ineffectively—to limit the size of their families.

The number of children most of the women wanted was four, and women who had already borne more than that number acknowledged that they would have preferred fewer children [*see* Figure 4]. More than 90 per cent of Taichung's wives (and their husbands too, according to the wives)

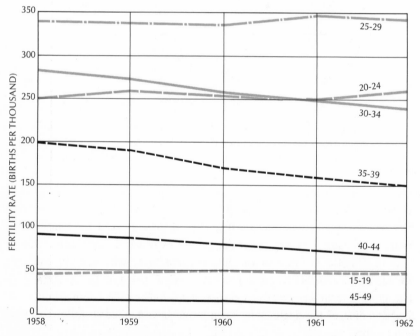

Figure 3. Fertility rates, shown here for Taiwan women in seven age groups (*figures at right*), have fallen since 1958 in the case of the older women, presumably because they are trying to limit their families. The rates are birth rates per 1000 women of the relevant age groups.

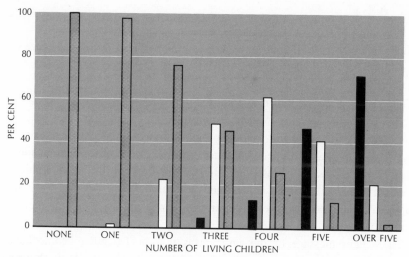

Figure 4. Family-size preferences are charted for Taichung wives according to the number of children they have. The chart shows the percentage of wives in each group who said they would have preferred fewer children (*black bars*) or more children (*gray bars*) than they had or that they were satisfied with the number of children they had (*white bars*).

were favorably inclined toward limiting family size. They had few objections in principle, they saw the value of such limitation for the economic welfare of their families and they did not believe that the number of children should be left to "fate" or "providence." In this regard (and the same has been found to be true in other countries) their attitudes are more advanced than some officials believe them to be.

The women were in general poorly informed about family-planning methods and indeed about the physiology of reproduction. About a fourth of them had employed some means of contraception, but in most cases only after four or five pregnancies and in many cases without success. The women expressed strong interest in learning and adopting better methods. And in their own minds family planning did not conflict with their traditional feelings about the Chinese family or its central role in their lives.

Experience with contraception or other methods of limiting family size was naturally most common in the "modernized" sectors of the population: the best-educated women, the most literate and those with an urban background. The women's actual and desired fertility were also related to these characteristics [*see* Figure 5], but we found that on every educational level the average women between 35 and 39, when childbearing is not yet over, had borne more children than she wanted. This was true even of

277

groups in which substantial numbers of women had tried to limit the size of their families: contraception had arrived on the scene too late and was too ineffective to enable such women to attain their goals.

The survey data made it clear that the women had become aware of the decline of infant mortality in their community. This is an important perception, and one that does not follow automatically on the event. (Other surveys have shown that women sometimes perceive a decrease in infant mortality as an increase in births.) Because they recognized that more children were surviving, the women appreciated that, unlike their parents, they did not need to have five to seven children in order to see three or four survive to adulthood.

The salient message of the survey was that in Taichung people have more children than they want. There are indications that the same thing is true in many similar societies. It seems clear that if throughout the world unwanted children were not conceived, a large part of the "population problem" would disappear.

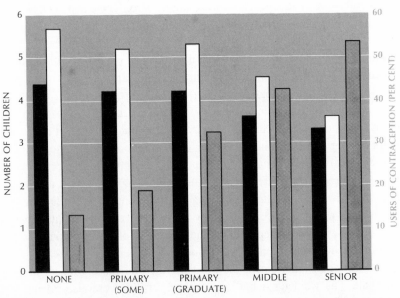

Figure 5. Education affects family size and the use of contraceptives. The chart groups women 35 to 39 years old according to the level of schooling they had reached. The bars show the average number of children they said they had wanted (*black*) and the number they had borne (*white*), and the percentage of each group practicing contraception (*gray bars*).

The next task was to facilitate the matching of behavior to attitude—to implement family planning. Several things were required beyond the mere wish to limit the number of children: information and knowledge, supplies and services, public acceptance and social support. To study how best to enable the people of Taiwan to do what they themselves said they wanted to do, the provincial health authorities undertook to develop a program of action to make the practice of family planning more readily available in the city of Taichung. This effort, we think, is one of the most extensive and elaborate social science experiments ever carried out in a natural setting. . . .

The city as a whole was exposed to only two aspects of the program: a general distribution of posters pointing out the advantages of family planning and a series of meetings with community leaders to inform them about the program, get their advice and enlist their support. That was the extent of the community-wide effort; the remainder of the program was designed as a differentiated experiment involving various kinds and degrees of effort. The objective was to learn how much family planning could be achieved at how much cost in money, personnel and time. To this end the local health authorities and a cooperating team from the U.S. devised four different "treatments," and applied one of them to each of the 2,389 lin's, or neighborhoods of 20 to 30 families, into which Taichung is divided. In order of increasing effort, the treatments were designated "Nothing," "Mail," "Everything (wives only)" and "Everything (wives and husbands)." . . . [See Figure 6.]

The program got under way in mid-February of 1963: the posters went up, meetings were held, 18 fieldworkers fanned out through the "Everything" lin's and the health stations prepared to receive inquiries. A set of educational materials was prepared for group and individual discussion, primarily visual aids dealing with the elementary facts about the physiology of reproduction, the reasons for practicing family planning and the major methods of contraception. The fieldworkers offered a wide choice of methods, encouraging couples to select whichever seemed most suitable: jelly, foam tablet, diaphragm, condom, rhythm, withdrawal, the oral pill and the new intra-uterine device. (The last is a recent development that holds great promise for mass programs to reduce fertility because it does not require continued supply, sustained motivation or repeated actions on the part of the user. A plastic ring or coil is inserted in the uterus by a physician and remains there; it is extremely effective as a contraceptive, although its mode of action is still unclear.) Contraceptive supplies were provided

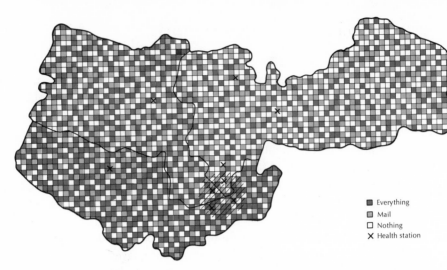

Figure 6. Concentration of effort in Taichung is mapped schematically. Each square represents a *lin* (although the correct number of *lin*'s is not shown). The city was divided into three sectors. The intensive "Everything" treatment was applied to half of the *lin*'s in the heavy-density sector (*lower left*), to a third of them in the medium-density sector (*upper left*), and to a fifth of the *lin*'s in the light-density sector (*right*). The remaining *lin*'s in each sector were divided equally between the "Mail" and "Nothing" treatments.

In the "Nothing" *lin*'s there was no activity beyond the distribution of posters and the meetings with leaders. In the "Mail" *lin*'s there was a direct-mail campaign addressed to newlywed couples and parents with two or more children. In the "Everything" neighborhoods the primary procedure was a personal visit to the home of every married woman from 20 to 39 years old by a specially trained staff of nurse-midwives. In half of the "Everything" *lin*'s the visits were made to wives only; in the other half the visits were extended to both husbands and wives, who were seen either separately or together.

at or below cost, or free if necessary; the pills sold for the equivalent of 75 cents for a cycle of 20. The same charge was made for the insertion of an intra-uterine device.

By the end of June fieldworkers had visited each of the nearly 12,000 designated homes at least once and more than 500 neighborhood meetings had been held. Between then and the middle of October follow-up visits were made to women or couples who had indicated interest and to women who had been pregnant or had been nursing infants earlier in the year. A final phase began in October and is still continuing; direct action has been terminated, but services and supplies are still available at the health stations. . . .

A program of this kind . . . apparently starts off reasonably well, builds up quite rapidly and achieves roughly half of its first year's return within the first four months. [*See* Figure 7.] The important thing is to develop a "critical mass" that can generate enough personal motivation and social support to carry on without further home visits. A poor country simply cannot afford visits to the entire population, so any realistic plan must rely heavily on personal and informal contacts from trusted sources; it may be that the job will have to be done by relatives, neighbors and friends or not at all. The task of a planned program will thus be to develop enough knowledgeable and convinced users of contraceptives to start a movement that reaches out to the ill-informed and unconvinced.

The indirect effects were extremely important in Taichung. The most dramatic indication is the fact that by the end of 1963 some 20 per cent of the acceptances had come from women who did not even live in the city. (That figure has since risen to almost 25 per cent.) Within the city about 60 per cent of the acceptances were from "Everything" *lin*'s; the other 40 per cent were divided about equally between the "Nothing" and the "Mail" *lin*'s. Even in the "Everything" neighborhoods about a sixth of those who accepted contraceptives actually came forward before their scheduled

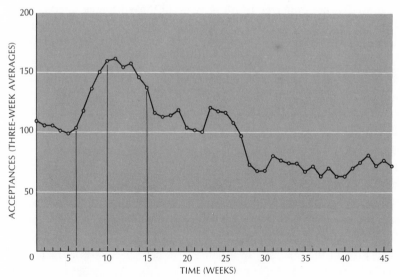

Figure 7. Progress of Action Program is traced by a curve showing the trend of "acceptances" of contraception in Taichung each week from the end of February 1963 to mid-January 1964. The three heavy vertical grid lines show (*left to right*) the points at which 40 per cent, 62 per cent, and 85 per cent of the home visits had been completed. The program reached a peak, then leveled off.

home visits had been made. Direct home visits, in other words, accounted for only some 40 per cent of the acceptances by the end of December.

As for the effectiveness of various concentrations of effort, the proportion of those who accepted contraceptives was indeed higher in the heavy-density sector, but this effect was almost completely within the "Everything" *lin*'s themselves. The indirect effect—the "rub-off" from the home-visit areas to the "Nothing" and "Mail" *lin*'s—was remarkably constant in the three sectors. Our tentative conclusion is that the maximum return for minimum expenditure can be obtained with something less than the heavy-sector degree of concentration. Finally, the added effect of visiting husbands as well as wives was not worth the expense, perhaps because in this program the preferred contraceptive method was one involving the wife alone.

The nature of the contraceptive method, as a matter of fact, has more of an effect on the success of a program than may have been generally recognized. A "one-time" method requires far less field effort over a long term than a method dependent on resupply and sustained motivation. In Taichung the choice turned out to be overwhelmingly for the intra-uterine devices, which were preferred by 78 per cent of those who accepted contraceptives; 20 per cent selected one of the more traditional methods (mainly foam tablets or condoms) and 2 per cent chose the oral pill (which was, to be sure, the most expensive method). The women themselves, in other words, elected the "one-time" method. This was particularly significant in view of the method's high effectiveness and what might be called its "accountability" through scheduled medical follow-ups. The six-month checkup shows that only some 20 per cent of the devices have been removed or involuntarily expelled, whereas about 30 per cent of the women who chose the traditional methods are no longer practicing contraception regularly.

The Taichung study revealed another significant advantage of the intra-uterine device: a striking tendency for information about it to be disseminated indirectly by word of mouth, obviating much of the task of communication and persuasion. Nearly 75 per cent of the new devices were accepted without the necessity of a home visit, compared with only 15 per cent in the case of the traditional methods. The intra-uterine devices "sold" themselves; what the home visits did, in effect, was to secure acceptance of the traditional methods. Since last October, when the action program proper was terminated, more than half of those who have accepted contraceptives have come from a widening circle around the city, and almost all

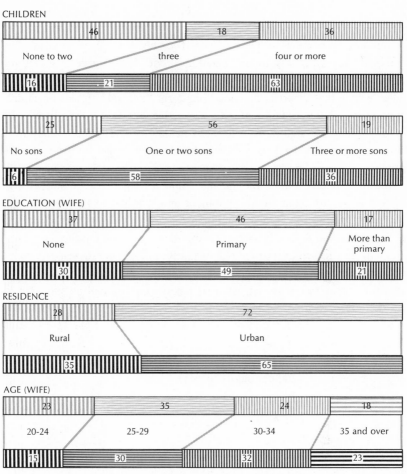

CHILDREN

None to two	three	four or more
46	18	36
16	21	63

No sons	One or two sons	Three or more sons
25	56	19
6	58	36

EDUCATION (WIFE)

None	Primary	More than primary
37	46	17
30	49	21

RESIDENCE

Rural	Urban
28	72
35	65

AGE (WIFE)

20-24	25-29	30-34	35 and over
23	35	24	18
15	30	32	23

Figure 8. Acceptance of family planning varied in different groups. In this chart the women are categorized according to various characteristics. The gray bars show the percentage of the "currently eligible" women who fell into that category. The black bars show the percentage of the new accepters of contraception who fell into the same categories as of the end of 1963.

of these women have chosen the new devices. This is presumably what happens when word of the method reaches women who are ready for family planning but want an easier and "better" way than they have heard of before.

Family planning does not, of course, diffuse evenly among the different kinds of people in a community. Acceptance varies with education and age and—in Taichung at least—above all with number of children and number

283

of sons. When couples in Taiwan have four children, they have all they want and they are ready to do something about it—if there is something available that is reasonably effective, inexpensive and easy to use. The evidence here is that whereas the slow long-term "natural" spread of contraception through a population reaches the better-educated people first, a deliberate and accelerated effort like the Taichung program can quickly have a major impact on the families that already have large numbers of children.

Taiwan is one of many low-income countries where rapid increases in population thwart economic development and threaten to slow further improvements in the standard of living. In the long run, to be sure, it seems likely that economic and social pressures combined with personal aspirations will lead individuals to limit their families. The underdeveloped countries, however, cannot wait for a long-term solution to their present crisis. The program in Taichung suggests that fertility control can be spread by a planned effort—not so easily or so fast as death control, but nevertheless substantially, in a short period of time and economically. (The cost of each acceptance was between $4 and $8, far below the eventual economic value of each prevented birth, which has been estimated as being between one and two times the annual per capita income.)

Editor's Note: *Since this article was written the birth rate has continued to decline in Taiwan. The crude birth rate dropped from 36.3 in 1963 to 32.1 in 1965. The most significant declines occurred in women over 30 years of age, the rates of decline increasing with age. Between 1959 and 1965 the declines for married women ranged from 29 per cent at age 30–34 to 56 per cent at 45–49, a pattern which is consistent with the spread of family planning. See "The Continuing Fertility Decline in Taiwan, 1965" by Ronald Freedman and Joanna Muller,* Population Index, *January–March 1967.*

Puerto Rico
RICHARD L. MEIER (1959)

Until a decade or so ago this island in the West Indies demonstrated very clearly all the characteristics of a population swollen far beyond the point

From Richard L. Meier, *Modern Science and the Human Fertility Problem,* John Wiley & Sons, New York. Copyright © 1959 by John Wiley & Sons. Reprinted by permission.

where it could feed itself. The efficient application of public health measures had led to a striking decline in the death rate, but the birth rate remained relatively unchanged from the former high levels. Poverty and unemployment were everywhere evident. American scholars, wishing to discover why fertility remained so high after mortality had long before made substantial declines all over the island, could conveniently begin their studies quite close to home. Since that time the Puerto Rican government has found its own remarkable solutions for both the economic problems and the population pressures. The prognosis as a whole is no longer disproportionately gloomy, even though a third to a half of the population is still living in relatively desperate straits that are reminiscent of the recent past. Thus, the earliest findings of the sociologists retain some degree of relevance to the solution of Puerto Rican population problems. It is known that cultural values in Puerto Rico are closely related to those held by almost all the former colonies of Latin countries . . .

Puerto Rican Background

How did it come about that such a large number of people reside on this island? The population density has already exceeded any European entity other than a major metropolitan area (for example, it is slightly denser overall than Belgium, but more than twice as dense if the most mountainous regions are ruled out of consideration). Part of the answer is to be found in the remarkable efficiency of sugar cane as a converter of sunlight, water, and fertilizer minerals into foodstuffs that are easily transported and marketed. The floor for the price of sugar on the world market has been set by the cost of carbohydrate rich foods elsewhere in the world. In this regard, an acre of sugar cane over the years can outproduce an acre anywhere else devoted to any other crop. In Puerto Rico the yields have gradually improved to a level approximating four tons of sugar per acre, which is considered to be a respectable but not remarkable level since considerably better yields are regularly recorded in Hawaii, Louisiana, and elsewhere. The sugar industry has often experienced skyrocketing demands for its product because it is a principal component of delicacies, confections, and soft drinks which persons with newly increased incomes are particularly eager to buy. Also, it can be stored easily in the event of military emergency. Therefore, sugar occasionally reaches price levels normally attained only by luxuries. During good times it was profitable for the sugar industries to

Table 1

Puerto Rico

(Dimensions and Magnitudes)

Area: 3423 sq. miles
Climate
  Average temperature: 76.0° F.; max. 78.9° F. (Sept.); min. 72.5° F. (Feb.)
  Annual rainfall: avg. 64.3 in.; max. 8.4 in. (Sept.); min. 2.5 in. (March)
Production *
  Sugar 10,900,000 tons (1953–54), $104 million
  Manufacturing (value added, 1952) $126 million
Population Growth *

Period	Population	Annual Rate of Increase (%)	Average Birth Rate/1000 Pop.	Rate of Natural Increase per 1000 Pop.
1899	953,243	1.50	45.7	14.3
1910	1,118,012	1.54	40.5	15.2
1920	1,299,809	1.56	40.4	16.4
1930	1,543,913	1.69	39.3	17.2
1935	1,723,534	1.95	39.0	18.9
1940	1,869,255	1.89	40.2	21.0
1941	....	....	39.8	21.2
1942	....	....	40.3	23.7
1943	....	....	39.6	24.9
1944	....	....	41.0	26.2
1945	....	....	42.3	28.2
1946	....	....	42.7	29.5
1947	....	....	43.3	31.3
1948	....	....	40.9	28.7
1949	....	....	39.1	28.6
1950	2,207,000	....	38.7	28.8
1951	2,233,000	1.20	37.6	27.6
1952	2,240,000	0.31	35.8	26.6
1953	2,229,000	0.49	34.7	26.6
1954	2,245,000	0.72	....	....
1955	....	....	36.1	....
1956	....	....	34.1	26.9
1957	....	....	32.9	....

Education *
  School enrollment (1953–4) 505,000; College level 13,250
Labor Force *
  631,000 (over 14 years); of these, 92,000 unemployed (1953)

Table 1 (*Continued*)
Family Income† (Net Family Income, 1950)

Income Component	Value, millions of dollars	Per Cent
Gross money income	738.5	. . . .
Minus taxes and other deductions	133.2	. . . .
Net money income	605.3	71.6
Net social income "free" services	135.8	16.1
Income "in kind"	85.4	10.1
Non-marketed net additions to private capital	18.8	2.2
Net family income (total)	845.3	100.0

Income Distribution † (Distribution of Net Family Income, 1950 ‡)

Per Cent of Families	10	20	30	40	50	60	70	80	90	100
Net Income, dollars	494	950	1030	1160	1370	1670	2100	2650	3680	. . .

* Sources: *Annuario Estadistico de Puerto Rico 1955,* Negociado de Economia y Estadistocos, San Juan, 1955; *New York Times,* June 27, 1954, IV, p. 4; March 25, 1957, p. 11; Jan. 25, 1958, p. 21.

† Source: "Puerto Rican Income Goals," unpublished manuscript of the Program of Education and Research in Planning, Harvey S. Perloff, Director, University of Chicago, June 1954, p. 43.

‡ Figures are given for family income groups by 10 per cent intervals and represent the value received by the highest income family of the given group.

buy up all the best irrigable land, employ field labor for the three to six months' season, and pay high enough wages to the workers to enable them to subsist upon imported rice, beans, flour, dry skim milk, lard, and salt fish until the next season. Many of the small farmers in the hills around the plantations found that a small patch of cane sold to the *central* was generally more profitable than the alternative native minor crops. By such means in Puerto Rico, as in other sugar economies, it became possible for three people to make a living, many of them one notch above subsistence, where before only one person could be supported at minimum levels.

Superimposed upon the spread of the sugar industry around the coastline, and into the richer valleys inland, was the need to control the water and to eliminate the unhealthful factors in the environment. Yellow fever, smallpox, typhoid, and malaria were overcome. With DDT and the improvement of drinking water supplies, dysentery diminished to a low level. Clinics and milk stations were established in the rural areas by the government. Thus, all of the previously important causes for mortality have been eradicated. The death rate has now dropped to a level below that of the United States, and infant mortality is now comparable with the more heavily rural areas in the United States.

The steady increases in population forced a subdivision of the hillside land, of the jobs in the sugar industry, of the niches within which commerce could be conducted, as well as all of the opportunities for selling services. Households expanded to the bursting point and then pushed adolescents into the labor market in order to make room for the new arrivals. The slums became infamous, and unemployment was rampant.

There were, however, some alleviating factors. Along with the improvement in health, schooling was extended so that, one way or another, a majority of the population achieved literacy. Other economic activities were added to sugar—some agricultural, and a few industrial. Certain kinds of welfare subsidies were channeled into the island from the United States. Before World War II, however, there seemed to be no way of overcoming the economic difficulties that beset the island. The needs of the ever-increasing population could not be met from the resources that were visible, so that it was then expected that economic conditions could only become steadily worse.

One of the commonplace observations of economic historians is that in the periods when economic opportunity became widespread, and urbanization proceeded, the family size became smaller. At one time they came to believe that this was a rather universal rule. It was noted that some societies achieved these reductions in births by postponing the age of marriage, others by the use of *coitus interruptus,* others with contraceptives, and some by the use of abortion. But eventually, in all the important regions, the birth rate was reduced by one-half, two-thirds, or even more within a span of two generations or so, so that the population again came into a crude equilibrium. The completed transitions occurred without plan, often in opposition to the laws and the public mores.

This generalization fitted neatly into the economists' views of personal motivations. A reduction in fertility was felt to be rational for all of those persons whose income would not permit both a higher level of consumption and a large family. For any normal population, of course, this class with limited income made up the predominant majority and determined the overall trend of the fertility. It was felt that public assistance and encouragement should hasten the transition to family limitation. But in Puerto

Rican families fertility has declined by less than 10 per cent in the 1935–1955 period, despite the visible costs, the remarkable opportunities, and the availability of free contraceptives. Such a picture does not make sense to the outside observer who believes that people will be rational in the long run. There are hints from elsewhere in the world that this unwillingness—perhaps it is an inability—to adjust fertility to the changes in the environment is characteristic not only of Puerto Rico but of many other populous cultures.

A series of clinics for maternal health was established in 1937, first in the cities and then in the rural areas, which made available various forms of contraceptives and gave advice as to their use. Three years later birth control clinics were sponsored by the government, first in the metropolitan area and later in other populous *municipios,* in the hope that an important proportion of the people would respond to the population pressure that was everywhere evident and would take up the use of family limitation techniques. Information and free materials were provided to all that asked for help. Despite the availability over many years, the demand did not accelerate and the birth rate was not significantly diminished! The noticeable drop starting in 1956 could easily have been due to a combination of other factors, including abrupt changes in immigration, taking effect over the preceding months. However, it may also be the first indication of a major decline.[1]

The overall picture was changed by the war in a great many ways. The military contacts, both of the young Puerto Ricans in the armed services and those of the local people with the military detachments stationed in their midst, broke through the insularism of the society. The submarine blockade brought with it considerable suffering but it also made possible capital accumulation through forced saving and nonconsumption. The war also accelerated the movement toward self-government and increased political and social responsibility. Accordingly, the island in 1945 became politically self-determinate. At the same time it was afflicted with rundown equipment for education and social services, but was blessed with some modern roads, harbor facilities and airports, and also with some $300,-000,000 of accumulated unspent credits. At this period its position was not greatly dissimilar from that of India, Burma, Ceylon, and Egypt, although on a smaller scale.

[1. More recent figures on live births per thousand in Puerto Rico show no major change: 31.2 in 1960–64 and 30.2 in 1965. Ed.]

The Puerto Rican government used these funds to build up the services necessary to industrialization, tourism, and improved economic efficiency. The well-publicized "Operation Bootstrap" was organized for attracting industries from the mainland. A relatively advanced form of economic and social planning was put into operation. The social and economic environment in the early stages of this effort are depicted by the statistics in Table I. Major determinants of the physical environments are also provided as a matter of convenience.

At the time these programs were still more in the discussion stage than actually functioning, some rather severe seasonal labor shortages were being experienced in commerical farms in the Atlantic states and in New York City. Ambitious young Puerto Ricans accepted impermanent jobs in the hope of finding something better before their money ran out. In one way or another they found means of surviving in Brooklyn and Manhattan, despite grave difficulties with the housing shortage. A large part of their savings was spent in helping kinfolk make the trip to New York. Non-scheduled airlines were created which charged only $50 per trip. This sum amounted then to only three or four weeks savings for a single, employed unskilled worker. The Puerto Rican immigrants seemed to be able to adapt to the American scene more rapidly than the ethnic groups that had preceded them, but this fact does not mean that the transition was without shock, demoralization, and distress.

In 1950 and thereafter, the flow to the mainland reached such dimensions that the accumulation of population on the island had virtually ceased. The Puerto Rican government worked out schemes to divert a large proportion of the stream to other American metropolitan areas where opportunities for employment were better, thus preventing the development of pressures and frictions which could easily bring the movement to a halt. The rate of migration was exceedingly sensitive to employment opportunities for unskilled labor on the mainland, particularly in New York City, so that even a minor economic recession could cause a 50 to 70 per cent dropoff in the new flow.

The mechanization of the sugar harvest was greatly accelerated by the emigration from the rural areas. An important fraction of the labor force, women more than men, found employment in the hundreds of small factories that were being set up in the vicinity of the Puerto Rican cities. Many of these persons acquired some elementary skill and then migrated to the mainland where the wage scale for such work was much higher.

Thus, Puerto Rico, rather unexpectedly, found a means of relieving its population pressures. A labor shortage in an accessible portion of the United States was carefully exploited, first by the individual workers, but later on with the aid of the insular authorities. It was handled in such a fashion that the economies of both the island and the mainland were able to profit from the movement. As a consequence, the level of underemployment on the island seems to have been greatly reduced, and the registered unemployment has dropped somewhat in the post war era. Such changes, when combined with the greatly increased productivity, have led to an average increase in real income per capita of about 8 to 10 per cent per year. This is a much more rapid increase than was registered on the continent, so that Puerto Rico has begun to catch up with the rest of the United States economy.

The particular solution that the Puerto Ricans discovered, however, is not open to any other overpopulated economy. It was only through a caprice of history that the island was brought under American hegemony. Since then its economy operated within the American tariff walls and its people were not subject to the immigration quota limitations. Some of the social services made available in the United States were extended to its overseas territories. . . . It is possible that a few features may be borrowed, as in the program for industrialization currently being developed in Jamaica, but these are at best superficial resemblances. Many new and equally ingenious conceptions will have to be added before any other migration-cum-industrialization programs can reach so hopeful a situation.

In Puerto Rico itself the effects of this improvement in income and outlook can be seen in many unexpected ways. The hills and mountainsides are much greener and less eroded now than they were before. This change has come about because most country people can afford kerosene for cooking instead of collecting faggots or making charcoal. The one-room palm-thatched houses that pocked the countryside in the interior have been largely abandoned, even many of the wooden ones, whereas those near the road have new lumber in them, or new roofs overhead. The additions to the cities contain neat *urbanisaciones* which are made up largely of two- to five-room concrete houses. El Fanguito, once said to be the largest and most disreputable slum in America, has had its worst edges trimmed and replaced with huge blocks of public housing, and good, strong buildings, able to withstand the fiercest hurricane, have been springing up here and there in its interior. Radios are found in almost every household and television antenna sprout up from the most unlikely spots. On the main boulevards in the metropolitan area the congestion is inexpressible, despite many expensive improvements.

The schools on the main bus lines are overcrowded until late at night. Undergraduate courses in the university are filled to overflowing. Young men in the lower income residential areas are to be seen wrestling with the disassembly and the reassembly of ten-year-old automobiles and twenty-year-old buses, activities which are felt to be one of the best means for developing their mechanical skill. Advertisements exhort self-improvement by acquiring one or another kind of diploma, mostly of a clerical nature. Lights in the governmental administrative offices often burn until 10 or 11 P.M. because so many of the responsible civil servants and their staffs work overtime. All these items are indicators of the kind of environmental conditions which have elsewhere been associated with postponement of marriage and widespread use of family limitation measures.

Not all parts of the society are equally affected. In the rural areas one sees little of this. The people are older there—or at least they seem to be older, but appearances can easily be misleading. Wherever poverty presses continuously, age comes on quickly. Tasks move more slowly in the country and the ins and outs are thoroughly discussed before any concrete action is taken. Very frequently the "action" assumes the form of a petition for help from the governor, the senator, or possibly even the principal *político* in the community. It is drawn up, of course, in very formal and ornate language so that no one could lose *dignidad* as a consequence of the appeal. Rural people are friendlier and less calculating in their human relations than the recent arrivals in the cities with their polite but pushing opportunism. Families and family connections remain both a burden and an asset in the countryside—a burden because the round of accumulated obligations uses up any windfall before it can be banked, and an asset in times of ill fortune. It is easier to understand why fertility has not changed significantly in the rural areas.

The Family Situation in the Poorer Classes

The Puerto Rican rural worker is known as an *jíbaro*. His culture and way of life has forms and standards which may be traced to Spain of the sixteenth century and earlier. These same forms and standards have been established, with many local variations, all over Latin America, much of the West Indies, the Philippines, and small parts of Africa. The *jibaro* and his family live by a special code for social relations called *respeto*.[2] The poorer people in the towns and the cities were almost all born in the country-side so that they were brought up to respect these same values, even though many adaptations have had to be made because of the new modes of behavior encountered when population reaches urban density.

Another important concept in the life of the poorer Puerto Ricans is that of *defenderse* (defending oneself). Any improvement in security, such as obtaining responsible godfathers and godmothers, an education, or a steady job, enables the individual to "defend himself better." Life is seen as a struggle, often against terrible odds, to maintain self-respect, health, and all of one's personal obligations. By far the most illuminating analysis of the family in this environment is provided by Stycos.[3] This study will be drawn upon very heavily in the next few pages.

It had been realized for a long time that the preferred size of a family in Puerto Rico ranged from two to four children, an average which was not far different from that of the United States.[4] The difficulties in "defending oneself" when encumbered with large families were widely recognized among rich and poor alike. Yet family limitation was not readily adopted among the poorer classes. That is the specific puzzle that provides the focus for this brief enquiry into the family situation.

Part of the explanation emerges from the patterns for child rearing that presently exist on the island.

> Baby boys are usually naked, or wear a waist length shirt, whereas girls have their genitals, as well as the upper portions of their bodies, covered. The masculinity of the boy child is a matter of considerable interest and parents and friends may play with the boy's genitals until he is around seven years old. (E. Padilla Seda, in *The People of Puerto Rico*, p. 291.)
>
> Even as an infant the male child is praised for being *macho*, "very male." *Macho*, which really means "male animal" rather than "man" (*hombre*) is thus used in a complimentary sense. The girl, on the other

2. An extensive description of this rural way of life is to be found in *The People of Puerto Rico*, Julian Steward, ed., University of Illinois Press, Urbana, Ill., 1956.
3. J. M. Stycos, *Family and Fertility in Puerto Rico*, Columbia University Press, New York, 1955.
4. E. Cofresi, *Realidad poblacional de Puerto Rico*, Imprensa Venezuela, San Juan, 1951; see also M. King, "Cultural Aspects of Birth Control in Puerto Rico," *Human Biology 20* (1948), and L. J. Roberts and R. L. Stefani, *Patterns of Living in Puerto Rican Families*, University of Puerto Rico Press, Rio Piedras, 1949. Smaller scale surveys conducted before World War II led to much the same conclusions.

hand, traditionally is sheltered, protected, chaperoned, and taught to believe that sex for her should be procreational rather than pleasurable.
Prior to marriage her relations to men are limited to mild and perhaps
somewhat clandestine flirtations. (R. L. Scheele, in *The People of Puerto
Rico,* p. 441.)

She is also shielded from the facts of life, because if she is not a virgin or
does not act like one, it is indecent for her to be married in church, and
then there is virtually no chance for her to improve her status:

> She has to be a *señorita.* It's clear that she should be. How could she get
> married if she wasn't? Ay, Virgen Santa! (Stycos, p. 61.)

A boy child is usually preferred by both husband and wife:

> . . . in case the father dies, the males can watch the females. (Why is
> that?) Because the man imposes respect everywhere. The girls would not
> be respected the same if they had no brothers. (Stycos, p. 45.)

The boys are initiated to sex at an early age, mainly with prostitutes and
undefended women. This pattern continues through the period of courtship
and often during marriage.

> A man makes love to every woman that passes his way. But if the wo-
> man is *señorita,* then he should let that one pass by because it is not good
> to fool with virgins. (Stycos, p. 79.)

The young men tend to choose their wives because of the similarity to the
mother and on the basis of presumed virginity. He marries a young woman
for whom he can have *respeto.* The highest standards are not absolutely
necessary, because consensual unions are common, but in the latter case
the idea of life-time commitment is not so keenly felt.

Marriage of one form or another tends to occur at an age two or three
years earlier than is felt to be desirable by either the husband or the wife,
when considering the ideal arrangement. The young men, it appears, are in
need of housekeepers, and the young women are impatient at being so rigidly cloistered and protected. As a consequence the women are married at
the age of twenty, on the average, and the men are married at the age of
twenty-three or four. Early marriage is one important reason for the high
birth rate in Puerto Rico, but it is hard to imagine any means for holding
the girls longer in such cramped quarters so that they are contented with
life and everyone can maintain *respeto.* The isolation of the women from
the outside world has been alleviated by the radio, which is perhaps the
major reason for its widespread popularity, but the radio tends ultimately

to increase the ferment because it introduces many strange and incompatible ideas from the city and from the outside world.

In the family the male is dominant. He makes all the major purchases and other decisions. His word is law. Every precaution is taken to assure that the wife is faithful, but the husband, of course, may do what he chooses, even to the point of setting up a new household or keeping a *querida* (concubine). The wife has too much *respeto* for the husband ordinarily to discuss matters of sex with him, including matters of contraception. The fraction of women that gain satisfaction from sexual intercourse is very small; indeed, it is spoken of with repugnance to persons filling the role of doctors and close confidantes, yet wives feel that they must submit as a duty and in order to keep their husbands from abandoning them.

There are other features of these motivations which also contribute to high fertility. We find the following arguments being made:

> A man is anxious to have his son early to prove his *hombria* (manliness) . . . I mean that he wants to have his first child to prove that he can make sons, that he is not barren (Stycos, p. 173.)

> I wanted a male son . . . so as to know I was a *macho*. (A *macho?*) Yes, to show that I am not like the men that have only females. (*Ibid.,* p. 179.)

> A large family proves the *hombria* of a man. (How?) Because it takes a real man to maintain and educate a large family. (*Ibid.,* p. 177.)

Thus a man needs a child quickly in order to prove that he is *un hombre completo,* and his pride in *macho* is often directed toward having a large family. It is generally felt that he should keep on having children until he has at least one boy.

For most women in Puerto Rico marriage and childbearing are occasions for repeated disenchantment and re-education. The wife comes to marriage quite innocent and thereafter acquires the knowledge as a series of surprises. The "good" wife is even ashamed at being examined by a physician, and hears only the barest and vaguest mentions of birth control. As the family increases in size some of the women become desperate and do take advantage of the free service, the barriers being broken down frequently by a need to visit the clinic for some other purpose.

> Many friends of mine invited me to the Health Unit, and I didn't dare go. (Why?) Because it was known by everyone that in town on Tuesday they give prophylactics in the Health Unit. Women are seen coming out of the Unit with their package and everybody knows what they have gone there for. (Stycos, p. 188.)

However, more often than not the husband may object (or it is suspected that he may object), in which case sterilization is considered, usually at the time of the delivery of the fourth, fifth, or later child. Religious objections were shown to be infrequent, and even then much more common among the few Protestants that were interviewed than among the Catholics, despite vociferous denunciation of the practice by the priests. Under conditions where the information is relatively adequate the application of measures for birth control still has an important barrier to overcome, because the husband is then less likely to trust the wife—she is felt to be less reluctant to have relations with other men if pregnancy can be prevented—and in addition to this there is prevalent a strong disgust in the use of most contraceptive materials.

Among the poor people in Puerto Rico a person must depend upon his family as a means of coping with insecurity. If the husband goes off to find work, the wife may move in with her parents. She may do this also if she is abandoned, which may occur in perhaps 20 per cent of the marriages, and also if she is widowed. If this is impossible she will have to look for some other liaison, or distribute the children to relatives and godparents. Thus, the normal household is seldom stable in terms of the number of individuals to be fed and provided with sleeping space.

Regardless of crowding, visiting back and forth, the not infrequent tantrums of the children, and the common domestic calamities, the interiors of these houses are kept remarkably clean. The area around the house may look cluttered and neglected, garbage and sewage disposal may be quite inadequate, and the house itself constructed of scrap lumber, corrugated iron, reeds, palm thatch, concrete blocks, or whatever else is available, but it is continually being improved, extended, or repaired. A majority of the poor people own the homes they live in, although they often do not own the land upon which it rests. The impermanence of location may also contribute significantly to the unregulated character of family life, including some of the difficulties experienced in planning that is to be found in a majority of households.

The sketches of Puerto Rican life provided in the preceding pages suggests that the mode of living, the economic insecurity of the mass of the population, and the need to move about to find some adequate means of support, combined with child rearing practices which emphasize *macho* and the overprotection of daughters, would lead inevitably to unions involving male dominance. Such conditions should in turn reproduce the traditional family pattern in an unending chain from generation to generation. These relationships are self-reinforcing and maintain themselves over time against many external changes. Experience over the past sixty years shows that the essential features are relatively impervious to the *Americano* acculturative forces, nor are they subject to legislation arising from the impatient element that wishes to proceed with all possible haste toward industrialization. Moreover, the established social institutions among the middle and upper classes are such that increases in family wealth, although they may remove the economic insecurity, tend to make the *respeto* system even more rigid. This tendency is made very clear in R. L. Scheele's contribution to *The People of Puerto Rico* (Julian Steward, ed.) referred to earlier.

The one institution which has tended to loosen the system and thereby increase the independence of women is the public school. Education enables them to obtain employment outside of the home in roles other than that of a servant, and it introduces them to a wider range of cultural contacts. The rapid increase in public education that has been under way seems to be bringing about a partial relaxation of the family relationships now observed.[5] The achievement of literacy made migration much easier but, surprisingly enough, the direct impact of the large-scale migrations since 1949 does not seem to have changed family life in any way that can be easily recognized. Perhaps the removal of the more venturesome element of the younger generation permitted the remainder to conform to prior standards. . . .

Family Limitation Experiences

In Puerto Rico, as in Europe, the idea of birth control has been introduced to a large part of the population by means of public controversy. The welfare workers, the Neo-Malthusians, and many of the Americanized intellectuals have been thumping the drums for birth control in conferences, public forums, articles in the newspapers, and letters to the editor. The opposition has come from the guardians of the old order, the classically trained jurists, those priests who were trained in the Spanish hierarchy of the Church, and a part of the medical profession. The subject was sometimes brought up in a manner calculated to embarrass the government at election time. Because people were curious—there is hardly anything more

5. R. Hill, "Impediments to Freedom of Mate Selection in Puerto Rico," *Journal of Home Economics 47*, 189 (1955).

interesting than a good fight, but it is even better to know what the issues are—they picked up a great deal of information, and misinformation, about contraception, alternative birth control practices, and their implications. However, the information that was spread about in the course of discussing the merits of the controversy was primarily received by men, so that it had very little immediate effect upon the birth rate. This is shown by the records of the first set of birth control clinics after they were established in 1937.

A survey of these early attempts to introduce contraception to the lower income families in Puerto Rico has been provided by Beebe and Belaval.[6] In the year 1938 the contraceptive services were contacted by 3851 families, which was perhaps 3 to 5 per cent of the population which had actual need of their services. Of these a sample of 1962 families was selected, more of them rural than urban. A third of these had already tried some form of contraception before contacting the clinic, almost all at the initiative of the male. The prior fertility was 60 per cent above that of the population as a whole, as judged by census data. The sample, although representing indigent families, was heavily weighted with families in which the wife was relatively well educated (they averaged five years of schooling completed) and husbands having better-than-average skills (45 per cent were larger farmers, skilled workers, and clerical workers). The mean family income was stated to be $7.80 per week, although the largest single class reported weekly incomes in the range of $2.50 to $3.50. The apparent fertility of the sample was markedly higher than had been noted in prior studies by Beebe and by Stix for various poor populations in North America when equivalent clinics were set up. Beebe and Belaval noted that the 644 families in the sample that had attempted one or another form of contraception at any time previously had a fertility 15 per cent less than the others. The high fertility of the sample, the relatively small reduction in fertility achieved, and its socio-economic status as compared to the population as a whole are all indicators that at this time Puerto Rico had made less progress on the path to low fertility than any of the other populations that had been studied previously by Beebe and Stix.

When reviewing two years of experience with their sample, Beebe and Belaval concluded that no appreciable fertility reduction occurred in the families where the wife had less than three years of schooling or the hus-

6. G. W. Beebe, and J. S. Belaval, "Fertility and Contraception in Puerto Rico," *Puerto Rico Journal of Public Health and Tropical Medicine 18,* 3–52 (1942).

band belonged to the ranks of the unskilled workers. The diaphragm and jelly method worked best in urban areas, while foam powder seemed to work best in many rural areas. For those families that persisted over the period of the study the overall pregnancy reduction was 50 to 60 per cent; nevertheless, the principal reason for dropping the service was that of pregnancy. Thus, after twelve months only about half of the families retained contact with the clinic. Because this sample represented an element in the population which most felt the need, and was relatively advantaged with respect to income and education, we could expect that an island-wide distribution of clinics would reduce fertility by only 10 to 30 per cent—if public confidence could be retained. The statistics indicate that a 10 to 20 per cent reduction in fertility did occur in the succeeding fifteen years, but only a small part of it came about because of improved contraception. Fertility among migrants in New York was estimated at 59 per 1000 by the public health authorities there (P. Kihss, *New York Times,* June 27, 1954, IV. p. 4), suggesting that more than half of the reduction on the island may be attributed to migration, since more than 400,000 Puerto Ricans were residing in New York at that time.

Contemporaneous with the maternal health clinics there was developed an alternative route to family limitation which has had a remarkable acceptance on the island. The gynecologists in a private hospital introduced a method for female sterilization at the time the child was born. The technique was of interest to doctors and was widely tried during the 1930's. The method was relatively inexpensive, a charge of $60 to $90 was made for hospital delivery followed by sterilization. This service quickly became so popular that the hospitals were swamped. By 1947 an island-wide survey showed that 6.6 per cent of all married women had already been sterilized, 8.3 per cent in the upper income category, and 2.7 per cent in the lower income category. For marital unions begun between 1930–1939 it was stated that 11.3 per cent had been sterilized by 1947.[7]

There is evidence to indicate that this proportion has been understated because of the delicate nature of the question when it is posed by a stranger. In the period after 1947 the rate of sterilization was stepped up considerably. For poor families the access to a bed in public hospitals required some "political pull" in many instances, and for this the cooperation of the husband was necessary. By 1953 one out of every five women in

7. P. Hatt, *Backgrounds to Human Fertility in Puerto Rico,* Princeton University Press, Princeton, N.J., 1952, p. 444.

contact with a Health Center (median age 29.4 years, median education 4.2 years, and median number of live births in present marriage 4.2) had already been sterilized. By that time the proportion sterilized had been equalized over the urban and rural areas.[8] Most of those in the rural areas were innocent about the techniques of birth control.

In the 1953 survey it was shown that sterilization was usually undertaken too late to have a very important effect upon overall fertility rates. It seemed to be mainly a means of preventing the hardships caused by abnormally large families. However, it was possible to show that this effect was nevertheless greater than the use of other means of birth control. If more facilities were available for hospital deliveries there would undoubtedly be a large increase in sterilizations.

The reasons for the popularity of sterilization are more difficult to understand. In part they stem from the esthetics of the culture, which assigns high values to personal cleanliness and, according to those standards, the available contraceptives were felt to be filthy and disgusting. *"La operacion"* is clean and, in addition, leaves no doubt as to the consequences. A large majority of the women are so harassed by their family responsibilities that they are quite sure that they will never regret the consequences, some are ambivalent, but a few do register regrets when interviewed later. As female sterilization becomes more common and is established as part of the standard expectations in this society, such regrets are likely to diminish still further. A very important feature of this means of family limitation is that it is permissible to talk about one's operations in polite society, which permits ready comparisons to be made in terms of the consequences. So easy is it to introduce the subject that it is a commonplace for an *Americano* woman visiting in a Puerto Rican home to be asked within an hour whether she has already had her "operation." The social pressures are coming to favor sterilization as soon as the maximum family desired is complete, especially in the middle classes where such rational arguments can be used and followed through successfully. The maximum family desired may be three children, but it is completed more commonly with four or five. Sterilization is usually not effected until the desired family size has been exceeded by one or two children.

In a developing country like Puerto Rico such concepts as family growth

8. J. M. Stycos, "Female Sterilization in Puerto Rico," *Eugenics Quarterly 1,* No. 2, 2–9 (1954).

cessation upon reaching ideal size can spread quickly to the masses. The educational plans in the Six Year Financial Program suggest that at least two-thirds of the girls born after 1950 will be educated a full six years or more. Those that migrate to the mainland tend to have neither the least nor the most education, therefore, the women that remain are expected to be literate and easily informed on these subjects. Middle-class views about family standards in the 1950's are rather likely to be transferred to the majority of the population by the 1960's—especially if the controversy with the local Catholic hierarchy continues, so that the issues are repeatedly publicized.

Various methods are being devised for bringing information about family limitation opportunities to those Puerto Ricans that are likely to be interested. Documentary films have been made and widely shown which emphasize that the small family tends to have fewer troubles and is, therefore, the happier family. Public health nurses will meet with small groups of women to give them details. Pamphlets have been prepared which have been designed to overcome the greatest deficiencies in knowledge and understanding that have been discovered in earlier studies. Every imaginable means that at the same time would not offend the public has been tried for overcoming the modesty barrier.

Early proponents of planned parenthood assumed that once easy and reliable methods of birth control were available, convenient, and legal the only remaining impediment to a rational solution of the problem would be that of religious or moral resistance. But in my opinion the existence of the ancient instinct deep in the biological organism is a more formidable enemy than religious dogma. In the United States at least the population has been increasing . . . at the same time that methods of birth control have become better known and more readily accessible. The only possible explanation is simply that people continue to *want* more children than is desirable now that the mortality rate has been so greatly reduced. Many who are intellectually convinced that population growth should be reduced nevertheless rejoice in at least their own large families because the impulse to increase and multiply was an instinct long before it was a biblical injunction. Man the thinker lags behind man the technician. No less important is the fact that his instincts lag, not years but millennia, behind even his thinking. The most crucial question is not can he be made to *believe* that too many children are undesirable, but can he conquer his instincts sufficiently to make him *feel* what his intellect has convinced him of?

Joseph Wood Krutch (1962)
"A Naturalist Looks at Overpopulation,"
Our Crowded Planet

The Voluntary Family:
Too Large or Too Small?

Editor's Note: *In the 1930's the steady decline in birth rates in the Western nations caused concern that voluntary parenthood would lead to race suicide.*

The Small Family Problem

A. M. CARR-SAUNDERS (1936)

The present situation is novel in human experience. It is true that a small family system prevailed in early times; the family was then small because married couples were under the compulsion of limiting the number of their children. Limitation was achieved by abortion which involved physical suffering, or by infanticide which was wounding to parental feelings or by abstention from intercourse which involved psychological tension. The primitive small family system, enjoined by convention, enforced by social pressure and involving suffering, has long passed away in Europe. But, though families were large in Europe during the Middle Ages and the succeeding centuries, they were not as large as they might have been; for the dependent section of the population was under the compulsion to delay marriage somewhat. This compulsion, though not involving methods as crude and painful as those which kept the primitive family small, was irksome; during the eighteenth century it ceased to exist, and men became free to marry as early as they liked and to have as many children as they wished. But men and women have never wanted as many children as "nature" sends; up to that time, however, they did not know of any effective method of limiting the family which involved neither suffering nor offence to moral sentiments. Then they became aware of the possibility of practising contraception. For a time they hesitated to employ this method

From A. M. Carr-Saunders, *World Population*, Oxford at the Clarendon Press, 1936. Reprinted by permission.

because it was repugnant to prevailing sentiment. Sentiment gradually changed; it is clear that to most people to-day contraception is not inherently repulsive. Hence came the modern small family system. It is novel because it is voluntary; all previous restrictions upon the size of the family were forced upon the parents. Parents had to be compelled because the only means by which limitation could then be achieved were all, in one way or another, painful or repulsive. But a painless, acceptable, and fairly effective method of family limitation now lies ready for use.

The result is of extraordinary significance. Since in former times the family was kept small by unwelcome means, there was always resistance to the use of those means. There was therefore no likelihood that the size of family would sink below the level needed for the replenishment of the community. The danger, which perpetually threatened, was that resistance would become too strong, and that in consequence the growth of population would be excessive. There is no resistance now. Therefore, if for any reason, however remote, trivial, selfish, or unsubstantial, parents do not want a child, the child does not come. Consequently there is no assurance whatever that children will come in numbers sufficient to prevent a decline of population and ultimate extinction.

This novel situation demands further inquiry. . . .

There are certain urges which lead people to desire children. They are deep seated, ineradicable, and incapable of complete satisfaction through any form of substitution. For the sake of convenience we may say that they constitute the parental instinct. Because the parental instinct will continue to exist, men and women will continue to desire children. It is clear that the satisfaction of the instinct does not require that the physiologically possible number of children shall be born; the family was large in former times, not because all the births were desired, but because births could not be avoided. Now that they can be avoided the size of family is determined by two contrary forces: on the one hand there is the parental instinct, on the other hand there are all those considerations which make a child or an additional child unwanted. . . .

We may say perhaps that in part the reason for the small size of family is that parents have gone on strike in protest against the neglect of their special problems. Parenthood has always involved trials and burdens; formerly, however, they were inescapable, and therefore parents were unable to force the attention of society upon them. Parents were enslaved, and slaves cannot withdraw their labour. Parents are now becoming free, and they take advantage of this freedom to bring the strike weapon into play. But the effectiveness of a strike depends upon the inconvenience which the community is made to suffer. In this case the community has not been in any way incommoded as yet. In fact the action taken by parents was welcomed; therefore the grievances of parents obtained, and still receive, little or no attention. Here the analogy fails, because the parents were not driven to return to work; they found themselves better off if they remained on strike.

It would be entirely mistaken, however, to suppose that these considerations represent more than a partial and subsidiary explanation of the present situation. If the special difficulties of parents were removed, more children would no doubt be wanted. But apart from these special difficulties incidental to parenthood which encourage limitation, there are numerous other considerations, worthy and unworthy, relevant and irrelevant, which lead in the same direction; the importance of these other considerations is evident when it is remembered that parents, who by reason of their favourable economic position suffer little from the difficulties incidental to parenthood, drastically limit their families. It follows that the major part of the explanation lies in the fact that the parental instinct is now satisfied when the average size of the family is not sufficient for the purpose of replacement.

If the parental instinct was a force of unvarying intensity and if the opposing considerations always exercised the same attraction, the position would be hopeless since extinction would be inevitable. But the parental instinct is a vague term which is used here merely to imply desire for children, and it is possible that the intensity of the desire for children may increase. The attraction exercised by the opposing considerations depends upon the scale of values, and the scale of values may also change. People may therefore come to desire the long run satisfactions of a moderate-sized family more than the short run satisfactions which are made possible when the family is small and the parents relatively free from parental cares.

There are reasons for supposing that under certain circumstances the parental instinct and the scale of values would undergo considerable changes. At present people are quite unaware of the implications of the new freedom. Hitherto throughout the whole history of the human race replacement has been automatic; indeed the danger has usually been in the direction of excessive reproduction. Replacement is no longer automatic, but of this fact there is no understanding. The most essential thing at the present time is to implant in the members of a modern community a firm grasp of the fact that they are responsible for its future in the sense that, if they do not replace themselves, the community will be extinguished. To achieve this end simple statistical demonstrations of the mode of recruitment of population in general and of the position of recruitment of the population in question from time to time should be made familiar to all. It will then become apparent that replacement is a social duty, a fact which at present is entirely unfamiliar to people at large. It will also become apparent that in many western communities the average size of family is now such that the duty is not being performed. . . .

In the light of this discussion it should not be difficult to understand the failure of the atttempts to raise the birthrate described in Part II. All that has been done by those attempts is to deal with a single aspect of a very involved problem and then only in a very inadequate manner. That family allowances, as given in France and Belgium, have been ineffective is no proof that family allowances have no part to play in the reconstruction that must take place. But there is another and very important reason for the failure of these schemes. They have been accompanied by attempts to make birth-control illegal. This is bad tactics. If anything is certain it is that people will resist being driven back under the tyranny of the unlimited family; therefore all measures are suspect which are associated with an anti-birth-control movement. But it is much more than bad tactics. It implies a complete misunderstanding of the only possible solution of the small family problem. The solution must begin by welcoming the voluntary small family system, and that means welcoming birth-control. For birth-control is not merely a practice which must be tolerated; it has positive functions of great importance to perform, such as, for example, making possible the proper spacing of the family. Let it be said clearly that the escape from the unlimited family makes a very great step forward in human history. The problem is to adjust outlook to the responsibility involved by the transition to the voluntary family system.

It should now also be possible to understand why the small family problem is so much more urgent and difficult than is generally realized. At the moment in this country the reproduction rate is about 25 per cent below replacement rate. If all children born were wanted (that is wanted before conception), the former rate would probably be 50 per cent below the latter. But the day when all children will be wanted children is certainly coming; for contraceptive methods are undergoing continual improvement. The perfect contraceptive, cheap, easy to use, and infallible, may be invented any day. Therefore, if things remain as they are, the reproduction rate will fall, and the prospect will be a reduction of the population to less than a quarter of its present size a century from now. But the coming of this catastrophic decline will be masked for a time by the fact that in any case the fall will not be large during the next two decades. The population will decline at the most by three or four millions in the next twenty years. This fall will be welcome to the many who believe that unemployment is due to over-population. Meanwhile people will come to think that they are rendering positive service by keeping their families small. All the habits connected with the small family system will harden into customs. Any suggestion that more births are desirable will meet with the impassioned opposition of birth-control enthusiasts. The prospect of so catastrophic a fall makes it urgent that steps should be taken at once, and the difficulties, which will be encountered in undertaking the social reconstruction that is necessary, are so formidable that the urgency is much enhanced.

Changing Family Size in the United States
COMMITTEE ON POPULATION, NATIONAL
ACADEMY OF SCIENCES (1965)

By the 1930's, the spread of family limitation in the American population had reached the point where, on the average, women were bearing only a little more than two children—barely enough to replace the parents. Note that the low point reached in the 1930's was a culmination of a decline in fertility that had lasted 130 years, through good times and bad. It is surely an oversimplification to consider the low fertility of the 1930's as primarily a product of the depression (see Figure 1).

Had the fertility rates of the 1930's continued until today, the growth of the American population would virtually have ceased. But fertility did not remain at its pre-war level, and the average size of the American family has risen by more than 50 per cent—from a little more than two to more than three children. Indeed, the number of children born per woman

From Committee on Population, *The Growth of U.S. Population,* National Academy of Sciences—National Research Council Publication No. 1279, pp. 4–6. Reprinted by permission.

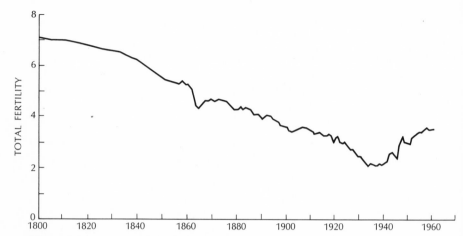

Figure 1. Average total fertility per child-bearing woman: U.S. white population
Source: Office of Population Research, Princeton University

of fertile age was as great in 1957, the year of highest post-war fertility, as it was at the turn of the century.

The recovery of the birth rate in the United States during the 1940's and the 1950's was not a simple reversal of the forces that had caused the birth rate to decline to its pre-war minimum. The post-war "baby boom" was not a return to the family-building habits of 19th century America. There were two reasons for it. First, among couples who consciously choose the number of children they have, a consensus developed in favor of moderate-size families instead of small ones. In the 1920's and the 1930's, couples with better education and higher incomes married late and had few children, but in the 1940's and the 1950's, young people generally married rather than remaining single, married at an earlier average age than did their parents, avoided childlessness, and rarely stopped with one child. Their preferences appear nearly evenly divided among two, three, and four children. There seems to have been a change in attitude among the more prosperous, better-educated segments of our population. The change represents neither a return to the very large family of the last century nor the abandonment of effective contraception, but does indicate a preference for more children than characterized the families of the 1920's and the 1930's.

The other reason for the great post-war increase in births lies in the lack of effective limitation of family size among the underprivileged, rela-

308

tively impoverished, and less-educated Americans. There has been an increase in fertility among the more-deprived segments of our population, caused partly by earlier marriage and partly by a decline in sterility.

Nevertheless, there seems little doubt that the rise in fertility in the United States is caused more by the preference for larger families among those who consciously choose the number of children they have than by the high fertility in the impoverished segments of the population. The importance of high fertility among the underprivileged lies not so much in its contribution to the national birth rate as in the difficulties that excessive fertility imposes on the impoverished themselves.

Fad

LINCOLN H. AND ALICE TAYLOR DAY (1964)

The importance attached to doing what everybody else is doing must be included in any consideration of the desire for more children. The American emphasis on schools, PTA, Scouts, organized recreation, and similar child-centered activities, particularly strong in the rapidly growing suburbs, may well result in the childless or one-child couple's feeling left out. For most Americans, except the very poor, no matter how large the family, a new baby is still an exciting event, heralded by gifts and visits from relatives and neighbors. A freshly bathed and laundered infant is most appealing and can easily evoke the desire to have one of one's own.

If the three- to four-child family is actually becoming established as the national norm, the parents of but one or two children may begin to feel uncomfortably out of step, that they have somehow made a mistake in limiting their family to this size. That the fastest growing areas in the United States are the new housing developments adds support to the fad theory. In these areas, where there is hardly an unmarried adult and only a handful of the middle-aged and elderly, the young couple is exposed to an unusual degree to people in the process of forming their families to whatever fashion there may be in family size. Literally everyone *is* having children. And because everyone is, parents are likely to find that these housing developments encourage additional childbearing not only by example, but also by providing ready access to playmates for their young-sters and, for themselves, other young parents with whom to share child-raising anecdotes and the duties of baby-sitting.

There is too much diversity in family size, even within the new suburbs, for the fad theory to explain *all* of the post-World War II changes in the size of American families; but it may be at least a partial explanation for the increasing concentration of family size within the narrow range of two to four children.

Since World War II new standards of family size have diffused rapidly throughout American society. Extremes in family size have been corre-spondingly diminished. These changes, together with the declines in the birth rate that preceded them, illustrate the fact that individual values, though highly important determinants of human behavior, are themselves part of a larger cultural setting. Changes in this cultural setting will bring with them changes in the proportions of the population holding various attitudes relevant to natality. With the means of family limitation almost universally available in this country, and with all groups coming under the potential influence of a single system of mass communication, one of the most crucial factors in any couple's decision about the number of its children may well come to be the desire to conform to prevailing cultural values about family building. It is this susceptibility of individual values to the cultural milieu as a whole that affords us a kind of cautious optimism concerning the practicability of voluntary limitation sufficient to stabilize the size of our population.

Declining Birthrate in the United States
PAUL WOODRING (1967)

In 1972 the number of children in the first grade in all U.S. schools will be 5 per cent smaller than it is today. This is not a guess but a fact, or a projection of a fact, for all the babies have been born and counted. Only a dramatic change in our immigration policy or a catastrophic rise in the infant death rate could change it materially. . . .

These facts have gone all but unnoticed, probably because of the wide-spread and legitimate alarm over the world-wide population expansion

From Paul Woodring, "There'll Be Fewer Little Noses," *Saturday Review,* March 18, 1967. Reprinted by permission.

which poses a threat of starvation in underdeveloped nations. But, in the United States the number of births each year has been falling steadily from its high of 4,308,000 in 1957. Between 1960 and 1965 the number dropped from 4,257,850 to 3,767,000. The 1966 estimate is 3,629,000. And this decline is not limited to states with stable populations—the number has declined even in California from 374,428 in 1964 to 352,146 in 1965 and an estimated 345,000 in 1966.

No one knows whether the decline will continue. Predictions of birthrates are so risky a venture that in the past nearly all forecasting has been erroneous. Textbooks written in the Thirties predicted that the low rate of that decade would continue and that the population of the nation would never rise above 150 million. In 1945 demographers rightly predicted that the rate would rise after the war, but they wrongly predicted that after just a few years the rate would decline to the 1936 level. Instead the high rate continued for fifteen years. By 1965, however, it had dropped to the 1940 level.

Today many demographers predict another upswing, in numbers if not in birthrates, in just a few years when the post-war babies themselves will become parents. Since 20,000,000 girls were born in the decade of the Fifties compared to only 15,000,000 in the previous decade, we can say with certainty that the number of women of childbearing age will rise during the decade of the Seventies, but it is possible that the drop in the number of births per potential mother will be so great as to offset that fact. (The fertility rate—number of births per 1,000 women aged 15 to 44—declined from 122.7 in 1957 to 90 in 1966.)

Many conflicting theories have been advanced to account for the rise and fall of birthrates. In the Twenties the declining rate was attributed to prosperity—it was pointed out that the birthrate was low in all the more advanced and prosperous nations. But in the Fifties the *high* birthrate was attributed to the affluence of that decade—it was said that parents had more children because they could afford more. Meanwhile, Japan, during a period of prosperity, has had a sharply falling birthrate.

One thing seems certain. Parents who know how to control birth, and have no religious objections to doing so, will have large families only when they want them. And wanting them or not has some of the characteristics of a fad or fashion. In the Fifties it was fashionable for young American parents to want many children as quickly as possible. Today it seems more fashionable to postpone childbearing and plan smaller families.

Obviously the pill has made birth control more effective. Its extended

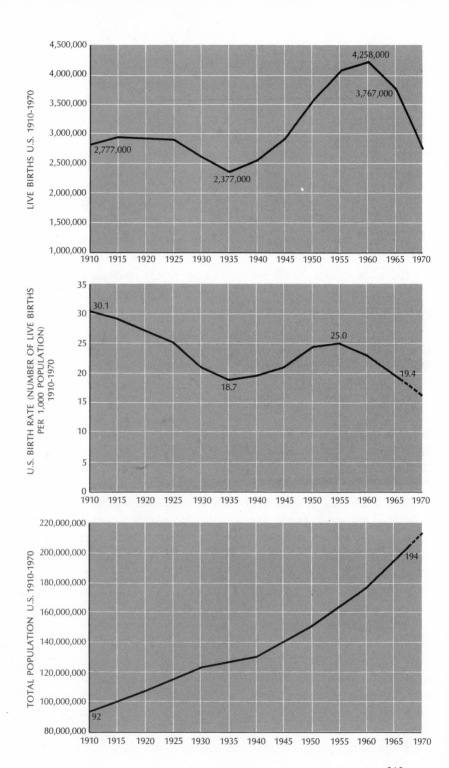

availability, combined with the apparent decrease in the desire for large families, seems likely to result in a continued decline in the number of births per potential parent. And if the "morning after" pill should become available, a still sharper decline may result.

In the essential matter of survival there are two things needed, the survival of the individual and the survival of the race. We are all very well endowed with deep instincts for both, and curiously enough we are ashamed of both these instincts. As to the survival of the individual we have a very strong, intimate and deep fear of death, evoked by any form of danger; it is not a thing we boast about, but it is certainly a very essential quality for survival, and as such it is to be regarded as important and valuable. For the reproduction of the race, there are two instincts needed, the sexual and the parental, and the way these are organized is to say the least curious. The sexual instinct, though much complicated by all sorts of taboos, is for most of mankind nearly as violent as the fear of death, though it has the advantage of being pleasant instead of unpleasant. Among animals it brings about the inevitable consequence of reproduction, and until very recently the same was true for man, so that the Malthusian increase of population was assured. This is still true for a large proportion of the human race, but the existence of birth-control has entirely altered the situation among the more highly developed peoples. The consequence has been to make reproduction depend for them not on an intense instinctive impulse, but rather on intellectual reasoning, and this for very many people is an exceedingly tepid motive.

Charles Galton Darwin (1952)
The Next Million Years

When we try to bring down birth rates, most human instincts work against us. It is not merely a question of the sex instinct; it is a question of the meaning of life—the joy of having children, the feeling that one is a complete human being only if he has children.

Roger Revelle
"Can Man Domesticate Himself?"

"Now is that sweet unwritten moment when all things are possible, are just begun."
Donald Culross Peattie, *Almanac for Moderns.*

Editor's Note: *Carl Sandburg once said, "A baby is God's opinion that life should go on." But when all babies are wanted babies then parents will actively share in the expression of this opinion about life. There may be some situations and some times when life seems too great a burden to pass on.*

Nightmare for Future Reference
STEPHEN VINCENT BENÉT (1938)

That was the second year of the Third World War,
The one between Us and Them.
                                        Well, we've gotten used.
We don't talk much about it, queerly enough.
There was all sorts of talk the first years after the Peace,
A million theories, a million wild suppositions,
A million hopeful explanations and plans,
But we don't talk about it now. We don't even ask.
We might do the wrong thing. I don't guess you'd understand that.
But you're eighteen now. You can take it. You'd better know.

You see, you were born just before the war broke out.
Who started it? Oh, they said it was Us or Them
and it looked like it at the time. You don't know what that's like.
But anyhow, it started and there it was,
Just a little worse, of course, than the one before,
But mankind was used to that. We didn't take notice.
They bombed our capital and we bombed theirs.
You've been to the Broken Towns? Yes, they take you there
They show you the look of the tormented earth.
But they can't show the smell or the gas or the death
Or how it felt to be there, and a part of it.
But we didn't know. I swear that we didn't know.

I remember the first faint hint there was something wrong
Something beyond all wars and bigger and strange,
Something you couldn't explain.
                              I was back on leave—
Strange, as you felt on leave, as you always felt—
But I went to see the Chief at the hospital,
And there he was, in the same old laboratory,
A little older, with some white in his hair.
But the same eyes that went through you and the same tongue
They hadn't been able to touch him—not the bombs
Nor the ruin of his life's work nor anything.
He blinked at me from behind his spectacles
And said, "Huh. It's you. They won't let me have guinea pigs
Except for the war work, but I steal a few.
And they've made me a colonel—expect me to salute.
Damn fools. A damn-fool business. I don't know how.
Have you heard what Erickson's done with the ductless glands?
The journals are four months late. Sit down and smoke."
And I did and it was like home.
                              He was a great man.
You might remember that—and I'd worked with him.
Well, finally he said to me, "How's your boy?"

"Oh—healthy," I said. "We're lucky."
                              "Yes," he said,
And a frown went over his face. "He might even grow up,
Though the intervals between wars are getting shorter.
I wonder if it wouldn't simplify things
To declare mankind in a permanent state of seige.
It might knock some sense in their heads."
                              "You're cheerful," I said.
"Oh, I'm always cheerful," he said. "Seen these, by the way?"
He tapped some charts on a table.

                              "Seen what?" I said.
"Oh," he said, with that devilish, sidelong grin of his,
"Just the normal city statistics—death and birth.
You're a soldier now. You wouldn't be interested.

But the birth rate's dropping."
          "Well, really, sir," I said,
"We know that it's always dropped, in every war."

"Not like this," he said. "I can show you the curve.
It looks like the side of a mountain, going down.
And faster, the last three months—yes, a good deal faster.
I showed it to Lobenheim and he was puzzled.
It makes a neat problem—yes?" He looked at me.

"They'd better make peace," he said. "They'd better make peace."

"Well, sir," I said, "if we break through, in the spring . . ."
"Break through?" he said. "What's that? They'd better make peace.
The stars may be tired of us. No, I'm not a mystic.
I leave that to the big scientists in bad novels.
But I never saw such a queer maternity curve.
I wish I could get to Ehrens, on their side.
He'd tell me the truth. But the fools won't let me do it."

His eyes looked tired as he stared at the careful charts.
"Suppose there are no more babies?" he said. "What then?
It's one way of solving the problem."
          "But, sir—" I said.
"But, sir!" he said. "Will you tell me, please, what is life?
Why it's given, why it's taken away?
Oh, I know—we make a jelly inside a test tube,
We keep a cock's heart living inside a jar.
We know a great many things, and what do we know?
We think we know what finished the dinosaurs,
But do we? Maybe they were given a chance
And then it was taken back. There are other beasts
That only kill for their food. No, I'm not a mystic,
But there's a certain pattern in nature, you know,
And we're upsetting it daily. Eat and mate
And go back to the earth after that, and that's all right.
But now we're blasting and sickening earth itself.
She's been very patient with us. I wonder how long."

Well, I thought the Chief had gone crazy, just at first,
And then I remembered the look of no man's land,
That bitter landscape, pockmarked like the moon,
Lifeless as the moon's face and horrible,
The thing we'd made with the guns.
                                        If it were earth,
It looked as though it hated.
                              "Well?" I said,
And my voice was a little thin. He looked hard at me.
"Oh—ask the women," he grunted. "Don't ask me.
Ask them what they think about it."
                                    I didn't ask them,
Not even your mother—she was strange, those days—
But, two weeks later, I was back in the lines
And somebody sent me a paper—
Encouragement for the troops and all of that—
All about the fall of Their birth rate on Their side.

I guess you know now. There was still a day when we fought,
And the next day the women knew. I don't know how they knew,
But they smashed every government in the world
Like a heap of broken china, within two days,
And we'd stopped firing by then. And we looked at each other.

We didn't talk much, those first weeks. You couldn't talk.
We started in rebuilding and that was all,
And at first nobody would even touch the guns,
Not even to melt them up. They just stood there, silent,
Pointing the way they had and nobody there.
And there was a kind of madness in the air,
A quiet, bewildered madness, strange and shy.
You'd pass a man who was muttering to himself
And you'd know what he was muttering, and why.
I remember coming home and your mother there.
She looked at me, at first didn't speak at all,
And then she said, "Burn those clothes. Take them off and burn them
Or I'll never touch you or speak to you again."
And then I knew I was still in my uniform.

Well, I've told you now. They tell you now at eighteen.
There's no use telling before.
                              Do you understand?
That's why we have the Ritual of the Earth,
The Day of Sorrow, the other ceremonies.
Oh, yes, at first people hated the animals
Because they still bred, but we've gotten over that.
Perhaps they can work it better, when it's their turn,
If it's their turn—I don't know. I don't know at all.
You can call it a virus, of course, if you like the word,
But we haven't been able to find it. Not yet. No.
It isn't as if it has happened all at once.
There were a few children born in the last six months
Before the end of the war, so there's still some hope.
But they're almost grown. That's the trouble. They're almost grown.

Well, we had a long run. That's something. At first they thought
There might be a nation somewhere—a savage tribe.
But we were all in it, even the Eskimos,
And we keep the toys in the stores, and the colored books,
And people marry and plan the rest of it,
But, you see, there aren't any children. They aren't born.

Population and Human Fulfilment

JULIAN HUXLEY (1957)

Man does not live by bread alone, nor should he live for bread alone. He needs power and shelter and clothing, and in addition to all material requirements he needs space and beauty, sport and recreation, interest and enjoyment. . . .

Indeed, once we start looking at the population problem as a whole and in all its implications, we find ourselves being pressed into a reconsideration of human values in general. First of all we must reject the idea that mere quantity of human beings is of value apart from the quality of their lives. . . .

From Julian Huxley, *Knowledge, Morality, and Destiny,* The New American Library of World Literature, 1957. Reprinted by permission of A. D. Peters & Co., London.

Just as the horrible destructiveness of atomic warfare is now prompting a reconsideration of warfare in general, and seems likely to lead to the abandonment of all-out war as an instrument of national policy, so I would predict that the threat of overpopulation to human values like health, standard of living, and amenity will prompt a reconsideration of values in general and lead eventually to a new value-system for human living. . . . The values we must pursue are those which permit or promote greater human fulfilment. Food and health, energy and leisure are its necessary bases: its value-goals are knowledge and interest, beauty and emotional expression, inner integration and outer participation, enjoyment and a sense of significance.

The Last Flower
JAMES THURBER (1939)

WORLD WAR XII, AS EVERYBODY KNOWS,

BROUGHT ABOUT THE COLLAPSE OF CIVILIZATION

TOWNS, CITIES, AND VILLAGES DISAPPEARED FROM THE EARTH

ALL THE GROVES AND FORESTS WERE DESTROYED

AND ALL THE GARDENS

AND ALL THE WORKS OF ART

MEN, WOMEN, AND CHILDREN BECAME LOWER THAN THE LOWER ANIMALS

DISCOURAGED AND DISILLUSIONED, DOGS DESERTED THEIR FALLEN MASTERS

EMBOLDENED BY THE PITIFUL CONDITION
OF THE FORMER LORDS OF THE EARTH,
RABBITS DESCENDED UPON THEM

BOOKS, PAINTINGS, AND MUSIC DISAPPEARED
FROM THE EARTH, AND HUMAN BEINGS
JUST SAT AROUND, DOING NOTHING

YEARS AND YEARS WENT BY

EVEN THE FEW GENERALS WHO WERE LEFT
FORGOT WHAT THE LAST WAR HAD DECIDED

BOYS AND GIRLS GREW UP TO STARE AT EACH OTHER
BLANKLY, FOR LOVE HAD PASSED FROM THE EARTH

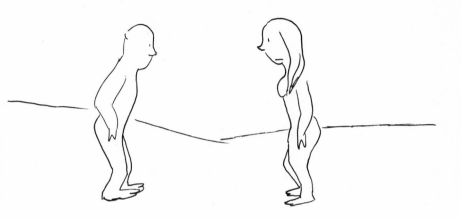

ONE DAY A YOUNG GIRL WHO HAD NEVER
SEEN A FLOWER CHANCED TO COME
UPON THE LAST ONE IN THE WORLD

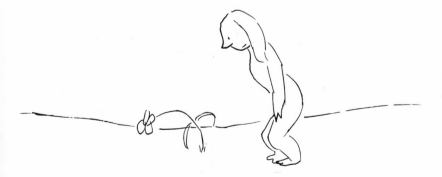

SHE TOLD THE OTHER HUMAN BEINGS
THAT THE LAST FLOWER WAS DYING

THE ONLY ONE WHO PAID ANY ATTENTION
TO HER WAS A YOUNG MAN SHE
FOUND WANDERING ABOUT

TOGETHER THE YOUNG MAN AND THE GIRL
NURTURED THE FLOWER AND IT BEGAN
TO LIVE AGAIN

ONE DAY A BEE VISITED THE FLOWER,
AND A HUMMINGBIRD

BEFORE LONG THERE WERE TWO FLOWERS, AND
THEN FOUR, AND THEN A GREAT MANY

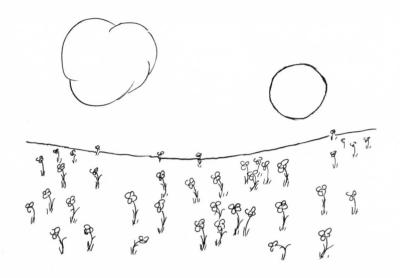

GROVES AND FORESTS FLOURISHED AGAIN

THE YOUNG GIRL BEGAN TO TAKE
AN INTEREST IN HOW SHE LOOKED

THE YOUNG MAN DISCOVERED THAT
TOUCHING THE GIRL WAS PLEASURABLE

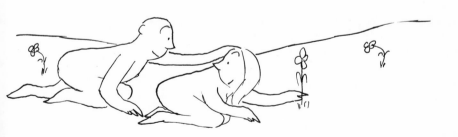

LOVE WAS REBORN INTO THE WORLD

THEIR CHILDREN GREW UP STRONG AND HEALTHY
AND LEARNED TO RUN AND LAUGH

DOGS CAME OUT OF THEIR EXILE

THE YOUNG MAN DISCOVERED, BY PUTTING ONE STONE UPON ANOTHER, HOW TO BUILD A SHELTER

PRETTY SOON EVERYBODY WAS BUILDING SHELTERS

TOWNS, CITIES, AND VILLAGES SPRANG UP

SONG CAME BACK INTO THE WORLD

AND TROUBADOURS AND JUGGLERS

AND TAILORS AND COBBLERS

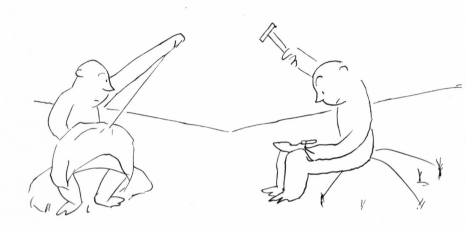

AND PAINTERS AND POETS

AND SCULPTORS AND WHEELWRIGHTS

AND SOLDIERS

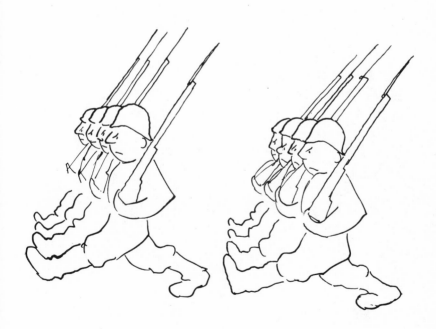

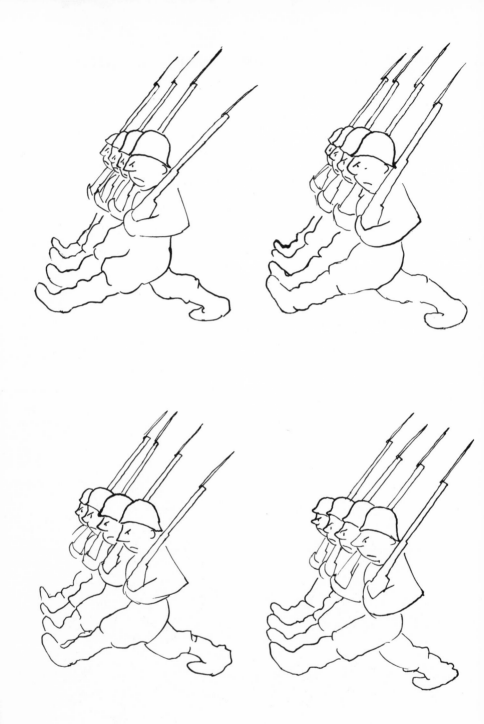

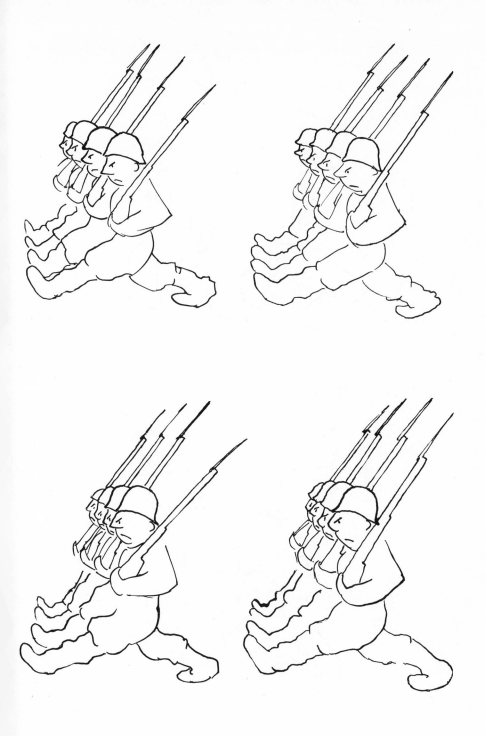

AND LIEUTENANTS AND CAPTAINS

AND GENERALS AND MAJOR-GENERALS

AND LIBERATORS

SOME PEOPLE WENT ONE PLACE TO LIVE,
AND SOME ANOTHER

BEFORE LONG, THOSE WHO WENT TO LIVE IN THE VALLEYS
WISHED THEY HAD GONE TO LIVE IN THE HILLS

AND THOSE WHO HAD GONE TO LIVE IN THE HILLS
WISHED THEY HAD GONE TO LIVE IN THE VALLEYS

THE LIBERATORS, UNDER THE GUIDANCE OF GOD, SET FIRE TO THE DISCONTENT

SO PRESENTLY THE WORLD WAS AT WAR AGAIN

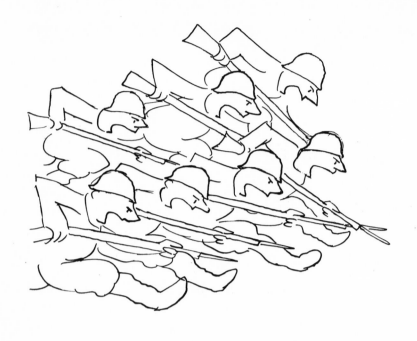

THIS TIME THE DESTRUCTION WAS SO COMPLETE...

THAT NOTHING AT ALL WAS LEFT IN THE WORLD

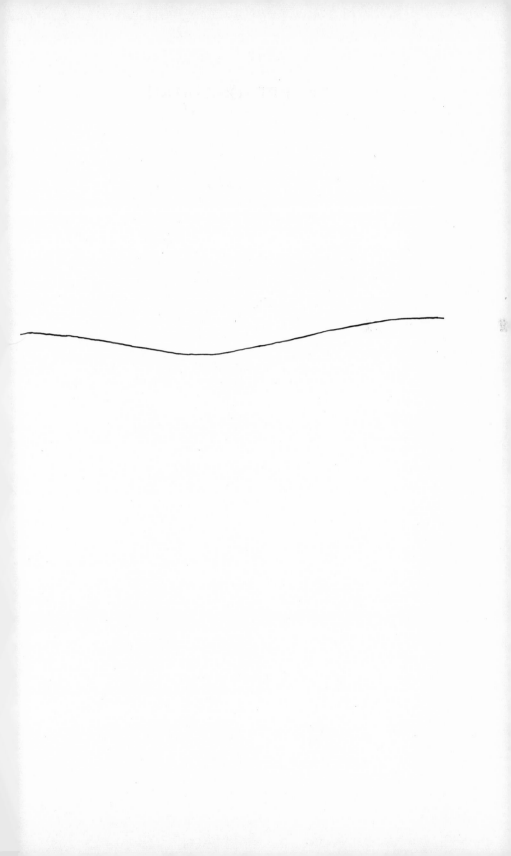

EXCEPT ONE MAN

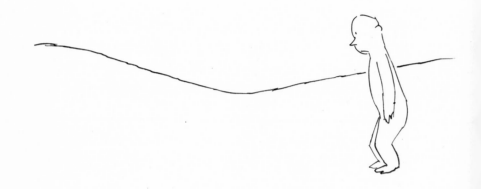

AND ONE WOMAN

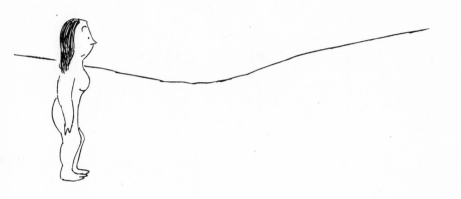

AND ONE FLOWER

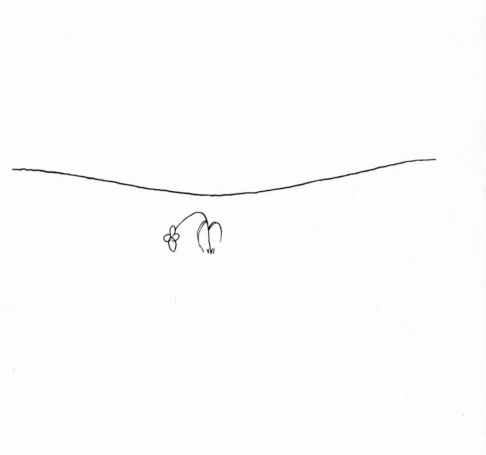

IV PROSPECTS FOR THE FUTURE

Introduction

At the opposite pole from the alarmists who tell us that in seven hundred years there will be no standing room left on earth and no place to bury the dead, are the apologists who protest that there is no cause for worry about the population problem. Science, the wonder-worker, will find a way out. Science will harvest the sea and feed us algae. Science will find ways of stacking us up so high above the earth's surface that we will all have room enough to stand. And, of course, science will dispose efficiently of the dead. We can all relax and go right on having as many children as we like. The scientists will take care of the problem.

Now, it is undoubtedly true that science will be able to increase our food supply and devise more efficient ways of using the limited space on the earth's surface. But it is also true that there are practical limitations beyond which science cannot go, or more importantly, beyond which we would not want it to go. It cannot replace wilderness once it has been destroyed. It cannot restore individuality and diversity in human life once they have been leached out by a flood of mass production.

There are ways, however, in which science can help solve the population problem. It can bring us a greater understanding of nature and ourselves so that we can predict with more confidence how certain courses of action are likely to develop. By opening up more choices and giving us the ability to realize the significance of these choices, science can immeasurably increase our ability to be responsible for our own future.

We have seen how Malthus's theory of population led to one of the most important biological theories and through this new understanding man was seen for the first time as an integral part of the natural world. Now through recent research on other living things we are beginning to gain new insights into the laws of natural increase. We are discovering, for instance, that animals do have ways of anticipating population densities, that in crowded conditions they are more often killed by stress than by starvation, that they adapt well to increased density up to a certain point but that there is a density beyond which they cannot go.

Of course, we must be cautious in applying results of experiments on animals to the human condition. There are many differences that must be taken into account. However, as our knowledge about nature grows, many ethologists are becoming convinced that "there is hardly any aspect of the behaviour of animals which may not have some reference to problems of human behaviour." [1]

One prospect for the immediate future which seems almost certain in the light of our present knowledge is that the world will be more densely populated than it is now. Understanding of the psychological and physical consequences of overcrowding will be helpful in planning for these changing conditions. The ways in which animals anticipate and regulate their populations may offer clues for controlling our own population growth.

By studying the ways in which natural processes work, science can find methods of altering these processes to bring about some desired result. Basic research on the human reproductive system, for example, could lead to new methods of family planning, methods which would be less expensive, more foolproof, or more acceptable to all religious doctrines. Similarly, research with sex determination may make it possible for parents to plan not only the number of children in their family but the sex of each child. It is interesting to speculate what effect this discovery would have on the birth rate. The old saying, "A boy in time saves nine," is particularly applicable to the most densely populated countries in the world. Furthermore, a higher proportion of boys would reduce the number of potential mothers for the next generation.

Thus, we see how the progress of scientific knowledge confers more freedom of choice and more possibilities of control over the future. It also places a greater burden of responsibility on the shoulders of the average man. The concept of responsible parenthood involves first, knowledge (through science and education), and second, courage and self-discipline to act on this knowledge. If the average man abdicates this right, if he turns the decisions over to scientists or politicians or computers, then the ideal of responsible parenthood will never be realized.

It has been suggested that the time will soon come when permission to

1. William H. Thorpe, quoted by Sally Carrighar in *Wild Heritage*.

have a baby must be obtained from the government. Accurate tabulations of births and deaths will make it possible for a computer to decide how many new births could be tolerated in any given period. This is one way of solving the population problem and may become necessary if responsible parenthood does not prove to be a practical solution. "Bit by bit," says Friedrich Sieburg, "we are abandoning what used to constitute the sovereignty of Western man. The private sphere, which was once surrounded by a certain sanctity, is dwindling. Man evacuates one field after another, and the state cannot be expected not to move into the empty space which we are unable to fill." [2]

Some writers argue that it is better to sacrifice a few areas of freedom in order that we may retain greater freedom in other areas. Keeping the population in balance with available resources both of nourishment and *Lebensraum* would free us of the tyranny of the machine-like efficiency which might become necessary in a very densely populated world. By preserving natural beauty, diversity, and individuality in human life, it may confer more freedom in the long run. Here again is a choice. Who will make it?

Dostoievsky's Grand Inquisitor suggests that the average man does not want the responsibility for making these choices. As freedom increases, the burden becomes intolerable and he wants to turn the responsibility over to someone else. Only the elect are strong enough to shoulder the burden, and they, therefore, must dictate to the many. Dubos, on the other hand, says that the freedom to choose is the fundamental human value. To abdicate it is to become less than human.

The growth of scientific knowledge which will open up new areas of freedom if the responsibility is accepted will also confer greater power on the dictator if the responsibility is rejected. Self-determination then becomes more and more difficult to recover. The choices we make today may well determine the degree of freedom, of individuality, and of personal dignity which our grandchildren will enjoy. "There is no more threatening and no more degrading doctrine," says J. Bronowski, "than the fancy that somehow we may shelve the responsibility for making the decisions of our society by passing it to a few scientists armored with a special magic. This is another dream . . . a modern version of the idle, harp-resounding heaven of other childhood pieties. But in fact it is the

2. Friedrich Sieburg, "The Self-Enslavement of Modern Civilization," *Atlantic Monthly*, March 1957.

picture of a slave society and should make us shiver whenever we hear a man of sensibility dismiss science as someone else's concern. The world today is made, it is powered by science; and for any man to abdicate an interest in science is to walk with open eyes towards slavery." [3]

3. J. Bronowski, *Science and Human Values,* Julian Messner, Inc., 1956.

Effect of Crowding and Stress:
New Insights from Biological Experiments

Throughout nature there is a balance between the reproductive rate of a given species of organism and the hazards of existence for that species. Elephants produce few young, while the spawn of oysters is innumerable. It is, to be sure, a teetering balance, so that there are often shifts in abundance from year to year or generation to generation. It is generally true, however, that biological systems have a great deal of "play" or flexibility. If the hazards of existence continue for any length of time to be greater than can be met by the reproductive rate, the species is started on the road to extinction. If reproduction exceeds mortality for any long period, the result is some sort of catastrophe—sometimes taking the form of mass suicide, as with locusts or lemmings.

Marston Bates (1962)
"Man as a Member of a Biological
Community," *Our Crowded Planet*

Nature's Balance, the Teetering See-Saw
SALLY CARRIGHAR (1965)

The very suggestion of overcrowding in a wilderness seems to contradict a favorite belief of nature-lovers: that nature manages her own world so well

From Marston Bates, "Man as a Member of a Biological Community," *Our Crowded Planet: Essays on the Pressures of Population*, edited by Fairfield Osborn, Doubleday and Company, Garden City. Copyright © 1962 by Doubleday and Company. Reprinted by permission.

From Sally Carrighar, *Wild Heritage*, Houghton Mifflin Company, Boston, and Hamish Hamilton Ltd., London. Copyright © 1965 by Sally Carrighar. Reprinted by permission.

that prey and predators always balance each other; that the hunting species weed out, as the saying is, the old and unfit and take enough of the young to prevent population explosions; that the normally smaller families of predators prevent the possibility of any one species of prey ever becoming exterminated completely. Nature's balance—we hear much about it, and it is a system of awesome efficiency. It is not perfect, however.

Some species over-produce quite consistently. Their numbers increase and then abruptly decline, in fairly regular cycles. Perhaps it simply takes about the same period for the populations to reach their peak every time; but it also is thought that the fluctuations may have some relation to extraterrestrial influences. The cycle of snowshoe hares, for example, is said to correspond to the eleven-year cycle of sunspots. During their times of superabundance the hares die by thousands from a disease which seems to result from stress and to be due to their overcrowded living conditions. Experiments with other species of animals show that the single factor of too many individuals in a given space, with no other privation whatever, sometimes causes symptoms such as enlarged adrenal glands. Heart disease also may result from crowding, as announced late in 1963 by scientists at the Penrose Laboratory of the Philadelphia Zoo. Herbert L. Ratcliffe, working with chickens, and Robert L. Snyder, observing captive wild woodchucks, found that caging too many animals within one enclosure can cause a drastic increase in fatal heart attacks. Physical contact is not necessary; even an excess of stimulation by voices can be disastrous. Heart disease has increased among other animals in the zoo, such as antelopes, deer, monkeys, and apes, since the practice began of displaying them in groups because the public likes to watch them that way.

Some animals cope with crowding in other ways besides dying. One of the most provocative, in view of the growing human urge to be on the move, is the method used by the small arctic rodents, the lemmings. Their population, like the hares', explodes periodically, the lemmings' reaching a peak every three or four years. At that time the lemmings are producing not only more litters but larger litters than usual. The cause of their abnormal fertility is not known, but whatever the explanation, the lemmings become extremely nervous during their months of excessive crowding. They run about frantically in the upper latitudes where they live, and some of them race away in their famous hordes, generally downhill on a course which brings them eventually to the sea, and they enter it, probably thinking it only a very wide river (they are good swimmers), and drown.

As their populations rise, many also are killed by their natural enemies, snowy owls, jaegers, foxes, and wolves. These species increase in numbers then—not due to undefined influences, only because they have found an abundance of easily captured prey. When the lemming population crashes, many of the predators also die, apparently from starvation rather than from the effects of overcrowding.

Since the pathological consequences of overcrowding have been understood, few biologists believe, as many once did, that the lemmings make their migrations and are impelled farther and farther because they have exhausted the vegetation on which they feed. When in 1953 a migration of lemmings came to the sea at Barrow, America's northernmost point of land, I arrived two days later and walked a long distance back on the tundra over which they had passed. The plants seemed of normal size. As described by the Eskimos and white members of the hospital staff, the lemming horde reached the shore on a front that would be nearly as wide as two city blocks, with the little animals running about eighteen inches apart. They were accompanied by their usual predators, and at Barrow the sled dogs were turned loose and caught many of the lemmings before they had reached the water.

During several previous years, at a location in Northern Alaska, I had had a captive colony of the lemmings (*Lemmus alascensis*) and had made a small, casual study of my own of the effects of crowding on the lemmings' temperament. They are extremely interesting creatures. Although rodents and only slightly larger than house-mouse size (but with long, silky fur), they are much more vocal than mice, more individual in their reactions, and more inventive in their play. To speak quite unscientifically, they give an observer the impression that they are enjoying life. They were supplied at all times with water and an abundance of food, including the arctic vegetation to which they were accustomed; they had moist earth to dig in, pieces of driftwood to climb and run on and chew (as they did, apparently, for the salt content); and they had nesting materials. As nearly as could be judged, they lacked none of the necessities of their normal living conditions.

They were confined in three enclosures of different sizes, and when the lemmings were distributed with sufficient space for each group, they thrived. Experimentally, then, I began putting more of them into one or another of the enclosures. They still had everything they needed and plenty of it—except elbow room, and elbow room proved to be an essen-

tial. Up to a certain limit of numbers a group would get along well together, with such signs of friendliness as little games and frolics and the
habit of sleeping three or four cuddled up in one nest. Up to a maximum
number, different for the various-sized enclosures, all went well, but the
addition of only a few more lemmings—sometimes only one—was an intolerable too many. With such crowding they all began to show irritability.
Instead of amiable pushing contests, nose to nose, they would stand on
their hind feet and box, trying to reach each other's throats, with their tiny
fangs bared. When I removed the lemmings that were the surplus population, the anger subsided, and I concluded that the pressure of too many
individuals in a given area was such a strain that the lemmings had been
trying to correct the situation in their own way—not analytically, of
course, but smaller numbers would have been the final effect of their fighting.

Population Control in Animals

V. C. WYNNE-EDWARDS (1964)

In population growth the human species is conspicuously out of line with
the rest of the animal kingdom. Man is almost alone in showing a long-
term upward trend in numbers; most other animals maintain their population size at a fairly constant level. To be sure, many of them fluctuate in
number from season to season, from year to year or from decade to
decade; notable examples are arctic lemmings, migratory locusts living in
the subtropical dry belt, many northern game birds and certain fur-bearing
animals. Such fluctuations, however, tend to swing erratically around a
constant average value. More commonly animal populations maintain a
steady state year after year and even century after century. If and when
the population does rise or fall permanently, because of some change in
the environment, it generally stabilizes again at a new level.

This well-established fact of population dynamics deserves to be studied
with close attention, because the growth of human populations has become in recent years a matter of increasing concern. What sort of mechanism is responsible for such strict control of the size of populations? Each

Figure 1. Massed maneuvers by starling flocks occur frequently on fine evenings, particularly in the fall. The maneuvers are an example of communal activity that appears to have the purpose of providing the flock with an indication of population density. If the density is too high or too low in relation to the food supply, the flock automatically increases the activities that will improve the balance.
Photograph by Joe Munroe. Reprinted by permission of Photo Researchers, Inc., N.Y.

animal population, apart from man's, seems to be regulated in a homeostatic manner by some system that tends to keep it within not too wide limits of a set average density. Ecologists have been seeking to discover the nature of this system for many years. I shall outline here a new hypothesis that I set forth in full detail in a recently published book, *Animal Dispersion in Relation to Social Behaviour*.

The prevailing hypothesis has been that population is regulated by a set of negative natural controls. It is assumed that animals will produce young as fast as they efficiently can, and that the main factors that keep population density within fixed limits are predators, starvation, accidents and parasites causing disease. On the face of it this assumption seems entirely reasonable; overcrowding should increase the death toll from most of these factors and thus act to cut back the population when it rises to a high density. On close examination, however, these ideas do not stand up.

The notions that predators or disease are essential controllers of population density can be dismissed at once. There are animals that effectively have no predators and are not readily subject to disease and yet are limited to a stable level of population; among notable examples are the lion, the eagle and the skua. Disease per se does not act on a large scale to control population growth in the animal world. This leaves starvation as the possible control. The question of whether starvation itself acts directly to remove a population surplus calls for careful analysis.

Even a casual examination makes it clear that in most animal communities starvation is rare. Normally all the individuals in the habitat get enough food to survive. Occasionally a period of drought or severe cold may starve out a population, but that is an accident of weather—a disaster that does not arise from the density of population. We must therefore conclude that death from hunger is not an important density-dependent factor in controlling population size except in certain unusual cases.

Yet the density of population in the majority of habitats does depend directly on the size of the food supply; the close relation of one to the other is clear in representative situations where both variables have been

Figure 2. Place in hierarchy is at stake in this contest between male black bucks in India. Many mammal and bird groups have a hierarchical system, or a system of defended territories. Successful individuals acquire food and breeding rights; the others leave, or perhaps stay as a reserve available for breeding if needed. By such means the group correlates its population with food resources.
Photograph by Ylla. Reprinted by permission of Rapho Guillumette Pictures, N.Y.

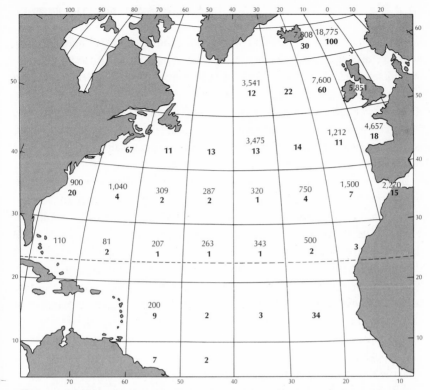

Figure 3. Population and food supply show a correlation in the North Atlantic Ocean. The figures in light type give the average volume of plankton found per cubic centimeter of water; the darker figures show the average daily count of ocean birds that feed on plankton.

measured (*see* Figure 3). We have, then, the situation that no individual starves but the population does not outgrow the food supply available in its habitat under normal conditions.

For many of the higher animals one can see therefore that neither predators, disease nor starvation can account for the regulation of numbers. There is of course accidental mortality, but it strikes in unpredictable and haphazard ways, independently of population density, and so must be ruled out as a stabilizer of population. All these considerations point to the possibility that the animals themselves must exercise the necessary restraint!

Man's own history provides some vivid examples of what is entailed here. By overgrazing he has converted once rich pastures into deserts; by overhunting he has exterminated the passenger pigeon and all but eliminated animals such as the right whale, the southern fur seal and, in many of their former breeding places, sea turtles; he is now threatening to exterminate all five species of rhinoceros inhabiting tropical Africa and Asia because the horns of those animals are valued for their alleged aphrodisiac powers. Exploiting the riches of today can exhaust and destroy the resources of tomorrow. The point is that animals face precisely this danger with respect to their food supply, and they generally handle it more prudently than man does.

Birds feeding on seeds and berries in the fall or chickadees living on hibernating insects in winter are in such a situation. The stock of food to begin with is so abundant that it could feed an enormous population. Then, however, it would be gone in hours or days, and the birds must depend on this food supply for weeks or months. To make it last through the season the birds must restrict the size of their population in advance. The same necessity holds in situations where unlimited feeding would wipe out the sources that replenish the food supply. Thus the threat of starvation tomorrow, not hunger itself today, seems to be the factor that decides what the density of a population ought to be. Long before starvation would otherwise occur, the population must limit its growth in order to avoid disastrous overexploitation of its food resources.

All this implies that animals restrict their population density by some artificial device that is closely correlated with the food supply. What is required is some sort of automatic restrictive mechanism analogous to the deliberate conventions or agreements by which nations limit the exploitation of fishing grounds.

One does not need to look far to realize that animals do indeed possess conventions of this kind. The best-known is the territorial system of birds. The practice of staking out a territory for nesting and rearing a family is common among many species of birds. In the breeding season each male lays claim to an area of not less than a certain minimum size and keeps out all other males of the species; in this way a group of males will parcel out the available ground as individual territories and put a limit on crowding. It is a perfect example of an artificial mechanism geared to adjusting the density of population to the food resources. Instead of competing directly for the food itself the members compete furiously for pieces of ground, each of which then becomes the exclusive food preserve of its owner. If the standard territory is large enough to feed a family, the entire group is safe from the danger of overtaxing the food supply.

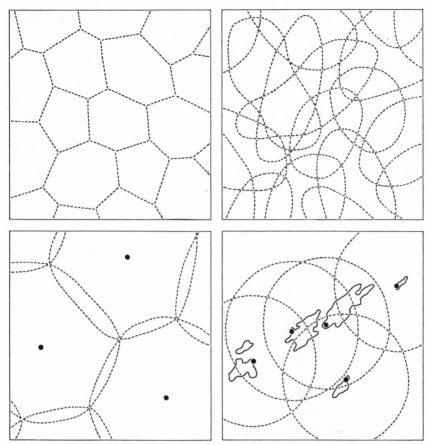

Figure 4. Population-control devices include the territory, of which the four basic types are depicted. Birds or mammals with territories have an established right to the available food; they also are the ones that breed. The others are in effect squeezed out. At top are two types of territory occupied by single males and their mates. At bottom are the types occupied by animals that live in colonies. One is virtually exclusive. The other is overlapping; shown here are islands from which five seabird colonies fan out within a maximum radius.

The territorial convention is just one example of a convention that takes many other forms, some of them much more sophisticated or abstract. Seabirds, for instance, being unable to stake out a territory or nest on the sea itself, adopt instead a token nesting place on the shore that represents their fishing rights. Each nesting site occupies only a few square feet, but the birds' behavior also limits the overall size of their colony, thereby restricting the number that will fish in the vicinity. Any adults that

367

have not succeeded in winning a site within the perimeter of the colony are usually inhibited from nesting or starting another colony nearby.

Other restrictive conventions practiced by animals are still more abstract. Often the animals compete not for actual property, such as a nesting site, but merely for membership in the group, and only a certain number are accepted. In all cases the effect is to limit the density of the group living in the given habitat and unload any surplus population to a safe distance.

Not the least interesting fact is that the competition itself tends to take an abstract or conventional form. In their contest for a territory birds seldom actually draw blood or kill each other. Instead they merely threaten with aggressive postures, vigorous singing or displays of plumage. The forms of intimidation of rivals by birds range all the way from the naked display of weapons to the triumph of splendor revealed in the peacock's train.

This hypothesis about the mechanism of population control in animals leads to a generalization of broader scope, namely that this was the origin or root of all social behavior in animals, including man. Surprisingly there has been no generally acceptable theory of how the first social organizations arose. One can now argue logically, however, that the kind of competition under conventional rules that is typified by the territorial system of birds was the earliest form of social organization. Indeed, a society can be defined as a group of individuals competing for conventional prizes by conventional methods. To put it another way, it is a brotherhood tempered by rivalry. One does not need to ponder very deeply to see how closely this cap fits even human societies.

A group of birds occupying an area divided into individual territories is plainly a social organization, and it exhibits a considerable range of characteristically social behavior. This is well illustrated by the red grouse of Scotland—a bird that is being studied intensively in a long-term research project near Aberdeen.

The grouse population on a heather moor consists of individuals known to one another and differing among themselves in social standing. The dominant males hold territories almost all year round, the most aggressive claiming on the average the largest territories. Their individual domains cover the moor like a mosaic (*see* Figure 5). The community admits as members some socially subordinate males and unmated hens that have no territories of their own, but with the onset of winter, or with

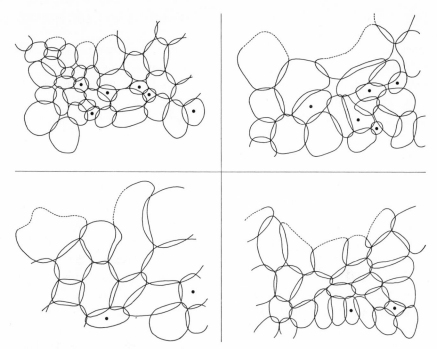

Figure 5. Territorial variations of Scottish red grouse males reflect a form of population control. The drawings show the territorial holdings of individual cocks in four successive springs (1958–1961) on the same 140 acres of moorland. Some of the smaller territories, marked by dots, were held by males who remained unmated. Average territory size varies from year to year, thus affecting the density of breeding; in these four years the number of territories ranged between 40, in 1958 (*top left*), and 16, in 1960 (*bottom left*). The density of breeding is correlated with the food supply, which is to say, with the quantity and quality of the heather.

a decline in the food supply for some other reason, these supernumeraries at the bottom of the social ladder get squeezed out. Only as many as can be supported by the lowered food level are allowed to stay. Thus the social hierarchy of the red grouse works as a safety valve or overflow mechanism, getting rid of any excess that would overtax the food resources. The existence of the peck-order system among birds has been known for some time, but its functional reason for being has been unclear; it now appears that the lowest members of the order serve as a dispensable reserve that can fill in as replacements for casualties among the established members or be dropped as circumstances require.

Certain definite rules mark the competition of the red grouse males for territory and status. One is that, at least in the fall, they crow and threaten only on fine mornings between first light and two or three hours later. So aggressive is this struggle that the stress forces some of the losers to make a break away from the moor; on unfamiliar ground and without their usual food they soon weaken and are killed by predators or disease. Once the early-morning contest is over, however, those birds that remain in the habitat flock together amicably and feed side by side for the rest of the day.

The convention of competing at dawn or at dusk and leaving the rest of the day free for feeding and other peaceable activities is exceedingly common among animals of various kinds. The changes of light at dawn and dusk are, of course, the most conspicuous recurrent events of the day, and this no doubt explains why they serve so often as a signal for joint or communal activities. There are many familiar manifestations of this timing: the dawn chorus of songbirds and crowing cocks, the flight of ducks at dusk, the massed maneuvers of starlings and blackbirds at their roosts as darkness falls; the evening choruses of almost innumerable other birds, various tropical bats, frogs, cicadas and fishes such as the croaker, and the morning concerts of howler monkeys.

All these synchronized outbursts give an indication of the numbers present in the respective populations. They provide an index of the popu-

Figure 6. Black grouse males are depicted in an "epideictic display," or ceremonial demonstration, that appears to be a form of population control. It evidently provides a measure of the population density within the area, because many males participate simultaneously on a communal strutting ground. It also serves as a means of excluding some less prominent males, who seldom display and often are chased away by the dominant birds. Epideictic displays also occur among many other bird and mammal species.

lation density in the habitat from day to day, and so feed to the group information that causes it, not deliberately but automatically, to step up those activities that may be necessary to restore the balance between the density and the food supply.

The daily community display puts a changing pressure on the members taking part. If the stress is great enough, a reduction in the population can be triggered off; if it is felt lightly or not at all, there is room for new recruits. Overcrowding will lead to expulsion of the population surplus, as in the case of the red grouse. In the breeding season the density index, in the form of the daily display, can influence the proportion of adults that mate and breed; likewise the number of young can be restricted in a variety of other ways to the quota that the habitat will allow.

In the light of this hypothesis one would expect these "epideictic" displays (that is, population-pressure demonstrations) to be particularly prominent at the outset of the breeding season. That is actually the case. In birds the demonstrators are usually the males; they can be called the epideictic sex. They may swarm and dance in the air (as many flying insects do) or engage in ritual tournaments, gymnastics or parades (characteristic of sage grouse, prairie chickens, tropical hummingbirds, manakins and birds-of-paradise). The intensity of these activities depends on the density of the population: the more males there are, the keener the competition. The new hypothesis suggests that this will result in greater stress among the males and sharper restriction of the size of the population.

In many animals the males have vocal abilities the females lack; this is true of songbirds, cicadas, most crickets and katydids, frogs, drumfishes, howler monkeys and others. Contrary to what was once thought, these males use their voices primarily not to woo females but in the contest with their fellow males for real estate and status. The same applies to many of the males' adornments and scent glands, as well as to their weapons. This newly recognized fact calls for some rethinking of the whole vexed subject of sexual selection.

Epideictic displays rise to a height not only as a prelude to the breeding season but also at the time of animal migrations. They show the scale of the impending change in the population density of the habitat and, during the migration, give an indication of the size of the flocks that have gathered at the stopping places, thereby enabling the migrants to avoid dangerous congestion at any one place. Locusts build up for a great flight with spectacular massed maneuvers, and comparable excitement marks the nightly roosting of migratory chimney swifts and other big gatherings of birds, fruit bats and insects.

Altogether the hypothesis that animal populations regulate themselves through the agency of social conventions of this kind seems to answer satisfactorily several of the major questions that have concerned ecologists. Basically the average population level is set by the long-term food resources of the habitat. A system of behavioral conventions acts as homeostatic machinery that prevents the growth of the population from departing too far from the optimal density. Fluctuations from this average can be explained as being due partly to temporary accidents (such as climatic extremes) and partly to the working of the homeostatic machinery itself, which allows the population density to build up when the food yields are good and thins it down when the yields fall below average. At any particular time the availability of food in relation to the number of mouths to be fed—in other words, the standard of living at the moment—determines the response of the regulating mechanism. The mechanism acts by controlling the rate of recruitment, by creating a pressure to emigrate or sometimes by producing stresses that result in large-scale mortality.

It has been particularly gratifying to find that the hypothesis offers explanations of several social enigmas on which there has been no good theory, such as the biological origin of social behavior; the function of the social hierarchy, or peck-order system, among birds; the chorus of birds and similar social events synchronized at dawn and dusk.

The theory has wide ramifications, which I have discussed at length in my book. The one that interests us most, of course, is its bearing on the problem of the unchecked growth of the human population. The hypothesis opens up to clearer view the differences between man's demographic history and that of other animals.

There are two outstanding differences. In the first place, the homeostatic control of animal populations is strictly automatic: even the social conventions of behavior are innate rather than deliberately arrived at. In part the density-dependent control in many animals, including some of the mammals, is exercised by means of a biological reaction—either reduction of the rate of ovulation through a change in the output of hormones, or resorption of the embryos in the uterus as a result of stress (as occurs in rabbits, foxes and deer). Man's fertility and population growth, on the other hand, are subject only to his conscious and deliberate behavior. The

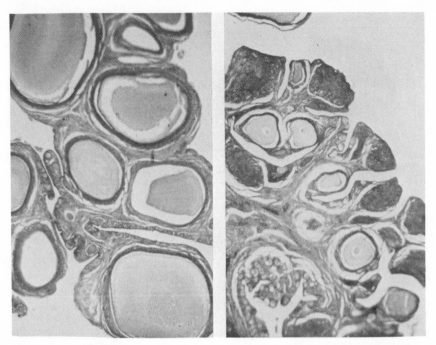

Figure 7. Ovary sections of nonbreeding fulmars indicate that population pressure may force a female to stop breeding. Section at left is from a young bird; that at right, from an older one as shown by dark resorbed ova. Older bird had bred as recently as the previous season.

second important difference is that modern man has progressively and enormously increased the food productivity of his habitat.

Primitive man, limited to the food he could get by hunting, had evolved a system for restricting his numbers by tribal traditions and taboos, such as prohibiting sexual intercourse for mothers while they were still nursing a baby, practicing compulsory abortion and infanticide, offering human sacrifices, conducting headhunting expeditions against rival tribes and so forth. These customs, consciously or not, kept the population density nicely balanced against the feeding capacity of the hunting range. Then, some 8,000 to 10,000 years ago, the agricultural revolution removed that limitation. There was no longer any reason to hold down the size of the tribe; on the contrary, power and wealth accrued to those tribes that allowed their populations to multiply, to develop farms, villages and even towns. The old checks on population growth were gradually discarded and forgotten. The rate of reproduction became a matter of individual choice

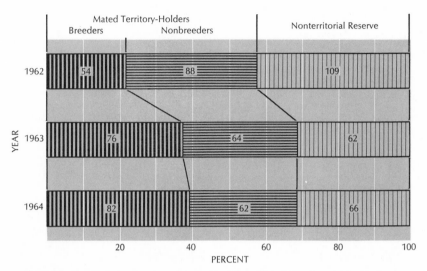

Figure 8. Population reserve exists among Scottish shelducks, as shown in data obtained by C. M. Young of the University of Aberdeen. The mated territory-holders all could have bred but many did not. The nonterritorial birds were denied even the opportunity to breed.

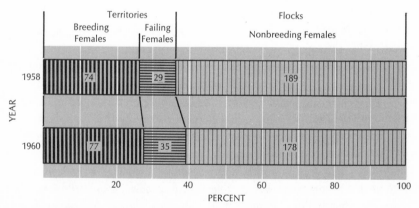

Figure 9. Similar data for the Australian magpie also show a breeding reserve. Females in flocks had no opportunity to breed; females in territories could have bred but many did not. The birds were studied over several years by Robert Carrick of the Australian government.

374

rather than of tribal or community control. It has remained so ever since.

Given opportunity for procreation and a low death rate, the human population, whether well fed or hungry, now shows a tendency to expand without limit. Lacking the built-in homeostatic system that regulates the density of animal populations, man cannot look to any natural process to restrain his rapid growth. If the growth is to be slowed down, it must be by his own deliberate and socially applied efforts.

Population Density and Social Pathology
JOHN B. CALHOUN (1962)

In the celebrated thesis of Thomas Malthus, vice and misery impose the ultimate natural limit on the growth of populations. Students of the subject have given most of their attention to misery, that is, to predation, disease and food supply as forces that operate to adjust the size of a population to its environment. But what of vice? Setting aside the moral burden of this word, what are the effects of the social behavior of a species on population growth—and of population density on social behavior?

Some years ago I attempted to submit this question to experimental inquiry. I confined a population of wild Norway rats in a quarter-acre enclosure. With an abundance of food and places to live and with predation and disease eliminated or minimized, only the animals' behavior with respect to one another remained as a factor that might affect the increase in their number. There could be no escape from the behavioral consequences of rising population density. By the end of 27 months the population had become stabilized at 150 adults. Yet adult mortality was so low that 5,000 adults might have been expected from the observed reproductive rate. The reason this larger population did not materialize was that infant mortality was extremely high. Even with only 150 adults in the enclosure, stress from social interaction led to such disruption of maternal behavior that few young survived.

With this background in mind I turned to observation of a domesticated albino strain of the Norway rat under more controlled circumstances indoors. The data for the present discussion come from the histories of six different populations. Each was permitted to increase to approximately twice the number that my experience had indicated could occupy the available space with only moderate stress from social interaction. In each case my associates and I maintained close surveillance of the colonies for 16 months in order to obtain detailed records of the modifications of behavior induced by population density.

The consequences of the behavioral pathology we observed were most apparent among the females. Many were unable to carry pregnancy to full term or to survive delivery of their litters if they did. An even greater number, after successfully giving birth, fell short in their maternal functions. Among the males the behavior disturbances ranged from sexual deviation to cannibalism and from frenetic overactivity to a pathological withdrawal from which individuals would emerge to eat, drink and move about only when other members of the community were asleep. The social organization of the animals showed equal disruption. Each of the experimental populations divided itself into several groups, in each of which the sex ratios were drastically modified. One group might consist of six or seven females and one male, whereas another would have 20 males and only 10 females.

The common source of these disturbances became most dramatically apparent in the populations of our first series of three experiments, in which we observed the development of what we called a behavioral sink. The animals would crowd together in greatest number in one of the four interconnecting pens in which the colony was maintained. As many as 60 of the 80 rats in each experimental population would assemble in one pen during periods of feeding. Individual rats would rarely eat except in the company of other rats. As a result extreme population densities developed in the pen adopted for eating, leaving the others with sparse populations.

Eating and other biological activities were thereby transformed into social activities in which the principal satisfaction was interaction with other rats. In the case of eating, this transformation of behavior did not keep the animals from securing adequate nutrition. But the same pathological "togetherness" tended to disrupt the ordered sequences of activity involved in other vital modes of behavior such as the courting of sex partners, the building of nests and the nursing and care of the young. In the experiments in which the behavioral sink developed, infant mortality ran as high as 96 per cent among the most disoriented groups in the population. Even in the absence of the behavioral sink, in the second series of three experiments, infant mortality reached 80 per cent among the corresponding members of the experimental populations.

The design of the experiments was relatively simple. The three populations of the first series each began with 32 rats; each population of the second series began with 56 rats. In all cases the animals were just past weaning and were evenly divided between males and females. By the 12th month all the populations had multiplied and each comprised 80 adults. Thereafter removal of the infants that survived birth and weaning held the populations steady. Although the destructive effects of population density increased during the course of the experiments, and the mortality rate among the females and among the young was much higher in the 16th month than it was earlier, the number of young that survived to weaning was always large enough to offset the effects of adult mortality and actually to increase the population. The evidence indicates, however, that in time failures of reproductive function would have caused the colonies to die out. At the end of the first series of experiments eight rats—the four healthiest males and the four healthiest females in each of two populations—were permitted to survive. These animals were six months old at the time, in the prime of life. Yet in spite of the fact that they no longer lived in overpopulated environments, they produced fewer litters in the next six months than would normally have been expected. Nor did any of the offspring that were born survive to maturity.

The males and females that initiated each experiment were placed, in groups of the same size and sex composition, in each of the four pens that partitioned a 10-by-14-foot observation room. The pens were complete dwelling units; each contained a drinking fountain, a food hopper and an elevated artificial burrow, reached by a winding staircase and holding five nest boxes. A window in the ceiling of the room permitted observation, and there was a door in one wall. With space for a colony of 12 adults in each pen—the size of the groups in which rats are normally found—this setup should have been able to support 48 rats comfortably. At the stabilized number of 80, an equal distribution of the animals would have found 20 adult rats in each pen. But the animals did not dispose themselves in this way.

Biasing factors were introduced in the physical design of the environment to encourage differential use of the four pens. The partitions separating the pens were electrified so that the rats could not climb them. Ramps across three of the partitions enabled the animals to get from one pen to

Figure 1. Effect of population density on the behavior and social organization of rats was studied by confining groups of 80 animals in a 10 x 14-foot room divided into four pens by an electrical fence. All pens (numbered 1, 2, 3, and 4 clockwise from door) were complete dwelling units. Conical objects are food hoppers; trays with three bottles are drinking troughs. Elevated burrows, reached by winding staircases, each had five nest boxes, seen in pen 1, where top of burrow has been removed. Ramps connected all pens but 1 and 4. Rats therefore tended to concentrate in pens 2 and 3. Development of a "behavioral sink," which further increased population in one pen,

is reflected in pen 2, where three rats are eating simultaneously. Rat approaching ramp in pen 3 is an estrous female pursued by a pack of males. In pens 2 and 3, where population density was highest, males outnumbered females. In pens 1 and 4, a dominant male was usually able to expel all other males and possess a harem of females. Dominant males are sleeping at the base of the ramps in pens 1 and 4. They wake when other males approach, preventing incursions into their territories. The three rats peering down from a ramp are probers, one of the deviant behavioral types produced by the pressures of a high population density.

another and so traverse the entire room. With no ramps to permit crossing of the fourth partition, however, the pens on each side of it became the end pens of what was topologically a row of four. The rats had to make a complete circuit of the room to go from the pen we designated 1 to the pen designated 4 on the other side of the partition separating the two. This arrangement of ramps immediately skewed the mathematical probabilities in favor of a higher population density in pens 2 and 3 than in pens 1 and 4. Pens 2 and 3 could be reached by two ramps, whereas pens 1 and 4 had only one each.

The use of pen 4 was further discouraged by the elevation of its burrow to a height greater than that of the burrow in the other end pen. The two middle pens were similarly distinguished from each other, the burrow in pen 3 being higher than that in pen 2. But here the differential appears to have played a smaller role, although pen 2 was used somewhat more often than pen 3.

With the distribution of the rats biased by these physical arrangements, the sizes of the groups in each pen could have been expected to range from as few as 13 to as many as 27. With the passage of time, however, changes in behavior tended to skew the distribution of the rats among the pens even more. Of the 100 distinct sleeping groups counted in the 10th to 12th month of each experiment, only 37 fell within the expected size range. In 33 groups there were fewer than 13 rats, and in 30 groups the count exceeded 27. The sex ratio approximated equality only in those groups that fell within the expected size range. In the smaller groups, generally composed of eight adults, there were seldom more than two males. In the larger groups, on the other hand, there were many more males than females. As might be expected, the smaller groups established themselves in the end pens, whereas the larger groups were usually observed to form in the middle pens. The female members of the population distributed themselves about equally in the four pens, but the male population was concentrated almost overwhelmingly in the middle pens.

One major factor in the creation of this state of affairs was the struggle for status that took place among the males. Shortly after male rats reach maturity, at about six months of age, they enter into a round robin of fights that eventually fixes their position in the social hierarchy. In our experiments such fights took place among the males in all the pens, both middle and end. In the end pens, however, it became possible for a single dominant male to take over the area as his territory. During the period when the social hierarchy was being established, the subordinate males in all pens adopted the habit of arising early. This enabled them to eat and drink in peace. Since rats generally eat in the course of their normal wanderings, the subordinate residents of the end pens were likely to feed in one of the middle pens. When, after feeding, they wanted to return to their original quarters, they would find it very difficult. By this time the most dominant male in the pen would probably have awakened, and he would engage the subordinates in fights as they tried to come down the one ramp to the pen. For a while the subordinate would continue its efforts to return to what had been its home pen, but after a succession of defeats it would become so conditioned that it would not even make the attempt. In essence the dominant male established his territorial dominion and his control over a harem of females not by driving the other males out but by preventing their return.

Once a male had established his dominion over an end pen and the harem it contained, he was usually able to maintain it. Although he slept a good deal of the time, he made his sleeping quarters at the base of the ramp. He was, therefore, on perpetual guard. Awakening as soon as another male appeared at the head of the ramp, he had only to open his eyes for the invader to wheel around and return to the adjoining pen. On the other hand, he would sleep calmly through all the comings and goings of his harem; seemingly he did not even hear their clatterings up and down the wire ramp. His conduct during his waking hours reflected his dominant status. He would move about in a casual and deliberate fashion, occasionally inspecting the burrow and nests of his harem. But he would rarely enter a burrow, as some other males did, merely to ferret out the females.

A territorial male might tolerate other males in his domain provided they respected his status. Such subordinate males inhabited the end pens in several of the experiments. Phlegmatic animals, they spent most of their time hidden in the burrow with the adult females, and their excursions to the floor lasted only as long as it took them to obtain food and water. Although they never attempted to engage in sexual activity with any of the females, they were likely, on those rare occasions when they encountered the dominant male, to make repeated attempts to mount him. Generally the dominant male tolerated these advances.

In these end pens, where population density was lowest, the mortality rate among infants and females was also low. Of the various social environments that developed during the course of the experiments, the brood pens, as we called them, appeared to be the only healthy ones, at least in terms of survival of the group. The harem females generally made good mothers. They nursed their young, built nests for them and protected them from harm. If any situation arose that a mother considered a danger to her pups, she would pick the infants up one at a time and carry them in her mouth to a safer place. Nothing would distract her from this task until the entire litter had been moved. Half the infants born in the brood pens survived.

The pregnancy rates recorded among the females in the middle pens were no lower than those recorded in the end pens. But a smaller percentage of these pregnancies terminated in live births. In the second series of experiments 80 per cent of the infants born in the middle pens died before weaning. In the first series 96 per cent perished before this time. The males in the middle pens were no less affected than the females by the pressures of population density. In both series of experiments the social pathology among the males was high. In the first series, however, it was more aggravated than it was in the second.

This increase in disturbance among the middle-pen occupants of the first series of experiments was directly related to the development of the phenomenon of the behavioral sink—the outcome of any behavioral process that collects animals together in unusually great numbers. The unhealthy connotations of the term are not accidental: a behavioral sink does act to aggravate all forms of pathology that can be found within a group.

The emergence of a behavioral sink was fostered by the arrangements that were made for feeding the animals. In these experiments the food consisted of small, hard pellets that were kept in a circular hopper formed by wire mesh. In consequence satisfaction of hunger required a continuous effort lasting several minutes. The chances therefore were good that while one rat was eating another would join it at the hopper. As was mentioned earlier, rats usually eat intermittently throughout their waking hours, whenever they are hungry and food is available. Since the arrangement of the ramps drew more rats into the middle pens than into the end ones, it was in these pens that individuals were most likely to find other individuals eating. As the population increased, the association of eating with the presence of other animals was further reinforced. Gradually the social aspect of the activity became determinant: the rats would rarely eat except at hoppers already in use by other animals.

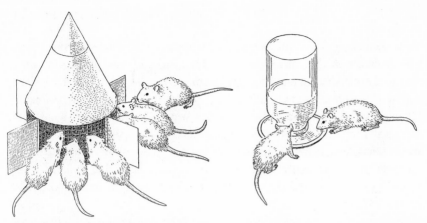

Figure 2. Food hopper used in first series of experiments is seen at the left in this drawing. Water tray is at the right. The hopper, covered with wire grating and holding hard pellets of food, made eating a lengthy activity during which one rat was likely to meet another. Thus it fostered the development of a behavioral sink: the animals would eat only in the presence of others, and they preferred one of the four hoppers in the room to all the others. In time 75 per cent of the animals crowded into the pen containing this hopper to eat.

At this point the process became a vicious circle. As more and more of the rats tended to collect at the hopper in one of the middle pens, the other hoppers became less desirable as eating places. The rats that were eating at these undesirable locations, finding themselves deserted by their groupmates, would transfer their feeding to the more crowded pen. By the time the three experiments in the first series drew to a close half or more of the populations were sleeping as well as eating in that pen. As a result there was a decided increase in the number of social adjustments each rat had to make every day. Regardless of which pen a rat slept in, it would go to one particular middle pen several times a day to eat. Therefore it was compelled daily to make some sort of adjustment to virtually every other rat in the experimental population.

No behavioral sinks developed in the second series of experiments, because we offered the rats their diet in a different way. A powdered food was set out in an open hopper. Since it took the animals only a little while to eat, the probability that two animals would be eating simultaneously was considerably reduced. In order to foster the emergence of a behavioral sink I supplied the pens with drinking fountains designed to prolong the drinking activity. The effect of this arrangement was unquestionably to make the animals social drinkers; they used the fountain mainly when other animals lined up at it. But the effect was also to discourage them from wandering and to prevent the development of a behavioral sink. Since rats generally drink immediately on arising, drinking and the social interaction it occasioned tended to keep them in the pens in which they slept. For this reason all social pathology in the second series of experiments, although severe, was less extreme than it was in the first series.

Females that lived in the densely populated middle pens became progressively less adept at building adequate nests and eventually stopped building nests at all. Normally rats of both sexes build nests, but females do so most vigorously around the time of parturition. It is an undertaking that

Figure 3. Water fountain used in second series of experiments is seen at the right in this drawing. Food hopper is at the left. The fountain was operated by pressing a lever. Thus it made drinking a lengthy activity, associated with the presence of others. But it did not create a behavioral sink. Although the rats would drink only if other animals were present, they engaged in this activity in their home pens, immediately after awakening. The fountain therefore acted to produce an even distribution of the population.

involves repeated periods of sustained activity, searching out appropriate materials (in our experiments strips of paper supplied an abundance), transporting them bit by bit to the nest and there arranging them to form a cuplike depression, frequently sheltered by a hood. In a crowded middle pen, however, the ability of females to persist in this biologically essential activity became markedly impaired. The first sign of disruption was a failure to build the nest to normal specifications. These females simply piled the strips of paper in a heap, sometimes trampling them into a pad that showed little sign of cup formation. Later in the experiment they would bring fewer and fewer strips to the nesting site. In the midst of transporting a bit of material they would drop it to engage in some other activity occasioned by contact and interaction with other individuals met on the way. In the extreme disruption of their behavior during the later months of the population's history they would build no nests at all but would bear their litters on the sawdust in the burrow box.

The middle-pen females similarly lost the ability to transport their litters from one place to another. They would move only part of their litters and would scatter them by depositing the infants in different places or simply dropping them on the floor of the pen. The infants thus abandoned throughout the pen were seldom nursed. They would die where they were dropped and were thereupon generally eaten by the adults.

The social stresses that brought about this disorganization in the behavior of the middle-pen females were imposed with special weight on them when they came into heat. An estrous female would be pursued relentlessly by a pack of males, unable to escape from their soon unwanted attentions. Even when she retired to a burrow, some males would follow her. Among these females there was a correspondingly high rate of mortality from disorders in pregnancy and parturition. Nearly half of the first- and second-generation females that lived in the behavioral-sink situation had died of these causes by the end of the 16th month. Even in the absence of the extreme stresses of the behavioral sink, 25 per cent of the females died. In contrast, only 15 per cent of the adult males in both series of experiments died.

A female that lived in a brood pen was sheltered from these stresses even though during her periods of estrus she would leave her pen to mate with males in the other pens of the room. Once she was satiated, however, she could return to the brood pen. There she was protected from the excessive attention of other males by the territorial male.

For the effect of population density on the males there is no index as explicit and objective as the infant and maternal mortality rates. We have attempted a first approximation of such an index, however, by scoring the behavior of the males on two scales: that of dominance and that of physical activity. The first index proved particularly effective in the early period of the experiments, when the males were approaching adulthood and beginning the fights that eventually fixed their status in the social hierarchy. The more fights a male initiated and the more fights he won, the more likely he was to establish a position of dominance. More than half the animals in each experiment gave up the struggle for status after a while, but among those that persisted a clear-cut hierarchy developed.

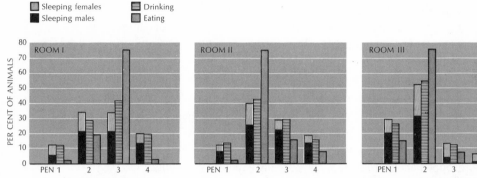

Figure 4. Behavioral sink developed in the first series of three experiments, drawing half the rats either into pen 2 or pen 3 of each room to drink and sleep, and even more into that pen to eat. Chart describes the situation in the 13th month of the experiment. By then the population distributions were fairly stable and many females in the densely populated pens had died. One male in room III had established pens 3 and 4 as his territory. Subsequently a male in room I took over pen 1, expelling all the other males.

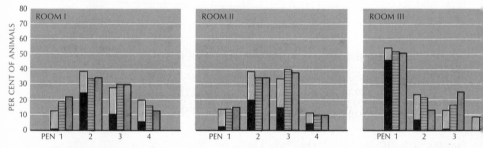

Figure 5. Population distributions in the second series of three experiments, in which no behavioral sink developed, were more even than they were in the first series, and the death rate among females and infants was lower. Chart shows the situation in the 13th month, when one male had established pens 3 and 4 of room III as his territory, and another was taking over pen 2, thus forcing most of the males into pen 1. Pen 1 in rooms I and II had also become territories; later pen 4 in room II became a territory.

In the crowded middle pens no one individual occupied the top position in this hierarchy permanently. In every group of 12 or more males one was the most aggressive and most often the victor in fights. Nevertheless, this rat was periodically ousted from his position. At regular intervals during the course of their waking hours the top-ranking males engaged in free-for-alls that culminated in the transfer of dominance from one male to another. In between these tumultuous changings of the guard relative calm prevailed.

The aggressive, dominant animals were the most normal males in our populations. They seldom bothered either the females or the juveniles. Yet even they exhibited occasional signs of pathology, going berserk, attacking females, juveniles and the less active males, and showing a particular predilection—which rats do not normally display—for biting other animals on the tail.

Below the dominant males both on the status scale and in their level of activity were the homosexuals—a group perhaps better described as pansexual. These animals apparently could not discriminate between appropriate and inappropriate sex partners. They made sexual advances to males, juveniles and females that were not in estrus. The males, including the dominants as well as the others of the pansexuals' own group, usually accepted their attentions. The general level of activity of these animals was only moderate. They were frequently attacked by their dominant associates, but they very rarely contended for status.

Two other types of male emerged, both of which had resigned entirely from the struggle for dominance. They were, however, at exactly opposite poles as far as their levels of activity were concerned. The first were completely passive and moved through the community like somnambulists. They ignored all the other rats of both sexes, and all the other rats ignored them. Even when the females were in estrus, these passive animals made no advances to them. And only very rarely did other males attack them or approach them for any kind of play. To the casual observer the passive animals would have appeared to be the healthiest and most attractive members of the community. They were fat and sleek, and their fur showed none of the breaks and bare spots left by the fighting in which males usually engage. But their social disorientation was nearly complete.

Perhaps the strangest of all the types that emerged among the males was the group I have called the probers. These animals, which always lived in the middle pens, took no part at all in the status struggle. Nevertheless, they were the most active of all the males in the experimental populations, and they persisted in their activity in spite of attacks by the dominant animals. In addition to being hyperactive, the probers were both hypersexual and homosexual, and in time many of them became cannibalistic. They were always on the alert for estrous females. If there were

 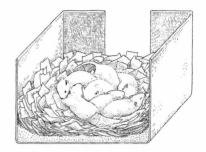

Figure 6. Normal maternal behavior among rats includes building a fluffy, well-shaped nest for the young. The drawing at the left shows such a nest, holding a recently born litter. The drawing at the right shows this same nest about two weeks later. It has been flattened by the weight of the animals' bodies but it still offers ample protection and warmth, and the remaining pups can still rest comfortably. In these experiments half the offspring of normal mothers survived infancy and were successfully weaned.

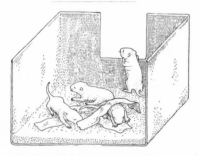 

Figure 7. Abnormal maternal behavior, shown by females exposed to the pressures of population density, includes failure to build adequate nests. The drawing at the left shows the recently born young of a disturbed female. She started to make a nest but never finished it. The drawing at the right shows her young about two weeks later. One pup has already left and another is leaving. Neither can survive alone. In these experiments, the mortality rate among infants of disturbed mothers was as high as 96 per cent.

none in their own pens, they would lie in wait for long periods at the tops of the ramps that gave on the brood pens and peer down into them. They always turned and fled as soon as the territorial rat caught sight of them. Even if they did not manage to escape unhurt, they would soon return to their vantage point.

The probers conducted their pursuit of estrous females in an abnormal manner. Mating among rats usually involves a distinct courtship ritual. In the first phase of this ritual the male pursues the female. She thereupon retires for a while into the burrow, and the male lies quietly in wait outside, occasionally poking his head into the burrow for a moment but never entering it. (In the wild forms of the Norway rat this phase usually involves a courtship dance on the mound at the mouth of the burrow.) The female at last emerges from the burrow and accepts the male's advances. Even in the disordered community of the middle pens this pattern was observed by all the males who engaged in normal heterosexual behavior. But the probers would not tolerate even a short period of waiting at the burrows in the pens where accessible females lived. As soon as a female retired to a burrow, a prober would follow her inside. On these expeditions the probers often found dead young lying in the nests; as a result they tended to become cannibalistic in the later months of a population's history.

Although the behavioral sink did not develop in the second series of experiments, the pathology exhibited by the populations in both sets of experiments, and in all pens, was severe. Even in the brood pens females could raise only half their young to weaning. Nor does the difference in infant mortality between the middle pens of the first and second series— 96 per cent in the first as opposed to 80 per cent in the second—represent a biologically significant improvement. It is obvious that the behavioral repertory with which the Norway rat has emerged from the trials of evolution and domestication must break down under the social pressures generated by population density. In time, refinement of experimental procedures and of the interpretation of these studies may advance our understanding to the point where they may contribute to the making of value judgments about analogous problems confronting the human species.

Cybernetics of Population Control
HUDSON HOAGLAND (1964)

There is an ambivalence about many scientific discoveries, and it is ironical that our best humanitarian motives in medicine and public health are primarily responsible for the grave dangers of the population explosion. I would like to consider some of the ways in which nature deals with overcrowding in other animal societies, since this may shed some light on our own population problems.

In multiplying cultures of microorganisms, the growth rate accelerates

From Hudson Hoagland, "Cybernetics of Population Control," *Bulletin of the Atomic Scientists,* February 1964. Copyright 1964 by the Educational Foundation for Nuclear Science. Reprinted by permission.

exponentially; but as toxic metabolic products such as acids or alcohols accumulate, the rate declines and the curve describing numbers of organisms as a function of time ultimately flattens off.

Insect populations are regulated in various ways. The fruit fly, *Drosophila*, above certain population densities, decreases its egg laying in an amount proportional to the density. In flour beetles, below a fixed number of grams of flour per beetle, cannibalism occurs in some species and egg production drops off; in one species, crowding results in females puncturing and destroying some of the eggs they have produced. Frequency of copulation also declines with crowding. There are some species of flour beetles with glands that produce a gas, the release of which is increased with crowding. This gas is lethal to larvae and acts as an antaphrodisiac at high densities of population. Flour contaminated with beetle excrement inhibits egg production of another species; mixing this contaminated flour with fresh flour decreases the rate of population growth, despite the ample food supply. . . .

Minnesota jack rabbit populations rise and fall through cycles of several years' duration. There is a build-up followed by a dying off. It was observed that when the animals died off there was usually plenty of food —they didn't starve. There was no evidence of excessive predators. Furthermore, the bodies showed no sign of any specific epidemic that killed them. To quote from a 1939 study of the dead animals: "This syndrome was characterized primarily by fatty degeneration and atrophy of the liver with a coincident striking decrease in liver glycogen and a hypoglycemia preceding death. Petechial or ecchymotic brain hemorrhages and congestion and hemorrhage of the adrenals, thyroid, and kidneys were frequent findings in a smaller number of animals. The hares characteristically died in convulsive seizures with sudden onset, running movements, hindleg extension, retraction of the head and neck, and sudden leaps with clonic seizures upon alighting. Other animals were typically lethargic or comatose." The adrenals were hypertrophied in some cases and atrophied in others. Such signs—liver disease, hypertension, atherosclerosis, and adrenal deterioration—are typical of the acute stress syndrome that results from overactivity of the pituitary-adrenal axis.

Studies of rodents showed that, after the severe stress of winter crowding in burrows when population densities were high, there was much fighting among the males, sex drives were at a low ebb, the young were often eaten, and the females produced premature births. There was also increased susceptibility to nonspecific infections—another byproduct of excessive production of adrenal corticoids. After such a colony has been depleted in numbers through effects of the stress syndrome, the colony then tends to build up again, and so it goes through repeated cycles of growth and decline.

A pair of deer were put on a small island of about 150 acres in Chesapeake Bay about forty years ago. The deer were kept well supplied with food. It was found that the colony grew until it reached a density of about one deer per acre. Then the animals began to die off despite adequate food and care. Examination of the dead animals again showed marked evidence of the adrenal stress syndrome. In studies of crowding in the Philadelphia zoo, it was found that in some species of animals there was a tenfold increase in atherosclerosis under conditions of severe crowding, and there were many other symptoms characteristic of stress. John Christian of the Naval Medical Research Institute made population studies in relation to crowding of mice. In his 1950 paper in the *Journal of Mammalogy,* "The Adrenopituitary System and Population Cycles in Mammals," he wrote: "We now have a working hypothesis for the die-off terminating a cycle. Exhaustion of the adrenopituitary system resulting from increased stresses inherent in a high population, especially in winter, plus the late winter demands of the reproductive system, due to increased light or other factors, precipitates population-wide death with the symptoms of adrenal insufficiency and hypoglycemic convulsions."

• • •

Stress in Human Populations

A question of immediate interest is to what extent the stress syndrome may be a factor in reducing the growth rate of human populations. As far as I know, there are no adequate data to answer this question. Studies from a number of laboratories including our own have demonstrated that the human pituitary adrenal system responds under stress in a way similar to that of other mammals. There is indirect evidence that inmates of concentration camps experienced acute forms of the stress syndrome that may have accounted for many deaths. Concentration camps are more appropriately compared with highly congested animal populations than are city slums, since even in very crowded cities, the poor do have some mobility. They can escape from their immediate congestion on streets and associate with other segments of the population. The incidence of street gangs and juvenile delinquency is especially characteristic of overcrowded city areas

and constitutes a form of social pathology. Several studies have also indicated a higher incidence of schizophrenia and of other psychotic and
neurotic behavior in congested urban areas than in more spacious environments, but other factors may be involved here. The increased incidence of
atherosclerosis and other cardiovascular pathology associated with urban
living and its competitive stresses may also be enhanced by crowding, although direct evidence for this is lacking. In underdeveloped countries
with high birth rates and recently lowered death rates, producing population growth of two to four per cent per year, any growth-retarding effect
of the stress syndrome is masked by the use of health measures that are
enhancing life expectancies. . . .

Many studies, other than those already mentioned, of mortality promoted by stress have been made. The white stork has been intensively
studied. Nestling mortality is often very heavy under crowded conditions
and individual chicks may be deliberately killed and sometimes eaten by
one of their parents, usually the father. This is most likely to happen
where the parents are beginners or young adults, and presumably of lower
social status in the pecking hierarchy. The killing off of the young under
prolific breeding conditions is characteristic of a great many birds and
mammals, and is a direct result of social stress. The killing of the young
and cannibalism are known to occur quite widely in mammals; for instance, in rodents, lions, and also in primitive man. Cases of cannibalism
are found in fish, spider crabs, and spiders and of fratricide in various insect larvae. *In all cases experimentally investigated, the mortality is found
to be dependent on population density and to cease below a certain critical population density.*

Mortality from predation has also been examined. This appears to be
density-dependent to the extent that the prey cooperates by making its
surplus members especially vulnerable to predators. The density-dependent elements in predation thus seem to arise on the part of the prey and
not on that of the predators. Because of lowered resistance to infective
agents following prolonged stress, disease as a form of predation may
effectively reduce excessive population. In this case a surplus of individuals predisposed to injury by their dominant fellows naturally experiences
a variable amount of uncontrolled mortality; this tends to fall most
heavily on the young, which are as yet unprotected by acquired immunity
from bacterial and viral infections. But social stress can lead to casualties
at all ages, both through direct and mortal combat and through stress-
induced disease. The victim of severe stress is likely to develop physiolog-

ical disorders affecting many organs, especially the lymphatic apparatus, including the spleen and thymus, and also the nervous system, circulatory, digestive, and generative organs, and the endocrine glands, especially the adrenal cortex, which serves an intermediary role between the stressor and the organs responding to adrenal cortical hormones. Social stress is sometimes partly physical, as when the exercise of pecking order rights leads to the infliction of wounds or to withholding food and shelter. But, as Wynne-Edwards points out, it may be largely mental, just as we find that man, in his simpler-minded states, may die from the conviction that he has been bewitched. Cases are known of birds, mammals, and amphibians similarly dying from nonspecific injuries apparently induced by social stress.

The Population Explosion

What about man? What can we do about the world population explosion? We could, of course, do nothing and just wait for the stress syndrome or a new virus to do its work. It has been said that until recently our politicians had washed their hands of the population problem but are now wringing their hands over it. We can leave the "solution" to some trigger-happy dictator with a suitable stockpile of nuclear weapons, or perhaps we can finally decide on an optimal population for the world and, by education and social pressure, try to see that it is not exceeded. At the present average growth rate of two per cent per year, there will be one square yard of earth per person in 600 years. Population growth depends only on the difference between birth rate and death rate. Man is the only animal that can direct its own evolution. Which of these two variables will he manipulate?

A Naturalist Looks at Overpopulation
JOSEPH WOOD KRUTCH (1962)

One of the many indications that the population explosion poses the most desperate problem of our day is the fact that it inevitably arises in connection with every approach to the analysis of our civilization and its prospects. To the critic of culture it is a part of our emphasis on quantity rather than quality. To the economist it raises the question of economic stability. To the political scientist it evokes the specter of wars for Lebensraum; to the conservationist the equally terrifying specter of universal starvation.

To the specialists in their various fields I leave the discussions appropriate to them and say only something about the situation as it appears to a naturalist; to one who is, of course, aware of its other aspects but tends to think first of man's place in nature and the consequences of modern man's refusal to accept the fact that he is indeed part of a scheme which he can to some extent modify but which he cannot supersede by a scheme of his own making.

It is true, of course, that man became man rather than simply a member of the animal kingdom when he ceased merely to accept and submit to the conditions of the natural world. But it is also true that for many thousands of years his resistance to the laws of animal nature and his modifications of his environment were so minor that they did not seriously interfere with natural law and required no such elaborate management of compensating adjustments as became necessary as soon as his intentions, desires, and will became effective enough to interfere with the scheme of nature.

It was not until well into the nineteenth century that his interferences did become extensive enough to force a dawning realization of the fact that you cannot "control nature" at one point without taking steps to readjust at another the balance which has been upset. Improved methods of agriculture exhaust the soil unless artificial steps are taken to conserve and renew it. You cannot destroy all the vermin without risking the destruction of useful animals. You cannot, as we are just discovering, poison noxious insects without risking the extinction of birds who are an even more effective control. It is not that we should not interfere with nature, but that we must face the consequences of this interference and counteract or ameliorate them by other interferences. You dare not, to put it as simply as possible, attempt to manage at one point and to let nature take her course at another.

Considered in connection with this fact the population explosion becomes merely a special (and especially ominous) example of a phenomenon characteristic of civilized man's peculiar place in nature where he is the only creature capable of effectively interfering with her operations while he remains at the same time not wise enough always to foresee the unwanted consequences of his interference. To reduce it again to the simplest possible terms, he has interfered with nature by preserving individual lives far more successfully than nature had ever been able to preserve them at the same time he has allowed nature to take her course so far as propagation is concerned. As a consequence either one of two things must happen. Either he must control birth as well as death or nature will step in and by her own rough but effective methods—starvation, disease, or the brutal death struggle for food and living room—eliminate the excess which failure to manage the consequences of his management has produced. No matter what fantastic increases technology may bring in the number of men the earth is able to support, the limit must be reached sooner or later. . . .

Many sociologists and political scientists recognize the fact that the question is not simply how many people the earth could possibly support, but what is the optimum number from the standpoint of the possibility of a good life. Just as it is foolish to ask what is the largest number of children a family could possibly consist of rather than how many constitute an ideal family unit, so it is foolish to ask how many could be crowded onto our globe rather than what number can live happily there. Men need not only food and a place to sleep but also room to move about in. It is at least possible to believe that cities are already too big and that life would become almost intolerable if they were both more densely crowded and so merged one with another that there was no escaping from them.

Of this the naturalist is often more acutely aware than either the sociologist or the political scientist because he is more completely convinced than they sometimes are that the best life for the human being is one which is led, partly at least, in the context of nature rather than in a context which consists exclusively of the man-made environment. For a large part of the existing human race in the centers of civilization, contact with the natural world is tending to diminish almost to the vanishing point while he has little experience with anything except bricks, steel and concrete on the one hand and mechanical contrivances on the other. As the cities spread and the country shrinks he is more and more imprisoned with his fellows in a world that has ceased to be even aware of many of the things of which he was once an intimate part. Already he has pushed into extinction many of the creatures with which he once shared the earth.

Those who feel that he has already begun to suffer from this fact, talk about recreational areas, about nature education, about national parks and even about wilderness areas. To some extent they can still meet the objections of those who say that we cannot afford to forego the use of any of our forests, or mountains, or deserts. But if our population continues to grow at its present rate, it will soon become evident that we do indeed need every available acre of possibly usable land either for agriculture or for building lots. Much of what is called conservation today is no more than a useful delaying action. The time may soon come when it will no longer be possible to protest against the despoliation of this or that park, or forest, or river. Hence the conservationist also must face the fact that behind almost every problem of today lies the problem of population. Unless that problem is solved, none of the others can be.

Let us suppose for a moment that those are in the right who say that the context of nature has ceased to be the most desirable context for civilized life, that man can live in a wholly man-made world and that he will in time forget all that he once drew from his contemplation of that world of which he has ceased to be a part. Let us suppose further that his increase in numbers stopped before space itself gave out, and that he has reached what some seem to think of as the ideal state, i.e., living in cities which are almost coextensive with the surface of the earth, nourishing himself on products of laboratories rather than farms, and dealing only with either other men or the machines they have created.

What will he then have become? Will he not have become a creature whose whole being has ceased to resemble Homo sapiens as we in our history have known him? He will have ceased to be consciously a part of that nature from which he sprang. He will no longer have, as he now does, the companionship of other creatures who share with him the mysterious privilege of being alive. The emotions which have inspired a large part of all our literature, music, and art will no longer be meaningful to him. No flower will suggest thoughts too deep for tears. No bird song will remind him of the kind of joy he no longer knows. Will the human race have then become men-like-gods, or only men-like-ants?

To this question the naturalist has his own answer just as he has his own answer to the question why population continues to grow so rapidly in a world already at least beginning to be aware that this growth is a threat. His approach may seem to others somewhat oblique, even distorted by his special interests. But at least his conclusions are the same as those to which many other approaches no less inevitably lead.

Research Which May Affect
Human Fertility

The Promise of Research

JOHN ROCK (1963)

In 1959, the Population Council and the Planned Parenthood Federation brought together some 150 investigators from twelve countries for a week of conferences to assess work-in-progress and point the direction for future investigations. . . .

In summing up this unique conference, the noted British anatomist Sir Solly Zuckerman, who served as general chairman, noted with the power of simple truth:

> By setting our knowledge into perspective, the conference also revealed very clearly that vast areas of the subject are still cloaked in an ignorance which prevents a rational and scientific approach to the problem of population control. It was undoubtedly startling to hear expert after expert declaring that little or nothing was known about this or that subject. . . . The first lesson of the conference is, therefore, that it is necessary to stimulate further basic research into almost every one of the topics that were discussed.[1]

From the transcript of the conference, Carl Hartman distilled and published a compendium of 154 important unanswered questions which "represent hiatuses in our knowledge of reproductive processes with partic-

---

1. S. Zuckerman: "Mechanisms Involved in Conception," *Science*, Nov. 6, 1959, p. 1263.

ular reference to man and other mammals." [2] The answers—which can be found only through a broadly conceived program of research such as was recommended to the N.I.H.—would undoubtedly lead to a variety of simple and acceptable methods of controlling conception.

This is clearly the scope of the research program which must be undertaken before man will be able to bring his fertility under rational—and moral—control. There is no private agency, or combination of agencies, which is able or willing to support a program of this magnitude. If it is to be done, it must be done by the U.S. government.

Of course, the dollar estimates submitted to the N.I.H. are only conjectures, for no one can know precisely how much such a program would cost. The important question is not how much such a program would *cost*, but how much it would be *worth* to the United States, and to the world, to develop one or more methods of family limitation which are both effective and acceptable to Catholics and non-Catholics alike.

Making the Rhythm Method More Accurate

There have been several instances in the past of long delays before pertinent scientific knowledge became adequate for the requirements of the theological process.[3] Therefore, it is indeed noteworthy that the morality of the so-called safe period, of the rhythm method of birth control, was propounded by the theologians more than a century ago, while its precise delimitation *still* poses a fundamental challenge to the scientists.

In 1853, the Bishop of Amiens, noting that many couples confined sex relations to what was then regarded as the sterile period of the menstrual cycle, asked the Sacred Penitentiary in Rome to rule on the practice. The Penitentiary, which is the Catholic Church's highest tribunal in matters of moral propriety, replied that the couples "should not be disturbed, so long as they do nothing to prevent conception."

2. C. Hartman: "Physiological Mechanisms Concerned with Conception—An Inventory of Unanswered Questions," *Perspectives in Biology and Medicine*, Vol. IV, No. 1 (Autumn 1960), p. 77.
3. There was one of more than 200 years between Galileo's substantiation of the Copernican solar system in 1611 and approval of the theory by Pope Pius VII in 1820. Economic science had been demonstrating the propriety of charging interest on loans for some time before Pope Clement V pronounced in 1311 that "he who shall pertinaciously presume to affirm that the taking of interest for money is not a sin, we decree him to be a heretic fit for punishment." Yet it was not until about 1745 that Benedict XIV allowed books defending the modern point of view to be dedicated to him. (See *Catholic Dictionary*, London: Addis & Arnald, 1951.)

This ruling apparently was not accepted unanimously in the Church. The same question was again presented in 1880, this time by a "Doctor L.," who reported approval of the practice by Cardinal Gousset and by writers in several theological journals but also called attention to condemnation by "a certain Spanish theologian." "In the judgment of learned physicians and physiologists," Doctor L. informed the Sacred Penitentiary, "women for the most part are not permanently able to conceive but only periodically able, that is, from the time at which the menstrual flow begins to the fourth day after it has ceased; in the rest of the month, they are usually sterile. They assert that this theory has been verified in 94 per cent of the women observed." The tribunal's reply reaffirmed the 1853 ruling and the moral basis for periodic continence was established.[4]

We know now, of course, that whatever it was that the "learned physicians and physiologists" had observed in 94 per cent of their women patients at the time of menstruation, it was certainly not ovulation; they were just about 100 per cent wrong in their determination of the fertile period. The error, it seems, stemmed from an extrapolation to man of observations in animals: In 1853, Theodor Bischoff, a German scientist, published his discovery of eggs in the genital tract of female dogs while they were "in heat" and had a bloody vaginal discharge. His conclusion, which seemed logical, was that women must also ovulate at the time of menstruation, for it is a similar discharge.

This misinterpretation had a profound influence on many nineteenth-century European investigators and "set gynecology back three quarters of a century."[5] Although evidence began to accumulate during the last decades of the century that the estrous (egg-time) bleeding of dogs and the menstrual bleeding of primates are two different processes, the association of ovulation and menstruation in women held on tenaciously.

In 1882, William Mensinga, a German physician, published a description of a device to be placed over the neck of the womb for conception control. This was the forerunner of the modern vaginal diaphragm and its popularization evoked the Church's formal condemnation. One year later another German, Carl Capellman, proclaimed with astonishing certainty that women are apt to be fertile during the first 14 days after menstruation

4. Both the 1853 and the 1880 opinions of the Sacred Penitentiary are quoted in Freedman, Whelpton, and Campbell: *Family Planning, Sterility and Population Growth,* pp. 416–7.
5. Carl G. Hartman: "A Half Century of Research in Reproductive Physiology," *Fertility and Sterility,* Jan.–Feb. 1961.

begins and 3 to 4 days before the next period. This "discovery" greatly influenced Catholic moralists of the pre-World War I era [6] and was widely disseminated as a natural method of birth control. Indeed it was still circulated in an edition of Capellman's book published in 1923.[7] Since it directed followers to have "safe" intercourse on the fourteenth day of the cycle, which we now know often marks the peak of fertility, it also helped to bring the rhythm method into disrepute.

This early background is instructive. As Dr. Carl Hartman pointed out in 1936 in a monograph sponsored by the National Committee on Maternal Health,[8] the errors of the nineteenth- and early-twentieth-century investigators stemmed from large generalizations based on inadequate data. It was only with the upsurge of detailed, minute investigations of reproductive physiology during the 1920's, particularly of the amazingly intricate hormonal mechanisms of the menstrual cycle, that a proper format for the rhythm method could be established.

The painfully slow accretion of data from many investigators led, in 1931, to a breakthrough. As so often happens in science, two men working independently in different parts of the globe simultaneously announced a new theory placing the time of ovulation approximately in the middle of the period between menses. An Austrian, Hermann Knaus, basing his findings on hormone-controlled variations in uterine contractions, concluded that ovulation always occurs 14 days before the onset of the next menstruation. Kyusaka Ogino, of Japan, after observing the condition of women's ovaries at carefully timed abdominal operations, came to similar, though less categorical, conclusions. Together they form the basis of the modern rhythm method of birth control.

These findings were greeted with interest by the birth-control movement. Dr. Hartman, one of the most distinguished of the scholarly pioneer researchers in reproductive physiology, who has always been an ardent protagonist of planned parenthood, published a review in 1933 in which he held out great hope for the Ogino-Knaus method. Hartman quarreled—and properly so—only with the absolutism in Knaus's statements. He noted that his own determination of ovulation in the rhesus monkey agreed "al-

6. W. J. Gibbons: "Medical Research and Fertility Control," *Catholic Mind*, Sept.–Oct. 1960, p. 434.
7. Quoted in Leo J. Latz: *The Rhythm of Sterility and Fertility in Women* (Chicago: Latz Foundation, 1950), p. 62.
8. C. G. Hartmann: *Time of Ovulation in Women* (Baltimore: Williams & Wilkins, 1936).

most to a day with Knaus' findings." He concluded that what the Church termed "the 'natural method' does offer Catholic women who avoid contraceptives out of religious scruples something that is likely, if followed closely, to reduce the incidence of pregnancies to a point approximating the record of our birth control clinics." [9]

But Hartman and other scientists insisted that additional research was needed to confirm the Ogino-Knaus findings, in contrast to the popularizers who immediately seized on them as the Church's—and nature's—"answer" to the birth-controllers. Hartman's own work on the rhesus monkey was an example of the kind of rigorous scientific proof required to establish the mechanism of ovulation with precision. . . .

Since the 1930's, the basic findings of Ogino and Knaus have been confirmed by other studies, the most notable of which was one that demonstrated that ovulation occasions a noticeable increase in basal body temperature.

While our present knowledge of ovulation is indispensable to the rhythm method, it does not automatically make it reliable in practice. During the years of our ovum study, Mrs. Lendon Snedeker and I established a rhythm clinic at the Free Hospital which was the only birth-control clinic in operation in Massachusetts. Our experience revealed the potentialities —and limitations—of the method. In 1940, with Dr. Stephen Fleck, we concluded "that the safe-period method constitutes a workable form of contraception for a selected group of women. On the other hand, it is doubtful whether the method is reliable enough ·for individual cases in which contraception is an essential safeguard of the patient's health." [10] A later appraisal of our results in 1951 brought forth the following: "The conclusion appears justified that the rhythm method offers a satisfactory degree of protection against unwanted pregnancy to rigorously selected and carefully instructed wives who, with their husbands, are intelligent and strongly motivated. For others and for those to whom pregnancy would be dangerous, the effectiveness of the method in preventing conception is not considered adequate." [11]

Thus, although the rhythm method is considerably more reliable today

9. "Catholic Advice on the 'Safe Period'," *Birth Control Review*, May 1933, p. 118.
10. Stephen Fleck, Elizabeth F. Snedeker, and John Rock: "The Contraceptive Safe Period, a Clinical Study," *New England Journal of Medicine*, Vol. 223 (1940), pp. 1005–9.
11. C. Tietze, S. R. Poliakoff, and John Rock: "The Clinical Effectiveness of the Rhythm Method of Contraception," *Fertility and Sterility*, Vol. 2, No. 5 (1951).

than it was before Ogino-Knaus, failures are still two to three times more frequent among couples using it than among those who use other methods. Moreover, in its present form, it requires learning, determination, and sexual restraint to a degree that limits its usefulness. Although the basic underlying physiology now has been known for some time and much of the fundamental research on the timing of ovulation has been done, science has not been able thus far to refine this knowledge so as to formulate simple procedures which people can use on a mass scale. I believe that a concerted effort, possibly under the auspices of the National Institutes of Health, could yield substantial progress toward this goal within a remarkably short period of time.

One of the major difficulties with rhythm is that ovulation in many women is not really rhythmic in occurrence. A complete cycle between ovulations may take 25 days on one round, and 32 days the next—depending on innate irregularities in organ functioning as well as on such accidental influences as tension, illness, or simple fatigue. Even among women whose menstrual cycles approach calendar regularity, any one or a combination of such factors may cause ovulation to occur as much as five or six days off schedule.

There seem to be two ways of perfecting the rhythm method so that it might work in all or almost all cases: by developing a cheap, simple, and accurate home test that any woman could use to *predict* the day of ovulation each month; or by developing an equally simple way to *induce* ovulation so that it could be made to occur on a selected day of each menstrual cycle. . . . I am forced to believe, on the basis of various biological, physiological, and chemical facts, that *both* approaches can succeed.

In humans as in other animals ovulation is controlled by the impressively versatile hypothalamus, a part of the floor of the brain, which causes the adjacent pituitary to secrete hormonal agents that stimulate the production of germ cells in both sexes. These agents are called gonadotropic hormones. Carried throughout the body, they induce the ovary to release a mature egg which is susceptible of fertilization. (As noted in a previous selection, the hormone progesterone, which is secreted in the ovary after ovulation and in the placenta during pregnancy, in turn suppresses in the pituitary the secretion of these gonadotropic hormones.)

One of them, often called LH (luteinizing hormone), is the substance that appears actually to trigger ovulation. But the pituitary does not discharge its periodic supply of LH into the blood stream all at once. During the early days of the menstrual cycle, the secretion is at first of small amounts; it increases steadily over a period of about 14 days, sometimes shorter, sometimes very much longer. Then there occurs a sharp rise, followed, probably in only a few hours, by the release of an ovum. In other words, when the concentration of this gonadotropic hormone reaches a critical level in the blood stream, ovulation results. Easy discernment of this gradual build-up, which, unfortunately, available test methods do not permit, would offer accurate forewarning that ovulation was imminent. . . .

Since an ovum remains susceptible of fertilization for not more than twenty-four hours, the timely *prediction* of ovulation would enable a couple to define the fertile period accurately and adapt their marital relations to it. Ovulation theoretically could be signaled at least two days in advance, whether or not it occurred in accordance with a customary schedule. Intercourse more than two days before ovulation would in all likelihood be ineffective, for spermatozoa do not ordinarily function longer than forty-eight hours after ejaculation.

The *induction* of ovulation, by administration of the pituitary hormones that evoke it, would shift the woman's role from passive to active. Science would put at her disposal the potent hormone to cause ovulation, if it was to occur at all, to take place at a particular time, in a perfectly natural way. She would, by virtue of her intellect and an available agent, "regularize" nature, to the benefit of her marriage and her family, much as the "pills" do by a reverse process.

For many years, ovulation has been easily achieved by injection of hormones in rabbits, monkeys, and other laboratory animals, and already we have had some published statements of success in inducing ovulation in a few women. Recently at the Yale University Medical School, Dr. C. Lee Buxton and his associates obtained results similar to those previously reported by others, when they caused five women to ovulate in response to injected gonadotropic hormones. There appeared to be no harmful side effects. This initial work requires extended investigation before firm conclusions can be drawn.

One of the major obstacles in the development of this ovulation-inducing technique lies in the source of hormonal material. To be sure, several useful organic products derived from one species of animal may yet be effective in another. The hormone ACTH, used in treating rheumatic fever and related diseases, is a striking example of this; it is obtained from sheep. But unlike ACTH, the female gonadotropic hormone, LH, is apparently more "species specific," medically speaking; as yet only the extract from human pituitaries, permissibly removed promptly at autopsies has proved to be effective in women. This method of drug procurement does not lend itself to mass production and widespread use.

Therefore, an immediate challenge to biochemists is to develop a way to purify animal products, or to synthesize human gonadotropin or an effective substitute—that is, to manufacture from easily available non-human ingredients a compound with the same, or nearly the same, molecular structure. This is how many remarkable drugs are produced in quantity.

Here again, the unity of research toward and away from fertility is evident. Development of an uncomplicated technique for inducing ovulation at will would be of great value not only for postponing pregnancies by improvement of rhythm-contraception but also for facilitating pregnancies as well, since a substantial proportion of childlessness is caused by constant or very frequent failure to ovulate. Surely this should be an added incentive for both the development and acceptance of a simple ovulation-inducing procedure.

New Contraceptives

RITCHIE CALDER (1962)

Although the surest way to plan a family is to leave it to the woman, so that she need not have the baby she does not want, anti-fertility researches have also been directed to the male. Certain chemicals taken orally in low doses which are not toxic inhibit the production of spermatozoa without impairing sexual activity.

Another important line of research, initiated by Professor M. C. Shelesnyak of the Weizmann Institute in Israel, is concerned with the "nidation moment." In the human being, the egg is laid in a nest. A ledge is formed in the wall of the uterus and the fertilized egg implants itself. If it fails to "nidate," there is no pregnancy and researches have shown that it is possible to prevent this nidation by a chemical means before coitus or after. This raises extremely interesting "philosophic" issues. What is "conception"? Is it when the egg is fertilized? This, biologically, makes no sense because the fertilized egg is non-viable until it attaches itself to the wall of the uterus. This nidation takes place in the week following fertilization. If this is accepted then "contraception" could properly be applied to measures taken before nidation. This has the great advantage of being retrospective. One of the desirable results of these researches would be a substance taken orally during the third week of the cycle, which would prevent nidation (or conception) without interfering with the menstrual cycle. It would never be known whether or not the egg had been fertilized.

Since we are faced with this epidemic, or pandemic, of children we might be justified in looking at this epidemiologically. In fact, there are possibilities of immunization. Just as the body creates antibodies against antigens (e.g. an invading germ) so it can produce antibodies against the male sperm. This is one of the explanations of sterility; antibodies have been discovered in one or other sex in certain cases of otherwise inexplicable sterility in human couples. The fact that the antibody can exist in the male as well as the female suggests that the husband might be so immunized. This could be done by injection, just as with vaccines and, as we know, multimillions of people in the countries where the population problem is so serious have no hesitation in accepting injections for their many ills.

Where a couple have decided that they have had enough children, one or other may submit to sterilization. This is neither a difficult nor a dangerous process, but as a British court case in 1961 showed, it is not consistently effective in women. In India, however, men are paid a gratuity to accept sterilization, which does not impair their sexual activity.

This is birth regulation at the family-planning level, but there are those who argue, again on the analogy of the epidemic, that there must be regulation on a demographic basis; that there should be measures taken by the community. The world-famous Indian scientist, Professor Homi J. Bhabha, has pointed out that the problem of India would be resolved by the simple reduction in over-all fertility of something in the neighbourhood of 33 per cent and suggested that there should be a search for some substance which would effectively do this to the whole population. He knew the outcry he was inviting but he suggested that such a substance might be introduced into the public water-supply, just as we chlorinate drinking water. He would be a daring, nay, reckless politician who would advocate such a policy of undiscriminating contraception. Everyone knows that psychologically the idea of losing virility or having sterility induced is one of the most disturbing. In two world wars, soldiers were convinced that the NAAFI tea was being doped to "take their minds off women" and one of the simplest tricks in psychological warfare is to convince the enemy that something which they are being given (e.g. the wide-awake pills for Luftwaffe pilots or Rommel's tank-drivers in the desert) would produce impotency, or sterility. Anyway, population cannot be turned on and off like a tap. (Professor Bhabha suggested that the water should be treated only for certain specified lengths of time, to produce the necessary 33 per cent reduction.)

This objection, however, would not rule out the possibilities either of "vaccination" against conception, where people would seek immunity, by their own choice, when they have had as many children as they desire, or the restraint of fertility (without sterility) by making oral inhibitors available, again at discretion, in rice, or salt, or any other form which would ensure the regimen, without dependency on pill-taking.

Sex Determination and Other Innovations

RICHARD L. MEIER (1959)

At this stage of the study the investigator . . . must find means for detecting new storm centers of potential change while they are still on the distant horizon. He must interpret what impact they are likely to have upon the territories in which a population problem exists. The effort need not be exhaustive—the methods of measurement are too poor to make this worthwhile—and may constitute no more than a search for relevant transitions. Then, once such items have been selected, estimates of the scope of the interaction with separate aspects of the population question must be prepared.

Diligent inquiry among circles of scientists and in the current journals reporting fundamental investigations revealed one such potential innovation which is still so new that it is difficult to appraise. The new work suggests that there may be means available in the not too distant future for controlling the sex of the children that are born. It is too early yet to argue the question from an assortment of preliminary investigations . . . even though the likelihood of the appearance of a means for controlling sex of human offspring is roughly the same as the achievement of an oral contraceptive to be used by males.

In any standard scholarly review this potentiality would be given an oblique reference with no further comment upon the implications. The responsibility that was accepted here, however, was one of portraying as complete a picture as possible of the conditions, technological and otherwise, likely to be associated with the introduction of oral contraceptives over the next two decades. The control of sex can be of significance because it is made feasible only by the existence of a convenient contraceptive. In many poor societies the importance of having sons (in a very few it can be a preference for daughters) is so great that contraception may be introduced to a very important extent through the exercise of that motivation. This is an excellent example of Ogburn's principle of convergence in social innovation.

According to the classical theory, as elaborated in the textbooks on genetics, it should be possible to separate the male-producing spermatozoa, containing a Y-chromosome, from the female-producing spermatozoa, containing in its stead an X-chromosome. These chromosomes are likely to influence to a very small degree the density, shape, and surface characteristics of the spermatozoa. Once instruments and tools in the laboratory have been perfected, these fine distinctions between the two types of cells can be used for their separation. The genetic theories which locate all sex-linked characteristics in the X- and Y-chromosomes are still open to question, but the alternative formulations suggest that minute external differences are to be found between male-producing and female-producing spermatozoa. Attempts to make this separation in the sperm of animals have been under way for more than two decades.

The prime motivation for such studies was a curious mixture of theoretical and practical interests. For a scientist the male/female ratio is a convenient means for measuring the effects of various experimental variables upon cells. Nevertheless, the detailed study of semen was stimulated by the demand, in certain parts of the world, for artificial insemination in animal breeding. It was also recognized that control of the sex of chickens, rabbits, sheep, or cattle would be a considerable convenience to the breeder and possibly even to the animal-raising industries.

The first success in this direction was registered in the U.S.S.R. by

V. N. Shreder.[1] She had discovered that by applying an electric field to diluted sperm, the cells migrating to one electrode, after artificial insemination, yielded litters that were as high as 80 per cent of one sex. Which sex it was depended upon the temperature at which the separation was carried out.

Shreder's work turned out to be difficult to confirm in other European laboratories. Other workers could clearly see the tailward migration of the sperm as soon as the current was applied, but once the separation of the two populations had been made there was disagreement as to whether sex differentiation had been achieved. However, the studies of M. J. Gordon at the University of California provided satisfactory statistical controls and proved conclusively that these electrophoretic techniques were capable of separating the male-producing from the female-producing spermatozoa. Gordon diluted rabbit semen in an appropriate buffer in 1:20 proportions and used a microelectrophoresis cell for 40 to 50 minutes, collecting 0.5 to 0.7 ml. at the pole for insemination. His results were still fairly uneven so that some litters yielded all of one sex while others were virtually equally balanced. This observation, combined with difficulties experienced by European investigators, suggests that a single important variable remains uncontrolled in the experiments to date.

An independent discovery in this same direction was reported by Lindahl.[2] He discovered that, although the X-chromosome was considerably larger than the Y-chromosome, it did not lead to an observably heavier spermatozoon, as might be expected. The observed densities seemed to increase with maturation, and such changes obscured any differences due to chromosome size. Nevertheless, when bull semen was centrifuged very carefully those cells which settled the most rapidly (5 to 7 per cent of the total) were used for artificial insemination and yielded all males, but the sample (11 calves out of 24 inseminations) was too small to make any strong assertions. Separation in this instance possibly depended upon difference in the shape of the spermatozoa. . . .

In reviewing the reports on the electrophoresis of semen an editorial in *Science* stated:

1. There is a series of articles in Russian and German starting in 1932. Only the most recent will be cited: V. N. Shreder, *Uspekhi Soveremennoi Biol.* (Moscow) *28*, 211 (1949); see also M. J. Gordon, "Control of Sex Ratio in Rabbits by Electrophoresis of Spermatozoa," *Proceedings of the National Academy of Sciences* (U.S.) *43*, 913 (1957).
2. P. E. Lindahl, "Counter-Streaming Centrifugation of Bull Spermatozoa," *Nature 178*, 491 (1956).

Human spermatozoa have likewise been observed to migrate tailfirst in an electric field. . . . The obvious problems that are likely to arise if successful control of human sex determination becomes practicable as a result of such experiments make one wonder whether human beings have yet acquired the wisdom to make use of such wide powers. (Nov. 22, 1957, p. 1059.)

An innovation of this sort has particular significance for those societies with land tenure systems, business organizations, and social status systems which depend upon male heirs for continuity. Many households are willing to pay heavily for the guarantee of a son. Once a second son is born, as a kind of insurance against the relatively high mortality rates, they may become disinterested in further additions to the family. Observers returning from such societies feel that if a doctor should set up a practice in which he would virtually guarantee the birth of a son if any child at all should be born, it seems likely that he would soon be swamped with clients. Other doctors would then feel it worthwhile to acquire the knowledge and the appropriate techniques.

Anthropologists and welfare workers from the smaller towns and villages were consulted about the possibilities. They suggested that the desire for sons is not limited to the major landowners and business classes. Many holders of small plots of two to ten acres would be willing to pay $50 or more for the guarantee of a son. A quarter to a half of the households in these poorer countries are in a position to decide consciously to alter the sex ratio. Whether they would avail themselves of the opportunity is another question. Several sociologists, when appraised of the technical possibilities, suggested that the necessity of artificial insemination imposed a social cost of major dimensions. In Puerto Rico, for example, what would become of *macho* and *hombria?* In Catholic countries artificial insemination is frowned upon as "unnatural." Yet we know from experience that such arguments have low predictive value for behavior. In Puerto Rico, for example, a man gets his way by being clever and opportunistic. Under such circumstances a slight twist of the conventional concepts would make him an enthusiastic taker of the offer. In other parts of the world doctors report that the success of epidemic control programs has been such that people now feel it is a privilege to be struck somewhere in the body with an instrument resembling a hypodermic needle, so that they have difficulty in introducing other kinds of treatment. For these people artificial insemination would be an understandable means for accomplishing a miracle. The chances of conception through the existing techniques are only about 20 to 30 per cent less than through normal exposure, so that artificial insemination would not be dropped due to loss of patience by the families concerned.

In many ways, determining the sex of a child by the parents or household seems to be a milder interference with nature than abortion or sterilization. Perhaps its acceptance, like these other well-known procedures, will be strong in some cultures and negligible in others. It is interesting to speculate upon the social effects of the adoption of this innovation in those societies where it becomes popular.

Initially, the service would be expensive, owing primarily to the costs of identifying the time of ovulation, and available only to the moneyed classes. Later, fees would be reduced and some of the clinics would devise "assembly line" methods. Therefore, the richest classes would be affected first, the middle classes thereafter, and the more prosperous farmers and tradesmen last of all. The normal rate of 50 to 52 per cent males could, within these social classes, easily rise to 60 per cent males and it would not be at all astonishing to see it reach 70 per cent males. The effects would probably not be too noticeable until twenty years later when a severe shortage of wives with proper family and upbringing would arise. This shortage would not be found in the lower classes, so ambitious fathers would be able to promote good marriages for their daughters. Instead of a dowry there might even be a marriage price for desirable girls. Thus, an excess of sons should stimulate social mobility in that society, if all other factors remained unchanged. It is a change that can be adjusted to rather readily, either through polyandry, immigration, or a social revaluation of girl-children. Publicizing the imbalances in sex-ratios should induce many families to make compensatory choices.

On the whole, the possibility of determining sex of progeny yields much more talk than direct action. The discussions are likely to be responsible for an increased sophistication about sex, including various methods of birth control. The doctors, whose reputations in these instances depend upon performance, could not take chances upon continence and so would prescribe and require one of the most dependable methods of birth control. Since the talk is certain to spread widely, even among the poorest classes —the subject is an exciting one to build daydreams around and to argue about with one's friends in the evening concerning the moral problems involved—the level of understanding that is created should prepare the way for greater rationality in family formation. In the long run these ancillary effects could easily become more important than the direct effects.

In the previous paragraphs a reasoned and conservative point of view was taken. However, this is the kind of innovation which easily leads to misapprehensions concerning the implications for society and, so, is liable to various forms of extremism on the part of persons having power. Such extremism, and the reactions to it, can yield surprises that have not been and cannot be anticipated. At the moment very little can be done to reduce the undesirable social consequences of the spread of the innovation. Any legislation directed against having sons sounds very silly, and would almost surely break down within a few years. Perhaps the wisest procedure would be that of requiring complete statistics upon directed conceptions and their outcomes.

Changes in the Technology of Spread

Perhaps the most important transformation on the horizon that will affect the rate of spread about birth control information is the current revolution in the science and technology of communications.[3] Already it is common to find a short wave radio in the coffee houses and tea shops of small isolated towns, and in the general stores of the villages. Many governments have exploited these opportunities for communication and have put up captive loud-speakers in the plazas and the bazaars, thus assuring that the government viewpoint is widely disseminated. With the advent of transistors the cost of radio in rural areas should be cut by a factor of at least three, and we might estimate that the numbers of sets would as a result multiply by ten or twentyfold. Television at that time should be no more expensive than radio is today and, by 1970, should have penetrated at least as far into the hinterland. The phonograph, which has already been introduced into some of the most isolated places in the world over the past few decades, is likely to be replaced by the transistorized tape recorder. It seems quite probable now that cinema film will be displaced by magnetic tape and portable large screen television equipment, greatly simplifying exhibition in out-of-the-way places. Textbooks, magazines, circulars, and newsbriefs could be transmitted by radio waves on demand and printed on the spot. We could go on describing equivalent opportunities in less well-known media for communications, but it is evident already that prospects are so varied that we must assume extensive contact between the cultural elite in the urban centers and every social class and isolated ethnic group of any

3. R. L. Meier, "Communications and Social Change," *Behavioral Science 1,* 43 (1956).

consequence. Remoteness is being conquered for a very reasonable price.

However, the extension of mass communications to the hinterland has implications not dissimilar from those of plucking the fruit from the Tree of Good and Evil. Whole new worlds of experience are opened up which inevitably introduce alternative explanations for commonplace events. This leads to doubt of the validity of tradition, to the conflict of old versus new, and to the acquisition of altogether new tastes. The specific effects that are forthcoming are unpredictable, even the categories of effects will vary widely according to time and place, so that the process cannot be carefully planned. Massive social change would then become inevitable. Innovations in agriculture, hygiene, public services, social organization, and education follow in the wake of acquaintance with the new worlds opened up by the technology of communications. Technical transformations of such scope have been gradually assimilated before with little net improvement by relatively static cultures, but henceforth their adoption may be expected to proceed far more rapidly because the delays due to lack of reinforcement are greatly reduced.

Many scientists think the day is not far off when parents will be able to choose the sex of their children. It will be interesting to see what effect this has on the population. There are already millions of people quite incapable of making a simple decision. How will this vast army of "don't knows" react when faced with so important a choice? . . . One of the drawbacks of increasing scientific knowledge is that it often brings increased responsibilities, but mankind's ability to accept its responsibilities does not necessarily increase at the same rate.

Susan Michelmore (1964)
Sexual Reproduction

Freedom or Control in Reproduction

Knowledge and Responsibility
JAMES ALFRED FIELD (1931)

The knowledge which has brought us power over human generation has brought with it one of the most portentous problems of modern society. Whether or not mankind shall be reproduced becomes in a new sense a question of volition, and consequently a question of responsibility. But the power to choose has come so suddenly that the sense of responsibility seems as yet inadequate. The new knowledge strains the old traditions: In other words, our problem of population involves a moral problem.

Alarmed by this situation, some persons demand a ban on knowledge. But the problem is not to be dealt with so summarily. There is no likelihood that it can be solved, in reactionary fashion, by exhorting the people to forget what they have learned and walk in the old ways, and by setting the police on them if they refuse. On the contrary, it is virtually inconceivable that the unsettling knowledge will be lost or the perilous power wholly relinquished. All over the world the trend of events has seemed to exclude such a possibility.

It thus becomes expedient to accept the knowledge, and to bend our efforts to working out new standards by which its exercise may be made to yield a clear preponderance of benefit. This is indeed no simple task; but its difficulties, viewed in a long perspective in which even now we begin to see them, may prove to be mainly difficulties of transition.

Meantime, the transition is none the less critical; for the numbers, and perhaps yet more the quality, of the race are at stake. If the readjustment is to be accomplished without excessive shock, it is imperative that the means of birth control should be made known wisely and temperately, and only so fast and so far as experience can bring with them the compensating influence of a readjusted sense of responsibility. The fanatical neo-Malthusian, the bigoted prude, the hysterical patriot who sees national greatness only in swarming numbers, must all give way to someone more highly endowed with the saving sense of proportion, and hence better able to fit the power of birth control into a proper place among the constructive forces of civilization.

Birth Control and Coercion

W. V. D'ANTONIO (1966)

One of the major surprises of the recent meeting of the Catholic Bishops in Washington was that they chose to issue, at the very outset, a strong denunciation of the Johnson Administration's efforts in the area of family planning. "Far from merely seeking to provide information in response to requests from the needy," the Bishops charged, "government activities increasingly seek aggressively to persuade and even coerce the underprivileged to practice birth control." This trend, they argued in their statement, threatens "the free choice of spouses" to determine the size of their families and seriously endangers the "inviolability of the right of human privacy." In sum, "government far exceeds its proper role."

Needless to say, the Bishops' statement caught many unprepared, especially Administration officials. They should not have been so surprised, for the Bishops' statement only followed hard on the heels of an earlier and very similar statement by Bishop John Wright of Pittsburgh and a concerted campaign by the Catholic Bishops of Pennsylvania. I want to focus my remarks on family planning and government policy around Bishop Wright's earlier statement, especially since he has long been thought of in Catholic circles as a progressive. Thus, his position cannot easily be dismissed as intransigent conservatism, something many might be prone to do with the statement of the American Bishops as a whole.

In reaction to an announcement in Pittsburgh last May that the city

From W. V. D'Antonio, "Birth Control and Coercion," *Commonweal*, December 2, 1966. Copyright © 1966 by *Commonweal*. Reprinted by permission.

would begin financing planned parenthood clinics, Bishop Wright said; "Directly moral considerations apart, the introduction of government power, policy and money into intimate family relations, especially those involving the expression of nuptial love and the sources of life, constitutes a clear peril to basic values, beginning with freedom." The Bishop went on to plead *for* government aid to help those already born to achieve personal autonomy and material well-being. Clearly, the Bishop is not opposed to government aid *per se,* but only government aid which may make effective contraceptive practices possible—on the ground that human freedom would be jeopardized in the process.

This is essentially the position taken by the Bishops in their Washington meeting, by spokesmen for the National Catholic Welfare Conference and by the Bishops of Pennsylvania in their more or less successful lobby against the recent Pennsylvania state government effort to institute broad-scale family planning aid in that state. Yet while NCWC has lobbied forcefully against government-sponsored family planning clinics, it has also forcefully argued for such government programs as aid to parochial schools. What is there about the one kind of aid which supposedly threatens human freedom, while the other aid is said to support and encourage freedom. In this important sense, the Bishops, Bishop Wright and NCWC are right: the basic issue is human freedom and how best to enhance it.

Human freedom consists in the ability to make choices. This means in the first place that there are a plurality of alternative choices available to an individual or group, and secondly, that the individual or group is aware of the choices and informed about their consequences. The ability to make choices is rather narrowly restricted by what sociologists call the socialization process, the process by which an individual becomes a predictable, role-playing, group-conforming creature. Freedom is not given, it isn't just there; it depends on the acquisition of knowledge about events and possible events and their consequences. And, I should add, it depends on the creative action of the individual to do something with this knowledge.

A major point to be made here is that the poor, the downtrodden, the underprivileged have little or no freedom—they lack *money* which permits certain kinds of choices, especially material choices; and they lack knowledge, language, ideas which permit a whole series of choices with social consequences. Government-sponsored family planning clinics at home and abroad would provide them with knowledge and facilities, thus widening their range of choices, and as I see it, their freedom.

But the argument of those opposed to government-sponsored family planning goes deeper. *They* say that government action in this area is an invasion of the most sacred right of privacy, the privacy of the bedroom. Somehow, it is argued, government programs inevitably mean government coercion—and in this case, the end of bedroom freedom. The argument seems specious on several counts.

It is not, for one thing, self-evident that government aid to family planning clinics would be more coercive than government aid to foster social security, medicare, college and university aid programs, and certainly aid to parochial schools. Who would be coerced? The word "coercion" in this context means that people are being forced to act against their will by people representing the government. The sociological data, from studies in the United States and abroad, show that people in the "deprived" sectors of the society would be glad to accept birth control help if they could get it. I know of no study which shows the opposite.

Dr. Donald Bogue, one of the country's most respected demographers, reported on a 1959 study of low-income population in Chicago that, "The most important finding was that despite their actual high fertility, these groups said they wanted smaller families than do more well-to-do people . . ." He also reported that, "The incidence of unwanted and accidental pregnancy is very high among these low-income and low-education groups; nevertheless, they endorse the idea of family planning more strongly than does the general population." Dr. Alberto Lleras Camargo, twice president of Colombia, said recently that, "Our population simply cannot be allowed to grow at the savage rate of the present (between two and one-half and three percent annually). . . . The humane, *Christian,* economic and political solution is birth control. And the sooner the better."

Freedom Welcomed

Thus, the evidence at hand shows that these people won't be coerced. They will welcome the chance to have some freedom in this matter. Most of them live now in the unfreedom of ignorance. There may be coercion, not in the law as such, but in its implementation! But this is an empirical question to be answered by experience, not accepted as an *a priori* assumption.

Another point in regard to this charge of invasion of privacy is more challenging. Actions of people may be said to be private (that is, of their own but no one else's concern) insofar as they have no further social consequences. There may have been a time in the history of this country when the begetting and rearing of children were private concerns of individual couples. *This is not the case today.* In our complex society the begetting of children can have great societal consequences. Family fertility patterns are inextricably bound up in the affairs of society. Hence, if there is evidence that the common good of all is threatened by large-scale unplanned, unwanted procreation in slum conditions, then the society is justified in acting to protect itself. The question then becomes one of asking what kind of action is necessary and desirable.

a) There is no argument against government aid on the ground that procreation is an absolute good that must be fostered at all costs;

b) There is substantial evidence that unplanned, unwanted procreation is detrimental to those born under such conditions, to the parents (at least the mother) and to the society which pays the cost of lives unfulfilled, or lived out in deviancy from accepted patterns. Perhaps the most persuasive evidence is found in the rising abortion rates throughout the world.

c) This point seems to be well understood by the Christian Democrats of Chile. They believe that in a pluralistic society the government should allow such programs for those who desire them. The Chilean women apparently desire them. The Christian Democrats of Chile appear to recognize population control as central to their aspirations for a better life for the Chilean people. The National Health Service is conducting an aggressive campaign against abortion, while permitting use of its facilities for birth control services. It was reported that some 120,000 IUD's were inserted during the past year.

There is an important additional point to be made; this involves the question of neutrality. Those opposing government action in family planning argue that the government should be neutral, that it has no business either promoting or discouraging family planning. I would disagree. The government is the agent *par excellence* of the people (i.e. society) by which they can promote their general welfare. In fact, given the size of the population involved, and the complex web of interrelationships which binds each to his fellows and makes it difficult if not impossible for any man or couple to be an island, the government should be concerned in this area of life.

Of course the dissemination of birth control information is not neutral. To ask people to consider an alternative to what they are doing is not a neutral request. It implies value judgments about the alternative(s) to be suggested. Nonetheless, the argument for governmental neutrality seems misplaced. Is the government neutral if it does not provide family planning help? Or is it being negligent in its responsibilities? I would argue that it is neglecting its responsibility when it ignores an urgent problem which no other agency of the society can cope with. We know empirically that 20–30 million Americans live deprived lives, and that the conditions of life elsewhere in the world are as bad or worse for more than one billion people. Because this problem touches on sexuality, should the government thereby be neutral? Can it be? Why is this area more sacred than the starving, educationally-deprived conditions of these people?

The opponents argue that this analogy is weak because birth control involves "The divinely conferred human personality, the mind of a person, the soul of a person, as well as the myriad strands of that person's relationship to other persons and to God." And these are no business of government, so they say. My response would be that God gives each person the potential of a mind and a personality, but that these potentials become human reality only when man interacts with his fellow man. Man is above all else social and he has created a social organization called the government, to help promote his well-being.

The position taken by Father Dexter Hanley, S.J., of the Georgetown Law School, in Testimony before the Gruening Committee in August, 1965, seems to provide a sound basis for government policy in this area, to wit:

"1) In a legitimate concern over public health, education and poverty, the government may properly establish programs which permit citizens to exercise a free choice in matters of responsible parenthood in accordance with their moral standards. 2) In such programs, the government may properly give information and assistance concerning medically accepted forms of family planning, so long as human life and personal rights are safeguarded and no coercion or pressure is exerted against individual moral choice. 3) In such programs, the government should not imply a preference for any particular method of family planning. 4) While norms of private morality may have special dimensions so affecting the common good as to justify opposition to public programs, private moral judgments regarding methods of family planning do not provide a basis for opposition to government programs. 5) Although the use of public funds for purposes of family planning is not objectionable in principle, the manner in which such a program is implemented may pose issues requiring separate consideration."

Here it seems clear in the present case that a vast majority of Americans approve of federal aid for family planning clinics—65 percent according to the Gallup Poll of October, 1965. Furthermore, 59 percent of American Catholics in this poll also approved of such aid. A majority also approved of using federal funds to support birth control programs abroad.

Indications are that the federal government is taking the cue that it has the support of the majority of the American population and is going ahead with the development of birth control programs both at home and abroad. Up to the present, the major focus of most activity, especially through the Children's Bureau and the National Institutes of Health, has been on basic research, with a large proportion of some 7 million dollars in fiscal 1967 geared to research related to fertility reproductive physiology and studies of motivations and attitudes of potential clients toward family planning services. Probably the most important government source of aid for family planning services is coming through the Offices of Economic Opportunity. It has been estimated that some fifty projects had been funded through OEO to provide family planning information and service to indigent women. It also appears clear that Title XIX of the Social Security Amendment Act of 1965 will become an important source of federal aid through state grants-in-aid in the years ahead. . . .

There are, perhaps a minimum of five million medically indigent, fertile women in the United States who are in need of or could make use of family planning services. In the year 1965, some 300,000 received help through public facilities; some 200,000 received service through Planned Parenthood Centers. Some four and one-half million remained unserved. Figured at the average cost of $20.00 per year per woman, family planning services for this population would come to some ninety million dollars annually.

The current budget for health and medical services at all government levels is approximately nine billion dollars. Obviously, family planning service for that segment of the population not able to afford it on its own, does not appear to be an onerous additional burden in itself. It seems well within our ability to foster the opportunity for a "good life" for the children of poverty in this country, and the government has made a firm commitment in this direction.

The scene at the international level is much more complicated, but is not without hope. Most of the world's governments are now seeking help. At present, we can be most effective by providing the technical assistance that is needed just to develop policies and programs. As our commitments abroad through AID and other programs increase, we will have to expand considerably a wide range of professional skills, in obstetrics and gynecology, demography and sociology and in agricultural and industrial technology. We can only hope to help others as they become aware of and perceive a need for help. The situation in Latin America, for example, seems to be changing rapidly. As a result, we have been able to develop demographic institutes there, to get the basic information that is needed before any effective proposals can even be considered. In this effort, private foundations such as Ford, and organizations like International Planned Parenthood can help, but increasingly, the government has come to be recognized as the agent of society most capable of and responsible for confronting this problem.

Concerning Equilibrium in Human Population
RICHARD L. MEIER (1959)

Recently a few scholars have recognized that voluntary controls upon family size, operated by the families themselves, do not guarantee a stable population, but one which, at least as likely as not, would continue to expand at an uneven rate. Wherever this latter probability has been felt to dominate, more oppressive measures have been suggested. Then it was pointed out that the state may need to interfere directly with individual choice in matters of procreation.[1]

1. Harrison Brown in his book *The Challenge of Man's Future* suggests that the state might intervene by imposing abortions or artificial inseminations so as to maintain the population in a steady state. Sir Charles Galton Darwin in *The Next Million Years,* Rupert Hart-Davis, London, 1952, chapter 8, feels that the natural reactions to such impositions perturb the system of intended controls so seriously that a population will inevitably break away from them. Both authors feel that strict, centralized controls over births would provide more human freedom than would be possible in

From Richard L. Meier, *Modern Science and the Human Fertility Problem,* John Wiley & Sons, New York. Copyright © 1959 by John Wiley & Sons. Reprinted by permission.

In spite of the strong personal bias in favor of freedom on the part of these scholars, they have chosen state-imposed restraints upon reproduction. They seem not to have considered very seriously the possibility of public action in the alternative direction, that of gradually increasing the choices available to prospective parents, but introducing the increments so that they reinforce whatever trend is needed to stabilize population. The range of new choices appear to be sufficiently large so that the best of them may simultaneously enhance social, economic, and psychological stability along with the attainment of population equilibrium.

Let us review this argument more fully. At a given moment in its existence each society has available to it a class of actions which, as a whole, tends to increase the freedom of choice of individuals, groups, communities, and institutions. It can also, for a time at least, reduce freedom in favor of some "higher end," and it has another class of actions available where human freedom seems to be a trivial component. Within the class that promotes freedom there ought to be a set which influences reproductive behavior. With this set there ought to be a subset of actions which bring declines in the birth rate. What items in this subset can be specified in sufficient detail so that doubters will be convinced and policy makers will be prevented from acting too hastily? This is a task worth undertaking now because . . . the information required for implementation is still incomplete and will require a considerable amount of investigation and analysis before it is possible to distinguish the better possibilities from the poorer ones. There seem to be many possible combinations open so that different cultures may safely choose freedom, each in a unique manner, at the same time that they seek to stabilize population.

Patterns of the Future
HARRISON BROWN (1954)

. . . if industrial civilization survives—if wars are eliminated, if the population of the world as a whole is stabilized within a framework of low death

societies subsisting at saturation levels and that such actions are to be preferred with that justification. By restraining some freedoms which are personally valued, they would hope to achieve others which are socially valued.

rates and low birth rates—will there continue to be a human history? The terms "stability" and "security" imply predictability, sameness, lack of change. And these terms further imply a high degree of organization—universal organization to avoid war, local organization to produce goods efficiently, and organization to control the distribution of goods. Organization in turn implies subjugation of the individual to the state, confinement and regimentation of the activities of the individual for the benefit of society as a whole.

Today we see about us on all sides a steady drift toward increased human organization. Governments are becoming more centralized and universal. In practically all areas of endeavor within industrial society—in our systems of production, in the fields of labor, capital, commerce, agriculture, science, education, and art—we see the emergence of new levels of organization designed to coordinate, integrate, bind, and regulate men's actions. The justifications for this increasing degree of organization to which man must accommodate himself are expressed in terms such as "stability," "security," and "efficiency." The end result of this rapid transition might well be the emergence of a universal, stable, efficient, industrial society within which, although all persons have complete personal security, their actions are completely controlled. Should that time arrive, society will have become static, devoid of movement, fixed and permanent. History will have stopped.

Here we indeed find ourselves on the horns of the dilemma. To what purpose is industrialization if we end up by replacing rigid confinement of man's actions by nature with rigid confinement of man's actions by man? To what purpose is industrialization if the price we pay for longer life, material possessions, and personal security is regimentation, controlled thoughts, and controlled actions? Would the lives of well-fed, wealthy, but regimented human robots be better than the lives of their malnourished, poverty-stricken ancestors? At least the latter could look forward to the unexpected happening—to events and situations which previously had been outside the realm of their experiences.

In a modern industrial society the road toward totalitarianism is unidirectional. In days gone by men could revolt against despotism. People could arise against their governments in the absence of legal recourse, and with muskets, sticks, knives, and stones as their weapons they could often defeat the military forces of the central authorities. But today our science and our technology have placed in the hands of rulers of nations weapons and tools of control, persuasion, and coercion of unprecedented power. We have reached the point where, once totalitarian power is seized in a highly industrialized society, successful revolt becomes practically impossible. Totalitarian power, once it is gained, can be perpetuated almost indefinitely in the absence of outside forces, and can lead to progressively more rapid robotization of the individual.

Thus we see that, just as industrial society is fundamentally unstable and subject to reversion to agrarian existence, so within it the conditions which offer individual freedom are unstable in their ability to avoid the conditions which impose rigid organization and totalitarian control. Indeed, when we examine all of the foreseeable difficulties which threaten the survival of industrial civilization, it is difficult to see how the achievement of stability and the maintenance of individual liberty can be made compatible.

The view is widely held in our society that the powers of the machine will eventually free man from the burden of eking out an existence and will provide him with leisure time for the development of his creativity and enjoyment of the fruits of his creative efforts. Pleasant though this prospect may be, it is clear that such a state cannot come into existence automatically; the pressures forcing man into devising more highly organized institutions are too great to permit it. If he is to attain such an idyllic existence for more than a transitory period he must plan for that existence carefully, and in particular he must do everything within his power to reduce the pressures that are forcing him to become more highly organized.

One of the major pressures that give rise to the need for increasing numbers of laws, more elaborate organization, and more centralized government is increase of population. Increase of numbers of people and of population density results in greater complexities in day-to-day living and in decreased opportunities for personal expression concerning the activities of government. But even more important, as populations increase and as they press more heavily upon the available resources there arises the need for increased efficiency, and more elaborate organizations are required to produce sufficient food, to extract the necessary raw materials, and to fabricate and distribute the finished products. In the future we can expect that the greater the population density of an industrial society becomes, the more elaborate will be its organizational structure and the more regimented will be its people.

A second pressure, not unrelated to the first, results from the centralization of industrial and agricultural activity and from regional specialization in various aspects of those activities. One region produces textiles, another produces coal, another automobiles, another corn, and another wheat. Mammoth factories require mammoth local organizations. Centralized industries must be connected, and this requires elaborate transportation systems. Regional localization of industries gives rise to gigantic cities, which in turn give rise to elaborate organization for the purpose of providing the inhabitants with the necessary food, water, and services. All of these factors combine to produce vulnerability to disruption from the outside, increased local organization and regimentation, more highly centralized government, and increasing vulnerability to the evolution of totalitarianism.

A third pressure results from increasing individual specialization and the resultant need for "integration," "coordination," and "direction" of activities in practically all spheres of vocational and leisure activity. It results in the placing of unwarranted trust in "integrators," "coordinators," and "directors." Early specialization results in lack of broad interests, lessened ability to engage in creative activity during leisure hours, decreased interest in the creative activities of other individuals, and lessened abilities to interpret events and make sound judgments. All of these factors combine to pave the way for collectivization, the emergence of strong organization, and, with it, the great leader.

Strong arguments can be presented to the effect that collectivization of humanity is inevitable, that the drift toward an ultimate state of automatism cannot be halted, that existing human values such as freedom, love, and conscience must eventually disappear.[1] Certainly if we used the present trends in industrial society as our major premises, the conclusion would appear to be inescapable. Yet is it not possible that human beings, recognizing this threat to the canons of humanism, can devise ways and means of escaping the danger and at the same time manage to preserve those features of industrial civilization which can contribute to a rich, full life? Is it really axiomatic that the present trends must continue and that in the long run industrial civilization and human values are incompatible? Here, in truth, we are confronted with the gravest and most difficult of all human problems, for it is one that cannot be solved by mathematics or by machines, nor can it even be precisely defined. Solutions, if they exist, can arise only in the hearts and minds of individual men.

1. These views have been forcefully and eloquently expressed by Roderick Seidenberg in his book *Post-Historic Man* (Durham: University of North Carolina Press, 1950).

The machine has divorced man from the world of nature to which he belongs, and in the process he has lost in large measure the powers of contemplation with which he was endowed. A prerequisite for the preservation of the canons of humanism is a reestablishment of organic roots with our natural environment and, related to it, the evolution of ways of life which encourage contemplation and the search for truth and knowledge. The flower and vegetable garden, green grass, the fireplace, the primeval forest with its wondrous assemblage of living things, the uninhabited hilltop where one can silently look at the stars and wonder—all of these things and many others are necessary for the fulfillment of man's psychological and spiritual needs. To be sure, they are of no "practical value" and are seemingly unrelated to man's pressing need for food and living space. But they are as necessary to the preservation of humanism as food is necessary to the preservation of human life.

I can imagine a world within which machines function solely for man's benefit, turning out those goods which are necessary for his well-being, relieving him of the necessity for heavy physical labor and dull, routine, meaningless activity. The world I imagine is one in which people are well fed, well clothed, and well housed. Man in this world, lives in balance with his environment, nourished by nature in harmony with the myriads of other life forms that are beneficial to him. He treats his land wisely, halts erosion and overcropping, and returns all organic waste matter to the soil from which it sprung. He lives efficiently, yet minimizes artificiality. It is not an overcrowded world; people can, if they wish, isolate themselves in the silence of a mountaintop, or they can walk through primeval forests or across wooded plains. In the world of my imagination there is organization, but it is as decentralized as possible, compatible with the requirements for survival. There is a world government, but it exists solely for the purpose of preventing war and stabilizing population, and its powers are irrevocably restricted. The government exists for man rather than man for the government.

In the world of my imagination the various regions are self-sufficient, and the people are free to govern themselves as they choose and to establish their own cultural patterns. All people have a voice in the government, and individuals can move about when and where they please. It is a world where man's creativity is blended with the creativity of nature, and where a moderate degree of organization is blended with a moderate degree of anarchy.

Is such a world impossible of realization? Perhaps it is, but who among us can really say? At least if we try to create such a world there is a chance that we will succeed. But if we let the present trend continue it is all too clear that we will lose forever those qualities of mind and spirit which distinguish the human being from the automaton. We have seen that population stabilization within a framework of low birth rates and low death rates is a major key to the avoidance of collectivization and robotization of humanity and to the perpetuation of machine civilization. . . .

In the first place, it is amply clear that population stabilization and a world composed of completely independent sovereign states are incompatible. Populations cannot be stabilized by agreement any more than levels of armament can be stabilized by agreement. And, as in the latter case, a world authority is needed which has the power of making, interpreting, and enforcing, within specified spheres, laws which are directly applicable to the individual. Indeed population stabilization is one of the two major problems with which a world government must necessarily concern itself.

Given a world authority with jurisdiction over population problems, the task of assessing maximum permissible population levels on a regional basis need not be prohibitively difficult. A rancher in Nevada usually puts no more cattle on a range than he believes can be adequately supported. Similarly, working on the basis that individual regions of the world should be self-sufficient both agriculturally and industrially, indices of potential productivity can be computed for all regions of the world, and maximum permissible population levels can be calculated on this basis.

The more serious difficulty is that of creating a situation in which the birth rate more or less automatically adjusts itself to the death rate. In nature, the death rate automatically adjusts itself to the birth rate, and the adjustment requires no conscious directed effort. In the artificial world that has been created by man, an artificial mechanism must be devised which can be incorporated with man's culture, which can operate automatically with a minimum of conscious effort, and which will permit birth rates to be determined by death rates.

If all babies were born from test tubes, as in Aldous Huxley's *Brave New World,* the solution would be fairly simple: The number of babies produced on the production line each year could be made to equal the number of deaths. In years of unusually high death rates, the production line could be speeded up; in years of low death rates, the line could be slowed down. Further, if we cared little for human emotions and were willing to introduce a procedure which most of us would consider to be reprehensible in the extreme, all excess children could be disposed of much as excess puppies and kittens are disposed of at the present time. But let us hope it will be a long time before a substantial number of our babies are born from test tubes. And let us hope further that human beings will never again be forced to resort to infanticide in order to avoid excessive population pressure.

We know from experience that social and economic pressures, coupled with widespread knowledge concerning birth-limiting techniques, can result in net reproduction rates that are very close to unity. We have seen that the net reproduction rate in England and Wales dropped to well below unity for a period of about 25 years, and that the net reproduction rate in the United States hovered around unity during the great depression. We have seen further that the net reproduction rate is a very sensitive index to social and economic pressures, and that these pressures can change greatly in but a short span of time.

Clearly a prerequisite for long-range population stabilization is stabilization of economic and social conditions to the point where birth rates will not fluctuate as widely as they do in industrial societies at the present time. Complete stabilization of such conditions is obviously difficult to achieve, and, from the point of view of individual freedom and human advancement, it is undesirable. Nevertheless, if economic and social pressures can be stabilized to the point at which the natural net reproduction rate does not fluctuate upward or downward by more than a few per cent from year to year, adequate control mechanisms are conceivable.

Birth rates obviously cannot fluctuate widely if population stabilization is to be achieved. Net reproduction rates which are constantly greater than unity, or which are only slightly less than unity, can quickly lead to enormous population pressures or to the danger of extinction. Ideally, the net reproduction rate should be kept at unity with a precision which borders on the fantastic: 1.0000. In the light of this rigid requirement, we must ask: If the natural uncontrolled net reproduction rate fluctuates by several per cent, how can the actual net reproduction rate be controlled with such accuracy?

Here we must examine the actual conception rate as distinct from the natural conception rate and as distinct from the birth rate. The actual conception rate can be divided into two parts—the conception rate which occurs as the result of the natural course of events, plus the addition to the natural rate which results from special treatments such as artificial insemination or hormone injections. Secondly, the birth rate depends upon the abortion rate, which we know is fairly high in most industrialized areas. It is clear that by maintaining rigid control over aids to conception, in particular artificial insemination, and rates of induced abortion, birth rates could be controlled with high precision—provided, of course, that the fluctuations in natural rates of conception do not exceed the requests for aids to conception and for abortions.

Briefly, such a control system would operate in the following manner. Let us suppose that in a given year the birth rate exceeds the death rate by a certain amount, thus resulting in a population increase. During the following year the number of permitted inseminations is decreased, and the number of permitted abortions is increased, in such a way that the birth rate is lowered by the requisite amount. If the death rate exceeds the birth rate, the number of permitted inseminations would be increased while the number of abortions would be decreased. The number of abortions and artificial inseminations permitted in a given year would be determined completely by the difference between the number of deaths and the number of births in the year previous.

It can be argued that such a procedure would be ruthless and would deprive many people of their individual liberties. Yet would it be any more ruthless than the policy which is now followed in the United States? Only a small fraction of the population would be affected. The vast majority of persons who might want to conceive would be able to do so, and the majority of those who might desire to terminate unwanted conceptions would be able to do so under hygienic conditions. Contrast this with the status quo, where abortions must be obtained frequently on kitchen tables, usually at great expense and under circumstances where the victims have the "freedom" to choose between giving birth to unwanted children and endangering their lives by subjecting themselves to illegal operations under insanitary conditions.

Control of aids to conception and of abortions could also provide a mechanism for slowing down the deterioration processes associated with the elimination of biological competition. Priorities for artificial insemination could be given to healthy women of high intelligence whose ancestors possessed no dangerous genetic defects. Conversely, priorities for abortions could be given to less intelligent persons of biologically unsound stock.

Such steps would undoubtedly contribute substantially to a slowing down of species deterioration. But it is clear that they would by no means be sufficient. A broad eugenics program would have to be formulated which would aid in the establishment of policies that would encourage able and healthy persons to have several offspring and discourage the unfit from breeding at excessive rates. Here, of course, we encounter numerous difficulties—what would constitute "fit" and what would constitute "unfit"? Where is the boundary between the mentally deficient person and the genius?

These are indeed grave problems, and the probability is high that they will never be solved. Yet the possibility cannot be excluded that solutions may be found. Our knowledge of human genetics, of human behavior, and of human biochemistry is fragmentary. Two or three generations of intensive research aimed at understanding the functioning of the human machine might well enable us to define terms such as "fit" and "unfit," as applied to human beings, with considerable precision. Although we realize that there is little likelihood that human beings will ever be able consciously to improve the species by carrying out a process of planned selection, there appears to be a finite possibility that, given adequate research and broad planning, deterioration of the species might eventually be halted.

Precise control of population can never be made completely compatible with the concept of a free society; on the other hand, neither can the automobile, the machine gun, or the atomic bomb. Whenever several persons live together in a small area, rules of behavior are necessary. Just as we have rules designed to keep us from killing one another with our automobiles, so there must be rules that keep us from killing one another with our fluctuating breeding habits and with our lack of attention to the soundness of our individual genetic stock. On the other hand, although rules of behavior which operate in such areas are clearly necessary if our civilization is to survive, it remains to be seen whether or not such rules can be reconciled satisfactorily with the ideal of maximum individual freedom.

• • •

If man is to find his way successfully through the labyrinth of difficulties that confront him in the years ahead, he must, above all, use his intelligence. He can no longer rely upon the unforeseeable fortunate circumstance; future mistakes will have consequences far more dangerous than past ones have been. He must divorce himself from unreasoned slogans and dogma, from the soothsayer, from the person whose selfish interests compel him to draw false conclusions, from the man who fears truth and knowledge, from the man who prefers indoctrination to education. Man must rapidly accumulate knowledge concerning both his environment and himself, and he must learn how to use that knowledge wisely. He must encourage the emergence of new ideas in all areas. He must learn not to fear change, for of one thing he can be certain—no matter what happens in the world of the next few decades, change will be the major characteristic. But it is within the range of his ability to choose what the changes will be, and how the resources at his disposal will be used—or abused—in the common victory —or ignominious surrender—of mankind.

Is Freedom Too Great a Burden?

It has been demonstrated that the overcoming of the problems of the modern age is inconsistent with an unrestricted measure of freedom. He who wishes to bring order into the world dare not place unlimited reliance on reason and good will. It is impossible to do without compulsion—not the compulsion that lies behind the law in the freest society, but the compulsion that does not trust the individual's goodness. Even the Western world has become deeply pessimistic, and in the long run that is inconsistent with the democratic organization of society. It is possible that man may be good, but we had better not put it to the test.

Friedrich Sieburg
"The Self-Enslavement of Modern
Civilization," *Atlantic Monthly*,
March 1957

The Grand Inquisitor
FEODOR DOSTOIEVSKY (1881)

. . . "My story is laid in Spain, in Seville, in the most terrible time of the Inquisition, when fires were lighted every day to the glory of God, and 'in the splendid *auto da fé* the wicked heretics were burnt.' Oh, of course, this was not the coming in which He will appear according to His promise at the end of time in all His heavenly glory, and which will be sudden 'as lightning flashing from east to west.' No, He visited His children only for a moment, and there where the flames were crackling round the heretics. In His infinite mercy He came once more among men in that human shape in which He walked among men for three years fifteen centuries ago. He came down to the 'hot pavement' of the southern town in which on the day before almost a hundred heretics had, *ad majorem gloriam Dei,* been burnt by the cardinal, the Grand Inquisitor, in a magnificent *auto da fé,* in the presence of the king, the court, the knights, the cardinals, the most charming ladies of the court, and the whole population of Seville.

"He came softly, unobserved, and yet, strange to say, every one recognized Him. That might be one of the best passages in the poem. I mean, why they recognized Him. The people are irresistibly drawn to Him, they surround Him, they flock about Him, follow Him. He moves silently in their midst with a gentle smile of infinite compassion. The sun of love burns in His heart, light and power shine from His eyes, and their radiance, shed on the people, stirs their hearts with responsive love. He holds out His hands to them, blesses them, and a healing virtue comes from contact with Him, even with His garments. An old man in the crowd, blind from childhood, cries out, 'O Lord, heal me and I shall see Thee!' and, as it were, scales fall from his eyes and the blind man sees Him. The crowd weeps and kisses the earth under His feet. Children throw flowers before Him, sing, and cry hosannah. 'It is He—it is He!' all repeat. 'It must be He, it can be no one but Him!' He stops at the steps of the Seville cathedral at the moment when the weeping mourners are bringing in a little open white coffin. In it lies a child of seven, the only daughter of a prominent citizen. The dead child lies hidden in flowers. 'He will raise your child,' the crowd shouts to the weeping mother. The priest, coming to meet the coffin, looks perplexed, and frowns, but the mother of the dead child throws herself at His feet with a wail. 'If it is Thou, raise my child!' she cries, holding out her hands to Him. The procession halts, the coffin is laid on the steps at His feet. He looks with compassion, and His lips once more softly pronounce, 'Maiden, arise!' and the maiden arises. The little girl sits up in the coffin and looks round, smiling with wide-open wondering eyes, holding a bunch of white roses they had put in her hand.

"There are cries, sobs, confusion among the people, and at that moment the cardinal himself, the Grand Inquisitor, passes by the cathedral. He is an old man, almost ninety, tall and erect, with a withered face and sunken eyes, in which there is still a gleam of light. He is not dressed in his gorgeous cardinal's robes, as he was the day before, when he was burning the enemies of the Roman Church—at that moment he was wearing his coarse, old, monk's cassock. At a distance behind him come his gloomy assistants and slaves and the 'holy guard.' He stops at the sight of the crowd and watches it from a distance. He sees everything; he sees them set the coffin down at His feet, sees the child rise up, and his face darkens. He knits his thick grey brows and his eyes gleam with a sinister fire. He holds out his finger and bids the guards take Him. And such is his power, so completely are the people cowed into submission and trembling obedience to him, that the crowd immediately make way for the guards, and in the midst of death-like silence they lay hands on Him and lead Him away. The crowd instantly bows down to the earth, like one man, before the old inquisitor. He blesses the people in silence and passes on. The guards lead their prisoner to the close, gloomy vaulted prison in the ancient palace of the Holy Inquisition and shut Him in it. The day passes and is followed by the dark, burning 'breathless' night of Seville. The air is 'fragrant with laurel and lemon.' In the pitch darkness the iron door of the prison is suddenly opened and the Grand Inquisitor himself comes in with a light in his hand. He is alone; the door is closed at once behind him. He stands in the doorway and for a minute or two gazes into His face. At last he goes up slowly, sets the light on the table and speaks.

" 'Is it Thou? Thou?' but receiving no answer, he adds at once, 'Don't answer, be silent. What canst Thou say, indeed? I know too well what Thou wouldst say. And Thou hast no right to add anything to what Thou hadst said of old. Why, then, are Thou come to hinder us? For Thou hast come to hinder us, and Thou knowest that. But dost Thou know what will be to-morrow? I know not who Thou art and care not to know whether it is Thou or only a semblance of Him, but to-morrow I shall condemn Thee and burn Thee at the stake as the worst of heretics. And the very people who have to-day kissed Thy feet, to-morrow at the faintest sign from me will rush to heap up the embers of Thy fire. Knowest Thou that? Yes, maybe Thou knowest it,' he added with thoughtful penetration, never for a moment taking his eyes off the Prisoner. . . .

" 'Hast Thou the right to reveal to us one of the mysteries of that world from which Thou hast come?' my old man asks Him, and answers the question for Him. 'No, Thou hast not; that Thou mayest not add to what has been said of old, and mayest not take from men the freedom which

Thou didst exalt when Thou wast on earth. Whatsoever Thou revealest anew will encroach on men's freedom of faith; for it will be manifest as a miracle, and the freedom of their faith was dearer to Thee than anything in those days fifteen hundred years ago. Didst Thou not often say then, "I will make you free"? But now Thou hast seen these "free" men,' the old man adds suddenly, with a pensive smile. 'Yes, we've paid dearly for it,' he goes on, looking sternly at Him, 'but at last we have completed that work in Thy name. For fifteen centuries we have been wrestling with Thy freedom, but now it is ended and over for good. Dost Thou not believe that it's over for good? Thou lookest meekly at me and deignest not even to be wroth with me. But let me tell Thee that now, to-day, people are more persuaded than ever that they have perfect freedom, yet they have brought their freedom to us and laid it humbly at our feet. But that has been our doing. Was this what Thou did? Was this Thy freedom?' . . .

" 'The wise and dread Spirit, the spirit of self-destruction and non-existence,' the old man goes on, 'the great spirit talked with Thee in the wilderness, and we are told in the books that he "tempted" Thee. Is that so? And could anything truer be said than what he revealed to Thee in three questions and what Thou didst reject, and what in the books is called "the temptation"? And yet if there has ever been on earth a real stupendous miracle, it took place on that day, on the day of the three temptations. The statement of those three questions was itself the miracle. If it were possible to imagine simply for the sake of argument that those three questions of the dread spirit had perished utterly from the books, and that we had to restore them and to invent them anew, and to do so had gathered together all the wise men of the earth—rulers, chief priests, learned men, philosophers, poets—and had set them the task to invent three questions, such as would not only fit the occasion, but express in three words, three human phrases, the whole future history of the world and of humanity— dost Thou believe that all the wisdom of the earth united could have invented anything in depth and force equal to the three questions which were actually put to Thee then by the wise and mighty spirit in the wilderness? From those questions alone, from the miracle of their statement, we can see that we have here to do not with the fleeting human intelligence, but with the absolute and eternal. For in those three questions the whole subsequent history of mankind is, as it were, brought together into one whole, and foretold, and in them are united all the unsolved historical contradictions of human nature. At the time it could not be so clear, since the future was unknown; but now that fifteen hundred years have passed, we see that everything in those three questions was so justly divined and foretold, and has been so truly fulfilled, nothing can be added to them or taken from them.

" 'Judge Thyself who was right—Thou or he who questioned Thee then? Remember the first question; its meaning, in other words, was this: "Thou wouldst go into the world, and art going with empty hands, with some promise of freedom which men in their simplicity and their natural unruliness cannot even understand, which they fear and dread—for nothing has ever been more insupportable for a man and a human society than freedom. But seest Thou these stones in this parched and barren wilderness? Turn them into bread, and mankind will run after Thee like a flock of sheep, grateful and obedient, though for ever trembling, lest Thou withdraw Thy hand and deny them Thy bread." But Thou wouldst not deprive man of freedom and didst reject the offer, thinking, what is that freedom worth, if obedience is bought with bread? Thou didst reply that man lives not by bread alone. But dost Thou know that for the sake of that earthly bread the spirit of the earth will rise up against Thee and will strive with Thee and overcome Thee, and all will follow him, crying, "Who can compare with this beast? He has given us fire from heaven!" Dost Thou know that the ages will pass, and humanity will proclaim by the lips of their sages that there is no crime, and therefore no sin; there is only hunger? "Feed men, and then ask of them virtue!" that's what they'll write on the banner, which they will raise against Thee, and with which they will destroy Thy temple. Where Thy temple stood will rise a new building; the terrible tower of Babel will be built again, and though, like the one of old, it will not be finished, yet Thou mightest have prevented that new tower and have cut short the sufferings of men for a thousand years; for they will come back to us after a thousand years of agony with their tower. They will seek us again, hidden underground in the catacombs, for we shall be again persecuted and tortured. They will find us and cry to us, "Feed us, for those who have promised us fire from heaven haven't given it!" And then we shall finish building their tower, for he finishes the building who feeds them. And we alone shall feed them in Thy name, declaring falsely that it is in Thy name. Oh, never, never can they feed themselves without us! No science will give them bread so long as they remain free. In the end they will lay their freedom at our feet, and say to us, "Make us your slaves, but feed us." They will understand themselves, at last, that freedom and bread enough for all

are inconceivable together, for never, never will they be able to share between them! They will be convinced, too, that they can never be free, for
they are weak, vicious, worthless and rebellious. Thou didst promise them
the bread of Heaven, but, I repeat again, can it compare with earthly bread
in the eyes of the weak, ever sinful and ignoble race of man? And if for the
sake of the bread of Heaven thousands and tens of thousands shall follow
Thee, what is to become of the millions and tens of thousands of millions
of creatures who will not have the strength to forego the earthly bread for
the sake of the heavenly? Or dost Thou care only for the tens of thousands
of the great and strong, while the millions, numerous as the sands of the
sea, who are weak but love Thee, must exist only for the sake of the great
and strong? No, we care for the weak too. They are sinful and rebellious,
but in the end they too will become obedient. They will marvel at us and
look on us as gods, because we are ready to endure the freedom which they
have found so dreadful and to rule over them—so awful it will seem to
them to be free. But we shall tell them that we are Thy servants and rule
them in Thy name. We shall deceive them again, for we will not let Thee
come to us again. That deception will be our suffering, for we shall be
forced to lie.

" 'This is the significance of the first question in the wilderness, and this
is what Thou hast rejected for the sake of that freedom which Thou hast
exalted above everything. Yet in this question lies hid the great secret of
this world. Choosing "bread," Thou wouldst have satisfied the universal
and everlasting craving of humanity—to find some one to worship. So long
as man remains free he strives for nothing so incessantly and so painfully
as to find some one to worship. But man seeks to worship what is established beyond dispute, so that all men would agree at once to worship it.
For these pitiful creatures are concerned not only to find what one or the
other can worship, but to find something that all would believe in and worship; what is essential is that all may be *together* in it. This craving for *community* of worship is the chief misery of every man individually and of all
humanity from the beginning of time. For the sake of common worship
they've slain each other with the sword. They have set up gods and challenged one another, "Put away your gods and come and worship ours, or we
will kill you and your gods!" And so it will be to the end of the world, even
when gods disappear from the earth; they will fall down before idols just the
same. Thou didst know, Thou couldst not but have known, this fundamental secret of human nature, but Thou didst reject the one infallible banner

which was offered Thee to make all men bow down to Thee alone—the banner of earthly bread; and Thou hast rejected it for the sake of freedom and the bread of Heaven. Behold what Thou didst further. And all again in the name of freedom! I tell Thee that man is tormented by no greater anxiety than to find some one quickly to whom he can hand over that gift of freedom with which the ill-fated creature is born. But only one who can appease their conscience can take over their freedom. In bread there was offered Thee an invincible banner; give bread, and man will worship Thee, for nothing is more certain than bread. But if some one else gains possession of his conscience—oh! then he will cast away Thy bread and follow after him who has ensnared his conscience. In that Thou wast right. For the secret of man's being is not only to live but to have something to live for. Without a stable conception of the object of life, man would not consent to go on living, and would rather destroy himself than remain on earth, though he had bread in abundance. That is true. But what happened? Instead of taking men's freedom from them, Thou didst make it greater than ever! Didst Thou forget that man prefers peace, and even death, to freedom of choice in the knowledge of good and evil? Nothing is more seductive for man than his freedom of conscience, but nothing is a greater cause of suffering. And behold, instead of giving a firm foundation for setting the conscience of man at rest for ever, Thou didst choose all that is exceptional, vague and enigmatic; Thou didst choose what was utterly beyond the strength of men, acting as though Thou didst not love them at all—Thou who didst come to give Thy life for them! Instead of taking possession of men's freedom, Thou didst increase it, and burdened the spiritual kingdom of mankind with its sufferings for ever. Thou didst desire man's free love, that he should follow Thee freely, enticed and taken captive by Thee. In place of the rigid ancient law, man must hereafter with free heart decide for himself what is good and what is evil, having only Thy image before him as his guide. But didst Thou not know he would at last reject even Thy image and Thy truth, if he is weighed down with the fearful burden of free choice? They will cry aloud at last that the truth is not in Thee, for they could not have been left in greater confusion and suffering than Thou hast caused, laying upon them so many cares and unanswerable problems.

" 'So that, in truth, Thou didst Thyself lay the foundation for the destruction of Thy kingdom, and no one is more to blame for it. Yet what was offered Thee? There are three powers, three powers alone, able to conquer and to hold captive for ever the conscience of these impotent rebels for their happiness—those forces are miracle, mystery and authority. Thou hast rejected all three and hast set the example for doing so. When the wise and dread spirit set Thee on the pinnacle of the temple and said to Thee, "If Thou wouldst know whether Thou art the Son of God then cast Thyself down, for it is written: the angels shall hold him up lest he fall and bruise himself, and Thou shalt know then whether Thou art the Son of God and shalt prove then how great is Thy faith in Thy Father." But Thou didst refuse and wouldst not cast Thyself down. Oh! of course, Thou didst proudly and well, like God; but the weak, unruly race of men, are they gods? Oh, Thou didst know then that in taking one step, in making one movement to cast Thyself down, Thou wouldst be tempting God and have lost all Thy faith in Him, and wouldst have been dashed to pieces against that earth which Thou didst come to save. And the wise spirit that tempted Thee would have rejoiced. But I ask again, are there many like Thee? And couldst Thou believe for one moment that men, too, could face such a temptation? Is the nature of men such, that they can reject miracle, and at the great moments of their life, the moments of their deepest, most agonizing spiritual difficulties, cling only to the free verdict of the heart? Oh, Thou didst know that Thy deed would be recorded in books, would be handed down to remote times and the utmost ends of the earth, and Thou didst hope that man, following Thee, would cling to God and not ask for a miracle. But Thou didst not know that when man rejects miracle he rejects God too; for man seeks not so much God as the miraculous. And as man cannot bear to be without the miraculous, he will create new miracles of his own for himself, and will worship deeds of sorcery and witchcraft, though he might be a hundred times over a rebel, heretic and infidel. Thou didst not come down from the Cross when they shouted to Thee, mocking and reviling Thee, "Come down from the cross and we will believe that Thou art He." Thou didst not come down, for again Thou wouldst not enslave man by a miracle, and didst crave faith given freely, not based on miracle. Thou didst crave for free love and not the base raptures of the slave before the might that has overawed him for ever. But thou didst think too highly of men therein, for they are slaves, of course, though rebellious by nature. Look round and judge; fifteen centuries have passed, look upon them. Whom hast Thou raised up to Thyself? I swear, man is weaker and baser by nature than Thou hast believed him! Can he, can he do what Thou didst? By showing him so much respect, Thou didst, as it were, cease

to feel for him, for Thou didst ask far too much from him—Thou who hast
loved him more than Thyself! Respecting him less, Thou wouldst have
asked less of him. That would have been more like love, for his burden
would have been lighter. He is weak and vile. What though he is everywhere now rebelling against our power, and proud of his rebellion? It is the
pride of a child and a schoolboy. They are little children rioting and
barring out the teacher at school. But their childish delight will end; it will
cost them dear. They will cast down temples and drench the earth with
blood. But they will see at last, the foolish children, that, though they are
rebels, they are impotent rebels, unable to keep up their own rebellion.
Bathed in their foolish tears, they will recognize at last that He who created
them rebels must have meant to mock at them. They will say this in despair, and their utterance will be a blasphemy which will make them more
unhappy still, for man's nature cannot bear blasphemy, and in the end always avenges it on itself. And so unrest, confusion and unhappiness—that
is the present lot for man after Thou didst bear so much for their freedom! Thy great prophet tells in vision and in image, that he saw all those
who took part in the first resurrection and that there were of each tribe
twelve thousand. But if there were so many of them, they must have been
not men but gods. They had borne Thy cross, they had endured scores
of years in the barren, hungry wilderness, living upon locusts and roots—
and Thou mayest indeed point with pride at those children of freedom, of
free love, of free and splendid sacrifice for Thy name. But remember that
they were only some thousands; and what of the rest? And how are the
other weak ones to blame, because they could not endure what the strong
have endured? How is the weak soul to blame that it is unable to receive
such terrible gifts? Canst Thou have simply come to the elect and for the
elect? But if so, it is a mystery and we cannot understand it. And if it is a
mystery, we too have a right to preach a mystery, and to teach them that
it's not the free judgment of their hearts, not love that matters, but a mystery which they must follow blindly, even against their conscience. So we
have done. We have corrected Thy work and have founded it upon *miracle,
mystery* and *authority*. And men rejoiced that they were again led like
sheep, and that the terrible gift that had brought them such suffering, was,
at last, lifted from their hearts. Were we right teaching them this? Speak!
Did we not love mankind, so meekly acknowledging their feebleness, lov-
ingly lightening their burden, and permitting their weak nature even sin
with our sanction? Why hast Thou come now to hinder us? And why dost

Thou look silently and searchingly at me with Thy mild eyes? Be angry. I don't want Thy love, for I love Thee not. And what use is it for me to hide anything from Thee? Don't I know to Whom I am speaking? All that I can say is known to Thee already. And is it for me to conceal from Thee our mystery? Perhaps it is Thy will to hear it from my lips. Listen then. We are not working with Thee, but with *him*—that is our mystery. It's long—eight centuries—since we have been on *his* side and not on Thine. Just eight centuries ago, we took from him what Thou didst reject with scorn, that last gift he offered Thee, showing Thee all the kingdoms of the earth. We took from him Rome and the sword of Cæsar, and proclaimed ourselves sole rulers of the earth, though hitherto we have not been able to complete our work. But whose fault is that? Oh, the work is only beginning, but it has begun. It has long to await completion and the earth has yet much to suffer, but we shall triumph and shall be Cæsars, and then we shall plan the universal happiness of man. But Thou mightest have taken even then the sword of Cæsar. Why didst Thou reject that last gift? Hadst thou accepted that last counsel of the mighty spirit, Thou wouldst have accomplished all that man seeks on earth—that is, some one to worship, some one to keep his conscience, and some means of uniting all in one unanimous and harmonious ant-heap, for the craving for universal unity is the third and last anguish of men. Mankind as a whole has always striven to organize a universal state. There have been many great nations with great histories, but the more highly they were developed the more unhappy they were, for they felt more acutely than other people the craving for world-wide union. The great conquerors, Timours and Ghenghis-Khans, whirled like hurricanes over the face of the earth stiving to subdue its people, and they too were but the unconscious expression of the same craving for universal unity. Hadst Thou taken the world and Cæsar's purple, Thou wouldst have founded the universal state and have given universal peace. For who can rule men if not he who holds their conscience and their bread in his hands. We have taken the sword of Cæsar, and in taking it, of course, have rejected Thee and followed *him*. Oh, ages are yet to come of the confusion of free thought, of their science and cannibalism. For having begun to build their tower of Babel without us, they will end, of course, with cannibalism. But then the beast will crawl to us and lick our feet and spatter them with tears of blood. And we shall sit upon the beast and raise the cup, and on it will be written, "Mystery." But then, and only then, the reign of peace and happiness will come for men. Thou art proud of Thine elect, but Thou hast only the elect, while we give rest to all. And besides, how many of those elect, those mighty ones who could become elect, have grown weary waiting for Thee, and have transferred and will transfer the powers of their spirit and the warmth of their heart to the other camp, and end by raising their *free* banner against Thee. Thou didst Thyself lift up that banner. But with us all will be happy and will no more rebel nor destroy one another as under Thy freedom. Oh, we shall persuade them that they will only become free when they renounce their freedom to us and submit to us. And shall we be right or shall we be lying? They will be convinced that we are right, for they will remember the horrors of slavery and confusion to which Thy freedom brought them. Freedom, free thought and science, will lead them into such straits and will bring them face to face with such marvels and insoluble mysteries, that some of them, the fierce and rebellious, will destroy themselves, others, rebellious but weak, will destroy one another, while the rest, weak and unhappy, will crawl fawning to our feet and whine to us: "Yes, you were right, you alone possess His mystery, and we come back to you, save us from ourselves!"

" 'Receiving bread from us, they will see clearly that we take the bread made by their hands from them, to give it to them, without any miracle. They will see that we do not change the stones to bread, but in truth they will be more thankful for taking it from our hands than for the bread itself! For they will remember only too well that in old days, without our help, even the bread they made turned to stones in their hands, while since they have come back to us, the very stones have turned to bread in their hands. Too, too well they know the value of complete submission! And until men know that, they will be unhappy. Who is most to blame for their not knowing it, speak? Who scattered the flock and sent it astray on unknown paths? But the flock will come together again and will submit once more, and then it will be once for all. Then we shall give them the quiet humble happiness of weak creatures such as they are by nature. Oh, we shall persuade them at last not to be proud, for Thou didst lift them up and thereby taught them to be proud. We shall show them that they are weak, that they are only pitiful children, but that childlike happiness is the sweetest of all. They will become timid and will look to us and huddle close to us in fear, as chicks to the hen. They will marvel at us and will be awestricken before us, and will be proud at our being so powerful and clever, that we have been able to subdue such a turbulent flock of thousands of millions. They will tremble impotently before our wrath, their minds will grow fearful, they will be quick to shed tears like women and children, but they will be just as ready at a sign from us to pass to laughter and rejoicing, to happy mirth and childish song. Yes, we shall set them to work, but in their leisure hours we shall make their life like a child's game, with children's songs and innocent dance. Oh, we shall allow them even sin, they are weak and helpless, and they will love us like children because we allow them to sin. We shall tell them that every sin will be expiated, if it is done with our permission, that we allow them to sin because we love them, and the punishment for these sins we take upon ourselves. And we shall take it upon ourselves, and they will adore us as their saviors who have taken on themselves their sins before God. And they will have no secrets from us. We shall allow or forbid them to live with their wives and mistresses, to have or not have children—according to whether they have been obedient or disobedient—and they will submit to us gladly and cheerfully. The most painful secrets of their conscience, all, all they will bring to us, and we shall have an answer for all. And they will be glad to believe our answer, for it will save them from the great anxiety and terrible agony they endure at present in making a free decision for themselves. And all will be happy, all the millions of creatures except the hundred thousand who rule over them. For only we, we who guard the mystery, shall be unhappy. There will be thousands of millions of happy babes, and a hundred thousand sufferers who have taken upon themselves the curse of the knowledge of good and evil. Peacefully they will die, peacefully they will expire in Thy name, and beyond the grave they will find nothing but death. But we shall keep the secret, and for their happiness we shall allure them with the reward of heaven and eternity. Though if there were anything in the other world, it certainly would not be for such as they. It is prophesied that Thou wilt come again in victory, Thou wilt come with Thy chosen, the proud and strong, but we will say that they have only saved themselves, but we have saved all. We are told that the harlot who sits upon the beast, and holds in her hands the *mystery,* shall be put to shame, that the weak will rise up again, and will rend her royal purple and will strip naked her loathsome body. But then I will stand up and point out to Thee the thousand millions of happy children who have known no sin. And we who have taken their sins upon us for their happiness will stand up before Thee and say: "Judge us if Thou canst and darest." Know that I fear Thee not. Know that I too have been in the wilderness, I too have lived on roots and locusts, I too prized the freedom with which Thou hast blessed men, and I too was striving to stand among

Thy elect, among the strong and powerful, thirsting "to make up the number." But I awakened and would not serve madness. I turned back and joined the ranks of those *who have corrected Thy work.* I left the proud and went back to the humble, for the happiness of the humble. What I say to Thee will come to pass, and our dominion will be built up. I repeat, tomorrow Thou shalt see that obedient flock who at a sign from me will hasten to heap up the hot cinders about the pile on which I shall burn Thee for coming to hinder us. For if any one has ever deserved our fires, it is Thou. To-morrow I shall burn Thee. Dixi.' "

Freedom and the Nature of Man

RENÉ DUBOS (1962)

The fundamental human value is the freedom to choose, and, if need be, to elect painful effort, dangerous risks, and responsibilities for the sake of some transcendental value. It is this way of life which differentiates man from the rest of creation. It corresponds to a faith more entrancing and more comprehensive than the view of the good life by the Greek philosophers, than the vision of heaven by the Medievalists, than the mathematical world conceived by the rational scientists, than the utopian societies imagined by political reformers. It is the largest possible faith, simply because it is open on an endless future with unlimited possibilities. . . .

Not only does man have a large degree of latitude in his decision to act or not to act, but, more importantly, he is often aware of the reasons that make him select the cause to which he dedicates his action. Free will, however, implies choice and a motive; and motive is a matter of faith. In final analysis, choice is rarely possible without some vision of the future. In fact, it is the possibility, nay, the inescapable need to choose, which gives its grandeur to the human condition, and which also accounts for its tragic quality.

In most cases, the choice that must be made is not between alternatives to be experienced personally and in the present; it is between courses of action which affect other human beings and which involve the future. For a cat, the decision to move nearer the stove or toward a sunny window may involve, chiefly, the perception of a more pleasant temperature. But for man, almost any kind of decision is likely to involve something more than his comfort; he must think of his neighbors, and he must consider the advisability of forgoing the pleasure of the moment for the sake of the morrow.

The need to choose is, perhaps, the most constant aspect of conscious human life; it constitutes both its greatest asset and its heaviest burden. In every person, now and then, and in most persons, very frequently, there arises the desire to escape the responsibility of having to make decisions which engage not only the self, but also one's fellow men and the future. In its crudest expression, this intellectual and emotional weariness takes the form of a longing to achieve the peace of mind symbolized by the passive gaze of the contented cow. In a more sophisticated manner, the same wish comes forth in the words that Thoreau wrote for his journal while drifting idly on Walden pond, and letting himself become a part of his surroundings, as if he were a completely passive creature. He thought then that man could be so much happier "just being" rather than "living." Like Thoreau on Walden pond, or a cat basking in the sun, man can indeed enjoy "just being," but usually he cannot bear the enjoyment for very long. Whatever the hardships and the efforts that living entails, men want to live, not just to be. Consciously or unconsciously, most of them take the attitude expressed by Secondhorn in Bernard Shaw's *Buoyant Billions:* "I don't want to be happy; I want to be alive and active." . . .

Like many romantics, Nietzsche claimed that he envied the animals because they did not know the past, were not concerned with the future, and lived only in the present. Hegel also stated that the periods of happiness are the "empty periods of history." In support of his statement is the fact that the pages of our era are filled to the brim, and that we are not particularly happy. But mankind will not go back; the moving force is not the search for happiness, but the desire to fill the pages of history.

Man exercises free will not only by conducting his life of the present for the sake of a future that he can barely imagine, but also by concerning himself with problems that have no obvious bearing on his selfish biological comfort and welfare. It is painfully obvious, of course, that cruelty based on selfishness still governs much of human action. Today as in the past, man is wolf to man. But it is equally true, and more interesting, that respect for life has become one of the tenets of philosophy in many cultures. It is a human ideal which extends in principle to all living forms —granted that it is often ignored in practice.

The skeptic does not lack arguments to defend the view that man is, after all, little more than an animal. In particular, he can point to the fact that the appetites of mankind are still much the same as they were before Paleolithic times. In prosperous refined cities, as well as in tropical forests or in arid deserts, the most common urge of the growing child is to eat as much and as often as possible; everywhere the dream of the young adult male is a woman all his own. But for mankind all over the world—including growing children and young adult males—food and sex and all instinctual hungers commonly take second place to emotions and adventures which are meaningless for animals. The universal appeal of Don Quixote's adventures for young, adult, and old alike is an expression of this "unnatural" aspect of human nature. Quixote embodies the peculiarly human willingness to risk danger and hardship for no better reason than achieving some feat memorable or noble. He is one of the great symbols of mankind because he stands for the desire to attempt the impossible for the sake of greatness without any hope of material reward.

Even in our times, which are said to be so materialistic and so scornful of ideals, what really excites the world is the account of a dramatic rescue at sea or in the bottom of a mine; of an idealist allowing himself to die of starvation for the sake of his country's political freedom; the struggles of an explorer reaching for the Pole or climbing Mount Everest; the daring of Lindbergh's first crossing of the Atlantic, or of astronauts shot into space. These events do not in any way affect the everyday life of the common man, nor have they any meaning that can be referred to the animal basis of mankind. But they bring to light two aspects of human nature which are more important than the traits that man has inherited from his animal past. One is the sense of belonging to a community—mankind—which, progressively, in the course of time, has come to encompass the whole world. The other is the sense of participation in a great adventure that transcends the search for the satisfaction of material needs and pleasures.

This unselfish manifestation of human nature is not new; in fact, it is as ancient as recorded history. In all cultures that we know of, there have been men who have shunned the abundant life and who have chosen instead asceticism, suffering, and otherworldliness. Some have been saints intoxicated with God, others have been very reasonable and otherwise ordinary persons obeying the dictates of their conscience. Socrates has become a legendary figure not so much by reason of his philosophy as by his willingness to accept death rather than violate the laws to which he owed the nature of his very self.

The spirit of human brotherhood and the urge to move forward and upward are not to be described in terms of chemical constitution and physical forces, but they are facts, nevertheless, just as real as the need for food, the love of comfort, or the fear of pain. As facts they differ from those of the so-called natural sciences, because they are concerned with consequences rather than being determined by antecedent causes. One could almost say that they are made not of matter, but of time and spirit because their chief constituents are memories of the past, anticipations of the future, and choice of values. But even though they arise from expectations, from visions of the mind, indeed from dreams, they are so real and powerful that they can sway human behavior and are thereby the most effective forces in changing the face of the earth. Thus it is certain that man cannot be completely understood merely by considering him as a piece of machinery to be dissected and analyzed objectively by the methods of the exact sciences. To be understood man must be "known" in the Biblical sense; he must be encountered and experienced as a dreaming and throbbing creature.

Biographies

Bates, Marston (1906–), Professor of Zoology at the University of Michigan since 1952. Field biologist and researcher with the Rockefeller Foundation, 1934–52.

Benét, Stephen Vincent (1898–1943), poet and dramatist. Especially noted for *John Brown's Body,* which won the Pulitzer Prize in 1929.

Berelson, Bernard (1912–), vice president of the Population Council since 1962. Has served as Director of the behavioral sciences program of the Ford Foundation, Professor of Behavior Sciences at the University of Chicago, and Director of the Bureau of Applied Social Research at Columbia.

Black, Eugene R. (1898–), special financial consultant to the Secretary General of United Nations. Formerly, senior vice-president of Chase National Bank and president of the International Bank for Reconstruction and Development.

Brown, Harrison Scott (1917–), chemist, author, and educator. Professor of Geochemistry at the California Institute of Technology since 1951. Taught at Institute for Nuclear Studies, 1946–51.

Calder, Ritchie (1906–), Scottish newspaper reporter and scientist. Professor of International Relations at the University of Edinburgh since 1961. He has served on United Nations missions of inquiry on population and natural resources.

Calhoun, John B. (1917–), research psychologist at the National Institute of Mental Health since 1954. Experimental researcher in behavior of Norway rats at Johns Hopkins University and Roscoe B. Jackson Memorial Laboratory in Bar Harbor, Maine.

Carrighar, Sally, naturalist and writer. Has done field research in Jackson Hole, the Sierra Nevadas, and Alaska.

Carr-Saunders, Alexander Morris (1886–1966), British sociologist. Fellow of the British Academy, Charles Booth Professor of Social Science at Liverpool University.

Coale, Ansley J. (1917–   ), Professor of Economics at Princeton and Director of the Office of Population Research. Has served as United States representative on the Population Commission of the United Nations.

Cook, Robert C. (1898–   ), president of Population Reference Bureau since 1959, and editor of *Population Bulletin*.

D'Antonio, W. V. (1926–   ), chairman of the Department of Sociology, the University of Notre Dame.

Davis, Kingsley (1908–   ), Professor of Sociology and chairman of International Population and Urban Research at the University of California at Berkeley since 1955. United States representative on the Population Commission of the United Nations, 1955–61.

Day, Lincoln H. (1928–   ), Research Associate at Harvard School of Public Health. Taught sociology at Mt. Holyoke College, Princeton, and Columbia. Recently a Visiting Fellow in Demography at the Australian National University. His wife, Alice Taylor Day, taught sociology at Mt. Holyoke and the University of Massachusetts.

De Castro, Josue (1908–   ), a Brazilian, was chairman of the executive council of the Food and Agriculture Organization of the United Nations, 1951–55.

Dostoievsky, Feodor M. (1821–81), Russian novelist. Convicted of conspiracy against the government in 1849 and sentenced to be shot. Reprieved at the last moment and sent to Siberia for five years of hard labor. His major works were written after his return to St. Petersburg in 1859.

Dubos, René (1901–   ), French bacteriologist and pioneer researcher in antibiotics. Professor of Pathology at Rockefeller University since 1957.

Fagley, Richard Martin (1910–   ), a minister of the Congregational Christian Churches. Executive Secretary of the Commission of the Churches on International Affairs, established by the World Council of Churches and the International Missionary Council, since 1951.

Field, James Alfred (1880–1927), Professor of Economy at the University of Chicago and president of the Illinois Birth Control League in its early years.

Freedman, Ronald (1917–   ), Professor of Sociology and Director of the Population Studies Center at the University of Michigan.

Fried, Morton H. (1923–   ), Professor of Anthropology at Columbia University since 1961.

Hauser, Philip M. (1909–   ), Director of the Population Research and Training Center and Chicago Community Inventory at the University of Chicago. Chairman of the Department of Sociology, 1956–65.

Hoagland, Hudson (1899–   ), Co-director of the Worcester Foundation for Experimental Biology since 1944. President of the American Academy of Arts and Sciences, 1961–64.

Hsu, Francis L. K. (1909–   ), Chinese anthropologist. Has taught and done field work in the Far East. Since 1955 Professor of Anthropology at Northwestern University.

Huxley, Julian (1887–   ), British biologist and author, Knight of the British Empire, grandson of Thomas H. Huxley. Director-General of UNESCO, 1946–48.

Krutch, Joseph Wood (1893–   ), drama critic, naturalist, and author. Brander Matthews Professor of Dramatic Literature at Columbia, 1943–50, and drama critic for *The Nation*. Retired to Arizona in 1950 to devote full time to writing.

Lorimer, Frank (1894–   ), Professor Emeritus of Sociology in the Graduate School of American University. Research Associate of the Office of Population Research, Princeton, 1961–64.

Lubbock, David, Special Assistant to the Director General of the Food and Agriculture Organization of the United Nations, 1946–51. Currently farming in Angus, Scotland.

Malthus, Thomas Robert (1766–1834), curate at Albury in Surrey when the first edition of his *Essay on the Principle of Population* was published in 1798. Became Professor of History and Political Economy at the East India Company's college at Haileybury in 1805.

Marx, Karl (1818–83), German political philosopher. Exiled twice from Germany for publications which were suppressed by the government. Settled in England in 1849. Agitated for social reforms and wrote *Das Kapital*, which was finished by his collaborator, Friedrich Engels.

Meier, Richard L. (1920–   ), organic chemist and sociologist. Research Associate at the National Institute of Mental Health and lecturer in the School of Natural Resources at the University of Michigan.

Organski, A. F. K. (1923–   ), political scientist and specialist in international studies. Associate Professor at Brooklyn College and teacher of graduate seminars at New York University and Columbia in American foreign policy and in Soviet administration. Katherine Organski, his wife, taught at Columbia, Barnard, Vassar, and New York University.

Orr, John Boyd (Lord Boyd Orr) (1880–   ), British food expert. Knight of the British Empire and Fellow of the Royal Society. Chancellor of Glasgow University in 1946. Director of the Food and Agriculture Organization of the United Nations, 1945–48.

Osborn, Frederick H. (1889–   ), trustee of the Population Council, the American Museum of Natural History, Princeton University, and the Carnegie Corporation. Editor of the symposium, *Heredity and Environment*.

Peattie, Donald Culross (1898–1964), botanist and naturalist, as well as poet and author of several books on nature.

Pike, James A. (1913–   ), Bishop of the Episcopal Diocese of California, 1958–66, author and editor.

Rock, John (1890–   ), Clinical Professor Emeritus of Gynecology at Harvard University and Director of the Rock Reproductive Clinic, Inc. His experiments with Drs. Gregory Pincus and Celso García led to the first oral contraceptive pill.

Sanger, Margaret (1883–1966), pioneer organizer of birth control movement in the United States, a trained nurse by profession. Indicted in 1915 for sending pleas for birth control through the mails. Opened first birth control clinic in the United States and organized the first American Birth Control Conference. Founder and first president of the American Birth Control League.

Sax, Karl (1892–   ), author and lecturer on genetics, horticulture, and demography. Professor of Botany at Harvard, 1935–59.

Thurber, James (1894–1961), journalist, cartoonist, and writer. Member of the staff of *The New Yorker,* 1927–61.

Vogt, William (1902–   ), field naturalist, lecturer, and author. Executive Secretary of the Conservation Foundation since 1964. National Director of Planned Parenthood, 1951–61.

Wells, George Philip (1901–   ), son of H. G. Wells. Professor of Zoology at the University of London since 1945.

Wells, Herbert George (1866–1946), British biologist, novelist, and journalist. Especially noted for science-fiction stories and two compendiums of knowledge, *The Outline of History* and *Science of Life,* written in collaboration with his son, George Philip Wells, and Julian Huxley.

Woodring, Paul (1907–   ), Education Editor of *Saturday Review* since 1960. Appointed Distinguished Service Professor of Psychology at Western Washington State College in 1962.

Wynne-Edwards, Vero Copner (1906–   ), British zoologist. Regius Professor of Natural History at Marischal College of University of Aberdeen since 1946.

Index

Abortion: in Bulgaria, 122; in Czechoslovakia, 122; in Hungary, 122; in Japan, 122, 123; in Poland, 122; prevalence of, 34, 118; punishment for, 153; in Romania, 142
Albania, natural increase in, 125
Alliance Nationale pour l'Accroisement de la Population (France), 149
An Almanac for Moderns (Donald Culross Peattie), selection from, 244
Animals, overproduction among, 359-62, 390-91
Aristotle, on population, 112
Australia, population growth in, 124

Balance in nature, 359, 359-62, 389-91, 394
Bates, Marston: on birth control movement in United States, 87-88; on controlling population, 30-49; on fertility and hunger, 76-78; on reproductive rate and balance, 359
Banks, J. A. (British sociologist), *Prosperity and Parenthood*, 120
Behavioral sink, 382; (figures), 378-79, 386
Belgium: birth rate in, 152; family allowances in, 150-51; population control in, 150-51
Benét, Stephen Vincent, "Nightmare for Future Reference," 314-18
Berelson, Bernard, on fertility control in Taiwan, 272-84
Besant, Mrs. Annie, trial, 86

Bhabha, Prof. Homi J. (India), on population control, 405, 406
Birds, territorial systems of, 366-70
Birth control: agitation for, 118; among Catholics, 215-16; in Chile, 417; in China, 270-72; in Communist countries, 169; among Jews, 211, 212; methods of, 100-106, 278, 282, 289-300, 397-404, 404-6; Papal Study Commission on, 222-30; Protestant view, 231-34; in Puerto Rico, 289, 297-301; and religious resistance, 193-94; responsibility in, 413-14; suppression of, 153; in United States, 419. *See also* Birth control movement, Family planning, Parenthood, *and* Population control
"Birth Control and Coercion" (W. V. D'Antonio), selection from, 414-20
Birth control clinics, 94, 401
Birth control movement: beginnings, 79-87; and Margaret Sanger, 88-94, 94-100; and the Roman Catholic hierarchy, 94-100; in United States, 87-88
Birth control pill, development of, 100-106
Birth rate: attempts to raise, 110, 143-53; Belgium and France compared (table), 152; changing (figure), 114; crude, defined, vii; decline in Europe, 118; declining in United States, 310-12; drop during war, 35-36; effects of famine, 77-78; in frontier countries, 124; in Germany, 145-48, 154; gross,